ARAB CONSTITUTIONALISM

After the 2011 uprisings started in Tunisia and swept across the Arab region, more than a dozen countries amended their constitutions, the greatest concentration of constitutional reform processes since the end of the Cold War. This book provides a detailed account and analysis of all of these developments. Individual accounts are provided of eight different reform processes (including Tunisia, Egypt, Libya, Yemen, and Sudan), with particular focus on the historical context, the political dynamics, the particular process that each country followed, and the substantive outcome. Zaid Al-Ali deconstructs the popular demands that were made in 2011 and translates them into a series of specific actions that would have led to freer societies and a better functioning state. A revolution did not take place in 2011, but it is inevitably part of the region's future, and Arab Constitutionalism explores what that revolution could look like.

Zaid Al-Ali is the Senior Adviser in Constitution-Building in the Arab Region for International IDEA. He has three law degrees from Harvard Law School, the Sorbonne University, and King's College London. He has been practicing international commercial arbitration since 1999 and has been advising on constitutional drafting in Arab countries since 2005.

Arab Constitutionalism

THE COMING REVOLUTION

ZAID AL-ALI

CAMBRIDGE
UNIVERSITY PRESS

Foreword

MONCEF MARZOUKI
PRESIDENT OF THE TUNISIAN REPUBLIC (2011–2014)

Constitutions are a product of the circumstances in which they are written. Their contents reflect the status of societies at a specific stage of their history, and the relationship between societal forces in their conflict over the distribution of wealth, power, and prestige. More particularly, constitutions indicate how much progress the peoples of particular countries have made in their effort to be recognized as citizens as opposed to subjects, and in their effort to establish a state that serves the public good rather than violent and corrupt minorities.

The revolutions of the Arab Spring represent a distinct moment in the history of this long struggle. I was honored and fortunate to have been a witness and actor to this sudden development after the revolutions began in late 2010. At 10 a.m. on January 27, 2014, in the plenary hall of the Tunisian parliament in the Bardo Palace, and in the presence of all of the Constituent Assembly's representatives, I signed the constitution that emerged from the revolution in my capacity as President of the Republic. My colleagues then added their signatures: Mustapha Ben Jaafar, in his capacity as Speaker of the Constituent Assembly, and Ali Laarayedh, in his capacity as head of the government that witnessed the birth pangs of this constitution.

This was a defining moment in the history of Tunisia and naturally in my own personal history. The 2014 Constitution was not the first in our modern history. It was preceded by the 1861 Fundamental Pact, and the 1959 Constitution that followed independence. There is, however, a fundamental difference between the 2014 Constitution and the two previous texts. The Fundamental Pact was enacted by Mohammed Bey, the former monarch. In it, he acknowledged for the first time that the population had a minimum amount of rights. This represented a quantum leap forward compared to the absolutism that prevailed in Tunisia and all Islamic Arab countries at the time. However, the Pact was granted to the people by the Bey, who himself was only acting because he had been forced to by European powers whose aim was to protect their own citizens.

In 1959, another tremendous step forward was made. For the first time, a constitution was drafted and adopted by a Constituent Assembly rather than by a single individual. The text was not imposed by a foreign power, but was developed pursuant to deep popular demands. The constitution was another step on the difficult, dangerous and long road that the Tunisian people have had to travel, but the journey was still incomplete. Despite the context, the constitution was still granted by the country's new leader, who acted virtually alone. For more than five decades, his party arrogantly claimed to be the people's representative and vanguard, making itself the sole guardian of a people that was considered incapable and too immature to exercise democratic rights. Although the 1959 Constitution was formally supposed to be a modern constitution advocating rights and freedoms, it was merely a cover for another round of absolutism, represented at best by Habib Bourguiba, and at worst by his successor, Zine El Abidine Ben Ali.

Most of the 1959 Constitution's provisions on rights and freedoms were just ink on paper. When we stood before the courts of despotism and demanded that its provisions be implemented, both we and the judges knew that they were just meaningless words to those in authority. Bourguiba and Ben Ali both tampered with the Constitution as they liked through changes and additions that allowed them to stay in power for life.

The revolution changed all this radically. The 2014 Constitution's most important feature was not its content but rather the way in which it came into existence. It was not granted by politicians or technocrats. Nor was it granted by a single leader or by a new vanguard party. On the contrary, the Constitution was the product of unprecedented dialogue between Tunisians, civil society organizations, and political parties. Countless hours of discussion and debates took place from 2011 to 2014. Detailed negotiations between political and community actors unaccustomed to such discussions took place until the very last moment. Some of these threatened to derail the entire process as they sought common ground rather than the conflictual and dictatorial approach that had prevailed throughout our history.

Some commentators have said that these discussions have not had any practical impact given that the population remains mired in poverty, and are still impacted by corruption and terrorism. This is incorrect. For the first time in their history, the people participated freely in constitutional discussions via their elected representatives. The people were represented by professional and civic organizations, and all discussion panels were open to every citizen. In my opinion, this phenomenon is the most important outcome to emerge from the 2014 Constitution. It cuts through the most important obstacles that prevent democratic states from emerging, and has impacted Tunisia at the following levels:

(i) For centuries, Sharia dominated the substance of Tunisia's social contract. Today, every political and social group that was involved in writing the 2014 Constitution accepts that the new social contract recognizes Islam as the state religion but that it is based on new concepts and values, including democracy and human rights. The word "Sharia" is not even mentioned in the text of the Tunisian Constitution, unlike most other Arab constitutions.

(ii) The Constitution also represents a clear break with outdated modes of governance, according to which power must be centralized in the hands of the president of the republic or the head of government. To prevent the return of tyranny, the Constitution distributes powers between the head of state, the head of government, and the speaker of parliament, and creates a number of independent bodies and a constitutional court to adjudicate disputes over the constitutionality of laws. The Constitution establishes a state that is defined by laws and institutions, not a tool of expropriation in the hands of a corrupt elite that serves only its own interests.

(iii) The Constitution recognizes the rights and freedoms of Tunisians that make them citizens, as opposed to subjects.

Despite all of the above, it would be naïve to assume that the Constitution by itself is capable of bringing about the social changes it advocates. It sets out objectives, mechanisms, and a roadmap, but the project remains in its infancy, and the threats to end it began from the moment of its birth. The path to a state of laws and institutions populated by citizens and not subjects remains long and perilous.

Religious parties have only reluctantly accepted that the source of legitimacy is first and foremost the will of the people, and that it is expressed by representatives who are freely elected. Moreover, the development model that was in place for decades, and that was imposed by the corrupt elites for their own interests, has not yielded the results that were originally promised. Today, as a result of legacies of the past, which include successive crises that continue to this day, the social and economic rights that are guaranteed by the Constitution remain mainly aspirational.

In addition, from the revolution's first moment, a counter-revolution was launched. Remnants of the previous regime, authoritarian parties, and the new populist movements have not hesitated to use democratic means to attack democracy itself, including through the corruption of media outlets and political parties, and by using financial means to influence elections. Their objective is to reimpose a presidential system that concentrates powers in the hands of a single individual. When this system was in place, the only means that we had to influence the head of state was prayer. If it were to reemerge, we would be left without recourse even if he or she were unstable or corrupt. All Arab peoples are following the same long, difficult, dangerous road albeit at different speeds. In a number of countries, blood has been shed to prevent them from establishing modern states.

Today, at the time of writing, the Constitution does not yet enjoy a consensus of support. Nevertheless, a historical turning point has clearly been reached. It has become possible to establish a social contract that is independent of religion. Also, there is no power today that can force Tunisians to return to the pre-2011 era. It is incumbent on us to continue the struggle for the Constitution to become a social contract that can last for generations, and that is embedded in hearts and minds of citizens, and in the state's institutions and policies. The night through which we have lived will pass.

Introduction

Protests and Reform: Ten years ago, millions of protesters in over a dozen Middle Eastern and North African countries took to the streets to demand radical change. In many cases, their purpose was to force longstanding dictators from office and to establish a democracy. In others, they demanded reform and clear action against corruption. Each country set a path of its own, but if there was one point of agreement between all actors it was that constitutional reform was an absolute necessity. What followed was the greatest concentration of constitutional reform efforts in the world since the end of the Cold War. Through this process, twelve out of the region's twenty countries either replaced their constitutions or amended them within just a few years, some more than once. In some countries, dictators who were about to be toppled promised constitutional reform, before ultimately ceding power to allow others to manage that process on their own. In others, chief executives organized constitutional reform efforts themselves, always carefully framing the scope of reform to a few limited issues. In addition, at least two other countries were deeply impacted by the protest movement and seriously contemplated constitutional reform efforts of their own.

Focus on constitutions: It is not immediately obvious why there should have been such wide agreement between virtually all actors on the need for constitutional reform. In nondemocratic settings, constitutions are not irrelevant but they play very particular roles. Nathan Brown convincingly established two decades ago that in Arab countries constitutions serve several important purposes, including to project state power and to organize the relationship between state institutions (which itself reflected the elite pact through which many countries were governed).[1] Since then, Nimer Sultany

[1] Nathan J. Brown, CONSTITUTIONS IN A NONCONSTITUTIONAL WORLD: ARAB BASIC LAWS AND THE PROSPECTS FOR ACCOUNTABLE GOVERNMENT, SUNY Press (2001).

has added that the texts of the constitutions also "expanded the political horizon" by "augment[ing] political culture."[2] But the question nevertheless remains: In countries where the general population has very little connection with their respective constitutions, why was there consensus in favor of amending or replacing them altogether? The explanation may simply be that national constitutions are closely associated with specific forms of rule to the extent that when those regimes are challenged it becomes inevitable that the constitution itself must be changed. After all, all states in the world, including those of the nondemocratic kind, seek to burnish their internal and international legitimacy by projecting a commitment to the law, of which constitutions are the most important element. Chief executives and senior state officials are expert at arguing that they are simply bound by the constitution and the law every time they engage in behavior that the general population finds abhorrent. The opposition to the pre-2011 constitutions was so prevalent that very few actors dared argue that they should be maintained or only slightly amended for fear of being labeled counterrevolutionary.

Outcome: The end result has been at best mixed. Some countries saw immediate improvements, others descended into war, while in others very little changed. In five out of the twelve processes, the former chief executive was forced out of office, leaving the new constitution to be negotiated through a political process that involved rival camps. In Tunisia and Sudan, the protests and subsequent negotiations yielded major changes to the system of government, but both countries are struggling in their efforts to stabilize their respective situations, while the general population's economic situation continues to deteriorate. In two cases, Libya and Yemen, the constitutional processes ended without having any impact. Meanwhile, Egypt has reverted to a form of rule that is similar to the pre-2011 period. In the remainder of cases, the new constitutions were drafted by appointed committees that preserved the same system of government with just a few differences, some of which have concentrated power even further in the hands of the chief executive. In Lebanon and Iraq, both of which experienced major uprisings of their own in 2019, the governing class has been broadly incapable of presenting any meaningful solutions, despite promises of wholesale reform, including constitutional amendment.

Impact: The impact on the general population of these countries has been dramatic. Ten years after the start of the 2011 uprisings, all of the circumstances and factors that encouraged the millions of protesters to take to the streets are

[2] Nimer Sultany, Law and Revolution: Legitimacy and Constitutionalism after the Arab Spring, Oxford University Press (2017), at 38.

still in existence. In some cases, the negative trends are even more acute than they were in 2011. In virtually all countries, inequality continues to increase. Even in Tunisia, which has made the most progress, regular bouts of protest and rioting take place in the peripheral parts of the country, which is where the uprising started in 2011. Official ceremonies to celebrate the adoption of the 2014 Constitution were boycotted by the unemployed. In other cases, living standards, such as they were, have collapsed. Meanwhile, thousands of young men and women still venture out to sea every year in an effort to reach Europe. Libya, Syria, and Yemen have endured years of brutal conflict, leading to millions displaced, famine, disease, and an unending list of other calamities with no end in sight. In Lebanon and Iraq, basic services such as electricity production, medical care, and education are collapsing. Demographic trends, the absence of macroeconomic reform, the general state of lethargy in government, and the prolonged period of nonreform are all pushing the region as a whole in a negative direction that is hard to ignore.[3]

Inevitability: There was nothing inevitable in this outcome. There was a period of time in all of the countries that were impacted by the 2011 uprisings where everything was possible. State officials who temporarily held the reins of power in 2011 and 2012 played a major role in shaping the transition. All were forced to improvise policies and transition roadmaps based on close to no planning or personal experience in the matter. A number of their decisions were very poorly considered, sometimes taken very quickly and unthinkingly, partially because they greatly underestimated the risks. They were also very uncertain of themselves, and often reversed themselves on major policies in response to relatively minor pressure. Often, they acted against their own personal interests without anyone forcing them to, and would only realize that they had done so months or sometimes years later. At the same time, individuals and groups who should have known better let their guard down at crucial moments, allowing these processes to veer off track right from the start. The result was that key legal documents, including interim constitutions, rules of procedure, etc. were rushed and poorly drafted. Some inexplicably left major areas untouched and unresolved, which allowed emerging powers in the years that followed to fight out a solution. The constitutional negotiations themselves, when they did take place, focused almost exclusively on how power would be shared between different factions. Barely any time was dedicated to the rights of the individual, or to the general population's clearly

3 See, for example, Intissar Fakir and Isabelle Werenfels, 'In Morocco, Benevolent Authoritarianism Isn't Sustainable', Carnegie Endowment for International Peace (July 29, 2020).

expressed desire to see social justice established. There is good reason to think that circumstances could have evolved very differently had a different set of decisions been taken, and if greater effort had been made to impose an agenda on the negotiations.

The Future: Given the circumstances set out previously, the phenomenon of mass protests in the region is very likely to continue in the years to come. Amid deteriorating socioeconomic circumstances on the ground, the level of political activity in each of these countries and the general population's own ambitions for themselves as individuals and as a society have only increased.[4] Whatever mass protests or uprisings take place in the future may not coincide in the way that they did in 2011, but the second wave that took place in 2019 (which impacted Algeria, Sudan, Lebanon, and Iraq) demonstrates that they do not take place in isolation from each other. However, when they do take place, whether it be on a regional scale on in an individual country, it is vital that the lessons of the post-2011 transitions be learned and be translated into a clear set of objectives that all progressive forces should strive to achieve. This book offers one perspective on what that may look like: a call to translate the clearly expressed desires of millions of protesters into constitutional principles that any constitutional reform effort should be built around; focusing constitutional negotiations not around power-sharing but around the relationship between the individual and the state, with a view to encouraging circumstances that individuals need to flourish; ending hyper-presidentialism, and introducing elements within the system of government that are designed to increase direct contribution of the individual; framing the constitutional reform effort around the need to avoid majoritarian outcomes; and finally structuring international assistance so that it properly responds to the needs of each specific country.

* * *

Terminology: I should offer some explanation of the book's title. The book is almost entirely inspired by the constitutional advisory work that I have been doing in the past fifteen years. From 2005 to 2010, I focused almost all of my time on Iraq, and from 2011 to 2020 I expanded to more than ten different countries. All of the countries that I have worked in since 2005 are bound together by several elements, one of which is that the majority of the people of each of those countries are Arabic speaking, and that the language of the legal

[4] See Elena Ianchovichina, Eruptions of Popular Anger: The Economics of the Arab Spring and Its Aftermath, World Bank Group (2018), at 120.

community is Arabic. Regrettably, over the past century, political movements have mobilized parts of the population under their control using racial politics, and politicized the word "Arab" in the process. To be clear, I categorically reject any ideology that is based on race or on the exclusion of the other. Very large numbers of people in all of these countries do not speak Arabic as a mother tongue, and many do not speak it at all. However, constitutions, legislation, and court decisions in all of these countries are all drafted in Arabic, which has made cross-border learning and comparisons from one country to another extremely fluid, and which has made it possible for me to work in all of these places without difficulty. Naturally, each country's history is unique, but there are a number of common features that bind all the countries that this book discusses together, including their Islamic and Ottoman heritage (with the exception of Morocco, which was never under Ottoman control), their colonial histories, and the manner in which all of these countries have been administered in the postcolonial period. Naturally, very many other countries in the world share some of these legacies and characteristics. However, it is the particular balance that exists in these countries that make them worthy of joint study and analysis.

Arab Spring: I should also clarify that I deliberately avoid use of the terms "Arab Spring," "Jasmine Revolution" (for Tunisia), or even "revolution" when describing the events that took place in 2011 and the years that followed. While the term "Arab Spring" is widely used both within and without the region, it remains highly imprecise. The term "spring" suggests (to me at least) that the populations of these countries were inactive and suddenly awoke from their slumber in 2011. However, in many of the countries that were affected by the 2011 uprisings, regular bouts of protest took place before 2011 and have continued to take place since. The two factors that made the 2011 uprising unique were that it was a regional movement (that was clearly inspired by the success of the Tunisian protesters) and its magnitude. I am also very uncomfortable with the term "revolution," mainly because, as I understand it, the term suggests a total reshaping of a country's system of government. However, for the most part, the systems of government in these countries has not changed considerably. In some cases, longstanding dictatorships were replaced by civil war, the outcome of which is still uncertain at the time of writing. For that reason, to describe the events that took place in 2011, I prefer the far less evocative but I hope more precise term "2011 uprisings," and avoid characterizing specific constitutional amendments as "revolutionary." In the case of Tunisia, which is so far the country that has experienced the most change, the term "Jasmine Revolution" is in fact not used officially (perhaps because the Jasmine flower is usually associated with summer recreation rather popular struggle for dignity). Tunisia's 2014 Constitution instead refers to the "Revolution for Freedom and Dignity."

Geographic Scope: This volume covers the main constitutional developments that have taken place since 2011 in Arab majority countries. It discusses each of the countries that have undergone major constitutional change through political negotiations (Tunisia, Libya, Egypt, Yemen, and Sudan). It also offers a more summary review of the constitutional amendment procedures that took place without political negotiations, all of which are discussed in a single chapter (Morocco, Algeria, and Jordan). The book also includes significant discussion of a number of other countries in its thematic chapters (Part II), including Lebanon, Syria, and Iraq. Post-2011 constitutional developments in those three countries do not merit their own chapters or sections for now, but they do provide important insights that I include in the analysis sections. Importantly, this volume is not a comprehensive review of all of all of the constitutional changes that have taken place since 2011. Some countries and developments have been omitted for a variety of reasons, some practical and others substantive. Mauritania is not discussed at all (with apologies to Omar Hammady), mainly for lack of time and resources, an omission that I promise to remedy if there is ever a second volume of this book. I also deliberately exclude any discussion of the Gulf countries. New constitutions have been adopted, others have been amended, and new practices have emerged in each of those countries, but political dynamics in that part of the world are too unique to be discussed in conjunction with the rest of the Arab region.

* * *

Outline: This book seeks to achieve two general objectives. First, it seeks to provide a detailed overview of the post-2011 transition processes with a view to providing a factual basis for the analytical sections that follow later on in the book. For all of the countries, the book follows the same general pattern, although the exact outline and focus for each country depends on its specific circumstances. In all cases, I provide a brief historical account of how each country was governed during the precolonial and colonial periods, and explore what impact they might have had on postcolonial governance. The book also describes the main procedural and substantive points of contention that each country had to resolve following the 2011 uprisings, and ends by evaluating the main substantive changes that were introduced in the new constitutional arrangement. Second, the book explores the major flaws in the region's constitutional frameworks thematically, mainly in order to suggest a path forward for those countries that are still undergoing constitutional reform today and those that will do so in the future. For each of these issues, the book explains its importance, explains in analytical form what was done in the post-2011 transitions, and what alternative approach might have been followed. As noted previously, the perspectives that are offered are not intended to be academic analysis, nor are they predictions of what may occur in the future. They are what I consider to be the best path toward resolving the region's constitutional frameworks if circumstances allow another opportunity similar to that which transpired in 2011.

Part I: Eight separate constitutional processes are explored in Part I, although not all to the same level of detail. Five of the processes were characterized by negotiations that took place between political forces, and these are covered in individual chapters, with the exception of Sudan. The three countries where constitutional reform was managed by appointed committees are all covered in the same chapter. Chapter 1 focuses on Tunisia, which is for now the country that has travelled the greatest amount of distance from its pre-2011 era. As the chapter seeks to explain, despite that progress, the transition was not without its difficulties and has left a number of issues unresolved. Chapter 2 discusses Egypt's turbulent constitutional process, including the adoption of an interim constitution and two permanent constitutions within a three-year period. It explains in some detail how decisions early on in the transition process by actors who probably did not appreciate what they were doing contributed to the chaos that followed in the years that followed. Yemen is covered in Chapter 3, which describes the elaborate process through which the transition was designed, and the faith-based approach that was followed during implementation. Despite deteriorating circumstances throughout the process, national and international officials pressed ahead, only adjusting the transition process by delaying implementation of every stage. Chapter 4 focuses on Libya. It commences with a detailed review of the country's colonial and postcolonial history, which deeply impacted the post-2011 transition in ways that are not immediately obvious. Aside from trying to recreate the process through which the 1951 Constitution was adopted, the substantive negotiations were also defined by dynamics that were first established in the late 1940s. Ultimately, the post-2011 negotiations that did take place were academic given that they were not supported by some of the country's main power brokers. Finally, Chapter 5 covers Jordan, Morocco, and Algeria, all three of which carried out limited constitutional changes through processes that were managed by the state. There are some differences between them, and some innovations were introduced in some respects, but generally speaking the chapter seeks to demonstrate that the system of government in all three countries remains unchanged. Chapter 5 also covers Sudan, despite its process standing far apart the other three countries that are covered in this chapter. Through a planned revolution, an organized civilian movement brought down an Islamist dictatorial regime, and forced a negotiation with the surviving security forces. Sudan is covered in Chapter 5 and therefore in shorter form than the other political processes merely because, at the time of writing, it was still at the start of its transition process, the outcome of which is uncertain. My hope is, if there is ever to be a second edition of this volume, that the transition will have been successfully completed, leading to the adoption of a progressive constitutional document that will contribute to peace and prosperity and which will allow more detailed consideration of the transitional process, hopefully in its own chapter. For now however the discussion on the Sudan is included in the same chapter as Morocco, Algeria, and Jordan even though it has very little in common with those processes.

Part II: The second part of the book is where I attempt to analyze all of these developments around a few themes, all of which are designed to support the argument that real revolution has yet to be achieved, and that reshaping society along more democratic lines is achievable. In Chapter 6, I challenge common assumptions about what a constitution's purpose should be. Despite the clear call for change that was expressed by masses of protesters in 2011, many decision-makers did not view their constitutions as instruments of transformation. In Chapter 7, I examine what I view as the principle failing point of Arab constitutions, which is the relationship between the individual and the state. Constitutional frameworks in the region were built around the notion that the state must exist for its own sake, and individuals who were not part of the state were treated as virtual nonentities. Post-2011 drafters were aware that the general population demanded change, but enacted only cosmetic changes with only a few exceptions. I offer some thoughts on the main issues that define the current relationship between individual and state and how it could evolve in the future. Chapter 8 examines the system of government and the legacies of the colonial era. The bulk of Arab countries are today hyperpresidential, granting huge powers to the executive without any meaningful accountability mechanisms. The challenge in 2011 and in the future will be to break away from that framework in a way that satisfies the demand for social justice. Chapter 9 discusses process issues, and argues that any negotiation process that is organized in the future must be built around a small number of key principles, including inclusivity that looks beyond politics, consensus building, interim arrangements, and an approach that sets aside faith and approaches developments objectively. Finally, Chapter 10 explores the ways in which international assistance is delivered to constitution negotiation processes and the types of adjustments that could be made to improve its impact.

What This Book Does Not Cover: This book's scope is limited. It does not seek to explain all of the circumstances that led to the uprisings, or to describe all the developments that took place during the transitions. Some scholars and analysts have sought to explain why the 2011 uprisings led to a change of regime in some countries, and why the harvest has been more modest in others. For example, it has been argued that regionwide factors, including religious legitimacy and the presence of natural resources, have played determinant roles in the post-2011 transitions.[5] Others have discussed the impact that the 2011 uprisings have had on societies, including discourses on revolt and national consciousness. These questions are beyond this book's scope for a combination of reasons, including that I am not properly equipped to discuss them. This book also does not posit a detailed or academic explanation of why major constitutional reform is still to be expected. The thesis that is offered is as stated earlier – that significant circumstances are pointing in that direction, and that progress toward democracy is difficult but certainly achievable with the right strategy and preparation.

* * *

Methodology: Some of my colleagues who have assisted in the drafting of this book (including Haykel Ben Mahfoudh) have insisted that I offer some thoughts on research methodology in this fast-changing world. I offer this modest contribution in the hope that they may be helpful to researchers who have an interest in the field. In my case, the accounts and insights that I offer in this book are in large part based on my own personal experiences over a ten-year period. Much of what follows assumes that such access is possible. There is little alternative to being in the countries that one is studying and to interacting with principle actors in their own language over a period of years. Having said that, I will mainly focus here on the online tools that I have used during the drafting of this book, and will not focus on traditional research methods.

Primary Material: Collecting primary resource material is now much easier than it was in the past. Many countries in the region now maintain online databases that are easy to search and include each country's constitutional history, as well as the full catalogue of legal documents (for example www.legislation.tn and http://iraqld.hjc.iq/). For the most part, these exist only in Arabic but some materials are also available in English and French.

5 Jason Brownlee, Tarek Masoud, and Andrew Reynolds, THE ARAB SPRING: PATHWAYS OF REPRESSION AND REFORM, Oxford University Press (2015).

These can be supplemented with other online databases that are maintained by foreign or international organizations (including www.constituteproject.org and http://constitutionnet.org/). Regrettably, for many countries one must now look beyond national legislation and also search through peace agreements and other related documents, for which there are also now increasing numbers of online databases (www.languageofpeace.org and www.peaceagreements.org). For court decisions, the situation is varied. Decisions by constitutional courts and supreme courts are typically published in official gazettes and are usually available online on the courts' websites (see, for example, www.cour-constitutionnelle.ma, www.sccourt.gov.eg, and www.iraqfsc.iq). Decisions are typically only available in Arabic. Many new websites offer access to searchable databases of court decisions (including https://qanouni.tn/). For lower courts, the situation is far more mixed. Depending on the country and the jurisdiction, some decisions are formally published. For the most part, however, practitioners and researchers have to rely on contacts to obtain decisions.

Secondary Sources: For the most part, one cannot rely on primary materials. At times, primary materials themselves only provide a partial picture of the dynamics that were at play, and to rely on them exclusively can lead to serious misunderstandings. The difficulty with secondary material is both access and quality. One of the key lessons that I have learned in writing this book is that one cannot rely on written accounts only, given that in many countries everything that has been published has been authored by one side of the political divide. As an example, a number of detailed accounts have been published by members of Tunisia's Constituent Assembly. However, to my knowledge, all of them were written in French and by members of the secular camp. Their insights are obviously a treasure but it would be wrong to rely exclusively on their accounts of the drafting process. Much therefore needs to be done to supplement the written account. Throughout the years, I have kept detailed notes of my meetings with negotiators, other officials, and activists, on which I have relied when writing this book. I have also kept my own archive of materials, including all the drafts of constitutions and legislation that I have been able to get my hands on through the years. Some of the drafts were given to me by the relevant actors, others were published in the press or through social media, but keeping a full and easily accessible archive of these materials as they become available is vital because with time they can become nearly impossible to find, which will make the history of events extremely difficult to reconstruct. To the extent that materials that have been published online have not been archived and need to be retrieved, one answer is the internet archive (https://archive.org/web/), which allows users to retrieve much (but not all) of what was posted online in the past, including materials that have been deleted. To recreate the political context or mood in specific countries and at specific periods of time, there are a variety of tools that one can use aside from traditional methods. One possibility is to carry out searches through online platforms including google and YouTube while narrowing down the time period, and ranking hits by numbers of views. For major constitutional or political events, this manner of proceeding can return a large number of articles or videos that will include contemporaneous extracts from formal sessions or interviews with many of the relevant actors. Some will have been viewed very large numbers of times, which will suggest their level of importance in the popular consciousness, and one can then use these to test possible bias in personal narratives that are offered by specific actors. When searching for commentary on specific issues or events, aside from the traditional means, one can now search through archives such as Google Books that can return results that would not otherwise have been available. The full text of individual results is not always available, but they at least serve to provide detailed references.

Arabic Materials: A large amount of material that is produced on Arab politics is written by individuals who do not understand Arabic, which can lead to highly questionable results. Often their interests are shaped by orientalist and cultural narratives (including, for example, the suggestion that Arab and Muslims cannot successfully negotiate a constitution because they are violent by nature). At times, authors simply misunderstand or confuse events because of language barriers or because they are forced to rely on partial accounts (for example, overreliance on locals who speak English or French, which leaves out the bulk of the population, including working-class communities. This in turn reinforces the impression amongst non-Arabic speakers that the main point of contention in these constitutional processes is about power, as opposed to the relationship between the individual and the state). Ideally, researchers who are interested in these issues should prioritize the use of materials that have been published in Arabic. For those who do not already know how to, learning to read Arabic is not as difficult as it sounds. If one focuses on legal materials, there is only limited terminology and phraseology that one has to learn. In terms of access, regrettably, despite many of the advances set out in this section, this still requires significantly more time than research in English or French, as much of the Arabic language material is not available in libraries or on online. In many cases, researchers will simply not even know that these materials exist. My intention when I started drafting this book was to mainly rely on Arabic language materials, including secondary sources, but the lockdown that followed the spread of COVID-19 reduced my productivity significantly, making it more difficult to see that commitment through. Hopefully, the next development in the technology of research will be to make all of these additional materials as easily available as the western sources.

Drafting: For the drafting process, the most important commodity is concentration. For this, the only solution so far as I can tell is to cut oneself off completely from the outside world. Today what this means is leaving one's phone at home or at least placing it far out of reach. It also means making frequent use of internet blockers (many of which are easily downloadable online), which are an extremely effective means of preventing time-wasting. My aim on the days when I was writing the book was to have at least six hours a day fully uninterrupted by phone calls, emails, and the Internet. I have also opted to label paragraphs throughout the book, for a combination of reasons. The book covers a wide range of countries and some readers may only be interested in specific countries, in specific topics, in specific periods of time. Labeling makes it easier for the reader to find what it is that they are looking for in case they hope to use the book for reference purposes and cannot afford the time to read the entire book from beginning to end. Secondly, labeling is a good drafting technique that I was taught many years ago as a young lawyer. Labeling helps focus the mind around the arguments that are being studied and the best order of ideas to make an argument. Finally, throughout the drafting process I have consulted with colleagues with specialized knowledge of specific countries or topics. I have aimed to have each section reviewed by at least two specialists. Given the wide range of countries and topics that are covered in this book, that step has significantly lowered (while not completely eliminating) the chances that I have mischaracterized or omitted the history of what happened or misunderstood its impact.

* * *

Acknowledgments: This book would not have been possible without very considerable assistance from a range of institutions and colleagues, who supported the work either through encouragement, by contributing ideas of their own, or by creating the space that I needed to make progress. First, my employer since the start of the 2011 uprisings, the International Institute for Democracy and Electoral Assistance, granted me a front row seat in just about every country in the region, something that would not have been possible elsewhere. My colleagues have encouraged me to play a proactive role wherever possible, which is what allowed me to travel extensively throughout the region, to develop my knowledge and relationships with senior officials, members of the legal community, and others. In particular, I am grateful to

Paulos Tesfagiorgis and Cheryl Saunders, who introduced me to the Institute, to Ayman Ayoub, who was my first regional director and who set me on my path to adopting a regional perspective on constitutional developments, Shana Kaiser, who supported my efforts in Yemen and elsewhere, and Adebayo Olukoshi, whose guidance and support over the past few years have played a major role in allowing this volume to be completed. I am also grateful to Shaker Badr, Yasmine Elmaghraby (who also reviewed some of the book's chapters), Hanen Beji, Monia Belarbi, and Aziz Mrad for carrying the burden of all our ongoing work in my absence, without which I would not have been able to focus to the extent that I was able. Finally, I must thank Sumit Bisarya, Kimana Zulueta-Fuelscher, and Adem Abebe, my colleagues at the Constitution Building Program in The Hague, from whom I learned so much. It goes without saying that none of the views that are expressed in this book should be attributed to the Institute.

Princeton: I first started working on this book in 2015–2016 at Princeton University, where I was a Law and Public Affairs fellow and a lecturer at the School of Public and International Affairs (formerly the Woodrow Wilson School). The environment created by the LAPA program was exactly what I needed in order to get started. For that I am principally indebted to my students, who (whether they realized or not) were the first people with whom I discussed many of the ideas that make up this volume. I am also grateful to Kim Lane Scheppele and Stan Katz, who first introduced me to the LAPA program, to Paul Frymer and Leslie Gerwin, who were respectively director and associate director during my year in Princeton, and to Jennifer Bolton and Judi Rivkin, whose assistance and good humor throughout that year made the burden of being so far from home considerably lighter. Menaka Guruswamy (a fellow classmate in law school) traveled to Princeton to serve as a commentator for the paper that I presented as part of my fellowship, and included the first draft of Chapters 6–8 of Part II of this book. She continues to offer precious insights into the world of constitutional transitions today.

Wissenschaftskolleg: Originally, this book was supposed to be completed in 2018, but a minor accident in which I broke a finger and fractured my right elbow forced me to delay those plans. I had already been making arrangements to spend the 2019–2020 academic year at the Wissenschaftskolleg zu Berlin (the Institute for Advanced Study in Berlin), during which I was hoping to focus on a new writing project on peace processes. My broken finger forced me to rearrange my plans and finish writing this book in Berlin. It was clearly for the best. The Institute's working environment, its collegial atmosphere, and the services that it provides are unparalleled and my writing benefited enormously as a result. In particular, I am grateful to Professor Dr. Barbara

Stollberg-Rilinger, Dr. Thorsten Wilhelmy, and Professor Dr. Daniel Schönpflug for their dedication to the Institute's mission and for creating exactly the type of environment that I needed to complete my work. Andrea Bergmann's and Vera Pfeffer's support, generosity, care, and attention throughout the year allowed my family and I to feel welcome every day of our stay in Berlin. Holger Spamann (also a former classmate and a fellow at the Institute during that year) offered very useful advice throughout the year as I struggled with the work. Finally, Sonja Grund and the entire library staff contributed enormously to this volume by making all the materials that I needed available to me within record time.

Academic Institutions: A number of other academic institutions have also hosted me with a view to discussing many of the ideas that are included in this volume with academic staff or students, or both. On each occasion, the comments that I received allowed for me to refine, correct, and sometimes abandon specific arguments. For that I am indebted to Professor Tarek Masoud at Harvard's Kennedy School of Government, Professor Tom Ginsburg at the University of Chicago Law School, Professor Asli Bali at UCLA Law, Professors Christine Bell and Stephen Tierney and Dr. Asanga Welikala from the School of Law at the University of Edinburgh, Professors Sanford Levinson and Zach Elkins at the University of Texas at Austin School of Law, Professor Kristen Stilt formerly of Northwestern University and currently of Harvard Law School, Professor Mohammad Fadel at the University of Toronto Faculty of Law, and the Constitution Unit at University College London.

Contributors: A very large number of friends and colleagues contributed to this book by reviewing specific sections and offering comments, by contributing to the development of my ideas through their guidance, or by speaking to me and sharing their own insights on the post-2011 constitutional processes over the years. I am thankful for the time that each of these individuals dedicated to supporting me. The full list is set out in alphabetical order, but I must begin by mentioning Professor Christina Murray, with whom I have now been working for many years. Her unparalleled experience, patience, and good humor is an inspiration to me (and to many others). It would not be an exaggeration to say that she has taught me half of what I know in this field. In addition, Fink Haysom, my first supervisor in the field of constitution-building fifteen years ago in Iraq, taught me (through example) the most valuable single lesson that I have learned in this field of work, which is never to forget one's own basic humanity no matter the circumstances. In addition, to the following individuals, I express my gratitude for all of their assistance and guidance: Abbas Zaid, Abdelkhalig Shaib, Abdelrahim al-Maslouhi, Abrak

Saati, Ahmed el-Gaili, Ahmed Ouerfelli, Alli Hugi, Amel Boubekeur, Amr Abderrahman, Amr Hamzawy, Amr Shalakany, Andrew Ladley, Anis Abidi, Anwar Darkazaly, Aymen Bikri, Cheryl Saunders, Chris Thornton, David Bilchitz, David Risley, Felix-Anselm van Lier, George Anderson, Haykel Ben Mahfoudh, Hedi Abdelkefi, Helen Lackner, Holger Spamann, Ian Martin, Intissar Kheriji, Ismail Wazir, Issandr el Imrani, Jamal Benomar, Jill Ghai, John Packer, Jonathan Murphy, Katia Papagianni, Kenny Gluck, Mahmoud Hamad, Marc Weller, Mark Fathi Massoud, Mehdi Foudhaili, Menaka Guruswamy, Merwan Lomri, Mohamed Makhlafi, Mohammed el-Ghannam, Monia Belarbi, Muin Shreim, Mustafa Ahmed Kamal, Nathan Brown, Neimat Abas, Niklas Kabel Pedersen, Nina Prasch, Nizar Saghieh, Oliver Wils, Olivier Pierre Louveaux, Omar Hammady, Peter Salisbury, Philipp Dann, Richard Stacey, Salsabil Klibi, Shadi Hamid, Sufian Obeidat, Sujit Choudhry, Stephanie Koury, Suliman Ibrahim, Tamer Nagy, Tom Daly, and Yash Ghai. Finally, Michaela Eckart supported the work more than most by providing research assistance, evaluating many of the arguments that are contained in this volume, and providing her own insight into the themes that it deals with. Naturally, I am solely responsible for the contents of this work, including any errors or misunderstandings.

Dedication: Finally, to my mother Samar Al-Ali from whom I learned the value of education, the art of self-discipline, and perseverance. To my wife, Rouba Beydoun, who had to endure lockdown due to COVID-19 with two children and me in Berlin. We struggled for a time, until she relented and allowed me to return to full-time work. And to my daughter Sama, from whom I hope to learn many things in years to come.

PART I

The Uprising

1

Tunisia

BACKGROUND

Ottoman Period: From the sixteenth to the nineteenth centuries, Tunisia was administered as a semi-autonomous province of the Ottoman Empire. Similarly to Algeria, in the seventeenth century, local officers increased their own powers without authorization from the central government. They established the post of "bey,"who became the territory's most important source of authority. The bey governed the territory through a familiar administrative framework. He maintained public order, collected taxes, and established a government that included four leading ministers, including a prime minister, a treasurer, a commander-in-chief, and a secretary. During the nineteenth century, the bey launched a campaign to modernize the country. A standing army was established, locals were recruited into the bureaucracy, and tax reform was enacted. The country fell into considerable debt, which allowed the United Kingdom and France to impose significant legal reforms. At the same time, significant numbers of Tunisia's own elite were demanding that the state adopt more modern methods of policy formation and some means of accountability.[1] A "Fundamental Pact" was adopted in 1857 and codified a small number of basic rights, including the right to security for all inhabitants of Tunisia regardless of religion, nationality, and race (Article 1), as well as specific rights for Jewish citizens, including the freedom of worship (Article 4). A constitution was adopted in 1861, which while undemocratic at first glance, also recognized a number of essential constitutional principles, including executive accountability before a legislative authority (Articles 11 and 64) and judicial independence (Article 28). The modernizing drive was

[1] See Theresa Lane Womble, Early Constitutionalism in Tunisia, 1857–1864: Reform and Revolt (PhD dissertation, Princeton University, 1997), at Chapter 2.

interrupted by a French invasion and occupation,[2] which led in May 1881 to the signing of one agreement that firmly established French military preeminence in the country,[3] and a second in June 1883 that placed Tunisia under a "Protectorate" according to which it was obliged to carry out any "administrative, judicial and financial reforms that the French government considered to be useful."[4] The impact of these two agreements is that while Tunisia formally maintained its sovereignty and its autonomy, it was in fact placed under French administrative control.[5] French authority was exercised through the Resident General, and through a number of "civilian controllers" who had full control over Tunisia's bureaucracy, including the ability to call on the use of force.[6] Ultimately, the colonial authorities maintained and further developed the state administration that had already been built by the Tunisian state.[7] Naturally, no legal recourse was afforded to ordinary Tunisians who wished to challenge specific actions that were taken by colonial authorities throughout that period.

Independence: In 1920 the pro-independence Destour party was founded. In the years that followed, it had little impact on colonial authorities, eventually growing sterile and moderate in its approach. In 1934 Habib Bourguiba, a lawyer and leading member of the independence movement, broke away from the Destour party to establish the Neo-Destour party. In 1956 Tunisia was formally granted independence after a long period of struggle. The country was immediately set on an undemocratic path when an electoral alliance that was led by the Neo-Destour party won all ninety-eight seats in the Constituent Assembly elections that were organized in March 1956 and when the French army intervened to quell Tunisian dissidents shortly before it was due to withdraw from the country.[8] Bourguiba assumed the presidency in 1957 and

2 Nominally, the French military stated that the invasion was intended to stop cross-border raids into Algeria, and then argued that it was forced to remain after initial withdrawals led to more attacks; Dominique Gaudiani and Paul Thiaucourt, La Tunisie: Legislation, Gouvernement, Administration, Librairie Administrative, Paul Dupont (1910), at 10.

3 See Treaty of Kasr Said, concluded between France and Tunisia (1881), Article 2.

4 See The al-Marsa Convention (1883), Article 1.

5 See Gaudiani and Thiaucourt (1910), at 13.

6 See Elisabeth Mouilleau, Fonctionnaires de la République et Artisans de l'Empire: Le Cas des Contrôleurs Civils en Tunisie, L'Harmattan (2000); and Gaudiani and Thiaucourt (1910), at 35.

7 See Lisa Anderson, The State and Social Transformation in Tunisia and Libya *(1830–1980)*, Princeton University Press (1986), at 226; Gaudiani and Thiaucourt (1910), at 15. Contemporaneous commentators argued that French control over the Tunisian state was analogous to the colonial form of government that France exercised in neighboring Algeria; see Ibid., at 29.

8 See Kenneth Perkins, A History of Modern Tunisia, Cambridge University Press (2004), at 131.

sought to remake Tunisia in his own image. He resisted the trend toward militarism and Arabism that imbued much of the rest of the region, favoring gradual institution building as well as the implementation of relatively progressive social and economic rights (including women's rights, education, and health care). Although that approach earned Bourguiba significant praise internationally, there was one regional trend that he did not resist, which was the monopolization of power and intolerance toward dissent.

1959 Constitution: Unsurprisingly, the constitution that was eventually drafted and that entered into force in 1959 established a system of government that was heavily biased in favor of the executive. It provided that the president was responsible for determining the state's national policy (Article 58), that the government was answerable to the president (Article 59), and that the president was responsible for selecting the prime minister (Article 50). The president could dismiss the government at any time and for any reason (Article 51), while the parliament could only do so if a two-thirds majority voted in favor (Article 63). The parliament also had no authority to recall the president or to hold him accountable for his actions. The president could declare a state of emergency without restriction, granting himself any authorities that he so desired and for any length of time (Article 46). The system of government was also highly centralized; the constitution included a single provision on local government (Article 71) and subsequent legislation ensured that important policy formation power was concentrated in the capital.

Legacy: Bourguiba remained president for thirty years until 1987. He was deposed by Zine El Abidine Ben Ali, a former director of national security and minister of the interior. Ben Ali had been appointed prime minister a few weeks before he removed Bourguiba from office and, citing Bourguiba's failing health, invoked Article 57 of the 1959 constitution relating to absolute disability to justify his actions. Ben Ali himself remained in power for twenty-four years until 2011. During his mandate, political opponents were exiled, arrested, and tortured or harassed by the security forces.[9] A series of fraudulent elections were organized, including the 2009 general election in which the ruling party won 161 out of 214 seats. The president's family also became heavily invested in the country's economy, to the extent that the regulatory process was rigged to benefit the president's relatives.[10] The Tunisian state

[9] See Final Report, Truth and Dignity Commission, March 26, 2019, available at www.ivd.tn/rapport/ (the Truth and Dignity Commission was established by Law 53 (2013) to "understand and remedy past human rights violations by revealing the truth and by holding officials accountable and offering reparations to victims" (Article 1)).

[10] See Bob Rijkers, Caroline Freund and Antonio Nucifora, "All in the Family: State Capture in Tunisia," The World Bank, Policy Research Working Paper 6810, March 2014.

claimed that it had achieved an "economic miracle," which was based on skewed economic data that deliberately ignored serious social and economic inequalities.[11] Almost all investment was concentrated in the northern coastal areas, leaving the center and south of the country with close to no opportunity for the growing number of unemployed youth.

UPRISING

Constitutional Rupture: On December 18, 2010, a popular uprising against poverty, corruption, and repression commenced in the impoverished center of the country, spread quickly throughout all provinces, and ended on January 17, 2011 when former President Ben Ali fled the country.[12] In conformity with Article 57 of the 1959 Constitution, the former speaker of parliament assumed the role of interim president, and immediately began constructing a road map to a more democratic form of government. One of the first questions that had to be addressed was whether to operate within the confines of the 1959 Constitution. During the initial period, an attempt was made to maintain constitutional continuity, in particular through reference to the 1959 Constitution in the first few post-uprising laws. By way of example, Law 5 (2011), which was issued on February 9, 2011, provided the interim president with decree-making authority in relation to a number of key issues, including the electoral system and political party law. Law 5 indicated that it was issued "pursuant to Article 28 of the Constitution," according to which the parliament "may authorize the President of the Republic, for a set period of time and for a specific purpose, to issue decrees" on the condition that they be submitted to ratification by the parliament. In the weeks that followed, the interim president's decree-laws continued to refer to the 1959 Constitution but a rupture was inevitable.[13] Decree-Law 14 (2011), which was adopted on March 23, 2011, and which temporarily reorganized public authorities, provided in its preamble that "current circumstances [...] prevent the regular functioning of public authorities, and make the full implementation of the Constitution impossible." Decree-Law 14 (2011) formally dissolved the parliament, the council of advisers, and the constitutional council (all of which had been

[11] See Béatrice Hibou, "La formation asymétrique de l'État en Tunisie. Les territoires d'injustice," in Irene Bono, Béatrice Hibou, Hamza Meddeb, and Mohamed Tozy (eds.), L'état d'Injustice au Maghreb: Maroc et Tunisie, Editions Karthala (2015), at 101.

[12] 338 people were killed and thousands were injured by security forces during the uprising.

[13] Decree-Law 10 (2011), which was adopted on March 2, 2011 and which established an independent national communications authority, made reference to Articles 28 and 57 of the 1959 Constitution.

firmly under the former ruling party's control), while at the same time granting the interim president both executive and legislative power.[14] Subsequent decree-laws made no reference to the parliament or the 1959 Constitution.[15] Most other state institutions continued functioning relatively normally and were not subject to the same extensive purges that many other Arab countries suffered.[16] Ultimately, shortly after it was elected, the Constituent Assembly formally provided in a law that the 1959 Constitution was suspended.[17]

Political Climate: The political climate in 2011 was already heavily polarized between Islamist and non-Islamist groups, partially as a result of historical legacies.[18] Ennahda, the country's largest Islamist party, had suffered the brunt of the previous regime's oppressive policies, and was therefore intent on establishing constitutional guarantees that would allow it to survive free from oppression. Ennahda accused some of its rivals of being in league with the same forces that had orchestrated their oppression under the previous regime, and so therefore greatly distrusted some of the more secular parties.[19] Many of the party's adherents were also planning to Islamize Tunisian society partially through a series of constitutional reforms.[20] The remainder of Tunisia's post-uprising political spectrum was diffused in a large number of small liberal, secular, conservative, and left-wing parties, many of which were joined together in a common distrust for Ennahda and Islamist trends in general. Many on the secular side of the divide considered Islamists to be the greatest threat to the country's security, and associated Ennahda with the Muslim Brotherhood and even with terror groups.[21] They also feared that a resurgent

14 See Decree-Law 14 (2011).

15 See, for example, Decree-Law 27 (2011), which was adopted on April 18, 2011, established a higher independent electoral commission, and made no reference to the 1959 Constitution.

16 The most extensive purge of former ruling party members took place in Iraq following the establishment of the De-Baathification Commission. See Miranda Sissons and Abdulrazzaq al-Saiedi, "A Bitter Legacy: Lessons of De-Baathification in Iraq," International Center for Transitional Justice, April 3, 2013.

17 See Article 27, Organic Law 6 (2011).

18 See Jamil Sayah, L'Acte de la Révolution tunisienne: La Constitution, L'Harmattan (2015), at 70–73.

19 See Yasmine Ryan, "This Tunisian Wants His Nation to Know Its Torturers," Foreign Policy, July 31, 2015; Naveena Kottoor, "Tunisia's Essebsi: The 88-year old Comeback Kid," BBC News, December 31, 2014.

20 See Azzam Tamimi, Rachid Ghannouchi: A Democrat within Islam, Oxford University Press (2001); and Ayman Mahdhab, "Disagreements on Sharia in Tunisia" (خلاف حول الشريعة في دستور تونس), Al-Jazeera (February 28, 2012).

21 Indeed, Ben Ali justified his 1987 palace coup on the basis that Bourguiba's health was preventing the state from taking action against a growing Islamist threat; see, for example, Andrew Borowiec, Modern Tunisia: A Democratic Apprenticeship, Praeger Publishers

Islamist movement would lead to a regression of many basic rights, particularly for women. Some of Tunisia's main political actors had clearly understood the danger that this dynamic created and engaged in a number of trust-building initiatives,[22] but the levels of distrust were so great that whoever reached out to the other side would often be ostracized by their own camp.[23] These tensions were significantly exacerbated by regional developments, including the ascendency of Islamist groups in neighboring countries, which gave greater confidence to Ennahda while at the same time increasing fears within the secular camp that they could be overrun. These dynamics meant that the relationship between religion and state would dominate the negotiations even though the uprisings were motivated by social and economic concerns.

High Commission: Decree 6 (2011) provided for the establishment of a "High Commission to achieve the goals of the revolution, on political reforms and democratic transition" that had as its objective to "study relevant legal provisions in the political system and recommend reforms to ensure that the revolution's objectives will be satisfied" (Article 2). The Commission was to be headed by a "national independent figure known for competence in legal and political affairs" and was to include representatives of "various political parties," civil society organizations and "groups that participated in and supported the revolution" (Article 3). The High Commission established two internal bodies: (i) an "Expert Committee," consisting of twenty members, which was responsible for drawing up legislative proposals; and (ii) a "High Authority Committee" (160 members who were formally appointed by the prime minister, and who included representatives from major political forces including Ennahda and more secular and progressive parties, as well as trade unions), which was responsible for debating the Expert Committee's proposals

(1998). The trauma of ten years of conflict in neighboring Algeria, ending in 2002, contributed to that sense of distrust.

[22] During the many years that they spent in exile prior to 2011, future President Moncef Marzouki (a prominent secular and left-wing member of the Tunisian opposition) traveled from France to the United Kingdom on twenty occasions to meet with Rachid Ghannouchi (leader of the Islamist Ennahda party); see Al Stepan, "Tunisia's Constitutional Debates: Inclusion or Exclusion?," presented at a conference entitled "Whither the Arab World? Revisiting Democratic Transition Theory," Paris (November 5–7, 2014).

[23] Following the elections in late 2011, Moncef Marzouki's Congress for the Republic (a coalition of leftists and islamists), Ettakatol (a left-leaning party), and Ennahda formed a tripartite alliance that allowed them to form a government and occupy the presidency and the speaker of parliament's position. Marzouki himself was indirectly elected president in December 2011 by the Constituent Assembly. During his tenure, Marzouki's support within secular and left-wing circles declined markedly, which was attributed to his alliance with Ennahda. Marzouki's Congress for the Republic had 29 seats out of 217 in the 2011 Constituent Assembly elections. In the 2014 parliamentary elections, the Congress' share of seats declined to 4 out of 217.

and for referring them to the interim president who would then adopt them in the form of a decree-law. The Commission's decisions were to be taken through consensus or by majority in case consensus was not possible (Article 5). The Commission organized its first session on February 2, 2011. The Commission's members agreed by consensus that a new constitution should be written by an elected Constituent Assembly.[24] On the other hand, Commission members also proposed a number of other initiatives that were divisive and arguably worsened the Islamist/secular divide. The Commission debated a proposal to adopt a "republican pact" that was supposed to enshrine a number of fundamental principles, including the separation of religion and state, as well as a political parties law that would have restricted fundraising opportunities for some parties.[25] Both of these proposals were adopted despite the divisions that they provoked within the Commission, ultimately causing some parties (including Ennahda) to withdraw altogether.[26] Many ordinary Tunisians considered that the Commission was not properly representative mainly because the Commission's members were drawn from elite circles, which meant that revolutionary circles were excluded.[27]

Electoral Results: Elections were eventually organized in October 2011, which saw the Islamist Ennahda win a plurality at 37 percent, an impressive result but far from a majority. The results stood in strong contrast to other regional outcomes. Ennahda formed an alliance with the two largest secular parties to form a government (which came to be known as the "troïka"), which was symptomatic of both its strength and its weakness. In Egypt, Islamist groups returned 69 percent of the vote, giving it a crushing advantage in the 2012 constitutional negotiations that ultimately caused them to overreach. In Libya, Islamists returned around sixty-one seats in the 2012 elections, but were not fully unified, while the remainder of the legislature was populated by a constellation of parties and individual candidates, massively complicating government formation and policy making. By that standard, the membership

[24] That recommendation was formally adopted in law through Decree-Law 27 (2011) (establishing a higher electoral commission to "supervise the elections of a national constituent assembly") and through Decree-Law 35 (2011) (establishing the legislative framework for the coming elections).

[25] The "republican pact," in particular, was widely interpreted as having as its purpose the curtailment of the types of reform that the future constituent assembly (which was expected to be dominated by the Islamist-leaning Ennahda) would be able to adopt; see, for example, "Tunisie, un pacte républicain motivé par la peur d'Ennahdha," Global Net (April 24, 2011).

[26] "Islamist Group Ennahda Quits Tunisia's Reform Commission, For Now," Agence France-Presse (June 28, 2011).

[27] See Héla Yousfi, "The Tunisian Constitution Tested against the Revolutionary Ideal," in Constitution of Tunisia, United Nations Development Programme (2017).

of Tunisia's Constituent Assembly was fortuitous as it meant that Ennahda was strong enough to negotiate the formation of a government and a policy agenda but far enough from a majority that it would be forced to compromise on key substantive issues. Nevertheless, the troïka made the mistake of assuming that electoral results were the only factor that should determine the negotiations' dynamics, which led to an attempt to impose majoritarian decision-making in the constitutional process. This was complicated by a number of factors, including that Ennahda on its own did not control a majority of the Assembly, and that the troïka was disunited on a number of fundamental substantive issues. In addition, Tunisia generally suffered from a weak political party culture, which manifested itself partly through the very large amount of floor crossing, party implosions, and formations that occurred within a relatively short amount of time.[28] The practical impact is that senior positions within substantive committees were allocated to the troïka early on in the Assembly's life, and were maintained even after Ennahda's partners were greatly reduced in size as a result of defections.

Mini-constitution: One of the National Constituent Assembly's first actions was to adopt an organic law that would organize the system of government during the interim period. The document that was ultimately adopted became known as the "mini-constitution" and served as a type of interim constitution. In contrast to both Libya and Egypt, Tunisia would be entirely governed through revolutionary legitimacy throughout this period. Egypt's and Libya's respective interim constitutions were drafted before elections were organized, and the elected bodies were constrained in their work by these frameworks and by the behavior of other institutions (including the courts and the security sector). In Tunisia, elected members of the Assembly, and more particularly the troïka, would be solely responsible for establishing the constitutional framework for the transitional period.[29] The only form of control and oversight over the Assembly's work would be political in nature, either within the Assembly itself or through mass protests. An ad hoc drafting committee, composed of members of the ruling coalition and of the opposition, was established to draw up the organic law. An initial draft was prepared by Ennahda, presented to the committee on behalf of the troïka, and subsequently debated and amended by the entire committee. Law 6 (2011) was

[28] Through the transitional period, significant numbers of Ennahda's own secular allies would defect to the opposition, which decreased Ennahda's ability to impose its agenda.

[29] By way of example, members of the troïka argued at the time that the High Commission to achieve the goals of the revolution on political reforms and democratic transition should be dissolved given that the only role that it could play would be to restrain the Constituent Assembly. Interview, Senior parliamentary staffer (February 28, 2020).

adopted by 141 out of 217 members, with 37 voting against, and served as an interim constitution that would remain in force until a new permanent constitution could be adopted. It established a fully parliamentary system (in keeping with the preferences of Islamist parties throughout the region). Under the law, the Assembly was to exercise two functions, that of a constituent power that would be responsible for drawing up a new constitution, as well as ordinary legislative functions (Article 3). After completing the constitutional negotiation process, the Assembly was to adopt each provision individually, pursuant to which it was to adopt the constitution as a whole by a two-thirds majority of all its members (Article 5), failing which a second vote would be held a month later in which the threshold would be lowered to an "absolute majority of all the Assembly's members" (Article 5). The interim president of the republic was indirectly elected by an absolute majority of the Assembly's members (Article 10), who would then nominate the largest parliamentary party's candidate to form a government (Article 15), which was then granted confidence by an absolute majority (Article 15). Meanwhile, the Assembly could withdraw confidence from the government by an "absolute majority of its members" (Article 19). In the years that followed, many commentators argued that the cabinet totally overshadowed the president, which played a role in the negotiations on the shape of the future system of government.[30]

PROCEDURE AND EARLY DRAFTS

Political Interests: As in other countries in the region, the Constituent Assembly's rules of procedure were a major source of contention throughout the entire process. The negotiations on the Rules of Procedure were far more contentious, which is reflected by the amount of time that it took to finalize the text. A second ad hoc committee, which included representatives from the troïka and the opposition, was established to prepare the rules. During the discussions, Ennahda prioritized mechanisms that would increase its own control over the process. In particular, Ennahda expected that the Assembly's general rapporteur would be elected from among its own ranks, and that most of the substantive committee heads would be drawn from the troïka. Ennahda therefore sought to establish a joint drafting committee that

[30] Earlier versions had provided that a withdrawal of confidence could only take place with a majority of two-thirds, a matter of significant controversy as it could mean that Ennahda could potentially remain in power even if most of its allies defected to the opposition; see Sélim Ben Abdesselem, Tome I: La Paranthèse de la Constituante – Du Rêve au Cauchemar, Nirvana (2018), at 127.

would have a very broad mandate and that would be dominated by friendly members and led by the general rapporteur. Ennahda and other groups were also concerned about the smaller parties' lack of negotiating and drafting capacity, and so therefore sought to impose short time frames. The concern was well founded, but a short time frame could not be a solution mainly because the Assembly's members were likely to be overburdened, particularly during the initial period, but also because procedural timeframes are largely ineffectual.[31] More creative solutions might have been more appropriate in the circumstances. Opposition members were equally concerned that a majoritarian approach to decision-making could allow Ennahda to determine the final outcome of the process, and so therefore pushed in favor of a more consensual approach. These dynamics played themselves out right from the start.

Initial Draft: The ad hoc committee decided not to rely on the previous parliament's internal rules as a starting point and to draw up an original draft that would also not be inspired from a particular party's perspective. Very early on, an Ennahda member presented a full draft of the rules that was 364 articles long.[32] That November draft provided for eight substantive committees (Rule 105) that were required to negotiate and draft the new constitution in two steps (Rule 113).[33] The first step stated that within seven weeks all committees were required to produce an initial report for discussion by the General Assembly (Rule 114) and which would have had to conform to a predetermined outline

[31] Each Constituent Assembly member was expected to be a member of a constitutional committee and an ordinary legislative committee. In addition, because the former ruling party had been dissolved, very few of the members would have any relevant experience to back themselves up. Finally, because of the revolutionary situation, the Assembly was under significant pressure to address a large number of issues, each of which required significant attention and took away the opportunity to focus on constitutional drafting.

[32] The November draft of the rules of procedure is in the author's possession. One member of the troïka have since written that they and some of their political leaders had not seen the draft rules until they were circulated to all members of the ad hoc committee; see Ben Abdesselem (2018), at 122–123. According to one former member of the Constituent Assembly, a legal adviser to the parliament had worked on amending the previous parliament's rules of procedure and had prepared a draft that was over 461 articles long prior to the revolution. According to that same account, after the Constituent Assembly was elected, the legal adviser in question worked with members of Ennahda to adapt the 461 article version to the Constituent Assembly's purposes; Interview with former member of the Constituent Assembly March 10, 2020.

[33] The substantive committees were as follows: fundamental principles; legislative authority; executive authority; judicial authority; local authority; independent agencies; constitutional oversight; constitutional amendment. Interestingly, the November draft did not provide which if any of the committees should focus on ordinary citizens rights and liberties.

(Rule 116).[34] The results and recommendations from the General Assembly's debate on the initial reports would then be transmitted to the relevant committees, which were to have another seven weeks to finalize another round of internal deliberations (Rule 117) and to submit a second report to the General Assembly (Rule 118).[35] Importantly, the November draft also provided for a joint drafting committee (Rule 106), which was to be a major source of controversy throughout the drafting process. The committee's mandate was defined as "the immediate and ongoing coordination of the work of the constituent committees to ensure that the final version of the draft constitution's provisions are consistent, coherent and unequivocal in its philosophy" (Rule 121). What was missing, however, was a clear indication as to whether or not the joint committee could overrule the substantive committees. The November draft was also very brief on the mechanisms of how the joint committee would operate, stating only that the substantive committees were required to "coordinate" with the joint committee (Rule 109). The November draft did not clearly indicate what steps should be followed after the General Assembly's second debate but it did provide that the joint drafting committee was responsible for "preparing the final draft of the constitution pursuant to the General Assembly's decisions" (Rule 121). This absence of detail increased the importance of the joint committee's composition (which was also a subject of major controversy). The November draft provided that the joint committee should consist of the Assembly's general rapporteur (who was to be the joint committee's chairman), and all of the substantive committees' heads and rapporteurs (Rule 122). Depending on the mechanisms through which these individuals were to be chosen, the joint committee could easily become dominated by specific political groups.

January 2012 Version: Over the weeks that followed, the draft was debated vigorously by the ad hoc committee. The joint drafting committee's mandate proved to be a major source of disagreement, with many members concerned

[34] Rule 106 provided that the committees' reports should consist of three parts, the first consisting of a general presentation of the issues of members' different views, the second a summary of the committee's process (including a list of all the references that it will have consulted, the opinions that it will have heard in its sessions, a summary of its cooperation with the joint drafting committee, etc.), and the third a summary of the committee's recommendations (including a first draft of the relevant sections, an explanatory document explaining the choices that the committee will have made, a separate explanation of contrary opinions from other committees, etc.).

[35] Rule 120 provided that the committee's second reports should consist of four parts. Rule 120 set out even more detail than Rule 106, requiring, for example, that the second report should include the relevant committee's first draft, its second draft, comments from other committees' members and from independent experts, etc.

about the influence that Ennahda could exercise through it. The final version of the rules was adopted on January 20, 2012 and constituted 143 articles, less than half the length of the original draft.[36] It reduced the number of constitutional committees to six, abandoned the strict timeframes, and also removed all the detail on how the committees should carry out their work.[37] On the mandate of the joint drafting committee, renamed the "Joint Committee for Cooperation and Drafting," members could not reach agreement on whether it could overrule the substantive committees and so therefore settled on a vague formulation as a form of compromise.[38] The final wording provided that the Joint Committee should "coordinate the work of the constitutional committees" and also "prepare the final draft of the constitution" (Rule 104). The wording left a number of issues unresolved: What should happen in the event of a contradiction between two separate committees' drafts? Should the Joint Committee be the ultimate arbiter of such a disagreement or should the members of the two committees be involved? Also, what should happen if the Joint Committee disagreed with arrangements or wording that one of the committees had adopted in its section of the constitution? Was it within the Joint Committee's mandate to amend that specific section, and if so could it make those amendments without referring back to the relevant committee? Or could it make recommendations to the relevant committee? The Rules of Procedure did not explicitly answer any of these issues, but did indicate in very broad terms that the Joint Committee could amend drafts that were referred to it by specific substantive committees and that it "could" refer those amendments back to the relevant committees, although it was not under an obligation to do so (Rule 65). Ad hoc committee members could not agree on any of these issues and so therefore deferred them to be resolved at a later date, which is to say after the emergence of a crisis surrounding the issue. In the meantime, the controversy shifted to the Joint Committee's composition and its decision-making process. The January 2012 version of the rules provided that the Joint Committee would consist of a number ex officio members,

[36] An unofficial English language translation of the Assembly's rules of procedures is available here: www.constitutionnet.org/vl/item/tunisia-constituent-assemblys-rules-procedure. For an analysis of the rules of procedure, see Bill Proctor and Ikbal Ben Moussa, "The Tunisian Constituent Assembly's By-laws: A Brief Analysis," International IDEA (2013), at www.idea.int/publications/tunisian-constituent-assemblys-by-laws/index.cfm.

[37] According to the January 2012 version, the substantive committees were as follows: governing principles and constitutional amendment; rights and freedoms; legislative and executive branches; legal, administrative, financial, and constitutional jurisdiction; constitutional authorities; and municipal and public authorities.

[38] A legal adviser to the Constituent Assembly who attended the *ad hoc* committee's sessions described them as "very tense"; Interview with the author (March 9, 2020).

including the President of the Constituent Assembly, the general rapporteur, the first and second assistants to the constitution general rapporteur, and the chairmen and rapporteurs of all constitutional committees (Rule 103).[39] In parallel, the Assembly decided that the chair and rapporteur positions would be allocated in proportion to each group's level of representation in the Assembly, which in turn meant that the Joint Committee would not be completely dominated by the troïka. However, Rule 60 provided that all committees should take their decisions by "majority vote" without any specific provision for the Joint Committee or for the drawing up of a full draft of the constitution. The combined effect of all these provisions was that, even though the opposition would have adequate representation in the Joint Committee, its minority status meant that it had no effective means to influence decision-making. The Rules of Procedure therefore set in motion a majoritarian system that would allow the troïka to impose its will in the constitutional negotiations. Despite the danger that they posed to the negotiations, the Rules of Procedure were adopted on January 20, 2012 and was by a near unanimity of members, with only two members abstaining.

Initial constitutional drafts and amendments to the Rules of Procedure: A first, very preliminary draft of the constitution was published in August 2012. The draft was incomplete, consisting in part of a table that included several options in crucial areas. Many commentators complained of a lack of progress and openly wondered what Assembly members had been doing for the previous 10 months. A second draft was published in December 2012, which caused additional criticism. A number of amendments to the Rules of Procedure were debated, including one proposal that was never adopted and that would have required the final constitution to take into account the "constitutional committees' final drafts" and "proposals from citizens and civil society through national dialogue."[40] The Rules of Procedure were ultimately amended in March 2013 for the purpose of accelerating the pace at which the substantive committees were working. New wording obliged the committees to "review comments and suggestions" received from the General Assembly within ten days (Rule 104(3)).[41] The amendment also for the first time provided a formal role for independent experts. It provided that, after the substantive committees completed their final drafts, the Joint Committee

[39] See, for example, Ben Abdesselem (2018), at 151–158.

[40] Proposed amendments to the Rules of Procedure (January 2013) (unpublished, in the author's possession).

[41] Under the new rule, if a committee failed to meet this deadline, then it would be obliged to carry out its work "with the assistance" of the Joint Committee and carry out its review within five days.

should review the drafts with the assistance of independent experts in no more than ten days, at which point the committees were to be given one final opportunity to review the drafts within two days (Rule 104(3)). A third draft of the constitution was published in April 2013. At that point, a number of issues had been agreed, but a number of important areas of disagreement remained to be resolved. For example, Article 141 of the draft provided that Islam's position as the state religion could not be changed through a constitutional amendment, which some opposition figures argued represented another attempt to Islamize Tunisia's constitution.[42] In addition, Article 73 of the June 1, 2013 draft provided that candidates for the position of president of the republic could not be dual nationals and could not be over seventy-five years old "on the day on which they present their candidature," wording that appeared designed to exclude a prominent opposition figure who was considering to contest the coming elections.

BREAKDOWN AND RESOLUTION

Narratives around the June 2013 Draft: On June 1, 2013, controversy erupted following the publication of a fourth draft.[43] Many opposition members accused Ennahda, and in particular the General Rapporteur (who became a hate figure in many circles), of manipulating the constitutional drafting process through its control of the Joint Committee for Cooperation and Drafting. Opposition members claimed that after the third draft had been published, the substantive committees reached agreement on a number of the longstanding points of divergence and also agreed to establish new institutional arrangements, much of which was ignored by the Joint Committee. By way of example, some members stated that the human rights committee reached agreement to amend the wording of the general limitations clause.[44] One opposition member stated that one committee had agreed to include wording that would establish a standing committee on democratic control of

[42] Yadh Ben Achour, Tunisie: Une Revolution En Pays D'islam, Cérès éditions (2016), at 321–322.

[43] See, for example, Rym Mahjoub, "From Division to Consensus: The Role and Contribution of the Consensus Committee," in Constitution of Tunisia, United Nations Development Programme (2017).

[44] Article 48 of the June 1, 2013 draft provided that limitations on fundamental rights could not "take away from the right's essence" without making reference to the principles of proportionality and necessity, which some opposition members had been demanding. In addition, Article 30 of the draft provided that freedom of expression could not be limited "except on the basis of law that protects the rights, reputation, security and health of others," which was not strong enough for some opposition members.

security and defense.[45] Opposition members alleged that both of these changes, as well as many others, were ignored by the Joint Committee and that other changes were introduced to the draft without consulting the relevant committees. Opposition members also complained that the published version of the June 1, 2013 draft was (for the first time) formally initialed, which suggested to some members that leaders of the troïka intended for it to be final pending adoption by the Assembly as a whole. An adviser to the Assembly also argued that the General Rapporteur deliberately violated the March 2013 amendments to the rules. Rather than review the draft constitution with the assistance of independent experts (Rule 104(3)), the Joint Committee prepared a new version of the draft on its own, which it then referred to the experts for comment, without indicating what had changed between the two versions.[46] In contrast, the General Rapporteur offered a radically different account of the Joint Committee's work, stating that it only made changes "if articles were not of the standard required for a constitution, or unnecessary details or repetitions existed, or there was an absence of content that required correction." He also wrote that on occasion, the Joint Committee "had to intercede" when the members of a specific committee "could not reach a resolution."[47] Finally, a second adviser to the Assembly was far less charitable to both sides. According to that account, the substantive committees' work was "confused," there was hardly any coordination between them, which meant that they adopted radically different working methods from each other, and they did not read any of the written submissions that were sent by members of the general public. The impact was that the Joint Committee "did not receive a single unified text. Instead it received six disjointed documents covering eight chapters." In the circumstances, the adviser argued that the Joint Committee "had no other choice" but to make amendments to the text.[48]

45 See Hatem M'rad, National Dialogue in Tunisia, Nirvana (2015), at 81.

46 The same legal adviser also indicated that the General Rapporteur selected sympathetic experts for the review process; Interview with the author, March 14, 2020.

47 See Habib Khedher, "The General Rapporteur of the Constitution and of the Joint Commission for the Coordination and Drafting of the New Constitution," in Constitution of Tunisia, United Nations Development Programme (2017). The General Rapporteur's narrative is supported by the Constituent Assembly's General Report on the Constitutional Draft (which, it should be said, the General Rapporteur most probably had a hand in writing), according to which the chairman of a key committee requested of the Joint Committee that it resolve a number of points of contention; see General Report on the Constitutional Draft, Constituent Assembly (June 14, 2013).

48 See Adel Bsili, "Beginning and Organization of the Work of the Constituent Committees," in Constitution of Tunisia, United Nations Development Programme (2017).

Consensus Committee: Pursuant to that controversy, the main parties in the Constituent Assembly agreed to form a "Consensus Committee." That body was formed in late June 2013 and met on a small number of occasions during July 2013 without having been formally established, and without its exact mandate and decision-making process having been determined. However, it was generally understood that the new Committee would seek to resolve all the substantive disagreements between the main parties that were represented in the Assembly. At first, the main blocs worked out the Committee's composition, making sure to allow adequate representation for opposition blocs outside of the ruling troïka. The Committee also negotiated a list of all the outstanding issues of contention that it would seek to resolve. The list included the relationship between religion and state (including Article 141, see earlier), the limitations clause (Article 48, see earlier), and a number of other discrete issues (including restrictions on candidates for president of the republic, government formation, composition of both the high judicial council and the constitutional court, etc.).[49] The Committee's deliberations were highly contentious. In a meeting that took place on July 24, 2013, the Committee debated specific formulations that impacted the relationship between religion and state. The members present debated the then draft of the preamble and of Article 141 and whether the specific wording that was still in the draft at the time established a civil state, or whether it was effectively allowing for religion to play a greater role in public life than it had in the past. The discussion was charged and ended without any progress having been made on this primordial issue that had absorbed so much attention since the start of the 2011 uprising.[50]

National and Regional Crisis: The negotiations were taking place against a backdrop of increased tensions both within Tunisia and across the region. At the start of July 2013, the Islamist president of Egypt was removed from office by the security services, which led to a significant spike in violence. On July 25, 2013, the day after the Consensus Committee failed to reach agreement on the relationship between religion and state, a prominent member of the Constituent Assembly and of the secular opposition was assassinated.[51] Given the circumstances, Tunisia's opposition decided to suspend its

[49] See Selma Mabrouk, 2011–2014: Le Bras de Fer, Arabesques (2018), at 429–430.

[50] For a detailed account of the meeting, see Ibid., at 436–452.

[51] The assassin's identity was not known at the time, but the act itself came at a time of growing violence against secular Tunisians. On occasion, specific acts of violence were openly carried out by Islamist groups. The assassination was therefore attributed to Islamists, and Ennahda was blamed either for orchestrating the assassination or at least for creating a permissive environment that encouraged attacks against secular interests. See, for example, Anne Wolf,

participation in the Assembly, the Consensus Committee's work was suspended, and major demonstrations and counter-demonstrations were organized, some of which called for the Assembly to be dissolved. Some Tunisians called for security services to intervene against Ennahda as in Egypt.[52] Shortly thereafter, on August 14, 2013, hundreds of supporters of Egypt's main Islamist party were massacred by security services in Cairo, emphasizing the fragility of Tunisia's own situation and the importance of reaching a solution.[53] In response to the country's deteriorating circumstances, the Speaker decided to suspend the Assembly's work while politicians and civil society leaders scrambled to find a solution.

National Dialogue: In response, a group of civil society organizations launched an initiative that they hoped would lead to a resolution. It was not the first time that civil society had intervened to help move the formal process along during the transitional period.[54] The main trade union, the bar association, a human rights organization, and the syndicate of employers formed what has become known as the "Quartet" for the purpose of proposing and encouraging the country's main parties to agree on a road map to end the transitional process. The Quartet focused on the main elements that would have to be agreed, including the electoral process, the formation of an interim and neutral government to oversee the electoral process, and the completion of the constitutional process. Each of these individual items required special consideration, as did the exact sequence in which the road map would be implemented. On August 22, 2013, several main parties including Ennahda announced that they had reached an agreement on some of the more contentious outstanding issues, including the relationship between religion and state. On September 18, 2013, the Quartet proposed a roadmap for the remainder of the transitional period. After having had the opportunity to consider the Quartet's proposition internally, the main parties met in the context of an organized National Dialogue starting in October 2013, which saw the parties meeting regularly with a view to trying to reach consensus on each of these four elements. In parallel, the Consensus Committee restarted its work. The two tracks were connected in a number of ways. With respect to substantive

"Religious violence in Tunisia three years after the revolution," CTC Sentinel, Vol. 7, No. 2 (February 2014), at 19.

52 "Will Tunisia's Rebellion Be Successful as in Egypt" (هل سيكتب لتمرد تونس نجاح التمرد المصري؟), France24 (July 4, 2013).

53 See, for example, Interventions by various representatives, July 8, 2013 session, National Constituent Assembly Minutes, Plenary Sessions, Tome 2, Assembly of the Representatives of the People (2020), at 1066–1070.

54 For more, see M'rad (2015).

discussions on the constitution, the National Dialogue reached broad agreement on a number of issues, leaving the details to the Consensus Committee.[55] Where specific substantive disagreements could not be resolved in the Consensus Committee, they were referred to the National Dialogue, which would then seek a resolution.[56] The sessions were not traditional mediation sessions, particularly given that Quartet members were leading protagonists in the discussions with their own interests (which were often not in line with Ennahda's own positions).[57] Ennahda was under pressure from all sides (its popularity within Tunisia was waning and regional dynamics were stacked against it, creating major risks for its survival) and so therefore conceded in favor of the majority of the demands that were made. By way of example, opposition members in the Consensus Committee argued that Article 46 on women's rights should include the principle of nonregression of accrued rights. Ennahda eventually accepted after having resisted the proposal for some time mainly because it feared a public backlash.[58]

Adoption: The Constituent Assembly's rules of procedure were eventually modified to recognize the establishment of the Consensus Committee and therefore the legitimacy of its decisions to be properly considered as having been taken by the Assembly as a whole.[59] A few days later, on January 26, 2014, the new Constitution was finalized and formally adopted by the Constituent Assembly by a large majority of its members.[60] There is significant debate on the factors that allowed the deadlock to be broken and its relative success in comparison to some other countries in the region. Some analysts attributed Tunisia's success to Ennahda's capacity and willingness to compromise on some of the key elements of its platform,[61] while others note more structural factors, such as the absence of oil wealth or of a hereditary system of government.[62] To this should be added the nonpolitical traditions of Tunisia's

55 See Mahjoub (2017).

56 See M'rad (2015), at 84.

57 See Hèla Yousfi, L'UGTT: Une Passion Tunisienne, IRMC (2015).

58 See Mahjoub (2017).

59 The Rules were amended on January 14, 2014. It amended Rule 41 to provide that the President of the National Constituent Assembly could exceptionally establish a committee known as the "Consensus Committee," which was subject to its own composition and decision-making rules. A new Article 106(bis) provided that the Committee's decisions were binding.

60 See Zaid Al-Ali and Donia Ben Romdhane, "Tunisia's New Constitution: Progress and Challenges to Come," OpenDemocracy (February 16, 2014).

61 See, for example, Monika Marks, "Convince, Coerce, or Compromise? Ennahda's Approach to Tunisia's Constitution," Brookings Doha Center Analysis Center, Number 10 (February 2014).

62 See Jason Brownlee, Tarek Masoud, and Andrew Reynolds, "Why the Modest Harvest?," Journal of Democracy, Vol. 24, No. 4 (October 2013), 29–44.

military and regional cross-border learning from violence that was developing in Libya and Egypt.[63] Ultimately, Tunisia's relative success can be attributed to a number of factors, including that political forces were relatively balanced throughout the process. Ennahda, the country's largest political force at the time, which at its high point represented 37 percent of the electorate, and was unable to gather any other significant fellow travelers to support its position, which meant that Ennahda had no choice but to compromise on a large proportion of its positions. In addition, the parties can be credited with adopting a pragmatic approach to the process' initial design. Over time, as the parties moved deeper into crisis, they abandoned many of the rules that they had established in favor of a negotiated, consensus-based arrangement that was detached from electoral outcomes.

CONSTITUTION

Impact of Political Divisions: The negotiations were defined by the risk of conflict between Islamist and non-Islamist members. The impact was that debates on national identity and the role of religion were reopened despite the fact that they had little or nothing to do with the uprising that had just taken place.[64] The risk also meant that much of the constitutional negotiations prioritized political stability, which meant that the Assembly was fixated on how to prevent any particular political grouping from capturing particular institutions and therefore dominating the state in its entirety. As a result, the composition of the country's highest judicial bodies (including the constitutional court) became a major source of contention between the parties. In contrast, social and economic considerations were deprioritized. On the other hand, negotiators were broadly aware of the need to formally advocate in favor of social justice but were not prepared to do anything other than reword existing provisions and perhaps also add to the list of rights without considering whether they should be directly enforceable. Decentralization garnered close to no interest in the Assembly. Published accounts of the negotiations indicate that very few proposals were made other than to make existing subnational units more independent, and that there was scarcely any debate between the members on how this should be achieved.[65]

63 See "Reform and Security Strategy in Tunisia," International Crisis Group, Middle East and North Africa Report Number 161 (July 23, 2015).

64 See, for example, Hédi Abdelkefi, The Tunisian Constitution: The Evolution of a Text, United Nations Development Programme (2017).

65 According to one account, there were disagreements on all of the draft constitution's provisions with the exception of the section on decentralization; see Mahjoub (2017).

Semi-presidentialism: As noted previously, in 2011, Tunisia followed a regional trend and transitioned from a presidential to a parliamentary constitutional system. Ennahda was the largest party in the Constituent Assembly and was expecting to perform well in future parliamentary elections. As a result, during the constitutional negotiations, it argued consistently in favor of increasing the parliament's mandate, including in areas that had traditionally fallen under the executive power's mandate. Conversely, many non-Islamist members argued in favor of a directly elected president who would exercise considerable responsibility. They also argued in favor of a two-round presidential electoral system, based on the expectation that secular and/or nationalist candidates would enjoy a majority of support. The two sides compromised in favor of a form of semi-presidentialism, so as to prevent the parliament or the president from dominating the other.[66] So therefore, while the constitution still provides for a directly elected president (Article 75), the president's influence is now balanced by a resurgent parliament. On government formation, the president must task the candidate of the largest electoral coalition with forming the government (Article 89).[67] The president and prime minister share responsibility on shaping government policy (Articles 91, 93). Parliament's oversight powers are now greatly increased, including through the ability to withdraw confidence from individual ministers based on an absolute majority of votes (Article 97). Meanwhile, the president's position is still highly secure, given that the only mechanism through which the president can be removed during his term of office is impeachment by a majority of two-thirds of the parliament's members (Article 88).

[66] For more on constitutional arrangements relating to semi-presidentialism, see: Sujit Choudhry and Richard Stacey, Semi-Presidentialism as Power Sharing: Constitutional Reform after the Arab Spring, Center for Constitutional Transitions and International IDEA (Spring 2014).

[67] The (now defunct) 2012 Egyptian constitution, and the 2014 constitution both provided for similar mechanisms, albeit each with its own specific modalities. Article 146 if the 2014 constitution provides, "The President of the Republic assigns a Prime Minister to form the government and present his program to the House of Representatives. If his government does not obtain the confidence of the majority of the members of the House of Representatives within no more 30 days, the President appoints a Prime Minister based on the nomination of the party or the coalition that holds a plurality of seats in the House of Representatives. If his government fails to win the confidence of the majority of the members of the House of Representatives within 30 days, the House is deemed dissolved, and the President of the Republic calls for the elections of a new House of Representatives within 60 days from the date the dissolution is announced. In all cases, the sum of the periods set forth in this Article shall not exceed 60 days." Article 47 of the new 2011 Moroccan constitution also provides that the King must appoint the prime minister from the largest political party in parliament, but does not specifically state that that individual must have been selected for the task by the party in question.

Balance within Parliament: The constitution also seeks to maintain a balance of interests within specific institutions. Article 60 provides that the parliament's powerful finance committee (which is responsible for reviewing the state's annual state budget before it is voted on in parliament) should be headed by a member of the opposition. This is based in large part on a practice that has been in place for some time in the United Kingdom's House of Commons, in which the Public Accounts Committee is by convention always headed by a member of the opposition.[68] Surprisingly, however, the president retains significant authority on security issues, which is probably attributable to the weight of constitutional tradition in Tunisia. Article 78 states that the president is solely responsible for appointing and dismissing senior military officers. Articles 18 and 19 establish the army and police's mandate in broad terms and also provide that both institutions should remain impartial, but does not set in place any mechanisms that would limit presidential influence. On states of emergency, the president may take "any measures" in the event of "imminent danger," the only limitation being that the president cannot dissolve the parliament (Article 80). Article 80 also does not specifically state how long a state of emergency may last. It merely states that an appeal may be made to the constitutional court thirty days after the emergency measures come into effect to determine if the circumstances that led to the initial declaration remain in existence.[69] The constitution also does not specifically state which rights, if any, cannot be derogated from during a state of emergency.

Constitutional Court: The Assembly's discussions on the constitutional court (which replaced a largely ineffectual constitutional council) were also highly revealing of the dynamics that dominated the drafting process. In other countries, the establishment of a new constitutional court is often regarded as an opportunity to redefine the role and place of the courts within the state's institutional structure.[70] In Tunisia, negotiators came to an agreement within

[68] The 2011 Moroccan constitution also provides the parliamentary opposition significant rights and arguably goes further than Article 60 in certain respects. For more on Morocco's constitution, see Mohamed Madani, Driss Maghraoui, and Saloua Zerhouni, THE 2011 MOROCCAN CONSTITUTION: A CRITICAL ANALYSIS, International IDEA (2012).

[69] In 2012, constitutional drafters in Egypt were so nervous about a possible return to Mubarak-era practices that they set out specific time limits for states of emergency and imposed the requirement that a referendum take place to allow any exceptional powers to continue past that time limit. The 2014 constitution also clearly specifies that a state of emergency can only extend as much as six months (Article 154).

[70] In South Africa, following the end of Apartheid, the new ruling authorities established a new and progressive constitutional court to serve as a model for the rest of the judiciary and to promote the spirit and purpose of the Constitution's bill of rights.

months of starting their work that the court's mandate should mainly consist of monitoring the constitutionality of draft bills and laws that are already in effect,[71] a change that was largely in keeping with a reform that had already been adopted in France in 2008[72] and in Morocco in 2011.[73] In so doing, an important opportunity was missed to go further by explicitly tying the court to the constitution's commitment to social justice. Instead, in conformity with the desire to maintain a semblance of neutrality, negotiators focused most of their attention on achieving some form of balance in the court's composition and in so doing may have contributed to tilting the court's outlook in favor of conservatism or judicial traditionalism. That lack of commitment could have been partially compensated by an appointment mechanism that would have established a progressive court. The 2014 Constitution provides that the president, the parliament, and the supreme judicial council should appoint four members each (Article 118). Under that arrangement, parliamentary and judicial nominations will necessarily depend on both institutions' makeup and their internal decision-making processes. For parliament, the electoral law ensures a highly fractured membership, which itself ensures that electing candidates to the court will be subject to political bargaining that will pay little to no interest in the nominees' positions.[74] In so far as the judicial council is concerned, what is most surprising is that Tunisia's revolutionary moment led to a complete reconfiguration of the executive and parliament's composition, but left the judiciary mainly intact despite the fact that many of its members are the product of the previous regime.[75] In current circumstances, the judicial council is likely to nominate to the constitutional court conservative members who will seek to maintain traditions dating from before the

[71] See, Article 5.20 of the August 2012 draft, and Article 117 of the December 2012 draft.

[72] France's Law 2008-724, which was adopted on July 23, 2008, introduced a number of reforms to the 1958 constitution, including but not limited to allowing for the first time the constitutional council to exercise a posteriori control over the constitutionality of laws.

[73] Articles 132 and 133, 2011 Constitution of Morocco.

[74] Organic Law 50-2015 provides that each of the parliament's candidates should be elected by a two-thirds majority of its members, a threshold that the parliament has thus far been unable to meet.

[75] See, for example, Samer Ghamroun, "In Memory of Mokhtar Yahyaoui (1952–2015): Lessons from Tunisia's Rebel Judge," Legal Agenda (November 30, 2015); "Repression of Former Political Prisoners in Tunisia," Human Rights Watch (March 24, 2010). In Kenya, the 2010 constitution established a mechanism that had as its purpose renewal of judicial culture. The Judges and Magistrates Vetting Board provided for the establishment of a judicial vetting commission, which was responsible for investigating all judges for the purposes of rooting out corruption and incompetence. See 2010 Constitution of Kenya, Schedule 6, Section 23(1).

2014 constitution entered into force, regardless of how the judicial council's leadership is composed.[76]

Limitations Clause: There are a few consolations, including the introduction of a robust limitations clause. Limitations clauses are designed to prevent parliaments and governments arbitrarily, unfairly, or inequitably curbing basic' rights. Previously, the 1959 Constitution provided that all citizens had rights, but did not establish any specific means or criteria to determine which limitations were legitimate and which were not. In other countries, the courts acted to develop tests that could be applied but this did not happen in a systematic way in Tunisia. The post-2011 negotiators therefore decided to adopt a limitations clause for this purpose.[77] Negotiators struggled to choose from among a series of options, and opted at the last moment in favor of a progressive formulation that specifically states that legislation curbing rights can only be passed if it is "necessary to a civil and democratic society" and the nature of the restrictions that the legislation envisages must be "proportional" to the objectives that the legislation seeks to achieve.[78] Crucially, Article 49 also provides that "[j]udicial authorities ensure that rights and freedoms are protected from all violations."

Assessment: In spite of a number of serious challenges, the Tunisian Constituent Assembly – under the people's ever watchful eye – successfully negotiated a new and modern constitution, which was finally approved by a

[76] Organic Law 2016-34 provides that the judicial council should consist of forty-five members of whom eighteen are elected judges and twelve will be ex officio members (to be drawn from senior ranks of the judiciary). Some analysts and pressure groups have argued that, in order to protect the judiciary's independence, the number of elected judges should constitute at least a majority of the council's members. See Human Rights Watch, "Tunisia: Law Falls Short on Judicial Independence," June 2, 2015. Comparative evidence suggests that a higher proportion is unlikely to actually make a difference in the council's performance. See Nuno Garoupa and Tom Ginsburg, JUDICIAL REPUTATION: A COMPARATIVE THEORY, University of Chicago Press (2015).

[77] For more on the doctrine of proportionality, see Aharon Barak, PROPORTIONALITY: CONSTITUTIONAL RIGHTS AND THEIR LIMITATIONS, Cambridge University Press (2012). See Chapter 7 for more.

[78] Article 49 of Tunisia's constitution provides as follows, "The limitations that can be imposed on the exercise of the rights and freedoms guaranteed in this Constitution will be established by law, without compromising their essence. Any such limitations can only be put in place for reasons necessary to a civil and democratic state and with the aim of protecting the rights of others, or based on the requirements of public order, national defence, public health or public morals, and provided there is proportionality between these restrictions and the objective sought. Judicial authorities ensure that rights and freedoms are protected from all violations. There can be no amendment to the Constitution that undermines the human rights and freedoms guaranteed in this Constitution."

large majority of the Assembly's members in 2014. In 2011 the political class was far from prepared for the changes that had been forced on them by the people. Important cleavages between conservative Islamist politicians on the one hand and liberal and secular politicians on the other complicated negotiations and grew worse over time. For a time, it was far from certain that the negotiating parties would be able to reach a final agreement and indeed negotiations and the drafting process broke down altogether in June 2013 and was only salvaged through the intervention of civil society organizations and through the use of informal negotiations procedures. By successfully negotiating a final agreement, the Tunisians have led the way in proving that ideological differences need not lead to conflict or stalemate and that they can survive in the context of a modern Arab state and society. The pragmatic and result-based approach that the Tunisian negotiators adopted will serve as a positive example of successful constitution-making and conflict resolution not just for the Arab region, but for much of the rest of the world as well.

In early 2021, Tunisia was widely considered to be a democracy, but still suffered from significant difficulties. Political parties were highly unstable. Nationalist, liberal, left-wing parties were constantly collapsing, merging, rising, and splintering from each other, all of which contributed to growing popular distrust of political parties. Ennahda had lost much of its popularity but remained relatively united. Parliament was populated by a plethora of parties, the largest of which barely controlled a fifth of seats, which meant that the cabinet consisted of an incoherent alliance that could not agree on any clear set of policy preferences. Economic reform proved close to impossible in the circumstances, leading to near paralysis despite growing challenges. The spread of COVID-19 throughout the country worsened this trend. By January 2021, nighttime rioting and looting by thousands of young Tunisians were taking place daily, leading to hundreds of arrests.

2

Egypt

BACKGROUND

Early Constitutionalism: During much of the nineteenth century, Egypt formally remained part of the Ottoman Empire, but enjoyed significant autonomy. It was ruled as an absolute monarchy by its own local dynasty, had its own bureaucracy and armed forces, but was not an independent state recognized under international law. In 1866 a consultative chamber consisting entirely of notables was established. The chamber was not formally established as a separate branch of government and did not exercise any oversight over the executive.[1] By 1876, public debt owed to both the United Kingdom and France reached unsustainable levels, prompting a default that caused major economic and social upheaval. By 1882, a nationalist uprising led to the adoption of an Organic Law that established a limited form of constitutionalism, in which the executive was nominally accountable before an elected council of representatives but in which there were very few mechanisms to enforce accountability.[2] The Organic Law provided that the council could question executive officials (Articles 19–21), that a law could not enter into force without the council's approval (Article 25), and that budgetary commitments also had to be approved by the council (Articles 30–31). However, in the event the government and the council disagreed on policy or budgetary matters, the council was to be dissolved (Articles 23 and 36). The Law did note that if the newly elected chamber maintained the same opinion as the

[1] F. Robert Hunter, Egypt Under the Khedives 1805–1879: From Household Government to Modern Bureaucracy, American University in Cairo Press (1999), at 51–52; and A. Schölch, "Constitutional Development in Nineteenth Century Egypt," Middle Eastern Studies, Vol. 10, No. 1 (January 1974), 3–14.

[2] Juan Cole, Colonialism and Revolution in the Middle East, Princeton University Press (1993).

first then that opinion would be binding (Articles 24 and 37), a very weak reassurance.[3]

British Domination: Shortly after the Organic Law entered into force, the United Kingdom invaded and occupied the country. From that point onward until 1952, the United Kingdom exercised varying levels of control over Egypt. Initially, British officials served only as advisers to the Egyptian authorities, but had the capacity to remove ministers who did not implement their policy. As a result, the United Kingdom involved itself in practically every aspect of Egyptian life, while maintaining the fiction of Ottoman sovereignty, and without there being any means through which it could held accountable for its actions.[4] In 1914, after the Ottoman Empire entered the war on the side of the Central Powers, the United Kingdom declared martial law in Egypt, deposed the monarch (who had sided with the Ottomans) in favor of a relative, and formally established the country as a protectorate.[5] Egypt was therefore formally recognized as an independent state. It adopted its own flag and currency and could enter into international treaties. However, its internal affairs, including financial matters, continued to be constrained by British authorities.[6] Despite promises to the contrary, the United Kingdom forced Egyptians to carry a significant burden during the conflict, which contributed to an independence movement that had started before the war.[7] In 1919, local elites formally organized as the Wafd, a liberal political party, led a revolution against the occupation. In response, the British unilaterally declared Egypt independent in 1922, while making sure to maintain full control over key interests (including the security of its own communications, the defense of Egypt against "all foreign aggression or interference, direct or indirect," and the protection of foreign interests).[8] In the decades that followed, the United

[3] Reprinted in Parliamentary Papers, Egypt, Number 7 (1882).

[4] Afaf Lutfi al-Sayyid, Egypt and Cromer: A Study in Anglo-Egyptian Relations, John Murray (1968), at 58. British advisers "kept no record of [their] proceedings or decisions; in theory [they] could issue only administrative orders but in practice [they were] all powerful, being responsible to the British Foreign Office alone"; see Harry J. Carman, "England and the Egyptian Problem," Political Science Quarterly, Vol. 36, No. 1 (March 1921), 55 and 57.

[5] See Malcolm Mcilwraith, "The Declaration of a Protectorate in Egypt and Its Legal Effects," Journal of the Society of Comparative Legislation, Vol. 17, No. 1/2 (1917), 238–259.

[6] Ibid., at 253.

[7] Carman (1921), at 68.

[8] See Declaration to Egypt by His Britannic Majesty's Government, February 28, 1922 quoted in "The Anglo-Egyptian Treaty Negotiations," Bulletin of International News, New Series, Vol. 4, No. 19 (March 17, 1928), at 3–11.

Kingdom maintained a military presence in the country, which it called on when its interests were under threat.[9]

1923 Constitution: In 1923, Egypt adopted its first formal constitution, which established a liberal constitutional monarchy that heavily favored the King. The text provided the monarch and his ministers with very significant powers, while providing only very limited checks against executive overreach. The King was solely responsible for appointing the government. The parliament nominally had the power to question ministers (Articles 107–108) and could also overrule the King on legislative matters, but both houses of parliament had to approve such a measure by a two-thirds majority (Article 36). That was essentially unreachable given that the King directly appointed two-fifths of the upper chamber (Article 75). In any event, the King's unlimited power to dissolve parliament served as a very strong disincentive for the parliament to take any drastic action (Article 38). Meanwhile, the 1923 Constitution's small number of provisions on the judiciary almost all deferred to legislation, which guaranteed that the judiciary would not be able to operate independently (Articles 124–131). Finally, the provisions purporting to grant basic rights to Egyptian citizens consisted almost entirely of clawback clauses, and therefore provided close to no protection against the state.[10] Despite the fact that the King's power was limited only very slightly by the text, the 1923 Constitution was formally suspended on three separate occasions, and was regularly violated when it was in force.[11]

Republicanism: In the decades that followed, the Wafd remained the country's preeminent political force, but by the early 1950s, its social capital had been largely spent. Wafd leaders abandoned their opposition to the

9 A treaty was signed in 1936 that formally ended the United Kingdom's military occupation (Article 1), but which provided that the Suez Canal was an "essential means of communication between the different parts of the British Empire" and therefore authorized the United Kingdom to "station forces in Egyptian territory in the vicinity of the Canal" (Article 8), and which obliged the Egyptian authorities to maintain various facilities for the United Kingdom's benefit, including "adequate landing grounds and seaplane anchorages" (Paragraph 14, Annex to Article 8). See "Treaty of Alliance between His Majesty, In Respect of the United Kingdom and His Majesty the King of Egypt," The American Journal of International Law, Vol. 31, No. 2, Supplement: Official Documents (April 1937), 77–90. The Treaty was described as having "liquidated a military occupation in principle while allowing it to continue in fact"; see Laila Morsy, "The Military Clauses of the Anglo-Egyptian Treaty of Friendship and Alliance, 1936," International Journal of Middle East Studies, Vol. 16, No. 1 (March 1984), 91.

10 For example, Article 21 on the right to form associations must be done through "means as established by law" with no indication of how far the law can go to restrict that right.

11 Nathan Brown, Constitution in a Nonconstitutional World: Arab Basic Laws and the Prospects for Accountable Government, State University of New York Press (2002), at 39–41.

monarch and to the United Kingdom's continued military presence. In 1942 the British Ambassador forced the Monarch to form a Wafd government at gunpoint, possibly the party's death blow in the population's eyes. By 1952, a wave of radicalism was sweeping the country, but there were no organized political forces capable of capitalizing on the situation. On July 23, 1952, a group of officers known as the "Free Officers" seized power, suspended the 1923 Constitution, exiled the monarch, established Egypt as a republic, dissolved parliament, and banned all political parties (including the Wafd). From 1952 until 2011 Egypt was ruled by four successive presidents, all of whom were drawn from the military and who paid lip service to democracy and to the rule of law at best, albeit not all to the same extent.[12] The first of the three presidents, Gamal Abdel Nasser, commanded very significant popular support in Egypt and beyond, which allowed him to govern the country without any significant restraints. During his tenure, a series of authoritarian constitutions was adopted by decree, none of which allowed any meaningful form of accountability. In 1971 his successor's political stability was far less certain, which prompted him to adopt a new constitution that aimed to partly reconcile with some of the country's various communities, while at the same time maintaining full control over government. The 1971 Constitution at first maintained the socialist form of government but was eventually amended in favor of an illiberal form of government that nominally maintained some of the procedural elements of a democratic system (elections, separation of powers, etc.) while at the same time ensuring that a single president would continue to dominate the system practically unchallenged.[13] The president had absolute authority to nominate the prime minister and all ministers (Article 141), could dissolve the parliament virtually without limitation (Article 136), could impose a state of emergency in perpetuity (Article 148), and could stand for an unlimited number of terms (Article 77). Meanwhile, the parliament could only withdraw confidence from the government if a

[12] There is disagreement on the extent to which the judiciary was able to operate independently from the executive during this period. For more, see Mahmoud Hamad, Judges and Generals in the Making of Modern Egypt: How Institutions Sustain and Undermine Authoritarian Regimes, Cambridge University Press (2019); and Tamir Moustafa, The Struggle for Constitutional Power: Law, Politics, and Economic Development in Egypt, Cambridge University Press (2009).

[13] An unofficial translation of the 1971 Constitution is available here: https://constitutionnet.org/sites/default/files/Egypt%20Constitution.pdf. The Supreme Constitutional Court did challenge the executive on a number of occasions, in particular by striking down electoral laws and dissolving parliament on more than one occasion, but ultimately the Court was easily brought under control by the president at the time through his unlimited appointments power; see Moustafa (2009), at Chapter 6.

majority of two-thirds of its members supported the motion (Article 127). The few sections that were dedicated to the judiciary barely provided any protection, given that most fundamental issues were left to subsequent legislation (Article 167). The Constitution recognized the Supreme Constitutional Court and even provided that members of the Court could not be dismissed (Article 177) but said nothing of how judges could join the Court or how it was to be organized. The 1971 Constitution mirrored the 1923 Constitution in granting rights to citizens while at the same time ensuring that they could be completely emptied of their meaning by subsequent legislation.[14]

Egypt on the Brink: On the whole, on the eve of revolution, the Egyptian state's history with constitutionalism remained limited. With a few notable exceptions, executive power had essentially remained unchecked for the bulk of the country's modern history. By the end of 2010, Egypt had been ruled by the same president for just under thirty years and there were strong indications that his son was being groomed to take over. A parliamentary election had just taken place in which the ruling National Democratic Party won 420 out of 518 seats, and in which the largest opposition party with parliamentary representation won just six. A state of emergency had been in effect for decades, contributing to a state of impunity for state institutions that routinely violated basic rights. The courts, which had just a few years before exhibited some signs of independence, had been brought under control. Socioeconomic conditions also appeared to be declining, with increased poverty and inequality, and worsening educational opportunities.

INTERIM CONSTITUTION

Constitution or Elections First: Following weeks of massive popular unrest, Hosni Mubarak was made to leave office on February 11, 2011 by the Supreme Council for the Armed Forces (SCAF), which assumed the functions of head of state until presidential elections were organized in June 2012.[15] As in many

[14] Articles 54 and 55 provided for freedom of assembly and association, respectively, and both state that they can only be exercised "within the limits of the law," without providing any meaningful indication of how far the law could go in restricting those rights.

[15] See Supreme Council of the Armed Forces, Statement Number 3 (February 11, 2011), available at www.sis.gov.eg/newVR/rev25th4/html/link12c.htm. The SCAF was established in 1954 and was chaired by the president of the republic, headed by the Field Marshal, and composed of virtually all of the country's most senior military officers; see Hamad (2019), at 205. When the SCAF met in February 2011, its sessions were not chaired or attended by the president of the republic. For a detailed explanation of how the SCAF forced Mubarak to leave office, see M. Cherif Bassiouni, Chronicles of the Egyptian Revolution and Its Aftermath: 2011–2016, Cambridge University Press (2017).

other countries in the region, the pre-uprising constitution was closely associated with the personalized form of rule that was established and maintained in the postcolonial period, and so there was little question in the minds of large numbers of Egyptians that it would have to be replaced in some way.[16] The SCAF immediately confirmed that tendency when, on February 13, 2011, it issued a "constitutional declaration" that suspended the 1971 Constitution (Article 1), dissolved parliament (Article 4), granted itself the authority to issue legislation by decree (Article 5), and promised to form a constitutional revision committee for the purpose of amending "some articles in the constitution."[17] The immediate question that needed to be answered was therefore what process should be followed to adopt that new constitution and also how the country would be governed in the meantime. On process, the main issue was whether and to what extent the future constitution's content should be influenced by electoral outcomes, which was to a large extent the same debate that dominated Tunisia's post-uprising transition. The debate on this issue immediately broke down into two camps, with one side arguing that the constitution should be drafted by an elected assembly ("elections first"), which would have meant allowing the Muslim Brotherhood's superior organizational capacity to determine the future constitution's content. The second camp argued that the constitution should be drafted before elections were to take place ("constitution first"), which would have allowed emerging political forces as well as groups, institutions, and communities that are not organized as political parties to play an equal role in the constitutional negotiations. The debate on this issue raged throughout the transition and was ultimately only resolved when the Muslim Brotherhood was physically eliminated from political life in mid-2013.[18] Interim governance attracted far less attention at this early stage mainly because most groups and institutions were more committed to limiting the power of their rivals through any means necessary than to respecting

[16] A number of key constitutional rules were constructed around the idea that the president controlled key institutions through his ruling party. After the uprising, the former ruling party ceased to function shortly after the uprising. Its headquarters were arsoned, its legal status was revoked, and all its property confiscated by a court order. See Hamad (2019).

[17] See Supreme Council of the Armed Forces, Constitutional Declaration (February 13, 2011), available at www.sis.gov.eg/newVR/rev25th4/html/link12f.htm. David Risley, "Egypt's Judiciary: Obstructing or Assisting Reform?," Middle East Institute (January 13, 2016) (according to whom the SCAF "allowed the declaration of a state of emergency to expire. The special emergency courts were disbanded, the Emergency Law itself was amended to add duration and scope limits, and extraordinary courts became constitutionally prohibited").

[18] See, for example, Mustafa Suleiman, 'Controversy Rages in Egypt on the Constitution First Dispute . . . and the Muslim Brotherhood Rejects Delaying the Elections' (الجدل يحتدم في مصر حول معركة الدستور أولا.. والإخوان يرفضون تأجيل الانتخابات), Al-Arabiya (June 19, 2011).

agreed governance rules.[19] The lack of interest in this fundamental issue was to have a deep impact on the remainder of the transition.

Political Dynamics: As in other countries, political dynamics in 2011 were highly charged and were marked by deep distrust between rival groups. The uprising had put everything into question, which meant that emerging groups considered that they had everything to gain while more traditional and established groups were more concerned about losing status and privilege. Despite these diametrically opposed prerogatives, some actors were nevertheless willing and able to collaborate and seek common cause with rival groups for temporary gain. On the negative side, however, all of these groups were internally divided, which had a major influence on the transition's outcome. On the conservative side, the SCAF was a primary actor throughout the transition.[20] The Egyptian republic was initially established by an army-led revolution, and all three of Egypt's presidents until the uprising were drawn from the armed forces, which translated into significant benefits for the military and other security services.[21] The SCAF's primary interest was therefore to return Egypt to a sense of normalcy, while at the same time protecting its autonomy from the civilian government, as well as maintaining and possibly even enhancing its mandate and prerogatives.[22] The constitutional, administrative, and criminal courts generally speaking could be considered to be part of the conservative camp throughout the transition.[23] Judges also

[19] This manifested itself in the main actors' behavior, which included sudden and drastic changes to both positive law or legal interpretation that had little to no basis in any form of legitimacy.

[20] For more on the SCAF, see International Crisis Group, "Lost in Transition: The World According to Egypt's SCAF," Middle East Report number 121 (April 24, 2012); Yezid Sayigh, "Above the State: The Officers' Republic in Egypt," Carnegie Endowment for International Peace (August 2012).

[21] Retired or active military officers held government positions, occupied a majority of the governorships, and controlled major institutions of state and significant parts of the economy. There was a sense of anxiety within the military in the years prior to 2011 that its position within the state was being undermined by a number of civilians and businessmen who were associated with Mubarak's son Gamal.

[22] The SCAF was also said to be internally divided along generational lines, with the older generation of officers that was generally reluctant to adopt a more visible political role but which was nevertheless more willing to respond to popular demands for change, and a younger generation who argued in favor of reasserting control through a more hardline response; see William C. Taylor, MILITARY RESPONSE TO THE ARAB UPRISINGS AND THE FUTURE OF CIVIL-MILITARY RELATIONS IN THE MIDDLE EAST: ANALYSIS FROM EGYPT, TUNISIA, LIBYA AND SYRIA, Palgrave Macmillan (2014), at 124–138.

[23] The courts have been described as belonging to a larger group known as the "deep state," which passively resisted all of the radical groups that were active during the transition. The deep state also included the police and the state bureaucracy among others. For more, see

enjoyed privileged status and significant stature within the state, similar to that of the military albeit with obvious differences. Throughout the transition, judges also wielded important influence by virtue of their stature and as a result of the very large number of high impact cases that were brought before them.[24] The courts' influence was such that at times other actors mobilized their own supporters to prevent judges from reaching the courts so as to prevent them from issuing decisions on specific matters.[25] The radical camp was divided between Islamist groups such as the Muslim Brotherhood on the one hand and revolutionary groups on the other. Both sought to fundamentally reshape state and society but had radically different objectives and methods. The Brotherhood's main interest was to move into a position of power through which it could dominate the state and Islamize society.[26] That entailed first that its members should be able to operate freely and openly, and without fear of repression, and second that the organization as a whole should dominate key state institutions. From a practical perspective, this entailed securing political guarantees from other powerful actors (including the security establishment) and establishing a constitution that would be best suited to their interests. Internally, the Brotherhood was far from democratic, however, which created its own divisions, and eventually caused large numbers of younger members and even some leaders to defect in frustration at their inability to impact the group's policies.[27] Revolutionary groups were diverse in nature and included a small number of radical political parties, activists, independent trade unions, academics, journalists, intellectuals, lawyers, and judges, and even organized football fans known as "ultras."[28] All hoped to introduce a progressive ruling order that would provide sustenance, freedom,

Risley (2016); and Issandr El Imrani, "Sightings of the Egyptian Deep State," Middle East Research and Information Project (January 2012).

24 Egypt's judiciary had already played an important role in challenging the Muslim Brotherhood's rule. See, for example, Zaid Al-Ali, "The Constitutional Court's Mark on Egypt's Elections," Foreign Policy (June 6, 2013); Zaid Al-Ali and Nathan Brown, "Egypt's Constitution Swings into Action," Foreign Policy (March 27, 2013).

25 There were significant divisions within the judiciary. Among other things, different jurisdictions were hearing claims in relation to similar issues but reaching radically different outcomes.

26 See Alison Pargeter, The Muslim Brotherhood: From Opposition to Power, Saqi Books (2013).

27 See Beverley Milton-Edwards, The Muslim Brotherhood: The Arab Spring and Its Future Face, Routledge (2016), at 41.

28 See Sherif Tarek, "Egypt's Ultras Go from Football to Politics," Ahramonline, April 13, 2011. For more on the Ultras, see Mohamed Gamal Besheer, Kitab al-Utras (كتاب الالتراس), Cairo: Dar Diwan (2011); for an English-language review of Besheer's book see Mahmoud el-Wardani, "The Ultras and the Egyptian Revolution," Ahramonline (February 4, 2012).

and dignity to ordinary citizens, and would establish social justice. Revolutionary groups were generally uncompromising in their principles and their approach. Much of their involvement took place outside the formal negotiation process, including through workers' strikes and the establishment of new independent unions, which often meant that their impact on the constitutional negotiations was limited. Finally, a small number of liberal and secular parties were lodged between the conservative and radical camps. These parties were mainly characterized by their general (although not absolute) commitment to democratic norms and to establishing constitutional guarantees that would prevent the Islamization of state and society. These parties did not attract significant popular appeal and so were only influential insofar as they were able to associate or ally themselves with other major actors.[29] The military, the courts, and all secular forces were concerned that the Muslim Brotherhood would return a majority in the coming elections that it would then use to force through a constitution entirely in its own image. In response, the Muslim Brotherhood sought to reassure all major political actors that it would not seek to dominate or dramatically alter the state, mainly by professing to prefer consensus and by committing not to contest more than 35–50 percent of parliamentary seats and not to contest the presidential elections.[30]

Drafting Committee: On February 15, 2011, the SCAF issued "Decision Number 1," in which it established a constitutional revision committee for the purpose of proposing changes to the 1971 Constitution and for developing a roadmap for the drafting of a new constitution.[31] The committee, which was named in Decision Number 1, consisted of eight men, including three who were drawn from the Supreme Constitutional Court, while the rest consisted of lawyers and academics.[32] Two committee members were linked to the

[29] See Mohamed el-Agati, Nick Sigler, and Nick Harvey, "Political Parties and Public Opinion in Egypt," Global Partners: Governance (February 2014), at 18.

[30] See Dalia Fahmy, "The Muslim Brotherhood: Between Opposition and Power," in Bessma Momani and Eid Mohamed (eds.), EGYPT: BEYOND TAHRIR SQUARE, Indiana University Press (2016), at 87.

[31] See Supreme Council of the Armed Forces, Decision Number 1, February 15, 2011, available at www.sis.gov.eg/newVR/rev25th4/html/link12x.htm. The SCAF's manner of proceeding was not in conformity with the 1971 Constitution. Article 189 of the 1971 Constitution provided that amendments should be approved by two-thirds of parliament's members before it could be submitted to referendum. Article 189 did not specify what process should be followed in the event parliament was in a state of dissolution, which suggests that the amendment process would have had to be delayed until a new parliament was elected.

[32] Members included Tariq al-Bishri (a former senior judge who had Islamist leanings), Hassan el-Badrawi (vice president of the Supreme Constitutional Court), Mohamed Hassanein Abdel

Brotherhood, while the rest did not have any clear political leanings, which constituted a clear indication that the SCAF had decided to seek an accommodation with the Muslim Brotherhood.[33] Despite the fact that they were at the height of their power, Egypt's revolutionary forces were not represented in the committee. Naturally, the Brotherhood participated enthusiastically, mainly with a view to influencing the transition roadmap in a way that would satisfy its own interests.[34] What this meant was that two committee members at least were bound to argue in favor of organizing an election first, and were also in a position to claim that they represented the views of a major political actor, while the remaining members were not known to have specific preferences and did not have any clear political affiliations. As a result, the SCAF was virtually guaranteeing that the outcome of the committee's work, and in particular the transition roadmap, would favor the Brotherhood.

The Committee's Roadmap: Decision Number 1 specifically provided that the committee should complete its work "within ten days" (Article 2). That deadline was respected, and the committee did not make an attempt to consult with groups or individuals outside of its membership, nor did it have a mandate to do so.[35] Decision Number 1 also listed eight specific articles that the committee was instructed to amend (which related to the process through which the president of the republic is to be elected, and a small number of other areas), which the committee respected.[36] It recommended that the eligibility requirements for presidential candidacy be tightened (Article 75), that the presidential election process be opened up to allow for a greater number of candidates to compete (Article 76), that presidential terms be reduced from six to four years and a two-term limit introduced (Article 77),

Al (former dean of Cairo University's law school), and Subhi Saleh (a lawyer, former member of parliament, and a member of the Muslim Brotherhood).

33 See Sherif Khalifa, Egypt's Lost Spring: Causes and Consequences, Praeger (2015), at 73. Mr. Sobhi in particular was elected to parliament in 2005 and was a prominent member of the Brotherhood. In 2007 Mr. Sobhi Saleh argued in a public conference that Article 5 of the 1971 Constitution should be interpreted in a way that would allow a religiously inspired party that is affiliated to the Muslim Brotherhood to operate legally; see "Political Group or Political Party? Can a Political Party Assimilate a Religious Frame of Reference?," Salon Ibn Rushd (March 15, 2007).

34 Mr. Sobhi Saleh described the roadmap as his and Mr. Tariq al-Bishri's "main accomplishment" during their work in the committee; see "Sobhi Saleh: What Tariq al-Bishri and I Planned Immediately after the Revolution Is Now a Practical Accomplishment" (صبحي صالح: ما خططت له مع المستشار طارق البشرى بعد الثورة مباشرة أصبح الآن إنجازات ملموسة), al-Ahram (December 30, 2012).

35 The Committee's proposed changes to the 1971 Constitution are on file with the author and are available at http://gate.ahram.org.eg/News/49461.aspx.

36 Hamad (2019), at 206.

that the process through which states of emergency are called be strengthened to prevent abuse (Article 148), and exceptions to due process rules for suspected terrorism-related crimes be eliminated (Article 179). The committee proposed to maintain the then-existing mechanism for simple constitutional amendment but also proposed that the president of the republic, with the approval of the council of ministers and a majority of the parliament's members, could form a constituent assembly to draft an entirely new constitution that would then be put to a referendum (Article 189). Most importantly perhaps, the committee proposed a new Article 189bis that proposed to automatically trigger a constitutional drafting process that was intended to lead to an entirely new constitution. Article 189bis provided in full that

> Within six months of their election, the non-appointed members of the first People's Assembly and Shoura Council [respectively, the lower and upper chambers of parliament] to follow the announcement of the results of the referendum on constitutional amendments shall select a constituent assembly that will be responsible for preparing a new constitutional proposal, in accordance with the provisions of Article 189 [according to which the proposal should be prepared within six months and a referendum on the proposal should be organised within fifteen days of its completion].

The committee's roadmap proposed to resolve the "constitution first" or "election first" debate in a way that was in accord with the Muslim Brotherhood's perspective. Article 189bis provided that the transition should commence with an election, and then proposed that the elected assembly appoint the drafting committee without providing any meaningful guidance on how the committee should be selected. It also provided that the committee had completely free reign to draft the constitution without providing members of the political minority, state institutions, or civil society with any guarantees that their views would even be considered. That type of arrangement automatically favors political movements with strong electoral appeal, and given the fact that the Muslim Brotherhood was by far the most organized political force in the country at the time, it was entirely predictable that the committee would be Islamist-dominated. State institutions, including the SCAF, may have had considerable influence but did not have a political party that could compete in the coming elections and represent their interests, which in turn meant that they could not be directly represented in the constitution drafting body.

Interim Governance: The committee's amendments to the 1971 Constitution and its proposed road map were put to a referendum on March 19, 2011, which is to say three weeks after the committee completed its work, leaving close to no time for Egyptians to reflect on the matter. The Muslim Brotherhood campaigned heavily in favor of the proposed road map, to the extent that it argued that it was every Muslim's duty to vote in favor of the text.[37] Ultimately, the amendments were approved by 78 percent of voters.[38] Remarkably, however, in the first of what was to become many sudden and unexplained shifts in the transition, the SCAF published an interim constitution on March 30, 2011 that did not correspond with the results of the referendum (the "2011 Interim Constitution").[39] The text included all the changes that had been approved (albeit with some changes; see later), but a large number of other changes were made, including many deletions,[40] as well as some reordering[41] and rewording.[42] While many of these changes did not appear to have a meaningful impact, many others would play a determinant role during transition. The executive's own powers were vastly increased. The SCAF (and then the president after an election was organized) was granted legislative powers (Article 56). That provision's impact was amplified as a result of other provisions that reduced the scope for oversight over the executive. By way of example, Article 33 provides that the parliament has the "authority to legislate and to determine public policy [...] and to oversee the work of the executive branch." No indication was given, however, on how that oversight should be exercised. The Interim

37 Heba Fahmy, "MB Faces Internal Divisions and Isolation from Opposition Groups," Daily News Egypt (March 28, 2011).

38 See Neil MacFarquhar, "Egyptian Voters Approve Constitutional Changes," *The New York Times* (March 20, 2011).

39 An unofficial translation of the 2011 Interim Constitution is available here: www.constitutionnet.org/files/2011_-_egypt_interim_constitution__english_.pdf. The identity of the interim constitution's drafters was never revealed. The interim constitution was published in the form of a "Constitutional Declaration," a legal instrument that has not been properly defined but which essentially consists of an executive decree that either replaces or adds to existing constitutions. There are no specific requirements that need to be satisfied in order for these documents to be legally recognized.

40 A large number of deletions were made, including the near totality of the 1971 Constitution's Part Two (on "fundamental principles"). Part Two included provisions on social solidarity (Article 7), motherhood (Article 10), public morals (Article 12), the fight against illiteracy (Article 21), and the just distribution of national revenue (Article 25), all of which were eliminated. The end result was that the interim constitution was about a third of the length of the 1971 Constitution, which meant that a considerable amount of important detail was left out.

41 Article 4 (on economic principles) and Article 5 (on freedom of association and political parties) were switched in the Interim Constitution.

42 The 1971 Constitution's Article 5 prohibited political parties from having a "religious reference or basis." The 2011 Interim constitution's Article 4 prohibited political parties from having a "religious basis," thereby abandoning the reference to the "reference." Both terms are not well-defined legal concepts and could easily be applied or interpreted interchangeably.

Constitution did not precisely indicate if the parliament's confidence was required to form a cabinet, whether confidence could be withdrawn from the full cabinet or from individual ministers, if ministers could be called to parliament for questioning, etc. In the absence of any wording to that effect, it would be reasonable to assume that the drafters intended for those powers not to exist.[43] Other institutions had their own constitutional guarantees reduced. For example, the 1971 Constitution's prohibition against dismissing members of the Supreme Constitutional Court (Article 177) was eliminated, which meant that the executive acquired very significant means to influence the Court's decisions. All of these arrangements served to reconfirm the tradition of limitless executive power, which both the SCAF and the soon to be elected president would use to redesign the constitution by decree (or "constitutional declarations"). This type of arrangement was not appropriate for such a volatile period. A particularly large number of actors were vying for control, which increased the importance of reaching consensus on key issues. The 2012 Interim Constitution tended in the opposite direction by giving one actor the power to impose its will at any point.

The SCAF's Roadmap: The transitional roadmap that was set out in Article 189bis was the only provision to have been approved in the referendum and subsequently revised in the 2012 Interim Constitution. Article 60 of the 2012 Interim Constitution provided that

> The members of the first People's Assembly and Shura Council (except the appointed members) [respectively, the lower and upper chambers of parliament] will meet in a joint session following an invitation from the Supreme Council of the Armed Forces within 6 months of their election to elect a constituent assembly composed of 100 members which will prepare a new draft constitution for the country to be completed within 6 months of the formation of this assembly. The draft constitution will be presented within 15 days of its preparation to the people who will vote in a referendum on the matter. The constitution will take effect from the date on which it is declared that the people approve it in the referendum.[44]

A number of elements were maintained, including the requirement that the first step in the transition be a parliamentary election, and that the second be

[43] See Reuters, "The Parliament Issues a Recommendation to Withdraw Confidence from al-Janzouri's Government" (مجلس الشعب يصدر توصية بسحب الثقة من حكومة الجنزوري) (March 11, 2012).

[44] An unofficial English language translation of the interim constitution is available is at www.constitutionnet.org/vl/item/egypt-constitutional-declaration-march-2011. The Arabic original is available at https://parliament2011.elections.eg/images/Laws/1_%20%202011%20-%20%202011.pdf.

the election of a constitutional drafting assembly by that same parliament. Article 60 did not specify when the presidential election should take place, which meant that the sequencing of some of the transition period's most important milestones was also left undetermined. Article 60 did introduce one major change in comparison to Article 189bis: It provided that it was the SCAF that should invite the two houses of parliament to elect the drafting assembly, whereas Article 189bis provided that the parliament could do so on its own initiative. The SCAF was therefore reserving a role for itself in the transition process that it could potentially leverage to extract advantages for itself. Article 60 also provided that the two houses of parliament were required to "elect" the members of the constituent assembly, whereas Article 189bis provided that they should be selected, an amendment that was unlikely to have a major practical impact, particularly given that it did not indicate how that election should be organized.

Constituent Assembly Composition: Crucially, Article 60 provided full discretion to the future parliament on how the Constituent Assembly should be composed, which is exactly what the Muslim Brotherhood wanted. This gave whichever parties dominated the future parliament important leverage to impose their preferred configuration. There was no general requirement to be inclusive, nor were there specific requirements that particular institutions or groups should be represented and in what proportion. Over time, secular groups would argue first that the electoral results should not necessarily be mirrored in the Assembly, and also that specific state institutions, social groups, and civil society organizations (collectively referred to as "corporate groups") were essential components of Egyptian society and should therefore be represented as well. Chief among these groups were the judiciary (including different jurisdictions within the court system), al-Azhar University (as the primary authority on personal status issues for Muslims), the Coptic Church, trade unions, employers' associations, and others. The Islamist and secular camps were left to negotiate this crucial issue, after the rules had already been established to one side's advantage. The negotiation process that was ultimately followed was chaotic and only lightly mediated by the SCAF, which in any event was not a neutral party.

SUPRA-CONSTITUTIONAL PRINCIPLES

Objective: Between the time when the Interim Constitution was adopted and the start of the parliamentary elections, the SCAF and secular forces attempted to reverse the gains that the Muslim Brotherhood had already secured in the Interim Constitution. A large number of parties, institutions, and groups circulated proposals on a set of principles that would be binding on any future constitution-drafting assembly, whatever its composition, and that also purported to predetermine how the drafting assembly would be composed. Most remained concerned that a constitutional assembly elected by the future parliament would be dominated by Islamists and would then proceed to reshape Egypt as an Islamic state. Liberal and secular parties therefore argued that any future constitutional assembly should respect a number of constants (including, for example, its republican nature). The Muslim Brotherhood and other Islamist movements were adamantly opposed to this initiative. The Brotherhood saw the effort to draw up the "Fundamental Principles" as an unprincipled afterthought that was purely designed to circumvent the popular will, and which essentially violated the terms of a roadmap that had already been agreed, and that was set out in Article 60 of the 2012 Interim Constitution. Revolutionary movements were also naturally highly suspicious of any attempt to curb the constitutional movement. Not entirely coincidentally, a similar debate was taking place in Tunisia at exactly the same time when the "High Commission to achieve the goals of the revolution, on political reforms and democratic transition" considered whether or not to adopt the Republican Pact, which was also originally intended to be a set of irrevocable principles that the yet to be elected Constituent Assembly would have to respect. Ennahda, Tunisia's main Islamist party, also refused to participate in the elaboration of the pact and for the same reasons.

Process: The deputy prime minister, a member of the liberal elite, adopted the initiative and organized dialogue and drafting sessions with other like-minded political figures with a view to drafting what ultimately would become known as the "supra-constitutional principles." Although very little was made clear at the time, supporters of the initiative probably intended the principles to be adopted as a "constitutional declaration" or for a referendum to be called so as to grant the principles democratic legitimacy. There were, however, a number of major difficulties in the manner in which the principles were developed. The process was not secret, given that drafts and other elements were regularly published in the press, but the general population was barely aware that such an initiative was underway let alone how it was proceeding. In addition, the process was far from inclusive and did not come close to resembling the type of effort that one would expect when developing binding and eternal principles that underpin the state. Initially, the process was decentralized. Starting in the Spring of 2011, a number of political groups, institutions, and civil society organizations each developed and circulated their own vision of what types of principles should be considered to be binding on any future constitutional assembly. After a number of these proposals had been published, the deputy prime minister launched an effort to consolidate these proposals into a single document.[45] In August 2011, a dialogue conference was organized under the auspices of the deputy prime minister and included another six individuals who appear to have met for approximately one week altogether.[46] Pursuant to these meetings a draft was circulated in September 2011 and another in November 2011.[47] The drafts included wording that strongly suggested that individuals who were linked to the military were either directly participating in the discussions or at least indicating to the drafters what the military was seeking to achieve. Some actors, including the Brotherhood, boycotted the process altogether and indicated that it would ignore whatever was agreed by the liberal and secular camp. Other actors, including Al-Jama'ah al-Islamiyyah (the Islamic Group), organized a major protest on July 29, 2011 to express their opposition.[48]

Substantive Provisions: Several draft documents were published and provide a very good indication of what the drafters' intent was at the time.[49] The drafts included ten individual "fundamental principles" and eleven "general rights and freedoms." The fundamental principles could be separated into three different categories. A number probably did enjoy sufficient support to be characterized as binding on the future constituent assembly, including a provision that Egypt's "political system is republican and democratic" (First (4)) and another that the "rule of law is the state's basis of government" (First (5)). A second category could be qualified not as "fundamental principles" but as as-of-yet unachieved aspirations, including one provision that stated that

[45] See Waheed Abdel Majeed, "Dr Waheed Abdel Majeed Narrates the Constituent Assembly's Most Dangerous Secrets" (أخطر أسرار الجمعية التأسيسية يرويها الدكتور وحيد عبد المجيد), Youm7 (June 11, 2013).

[46] See Tahany El Gebaly, "Constitutional Principles: Documents on Post-revolution Egypt," Alif: Journal of Comparative Poetics No. 32 (2012), 228–253.

[47] More than a year after the initiative ended, the by then-former deputy prime minister indicated in statements to the press that two senior members of the judiciary were responsible for drafting the two drafts, something that was not known at the time; see Hamad (2019), at 218.

[48] Muhammad Khayyal, "Islamic Group: Egypt to Witness Biggest Ever Massive Gathering in History on Friday," Al-Shuruq al-Jadid (July 24, 2011).

[49] Several drafts were produced and circulated to the press. An unofficial translation of the last draft that was produced, which was published in November 2011, is available at www.constitutionnet.org/vl/item/egypt-draft-constitution-november-2011-english. The Arabic original is available at www.constitutionnet.org/vl/item/egypt-draft-constitution-november-2011-arabic. For a detailed analysis of the Fundamental Principles, see Zaid Al-Ali, "Declaration of the Fundamental Principles for the New Egyptian State: A Commentary," International IDEA (November 23, 2011), at www.constitutionnet.org/news/commentary-november-draft-egypt-fundamental-principles-document.

"the state is committed to improving the Nile's administration and its protection from pollution" (First (7)). Once again, very few if any future constitutional negotiators would likely oppose this type of wording, despite the fact that most Egyptians were aware that the state had in fact not been satisfying that aspiration. Finally, some of the principles were in fact not fundamental at all but related to fundamental issues that were heavily contested. Article First (1) described Egypt as a "civil state." Many Egyptians agreed with the formulation, but there was in fact a deep disagreement on what the term meant, including the extent to which it limited the influence of religion on the state. Article First (9) provided that the armed forces "have as their mission to protect the country, the integrity, security and unity of its land, and to defend constitutional legitimacy," without providing any indication as to what was meant by constitutional legitimacy or what measures the military could use to protect it. This lack of detail and clarity raised the possibility that, if the November draft were adopted, Egypt's military could legally intervene in the political process any time in the future and in the manner that it chose.[50] Article First (9)'s second paragraph was even more problematic. It provided that, "The Supreme Council of the Armed Forces is solely responsible for all matters concerning the armed forces, and for discussing its budget, which should be incorporated as a single figure in the annual state budget. The Supreme Council of the Armed Forces is also exclusively competent to approve all bills relating to the armed forces before they come into effect." A number of Egyptians rightly saw this draft provision as evidence of the SCAF's intentions to isolate it from any form of civilian oversight. In contrast, the eleven "general rights and freedoms" offered almost nothing new in comparison with past Egyptian constitutions. By way of example, Article Second (22), the last provision of the section, provided for both freedom of association and assembly in three lines, most of which consisted of a vaguely worded limitation that could be used to empty those two rights of all meaning.

Procedural Rules: The draft principles also purported to predetermine the Constituent Assembly's composition, and to limit its substantive scope of action. Article Third (1) of the final version of the principles to have been published was a radical departure from Article 60 of the Interim Constitution given that it provided that eighty members of the Constituent Assembly should be representatives of corporate groups. Article Third (1) provided that the

[50] One of the only modern constitutions to adopt similar wording is the constitution of Spain, which provides that the armed forces have as one of their obligations to defend "the constitutional order" (Section 8). That provision is considered by many to have partially inspired segments of the Spanish military to carry out its failed coup d'état in February 1981.

Assembly should include fifteen representatives of judicial bodies, fifteen should be university professors, fifteen should be trade unionists, etc. It also provided that twenty members only should be drawn from the soon-to-be-elected parliament. Article Third (2) sought to limit the Constituent Assembly's mandate by allowing the SCAF to object to the coming draft constitution if it found that "one or more provisions are contrary to the basic tenets of the state and of Egyptian society." Finally, the same article provided that the Supreme Constitutional Court would have the final say if the constitutional drafters refused to amend their draft pursuant to the SCAF's objection. Although a more complex and multi-stage constitutional drafting process than that provided for in Article 60 of the Interim Constitution would have been welcome, the fact that these suggestions were made after the Interim Constitution had been formally adopted pursuant to a referendum (even if the people were not made to vote on the final text) made it unlikely that they could be adopted. Also, the fact that the draft principles proposed to allow the SCAF to make its own evaluation on the substantive content of the future constitution was bound to be highly controversial, mainly given that it gave special arbitral powers to an interested party.

Public Response: The public response to the November draft was overwhelmingly negative. The Muslim Brotherhood maintained its position that only a democratically elected body could determine the substantive content of the future constitution. Revolutionary parties objected to the privileges that the principles sought to grant to the military. Significant violence broke out in mid-November, mainly between revolutionary forces and the police. Several hundred protesters were killed and wounded and the effort to draft the Fundamental Principles was subsequently abandoned.[51]

THE 2012 CONSTITUTION

Composition (First Iteration): Parliamentary elections were organized in several rounds that took place in late 2011 and early 2012.[52] The Muslim

[51] See Heba Fahmy, "Thousands Rally in Tahrir on Friday of 'Protecting Democracy'," Daily News Egypt (November 18, 2011). The protests led to significant violence between demonstrators and police, resulting in hundreds of dead and wounded civilians. The intensity of the violence was partially recorded in amateur videos uploaded online; see, for example: www.youtube.com/watch?v=T9JmBTotCWQ. Those events have subsequently become an iconic moment for Egypt's revolutionary movement; see, for example, Amira Howeidy, "How to Mark the Battle of Mohamed Mahmoud?," Ahram Online, November 16, 2013.

[52] See Carter Center, "Final report of the Carter Center Mission to Witness the 2011–2012 Parliamentary Elections in Egypt," September 21, 2012.

Brotherhood contested the elections through its newly established Freedom and Justice Party (FJP). A group of Salafis, a more radical and puritanical branch of the Islamist community, established the Nour Party.[53] Together these two parties won 391 out of 508 seats, while the remaining seats went to a disparate group of liberals, secularists, left-wing revolutionary parties, and remnants of the previous regime. The Islamists returned practically double the results that their Tunisian counterparts obtained in the October 2011 elections, presenting them with a historic opportunity to consolidate their position and reshape society. The parliament immediately set about composing the Constituent Assembly in accordance with Article 60 of the Interim Constitution. There was significant controversy on how the 100 members should be elected and in particular how many should be drawn from parliament and how many should represent corporate groups. The Muslim Brotherhood was aware of the levels of concern that the electoral results would create amongst non-Islamists and so sought to reassure them by arguing that the Assembly should consist of sixty parliamentarians and forty representatives of corporate groups. Secular groups argued a number of positions in response, most of which allowed between twenty and forty parliamentarians altogether. On March 24, 2012, a slate of 1,000 candidates, most of them completely unknown, was presented to a joint session of parliament. Many members requested a delay so as to be able to properly evaluate the candidates, but the election went ahead and resulted in an Assembly that included sixty-five Islamists. Some opposition members accused the Muslim Brotherhood and the Salafi Nour Party of having drawn up the candidate list and their preferred candidates beforehand, which would have meant that what was portrayed as being a consensual constituent assembly was in fact determined entirely by the two main Islamist parliamentary parties.[54] Within a few weeks nearly a third of all of the Assembly's members (including all secular and liberal members and representatives of al-Azhar and the Coptic Church) withdrew in protest at the Assembly's composition. A mediation and dialogue committee was formed to resolve the matter and a preliminary agreement was reached according to which the Assembly's membership should be tweaked to bring non-Islamists back on board, although a number of procedural limitations had to be overcome. However, before any meaningful progress could be made, an administrative court dissolved the Assembly on the grounds that

[53] Emmanuel Karagiannis, The New Political Islam: Human Rights, Democracy and Justice, University of Pennsylvania Press (2018), at 108.

[54] Waheed Abdel Majeed, "The Full Story of the Struggle for the Constituent Assembly" (القصة الكاملة لمعركة الجمعية التأسيسية), Shourouk News (June 20, 2012).

parliamentarians are not permitted to elect themselves to serve on state institutions.[55] The FJP accepted the court's decision, which meant that the conversation moved from adjusting the Assembly's membership to completely reconstituting it.

Composition (Second Iteration): A number of ad hoc meetings took place during April 2012 to negotiate the Assembly's new composition, which were almost entirely dedicated to discussing how many Assembly members should be political party members and what exact number of seats should be allocated to each party. During these discussions, a number of parties linked composition to voting rules within the Assembly. Secular parties argued, for example, that a higher number of Islamist members would only be acceptable if there was a supra-majority voting requirement that would make it impossible for Islamist members to impose their view. Meanwhile, both the FJP and the Nour Party argued both that parliamentary parties should have a higher proportion of the Assembly's membership and that the voting threshold should be at 50 percent. Ultimately, the voting requirement was settled first, when a senior liberal politician suggested a decreasing majority rule according to which a first vote should require a two-thirds majority, which if not met would then allow for the same issue to be adopted by a 57 percent majority. On June 7, 2012, an agreement was reached according to which thirty-nine seats would be reserved for parliamentarians (including sixteen for the FJP, eight for the Nour Party, and the remainder for an assortment of liberal, secular, and other non-Islamist parties).[56] The remaining sixty-one seats would be allocated to corporate interests (including fifteen for members of the judiciary, the largest group). Despite the progress that had been made, the agreement was still missing significant detail. For example, it did not specify how representatives of corporate groups would be selected, and also did not specifically define what constituted an Islamist.[57] Nevertheless, an election was organized on June 13, 2012, despite the fact that most of the 1,300 candidates were once again unknown. The end result was that the number of Islamists within the second Assembly was lower than its original configuration, although it is not exactly clear by how many, mainly because many non-Islamist members,

[55] See Decision 26657/66 (April 10, 2012) (in the author's possession).

[56] The new composition was clearly not in conformity with the administrative court's decision, but the negotiators proceeded nevertheless. The new composition opened the door to more legal challenges in the weeks and months that followed.

[57] Secular members were hoping to further reduce the Muslim Brotherhood's level of representation by including moderates within the Islamist quota. The Muslim Brotherhood meanwhile insisted that all Islamists should be members of the FJP and of the Salafi Nour party; see Majeed (2012).

particularly some representatives of specific corporate interests, had identical positions on many issues. A number of secular members refused to participate on the basis that the Assembly was still dominated by Islamists, while others expressed satisfaction with the Assembly's second iteration.[58]

Rules of Procedure: Shortly after it commenced its work, the Assembly adopted its Rules of Procedure. The Rules provided for a president who should chair and determine the agenda of plenary sessions (Article 7). A Secretary General was responsible for managing the Assembly's secretariat, which was responsible for managing the Assembly's internal administration, including preparing draft agendas, taking attendance, preparing comparative studies for the committees, overseeing the work of the committees' rapporteurs, and providing assistance in the drafting of reports (Article 11). Four substantive committees were established, each of which would have a rapporteur (Articles 14 and 15).[59] The drafting effort was supported by a drafting and research committee whose membership consisted of legal and language experts from within and without the Assembly, and which was responsible for presenting suggestions to the substantive committees (Article 19). The Assembly's quorum was set at 50 percent of its members, and decisions on procedural matters were to be decided by a majority of members. Article 5 set out the process through which the constitution was to be adopted, which was in conformity with the agreement that was entered into during the negotiation for the Assembly's second iteration

> The Assembly adopts draft provisions one by one and through consensus. If consensus cannot be reached, the draft provision is sent to a joint committee composed of the Assembly's chair and the relevant specialised committee in order to review the provision's wording in accordance with the objections that will have been made. The provision's new version will be presented to the Assembly in a subsequent meeting, and will require the support of 67 members at least to be adopted. If that level of support is not achieved, the provision is voted on again in a subsequent meeting and may be adopted with the support of 57 members.[60]

58 On 18 June 2012, at the Constituent Assembly's first session, Ayman Nour, a leading liberal politician, stated that the Constituent Assembly's composition "is much better than is being suggested in the media"; see Constituent Assembly minutes, unpublished (in the author's possession).

59 The substantive committees were as follows: (i) shape of the state and fundamental principles; (ii) rights, freedoms, and public obligations; (iii) system of government and public authorities; and (iv) oversight and independent agencies.

60 The Assembly's rules of procedure are available, in Arabic, at http://tinyurl.com/od4p28q.

Majoritarianism: The FJP leadership stated on a number of occasions that it would not be satisfied unless the future constitution was approved by all of Egypt's main constituencies and in particular that it would not be adopted over the objections of secular groups. Shortly before the results of the 2012 presidential elections were announced, the Muslim Brotherhood candidate signed a joint declaration with secular and liberal political figures in which they all committed to composing the Constituent Assembly in a way that would "guarantee that the constitution will be drafted for all Egyptians."[61] At the Assembly's opening session, a leading member of the Brotherhood stated that he would strive not for consensus but for unanimity.[62] Leaders of the Muslim Brotherhood also stated that its aim was for the constitution to be adopted by a large majority of at least 80 percent of the voting public in the referendum, and that negotiations would continue for as long as necessary until an agreement was reached on all issues.[63] However, given the Assembly's composition, Article 5 allowed for the FJP and its allies to push through any wording that they chose regardless of any objections by the opposition. Instead, the rules contained no other mechanism to overcome disagreements or to protect individual rights.[64] The rules guaranteed for the majority an opportunity to impose a majoritarian outcome. In the months that followed, several attempts were made to develop alternative and ad hoc mechanisms that could check this majoritarian tendency, none of which were successful.

Negotiations: The Assembly held its first session on June 18, 2012. Instructions were issued to the committees by the secretariat that they should strive to satisfy the (as of yet undefined) goals of the 2011 "revolution" while at the same time seeking inspiration from Egypt's constitutional history. The fact that at least fifteen Assembly members were judges reinforced the tendency to rely on the 1971 Constitution as a main source of inspiration.[65] Very quickly, the bulk of the negotiations centered on a small number of issues, including the separation of powers between the executive and the parliament, the

61 See "Fairmont Agreement" (June 22, 2012), available at www.shorouknews.com/columns/view.aspx?cdate=06072012&id=a87dcc81-d96c-42f1-afe4-d2b5db538938.

62 See Statement by Ali Fateh al-Bab, Constituent Assembly minutes (June 18, 2012), unpublished (in the author's possession).

63 Interview with the author (June 2012).

64 Article 5 was reminiscent of the process through which Syria's 1973 Constitution was drafted. The People's Assembly that was appointed to draft the Constitution consisted of 173 members, 87 of whom were Baath party members; see Karim Atassi, Syria, The Strength of an Idea: The Constitutional Architectures of Its Political Regimes, Cambridge University Press (2018), at 301.

65 The Assembly's president was a senior judge, who has served as head of the court of appeals and of the judicial council.

powers of the military, and the relationship between religion and state. The FJP professed to favor a parliamentary system of government on the basis that it would help deconcentrate power away from Egypt's imperial presidency, and so therefore tilted the balance of power away from the president in favor of the parliament. Assembly members argued about detailed issues, including term limits, the situations in which the president could dissolve parliament, and the means through which parliament could exercise oversight, and eventually settled on a mixed system. Ultimately, the conversation was without major consequence given that the Brotherhood was confident that the Islamist camp would continue to dominate both branches of government in the foreseeable future. The only major difference that was introduced to the system of government was to grant the military all the privileges that it had tried and failed to grant itself during the drafting of the supra-constitutional principles document. Among other things, the final constitution provided for the first time that the minister of defense had to be drawn from the officer class (Article 195), that a special council dominated by the security services was solely responsible for debating the military's budget (Article 197), and also established the principle that civilians could be tried before military courts (Article 198). Also, the new constitution maintained the 1971 Constitution's system on decentralization, which meant that a large proportion of governors would continue to be drawn from the officer class and that there would be very little oversight of their work. The main issue of contention during the negotiations was the relationship between religion and state and how Islamic Shari'a should impact fundamental rights. Early on during the transition, some of the FJP's more senior officials committed to leaving the 1971 constitution's Article 2 (according to which the "principles of Islamic Sharia" were the principle source of legislation) untouched, which set many nerves at ease.[66] However, as the Assembly commenced discussions on the issue, the Nour Party made a series of demands, including that Sharia be made the only source of legislation, that al-Azhar be the only authority for interpreting the principles of Islam, and specific rights including gender equality rights be curbed. This set off very tense and unsuccessful negotiations with the secular camp lasting weeks.

Ad Hoc Committees: In an effort to repair relations between the two camps, at least two ad hoc bodies were established. A consensus committee consisting of a limited number of Assembly members and political leaders was formed. The committee resolved to attempt to resolve fundamental issues, including but not limited to the relationship between religion and state and

66 "Egypt's Brotherhood Closer to Announcing Their Party" (إخوان مصر يتقدمون لإعلان حزبهم), Al-Jazeera (May 18, 2011).

the system of government. An initial meeting was organized on August 28, 2012, at which members tried to bridge the gap between the Nour Party's and the secular camp's positions. A secular member suggested specific wording for Article 2 according to which no law should contradict the constitution's provisions on fundamental rights, but the matter was left for future discussion. The committee only met on a handful of other occasions and did not make any significant progress.[67] In an effort to encourage some of the secular members who had been boycotting the Assembly to end their boycott, the Assembly's leadership also established a ten-member "technical advisory committee" composed essentially of prominent Egyptians, and in which there were only two Islamists. The Assembly's rules were never formally amended but the committee received written instructions from the Assembly's leadership inviting it to develop comments on the existing draft. By mid-November, the eight secular members withdrew on the basis that the Assembly did not set aside any time to consider the committee's comments, a charge that the Assembly's president denied.[68]

Breakdown: As negotiations progressed, secular members raised a series of complaints against the Brotherhood-controlled Assembly. They alleged that Islamist members considered themselves to be the sole legitimate owners of the constitutional process and viewed all others merely as an "opposition," to the extent that secular members would sometimes not even be allowed to speak for a variety of pretexts (including that sessions would have to be lifted for prayers).[69] Secular members also claimed that the Assembly's Secretariat had been captured by the Brotherhood and was publishing drafts of the constitution on the Assembly's website that had not in fact been formally approved, and that coincided with the Brotherhood's views.[70] On the other hand, the FJP suspected that secular members were more interested in undermining the then-dominant Islamist political parties than resolving substantive disputes on the constitution. The FJP was also seriously concerned that secular members were attempting to delay the negotiations so as to give

[67] See Majeed (2013).

[68] Assembly members made a small number of references to the technical advisory committee's suggestions during plenary sessions; see, for example, Constituent Assembly minutes (November 4, 2012), unpublished (in the author's possession).

[69] See, for example, Statement by Amr Moussa, Constituent Assembly minutes (September 5, 2012), unpublished (in the author's possession); and Statement by Amr Moussa, Constituent Assembly minutes (November 5, 2012), unpublished (in the author's possession).

[70] Waheed Abdel Majeed, "The Brotherhood's Attempts to Avoid Its Commitment to Reach Consensus in the Assembly" (أسرار محاولات الإخوان للإفلات من الالتزام بالتوافق داخل التأسيسية), Youm7 (June 12, 2012).

the courts sufficient time to complete a number of proceedings that were pending and that would have a major influence on the Assembly's work. The Supreme Constitutional Court dissolved the parliament on June 14, 2012 on the basis that the electoral law was not in conformity with the Constitution.[71] In addition, the courts were considering claims that had been raised against the Constituent Assembly's second iteration and that threatened to lead to a second dissolution, based on the same rationale that was applied to its first iteration. The FJP was concerned that a second dissolution would result in a significant fall in their popularity. In addition, any attempt to form a new Assembly would likely require a new parliamentary election, in which it was possible that the Brotherhood would not return the same impressive result. In any event, the Muslim Brotherhood viewed Egypt's secular parties as a small community with very limited legitimacy that they could dispense with if necessary. The Brotherhood therefore decided to accelerate the work, which meant securing fast and convenient political agreements with sufficient members simply with a view to moving on with the referendum. An agreement was reached with the Nour Party on matters relating to religion. Provisions were included in the draft that al-Azhar would be responsible for interpreting the principles of Islamic Sharia (Article 4), and the term "principles of Islamic Sharia" (which was previously interpreted as being fairly limited in scope) was redefined in very broad terms to include the entire range of Islamic rules dating back centuries (Article 219). Then on November 6, 2012, the Assembly's leadership circulated a three-week timetable toward completion of the drafting process. This was regarded by secularist members as a betrayal by the FJP, and also clearly illustrated to them a preference by the FJP in favor of accommodating Islamic fundamentalists rather than the other end of the political spectrum. Thus, despite the fact that a "constitutional declaration" was issued that extended the deadline for completion by an additional two months,[72] on November 29, 2012, the Assembly's leadership suddenly and without prior notice moved to complete the constitution in a remarkable overnight session that took place before the original six-month deadline had even expired.[73] By then, virtually every non-Islamist

[71] Decision 20/34 (June 14, 2012).

[72] For an unofficial translation of the Constitutional Declaration, see http://english.ahram.org.eg/NewsContent/1/64/58947/Egypt/Politics-/English-text-of-Morsis-Constitutional-Declaration-.aspx.

[73] See Constituent Assembly minutes (November 29, 2012), unpublished (in the author's possession).

member had either withdrawn from the Assembly or boycotted the session.[74] Their decision to withdraw was made easier by the then-Muslim Brotherhood affiliated president's declaration that his executive decisions were above judicial review.[75] In December 2012, the final draft constitution received the support of 63 percent of voters, but turnout was particularly low at around 33 percent.[76] By way of comparison, turnout in the March 2011 referendum and in the 2011 parliamentary elections were 42 percent and 54 percent, respectively. In addition, the 2012 Constitution received ten million and seven hundred thousand favorable votes, whereas the 2011 constitutional amendments received fourteen million and two hundred thousand. After the referendum results were published, the Muslim Brotherhood's leadership changed its discourse on the importance of consensus, arguing that the level of approval that the 2012 Constitution achieved was higher than international norms for referenda and was therefore sufficient.[77] Meanwhile, after the 2012 Constitution entered into force, the president of the republic once again called for dialogue, which was promptly rejected by the opposition.[78]

THE 2014 CONSTITUTION

Interim Constitution: The 2012 constitution remained in force for only six months. On July 3, 2013, the president of the republic (who was a leading member of the Muslim Brotherhood) was removed from office by the military following large-scale demonstrations that took place in many parts of the country. The Muslim Brotherhood and the FJP were driven underground by a resurgent security state following significant violence.[79] A statement by the "General Command of the Armed Forces" suspended the 2012 Constitution (Paragraph 6(a)) and called for the formation of a committee

74 "The Constituent Assembly Approves Egypt's New Constitution before It Is Put to Referendum; The Opposition Rejects the Text" (الجمعية التأسيسية تقر دستور مصر الجديد قبل عرضه على الاستفتاء والمعارضة ترفضه), al-Hurra (November 30, 2012).

75 Hisham al-Mayani, "Morsi Immunizes His Decisions in a Constitutional Declaration and Forbids the Dissolution of the Upper Chamber" (مرسي يحصن قراراته بإعلان دستوري ويمنع حل التأسيسية والشورى), Al-Ahram (November 22, 2012).

76 The referendum was organized in two rounds. An unofficial translation of the final 2012 constitution is available at www.constitutionnet.org/vl/item/new-constitution-arab-republic-egypt-approved-30-nov-2012/. The original Arabic is available at www.constitutionnet.org/vl/item/msr-lnskh-lnhyy-lmshrw-ldstwr-ljdyd-hsb-30-tshryn-thnynwfmbr-2012-ljmy-ltsysy-2012. The referendum's official results are available at https://referendum2012.elections.eg/results/referendum-results.

77 Interview with the author (January 2013).

78 See See Khalifa (2015), at 154.

79 See "All According to Plan," Human Rights Watch (August 12, 2014).

to propose amendments to the 2012 Constitution (Paragraph 6(f)).[80] The statement was followed on July 8, 2013 by a new constitutional declaration that was designed to operate as a new interim constitution (the "2013 Interim Constitution"), which would be in force during the duration of yet another transitional period.[81] The text was clearly still inspired by Egypt's constitutional tradition but was around half the length of the 2011 Interim Constitution at thirty-three articles altogether. It provided for the bare minimum of civil and political rights without mentioning any social and economic rights (Articles 4–14); a small number of institutions including the Supreme Constitutional Court, the State Council, and the armed forces (Articles 16–22); and the executive branch of government without any mention of a legislative branch (Articles 20–26). The president of the republic was granted very significant powers, including the right to issue legislation and the right to form the cabinet unilaterally (Article 24).[82] The president had the authority to declare a state of emergency lasting only three months, renewable only after approval by the people in a referendum (Article 27).

Constitution First: Most importantly, the 2013 Interim Constitution provided for a new transitional roadmap that adopted a "constitution first" approach that did not provide for any meaningful input by the general population. The first step of the process was that an expert committee would have one month to suggest changes to the 2012 Constitution (Article 28). The committee was composed of six judges and four academics, three of whom were retired, all of whom were selected more for their conservatism than for their expert knowledge. Their suggested changes to the 2012 Constitution essentially proposed to shift constitutional practice back in favor of the 1971 Constitution in many respects (including by watering down the role of religion and by removing some of the few clear improvements that the 2012 Constitution had introduced).[83] Second, a fifty-member constitutional

[80] See Statement of the General Command of the Armed Forces (July 3, 2013) (in the author's possession).

[81] For an unofficial translation of the constitutional declaration, see www.constitutionnet.org/vl/item/unofficial-english-translation-constitutional-declaration-egypt-july-08-2013. For the Arabic original, see www.constitutionnet.org/sites/all/themes/const4/svg/download.svg.

[82] The statement by the "General Command of the Armed Forces" provided that the Chief Justice of the Supreme Constitutional Court should serve as interim president (Paragraph 6 (b)). Although not stated explicitly, it was clear that the interim president should serve until presidential elections were organized in accordance with Article 30 of the 2013 Interim Constitution.

[83] In a clear instance of self-dealing, Article 158 of the expert committee's proposed changes provided that the judiciary's budget should appear as a single figure in the annual state budget, something that had never been provided for in Egyptian constitutional tradition. For an

committee would have sixty days to prepare a final draft of the constitution (Article 29).[84] Article 29 provided that the committee's members should represent "all segments, sects and demographic diversities of society, especially parties, intelligentsia, labourers, peasants, members of trade unions, specialized federations, national councils, al-Azhar, the Egyptian Churches, Armed Forces, the police and public figures, provided that ten members at least be young people and women." On September 1, 2013, the full list of members was announced, and consisted almost entirely of representatives of specific corporate groups, many of which were originally listed in Article Three of the supra-constitutional principles document.[85] Institutions such as the Chamber of Tourism, the Plastic and Applied Arts Sector, and the Egyptian Book Union were represented in the constitutional committee. Most of these representatives of corporate groups were only involved in the negotiations when the substance of the discussions concerned their own group (e.g. representatives of religious institutions were mainly interested in religion and national identity and had very little to say about other issues). Six members were drawn from political groups, including two Islamists, one of whom was a member of the Nour Party while the other was an independent. The largest proportion of members consisted of what was termed "public figures," very few of whom had any previous experience with constitutions. The expert committee was also required to be present at all of the constitutional committee's sessions both to explain their written proposal and to "make any other opinions or propositions" (Article 6). The constitutional committee adopted its rules of procedure on September 11, 2013, which provided for the establishment of three substantive subcommittees and one drafting committee (Article 12).[86] The rules also provided that the final draft of the constitution should be adopted by consensus, absent of which a three-quarters majority of members would suffice (Article 5). Ultimately, there was little scope for disagreement within the constitutional committee, partly as a result of the fact that discussions were dominated by conservative members who generally worked against any major

unofficial translation of the C10's proposed changes to the 2012 constitution, see www.constitutionnet.org/vl/item/egypt-proposed-amendments-constitution-2012. For the Arabic original, see www.constitutionnet.org/node/11730.

84 The timeframe was ultimately interpreted as referring to working days and not calendar days, which allowed the constitutional committee to extend the entire period to three months altogether.

85 Presidential Decree 570/2013 (September 1, 2013).

86 The substantive committees were as follows: (i) the state and fundamental characteristics; (ii) rights and freedoms; and (iii) system of government and public authorities. See Decision 4 (2013), President the Constitutional Committee (September 11, 2013), Official Gazette Number 210 (2013).

reforms. The final draft that was adopted by the C50 was little more than a reformulation of the 2012 constitution based on the negotiations that took place between special interests. The final draft was put to referendum on January 14 and 15, 2014 and was approved by 98.1 percent of voters, with a 38.6 percent participation rate.

Outcome: The 2014 Constitution introduced a number of changes, most of which made little difference to the lives of ordinary citizens.[87] Rights and freedoms were formulated restrictively, allowing parliament to enact limitations almost without restriction.[88] Military trials of civilians were once again maintained, despite promises to the contrary (Article 204). The relationship between the president and the parliament was rebalanced back in favor of the president but, as in 2012, these changes were unlikely to have any practical impact given that all the levers of state were under the control of the security services.[89] The courts' independence was also expanded, in particular by allowing the judiciary's annual budget to appear as a "single figure" in the annual state budget (Article 185). The one possible consolation for the general population was that the 2014 Constitution provided that specific proportions of the annual state budget should be invested in health and education.[90] In practice, however, these provisions have been ignored. In 2019 political forces that supported the president drew up amendments to the 2014 Constitution that were approved in a referendum by 88 percent of voters. The amendments reset the clock on presidential term limits (Article 244bis), and granted the president the power to appoint the president of the Supreme Constitutional Court (Article 193(3)).

[87] For an unofficial translation of the final constitution, see www.constitutionnet.org/vl/item/egypt-constitution-2014. For the original Arabic language version, see http://egelections-2011.appspot.com/Dostour/Dostour_update2013.pdf.

[88] By way of example, Article 15 provides that "[s]triking peacefully is a right that is organized by law."

[89] See Amr Hamzawy, "Egypt's Consolidated Authoritarianism," Brown Journal of World Affairs, Vol. XXVI, No. I (Fall/Winter 2019), 73–88.

[90] By way of example, Article 18 provided that the equivalent of 3 percent of GNP should be allocated to education. That target has not been met.

3

Yemen

BACKGROUND

Territorial Consolidation: Prior to the nineteenth century, the territory that is today part of the state of Yemen was not subject to centralized rule. The Ottoman Empire had established a presence in most of the territory in the sixteenth century only to be expelled a century later, after which most of the country's regions were subject to their own local administration (some of which withdrew inward, while others became important international trading centers).[1] The process of centralizing authority in Yemen, albeit in two separate territories each subject to its own administration, began in the first half of the nineteenth century. In 1839 the British Empire seized control of the southern port of Aden, and gradually expanded its authority to include other territories around Aden. In 1849 the Ottoman Empire had reestablished its presence over much of the remainder of Yemen's territory, including the northern highlands and Sana'a city (which was eventually to become the capital of a united Yemen). These two territories slowly consolidated inwardly over a period of decades, much of which was marked by armed revolts against foreign rule. They both also introduced their own respective legal systems, while making sure to adapt to the local context.[2]

Institutionalization: The British initially maintained "friendship treaties" with tribal authorities, but moved to institutionalize its rule in the twentieth century. Aden city was established as a colony that was directly administered

[1] See Jane Hathaway, "The Ottomans and the Yemeni Coffee Trade," Oriente Moderno 25 (86), no. 1 (2006), 161–171. For the development of administrative structures under the Ottoman Empire, see Thomas Kuehn, Empire, Islam, and Politics of Difference: Ottoman Rule in Yemen, *1849–1919*, Leiden and Boston: Brill (2011).

[2] For more, see Paul Dresch, Tribes, Government, and History in Yemen, Clarendon Press (1994).

by British officials. A legislative council was established, and ordinary legislation was enacted by a governor. Some slow movement was made during that time to increase local participation in governmental affairs, including through the appointment of locals as council members. The rest of the territories that were under British control were organized as a protectorate, in which local institutions were generally preserved to the extent that they did not conflict with British security interests. Some of the territories were administered by local government while others were more traditional sheikhdoms. There were several state councils. In 1951 Lahej Sultanate, which was part of the protectorate, adopted a written constitution, which included a catalogue of civil rights and guarantees for judicial independence.[3] The Ottoman Empire introduced the Tanzimat system in 1872 through a clearly defined hierarchy of administrative sub-divisions with an administrative council at each level of provincial government and a municipality in Sana'a.[4] Many local leaders remained deeply opposed to Ottoman rule, however, and organized a series of armed uprisings. In response, the Ottoman Empire, partially inspired by the British Empire's ability to rule over Southern Yemen with significantly less resistance, opted in favor of instituting a type of indirect rule that would allow for greater local autonomy.[5]

Fragile Constitutionalism: After the Ottoman defeat in the First World War, sovereignty over northern Yemen was surrendered to Imam Yahya, who ruled the territory as an absolute monarchy. In 1962 a group of revolutionary military officers seized power in a coup d'état and established the Yemeni Arab Republic, which triggered a brutal eight-year war between republicans and monarchists, both of whom were supported by a number of foreign sponsors, that ended in 1970. In that same year, a new constitution was adopted that provided for an elected consultative council (Articles 44, 48), a three to five-member executive council with a rotating chairmanship (Articles 73, 78), some oversight mechanisms including the right to withdraw confidence from the government (Article 65), an independent judiciary (Articles 144, 145), and a series of rights and freedoms (Articles 8–43). The constitution

[3] For the administrative development in Aden, the Colony, and the protectorate see Herbert J. Liebesny, "Administration and Legal Development in Arabia: Aden Colony and Protectorate," Middle East Journal, Vol. 9, No. 4 (1955), 385–396.

[4] Law of provincial administration (1871). The Tanzimat system was partially motivated by a desire to act against rising nationalism in various parts of the Ottoman Empire by reimposing central rule in all parts of the Empire. See Reşat Kasaba (ed.), The Cambridge History of Turkey, Volume 4 Turkey in the Modern World, Cambridge University Press (2008).

[5] The Da'an Agreement was signed in 1911 between the Ottoman authorities and Imam Yahya, who was a spiritual leader in northern Yemen. See Abdol Rauh Yaccob, "Yemeni Opposition to Ottoman Rule: An Overview," Proceedings of the Seminar for Arabian Studies, Vol. 42 (2012), 411–419.

did not lead to stable governance, partly because it did not offer any genuine guarantees, including the fact that all political parties were formally banned (Article 37). In the years that followed its adoption, an intense and violent competition for power took place, which saw the constitution suspended in 1974 and reinstated in 1978. Ali Abdullah Saleh, an army officer, assumed the presidency in 1978, which he was to maintain for over three decades. Meanwhile, British control over southern Yemen ended in 1967, which led to the establishment of the Soviet-supported People's Democratic Republic of Yemen, with Aden as its capital. In 1970 a constitution was adopted that reflected Soviet preferences, and which also banned partisanship.[6] Southern Yemen remained highly unstable during this period, which resulted in another round of bloodletting that took place in 1986.

1991 Constitution: An initiative to unify the two countries was formally launched in 1990, with the newly established Republic of Yemen to be governed by a constitution that entered into force in 1991.[7] That text established a highly centralized system of government, which barely took into account that the Republic was a merger of two countries.[8] It also provided for a semi-presidential system that leant in favor of parliamentary authority. The presidency was occupied not by a single individual but by a five-member council, which was indirectly elected by the parliament (Article 82); although the text does not explicitly say so, the drafters clearly meant for the presidency council to act as a power-sharing mechanism between the country's north and south. The presidency council appointed a prime minister and government (Article 94(4)), which itself had to obtain confidence (Articles 72 and 104) and could have confidence withdrawn from parliament (Article 74). Importantly, much of the 1991 constitution was never implemented, and little was done to integrate northern and southern institutions. In 1991 a political parties law was adopted that liberalized party activity, but which did little to improve the overall governance framework.[9] By 1994, significant problems had emerged, including serious accusations against Saleh (who was appointed chairman of

[6] See Article 37. The 1970 Constitution is available at http://yemenparliament.gov.ye/Details?Post=954. An unofficial translation of the 1970 Constitution is available at https://al-bab.com/constitution-yemen-arab-republic-1970.

[7] An informal English-language translation is available at www.constituteproject.org/constitution/Yemen_2001.pdf

[8] There were no formal power sharing arrangements and there were practically no provisions relating to decentralization. Articles 117 to 119 were the only provisions that mentioned the existence of "municipal governments." Law 4 (2001) purported to introduce only very limited decentralization but was never implemented.

[9] Law 66 (1991).

the presidency council) and his entourage of corruption, nepotism, and ineffective government. The then-ruling party in the south decided to secede, which led to a civil war that eventually led to a complete takeover of the entire country by the north. The 1991 constitution was amended to replace the presidency council with a single president (Article 104), and to eliminate any reference to municipal councils. In 2000, a decentralization law was adopted that placed very little real authority in the hands of local administrations and locally elected councils, all of which were obligated to implement or respect policies that were developed by the central government.[10]

Yemen on the Brink: Yemen's modern history has been particularly turbulent, even by regional standards. Colonial powers were either unwilling or unable to fully pacify the country, allowing local identity to thrive. Meanwhile, continuous conflict prevented stable institutions and the rule of law from emerging. After unification, an attempt was made to implement centralized rule in the absence of a solid basis to do so, and for undemocratic purposes. From 1994 until 2011, the country was ruled by the Sana'a-based authorities, which established a highly centralized and undemocratic system of government.[11] President Saleh monopolized power, including through his relatives, who controlled much of the security sector, profited from weak oversight frameworks,[12] and launched a series of internal conflicts in various parts of the country (including six separate wars in Saada province between 2004 and 2010).[13] The result was that Yemen was in a desperate situation. The already limited oil resources as well as foreign aid were declining, worsening an already serious budgetary crisis, which itself led to an increase in poverty and unemployment (particularly among the very large numbers of young people); water resources were also in decline, a major cause for concern given that Yemen is one of the world's most water-stressed countries; resentment

[10] The Arabic original and an unofficial translation are available here: https://constitutionnet.org/vl/item/yemen-law-concerning-local-authority-august-2000.

[11] In the 1999 presidential elections, President Saleh was awarded 96.2 percent of the vote.

[12] See "Letter Dated 20 February 2015 from the Panel of Experts on Yemen Established Pursuant to Security Council Resolution 2140 (2014) Addressed to the President of the Security Council, S/2015/125," February 20, 2015 ("Ali Abdullah Saleh, on the other hand, is in a very different situation. Ali Abdullah Saleh was President of Yemen for 33 years, until 2012, and during that time he is alleged to have amassed assets between $32 billion and $60 billion, most of which are believed to have been transferred abroad under false names or the names of others holding the assets on his behalf. These assets are said to take the form of property, cash, shares, gold and other valuable commodities. At the time of writing this report, these assets were believed to be located in at least 20 countries").

[13] See Victoria Clark, Yemen: Dancing on the Head of Snakes, Yale University Press (2010); and Stephen Day, Regionalism and Rebellion in Yemen: A Troubled National Union, Cambridge University Press (2012).

among southern Yemenis against the central government was organized and had grown considerably; both Ansar Allah and al-Qaida in the Arabian Peninsula were growing in prominence and strength, worsening security risks in much of the country.[14] On the eve of the uprising, poverty stood at 42 percent of the country, with ten million Yemenis being food insecure and one million children under the age of five acutely malnourished.[15] On the eve of its uprising, Yemen therefore had very fragile institutions, was highly divided, was threatened by multiple security threats, and was suffering from an acute and worsening economic and humanitarian crisis.

NEGOTIATIONS

Political Dynamics: By early 2011, Yemenis were already mobilized against state policies and declining standards of living. Events in Tunisia encouraged protest movements to take their action even further. Yemenis took to the streets in their thousands all over the country starting on January 27, 2011. Many of these initial protests were met with violence by the security forces. A tent city was established in one of the capital's main squares where different groups of protesters debated the type of reforms that they wanted to see introduced. On March 18, 2011 fifty protesters were killed by snipers, which led to an immediate escalation. Several components of the regime and the armed forces defected, leading to military confrontations in various parts of the capital. This led to several months of negotiations that were limited to traditional elite circles who limited themselves to exploring how conflict could be avoided by determining how and when Saleh would leave power. Improved living conditions and governance were not part of these initial discussions, and groups (many of which were radical) that were not directly involved in the standoff in the capital were also not involved.[16] President Saleh's main objective appeared to be either to remain in power or to maintain sufficient authority to protect his interests, possibly with a view to returning to power sometime in the future. He was supported in that by his family members and by the General People's Congress (GPC), the ruling party that he had established in 1982 and that was still at that time the leading

[14] Ansar Allah is also known as the Houthi movement, or simply the Houthis.

[15] "Facing the Hard Facts in Yemen," The World Bank (September 26, 2012).

[16] See Helen Lackner, "Yemen's 'Peaceful' Transition from Autocracy: Could It Have Succeeded?," International IDEA (2016), at 23–29. Helen Lackner, "The Change Squares of Yemen," in Adam Roberts, Michael J. Willis, Rory McCarthy, and Timothy Garton Ash (eds.), Civil Resistance in the Arab Spring: Triumphs and Disasters, Oxford University Press (2016).

political force in the country. He was mainly opposed by the Joint Meeting Parties (JMP), a coalition of opposition parties that included Islamist, socialist, and nationalist forces.[17] These parties mobilized heavily to oust President Saleh from power but were relatively conservative when it came to governance reform. International actors were also involved, including regional players that were concerned about potential spillover effects from a conflict in Yemen and world powers including the United States that were intent on preventing any disruptions to international security. Groups on the outside of the negotiations were far more radical by nature, and their exclusion from the negotiations increased the likelihood of a conservative outcome. This included the protest movement that sparked the 2011 uprising. Ansar Allah, a revivalist Islamist group that at the time was concentrated in northern Yemen and was not present in the halls of power in Sanaa, also did not participate.[18] The Hirak was a grassroots protest movement that emerged in 2007 in southern Yemen to demand better treatment of southern interests, parts of which were adopting an increasingly militant and separatist position. Much of the Hirak considered the entire Yemeni state to be illegitimate and did not feel directly concerned by tensions in Sana'a. Later in the transition, all three of these groups were to play important roles in the discussions albeit in different ways and to different extents.

GCC Initiative: As the country edged closer to civil war, rival political forces attempted to negotiate a resolution. In April 2011, an initiative was tabled to resolve the crisis among the forces that were still loyal to President Saleh, those that had defected, and the JMP (the GCC Initiative).[19] The one-page document proposed to set in motion a negotiated transition through

[17] See Vincent Durac, "The Joint Meeting Parties and the Politics of Opposition in Yemen," in Hendrik Jan Kraetzschmar (ed.), The Dynamics of Opposition Cooperation in the Arab World, Routledge (2015). Michaelle Browers, "Yemen's Joint Meeting Parties: Origins and Architects," International Journal of Middle East Studies, Vol. 39, No. 4 (2007), 565–586.

[18] Helen Lackner, Yemen in Crisis: The Road to War, Verso (2019), at Chapter 5.

[19] According to a senior western official who was based in Sanaa, Qatar and the UAE were responsible for most of the GCC Initiative's contents; Senior western official, interview with the author (March 2014). Two other senior western officials stated that the GCC Initiative was in fact drafted by the United States and translated from English into Arabic; see Senior western official, interview with the author, May 10, 2020, and the unpublished account of a senior western official (in the author's possession). This account is supported by Charles Schmitz, "Yemen's National Dialogue," Middle East Institute, MEI Policy Paper 2014-1 (February 2014), at 4. This account is contradicted by a Western academic who was present in Yemen at the time and who maintains that the text of the GCC Initiative was in fact drafted by a group of senior Yemeni officials; Interview with the author (May 27, 2020).

which President Saleh would leave office and a new constitution would be developed.[20] It proposed that from the first day of its entry into force, President Saleh would require of the opposition that it form a government of national unity, half of which would be drawn equally from the-then ruling party and the opposition (Article 1). Crucially, the Initiative also proposed that twenty-nine days after it was to enter into force the parliament should grant the president and his collaborators "immunity against legal and judicial proceedings" (Article 3). The day after, the president would resign in favor of his Vice President (Article 4).[21] The vice president would then call for presidential elections within sixty days, in accordance with the Constitution (Article 5). Finally, the Initiative proposed that a new constitution should be drafted (Article 6) and be put to a referendum (Article 7), following which elections should be held (Article 8). The GCC Initiative as it then existed was designed to bring an end to the president's rule while keeping as much of the political system in place as possible. However, the document was missing crucial detail that could not be resolved other than through prolonged negotiations. For example, the document did not indicate how decisions would be made during the transition process in the event consensus could not be reached. There was also no detail whatsoever on how the new constitution would be drafted or who would determine its content. Both of these issues would ultimately be highly controversial throughout the transition process. President Saleh initially accepted the initiative but refused to attend the signing ceremony at the last moment, formally on the basis that he was opposed to foreign intervention in his country's sovereign affairs but possibly also because he was hoping to negotiate better terms for himself.

Stalled Negotiations: The months that followed were witness to intense negotiations between Yemen's main political forces, as well as mass protests, civil disobedience, and continued deterioration in overall security in the country. On June 3, 2011, President Saleh himself was seriously injured in an assassination attempt, and was taken to Saudi Arabia for treatment for close

[20] See The Gulf Cooperation Council Initiative (November 23, 2011). The Initiative was endorsed by United Nations Security Council Resolution 2014, S/RES/2014 (2011) (in the Resolution, the Security Council noted "the commitment by the President of Yemen to immediately sign the Gulf Cooperation Council initiative and encourages him, or those authorized to act on his behalf, to do so, and to implement a political settlement based upon it, and calls for this commitment to be translated into action, in order to achieve a peaceful political transition of power").

[21] Abdrabbuh Mansur Hadi was a military officer originally from the southern Yemen province of Abyan, who fled into exile in north Yemen after the fighting that took place in 1986. Vice President Hadi (who eventually became President Hadi) would eventually play a leading role in the transition.

to four months. Shortly after he departed, Jamal Ben Omar, who was then a Special Adviser to the Secretary General of the United Nations, arrived in the country with a handful of experts to assist in the negotiations.[22] Importantly, although many Yemenis considered that the GCC Initiative was flawed, they also considered that its mere existence made it almost impossible to step back from what it already included, which meant that all that could reasonably be done was to add to it. There were deep substantive divisions between the different sides on what that additional detail should consist of, including how specific some of the arrangements should be. Some actors were determined to see a new president take office within a very narrow timeframe, while members of the ruling party not only resisted that tendency but were also reluctant to commit to any specific position while the president's health and survival remained in doubt. In July 2011, a closed group of senior political leaders circulated a draft agreement that they had negotiated, but which was never formally adopted.[23] That document provided that the president should call for early presidential elections "by the end of 2011" (Article 4(a)). The document was also the first to provide that a national dialogue council would be responsible for "developing a transition roadmap and monitoring its implementation" (Article 8). The body should be "as inclusive as possible" (Article 9) and should reach decisions through "sufficient consensus," a term that was only loosely defined (Article 10). Negotiations continued during the weeks that followed and subsequent drafts introduced new arrangements that favored the president (including a requirement that the president would have to formally approve the power-sharing government, and the fact that a firm deadline for early elections was missing), thereby increasing concerns that the president was seeking to remain in office.

Final Agreement: In September 2011, President Saleh unexpectedly returned to Yemen, which allowed him to take back control over his own negotiation position. He delegated his vice president to negotiate an implementation mechanism (including early presidential elections) with all factions, to sign the initiative, and to supervise its implementation (Article 1).[24] Crucially, the decree did not indicate when the presidential elections should take place, which raised concerns even further. In the weeks that followed, negotiations continued without any meaningful progress. On October 21, 2011,

22 In 2012 the Special Adviser was promoted to Special Envoy and was permitted to keep a small number of staff in Yemen on a full-time basis. Until that time, the Special Adviser travelled in and out of the country, which some observers noted was an effective manner of proceeding as it encouraged Yemenis to make progress in time for one of the Adviser's departures or arrivals.

23 In the author's possession.

24 Presidential Decree 24 (2011).

the United Nations Security Council adopted Resolution 2014, which required that the Secretary General report back on the negotiations within thirty days.[25] The Resolution carried with it the implicit threat of sanctions, which was also reinforced by statements by some western officials. By late November, as the deadline for completion approached, the negotiators accelerated their work but could still not reach agreement. The embassies of the United States and United Kingdom submitted a draft document that they had drawn up, but the Yemeni negotiators were uncomfortable with that input.[26] The parties therefore enquired with the United Nations Special Adviser if he could present a proposal to both sides of the negotiations that they could then use to reach an agreement. The Special Adviser and his small number of advisers had in fact, over the previous few months, been carrying out consultations with a wide group of political and civil society leaders and had a draft implementation plan that they hoped might be acceptable to the parties ready to be presented. The negotiators dedicated the little time that was remaining to discussing, amending, and also shortening the Special Adviser's draft.[27] On November 23, 2011, the president and opposition leaders signed both the GCC Initiative (which remained substantively unchanged since April 2011) and the second additional text, which became known as the Implementation Mechanism.

ROADMAP

Objective: Formally, the Implementation Mechanism was adopted merely to provide additional detail on how the GCC Initiative would play out in practice. For many national and international actors, therefore, the Mechanism's role was limited to assisting Yemen to transition away from the former president's rule in favor of a new president, who would not introduce any major changes to the political system. However, for other actors, including many emerging groups and the United Nations Special Adviser, the Implementation Mechanism was designed to allow Yemen to transition to

[25] United Nations Security Council Resolution 2014, S/RES/2014 (2011).

[26] On the issue of decision-making, the draft provided that all decisions should be taken through consensus, absent of which the matter would be referred to the vice president and to the prime minister, and if those two parties could not reach agreement "the issue would be reverted to a jury the formation of which is agreed" (Article 8); it also provided that a national dialogue conference should focus on four issues, one of which was "the phenomenon of terrorism" (Second Phase, Article 2(d)). See unpublished draft (in the author's possession).

[27] Based on the written and unpublished account of a senior western official (in the author's possession).

democracy.[28] For them, this would be achieved through a number of means, including but not limited to providing for a National Dialogue Conference (NDC) on a far more open basis than anything that Yemen had done in the past and for the contents of the new constitution to be determined by the outcomes of that dialogue process.

Phased Approach: The final version of the Implementation Mechanism provided that the transition should take place in two stages. Altogether the transition was due to last for around two years and three months, although an exact length was not specified. The first phase would start immediately upon signing of the GCC Initiative, and would end ninety days later when early presidential elections were organized. During that time, a number of bodies and institutions were due to be established. The second phase was organized in three separate steps. At first, a technical committee would determine how the dialogue process would take place, including who would take part, what they would discuss, how they would take decisions, etc. The NDC was envisaged as the centerpiece of the transition period, which would change the country's politics for generations to come. The Implementation Mechanism provided that the substance of the NDC's discussions should be captured in a series of interim and final reports that would be published online and circulated to the public. After the completion of the National Dialogue, a constitutional drafting commission (CDC) was to be composed to "prepare a new draft constitution within three months of the date of its establishment." The CDC's work would be limited to repackaging and redrafting the NDC's outcomes in the form of a new national constitution. A referendum would then be organized and, if successful, be followed by elections. The Mechanism did not specify how soon the referendum should be organized, which potentially meant that the transition could be open ended.

Unique Features: In comparison with other transition processes in the region, the GCC Initiative and its Implementation Mechanism were by far the most ambitious and sophisticated for at least two reasons. First, the roadmap deliberately avoided organizing any competitive elections during the transition. Many of the main actors were conscious that an election organized immediately after a long period of undemocratic rule would lead to a skewed result, particularly in a negotiated transition in which the former ruling party was unquestionably still the most important political force in the country.[29]

[28] Senior international official, interview with the author (March 2014).

[29] See, for example, Zaid Al-Ali, "Constitutional Legitimacy in Iraq: What Role Local Context?," in Rainer Grote and Tilmann J. Röder (eds.), CONSTITUTIONALISM IN ISLAMIC COUNTRIES: BETWEEN UPHEAVAL AND CONTINUITY, Oxford University Press (2011). The authors of Sudan's

The negotiating parties therefore adopted a mechanism that would allow groups and communities, that would otherwise not have had the opportunity to do so, to participate in governance. The 2012 presidential elections did not constitute an exception to that approach, given that it was not competitive and was solely designed to offer some form of democratic legitimacy to an elite bargain. Second, throughout the region, the transition process was almost always designed to be unidimensional. Appointed committees or elected assemblies were responsible for drafting a constitution, and as soon as they were finished their drafts would be submitted for approval. Yemen's approach of a wider dialogue conference (that, importantly, was to include a relatively good representation of women and youth) was therefore more likely to lead to a broader range of contributions, which in theory was supposed to lead to a more consensual final constitution and a better quality draft than regional peers.

Design Flaws: At the same time, the Implementation Mechanism suffered from a number of flaws, some of which may have been inevitable in the circumstances but that would ultimately prove to be fatal to the entire transition (see later). Dialogue conferences are extremely important and can be catalysts for change but they also cannot achieve everything that needs to be done to transition from conflict, volatility, and undemocratic rule to peace and democracy. To resolve conflict, high level negotiations between political and military leaders must take place. To establish democratic institutions, legitimate political leaders must negotiate a new state structure with input by technical experts, which is a complex exercise. Neither of these two processes had been specifically provided for in the Implementation Mechanism, which may have been because the negotiators were hoping that they would either take place in the NDC or that they would take place alongside it. As the case may be, however, they did not take place at all. The longstanding conflicts within Sanaa and between Sanaa and other parts of the country could not be resolved given that discussions between the relevant leaders never took place or at least did not reach a solution. Instead, the Implementation Mechanism and the NDC's internal arrangements and the general context created the impression in the minds of many that the NDC would be a forum in which all issues would be resolved, while at the same time explicitly allowing the president to impose outcomes at crucial junctures (see later). That combination of factors essentially ensured that the transition would not succeed.

2019 Constitutional Charter were also aware of this problem, and so therefore opted not to hold elections for the first several years after the Charter entered into force.

INTERIM ARRANGEMENTS

Existing Constitution: Post-uprising governance was dealt with only indirectly in Yemen, contrary to Egypt, Tunisia, Libya, Sudan, and others. The result was highly inadequate, particularly for a country with such a weak institutional framework. The negotiating parties and the Special Adviser were conscious that they could not in the circumstances negotiate and draft an entirely new interim constitution and so opted to maintain some form of constitutional continuity, even if only imperfectly. The Implementation Mechanism provided that it and the GCC Initiative "superseded any current or legal arrangements" and that they "could not be challenged before state institutions" (Article 4). What this meant is that during the transitional period, the 1991 Constitution remained in force but was considered to have been amended by the GCCI Initiative and the Implementation Mechanism. However, it was never made clear which of the 1991 Constitution's provisions were being amended, and what impact an amendment should have. By way of example, Article 119(4) of the 1991 Constitution provides the president with an absolute right to name the prime minister and all the members of the cabinet. As noted previously, the Implementation Mechanism provided that a national unity government was to be headed by a prime minister nominated by the JMP. In the event that individual resigned from his position, or could no longer exercise his functions, would Article 10 of the Implementation Mechanism apply or would Article 119(4) of the 1991 Constitution? This type of ambiguity only became apparent as the transition progressed, and as events that were unforeseen at the start of the transition imposed themselves and forced senior officials to improvise solutions based on their own readings of the legal instruments. In another example, the Implementation Mechanism purported to amend the 1991 Constitution without conforming to the formal amendment procedure (Article 158), which opened the door to future extra-constitutional amendments (see later). Finally, the Implementation Mechanism did not make any provision for what should happen in the event the two-year transition period expired before the new permanent constitution entered into force. Would the transition be automatically extended, would it have to be formally extended, or would the 1991 Constitution come back into force in its original form? If the transition could be extended, then who would have to agree to such an extension? What ended up happening is that, in its final report, the NDC decided that the transition should be extended by a year in order to allow a number of steps to be completed (including the drafting and adoption of legislation, the drafting of the constitution, the constitutional referendum, etc.) without formally stating that the Implementation

Mechanism was amended.[30] By the end of that one year extension, very few of those steps had been completed, which reopened the question as to whether and if so how the transition period should be extended. The question was further complicated by the fact that the NDC had completed its work, which meant that whatever legitimacy it could offer to a further extension was not available.[31]

Hyperpresidentialism: Some of the Implementation Mechanism's explicit amendments to the 1991 Constitution reinforced the presidential system that was already in place. Combined with the fact that the NDC had such a wide mandate and was so formalized, the president's vastly expanded powers allowed him to impose an outcome at a time when the general expectation was that a negotiation was taking place. The Mechanism provided that all of the government's decisions should be taken through consensus, absent of which the matter would be referred to the vice president (or the president after the elections) and to the prime minister, and if those two parties could not reach agreement, the vice president (or president) should "take the final decision" (Article 12). The parliament was also required to function through consensus, barring which the Speaker "shall refer the matter for decision" by the vice president (or president) (Article 8). There is some question as to whether placing almost unlimited power in the hands of a single individual was appropriate for a transitional period, particularly one that was supposed to be governed through a power-sharing arrangement.[32] As it turns out, the vice president's military background and the instincts that he developed in that context made him especially unprepared for the role of consensus builder, which eventually caused significant damage. To cite one example, Article 16 of the Implementation Mechanism provided that a Committee on Military Affairs for Achieving Security and Stability should be established, and that it should have as its mandate to "end the division in the armed forces and address its causes." The Mechanism did not indicate how the Committee should be composed or what exactly its powers would be. In the end, only those individuals who were closely aligned with former President Saleh, President Hadi, and a powerful general were included, which meant that a range of forces, including the southern forces and Ansar Allah, were excluded.[33] However, throughout the transition, President Hadi removed a significant number of

30 NDC Outcomes, The Republic of Yemen (2013–2014), at 290.

31 As it turns out, at the end of that one-year extension, Ansar Allah had taken control of the capital, bringing the entire process to a halt (see later).

32 See Maged al-Madhaji, "How Yemen's Post-2011 Transitional Phase Ended in War," Sanaa Center for Strategic Studies (May 19, 2016).

33 Presidential Decree 29 (2011).

officers from their positions by decree without giving any indication what his strategy was. The Committee was not consulted and many of its recommendations were ignored. In another example, in 2014, the President eliminated all fuel subsidies overnight despite having been advised to phase them out gradually. Even more importantly, in January 2014, the President established a "regions committee" to finalize crucial issues relating to the future federal arrangement, which he personally headed and which reached a conclusion within a few days, that met with considerable opposition (see later). Other actors were at best estranged by the President's actions and at worst were antagonized by them.[34]

Governance: As noted previously, Yemen was facing a number of economic, security, and social challenges, many of which did not specifically relate to the transition but which nevertheless required urgent attention by state authorities. The need for action and the already unfavorable circumstances should have translated into robust institutional arrangements that could have improved policy formation and the chances that specific policies would be implemented within a reasonable timeframe. The Implementation Mechanism presented an opportunity to achieve this even if only partially. Regrettably, the Mechanism's drafters, including the Special Adviser, paid almost no attention to transitional governance and to matters of political economy.[35] The Implementation Mechanism established a government of national unity in a country where governance was already in crisis.[36] Thus, rather than introducing meaningful change, the new government was populated by senior political figures who had very little in common (at best) and who were not properly equipped to address the country's many security and economic challenges. It was entirely foreseeable that these parties would transform government appointments and procurements into spoils for themselves (as in Lebanon and Iraq) that would worsen governance in the short term.[37] Inclusivity may have been inevitable in the circumstances but there was nothing inevitable about the absence of clear rules for governance. The Implementation Mechanism missed a number of important opportunities and possibly also unnecessarily worsened governance in other ways. In other post-conflict situations around the world, peace agreements and power-sharing

[34] For more on this issue, see "Yemen's Military-Security Reform: Seeds of New Conflict?," International Crisis Group, Middle East Report 139 (April 4, 2013).

[35] Senior western official, interview with the author (May 10, 2020).

[36] The fact that the former president would remain free in the country to seek a path to return to office was also to have a major destabilizing effect.

[37] See "Yemen's Southern Question: Avoiding a Breakdown," International Crisis Group, Middle East Report Number 145 (September 25, 2013), at 8.

arrangements have provided coordination mechanisms that had as their purpose improvement of governmental performance at a time of great fragility and had a positive impact in the short term.[38] Such arrangements were never seriously considered during Yemen's negotiations. In addition, the Implementation Mechanism arguably worsened governance by not clearly indicating whether and, if so, to what extent the president's extraordinary power extended past transitional issues and into issues of regular governance. The result was very significant confusion, which caused crucial institutions to break down altogether and lengthy litigation before the administrative courts.[39] Finally, the Mechanism downgraded the government of national unity to the status of a caretaker government, particularly as it limited its mandate to "customary functions as set forth in the Constitution" as well as a small number of transitional issues, without listing any specific areas that should be prioritized (Article 19).[40] The Mechanism set out a small number of issues that the government was expected to prioritize, but the items that were included in the list were so mundane ("economic stabilization," "good governance," "rule of law") that they hardly made any difference (Articles 13 and 15).

Dispute Resolution: To make matters worse, neither the 1991 Constitution nor the Implementation Mechanism established a convincing mechanism for dispute resolution during the transitional period. The 1991 Constitution provided for a Supreme Court (Article 153), but that body did not have a mandate to interpret the Constitution. In any case, given the influence that the president had on the Supreme Court's composition, it could not have served as a neutral venue for dispute resolution on issues relating to the transition.[41] Article 25 of the Implementation Mechanism provided that an "Interpretation Committee" should be established, which was mandated to "resolve any dispute regarding the interpretation of the GCC Initiative or the Mechanism." The Mechanism did not provide any indication of how the Committee was to be composed or how it would function. In any event, President Hadi refused to establish it despite being pressured to do so on a

[38] See Tobias Thiel, "Governance in Transition: The Dynamics of Yemen's Negotiated Reform Process," in Marie-Christine Heinze (ed.), Yemen and the Search for Stability: Power, Politics and Society after the Arab Spring, I. B. Tauris (2018).

[39] See Ibid.

[40] Charles Schmitz, "Yemen's National Dialogue," Middle East Institute, MEI Policy Paper 2014-1 (February 2014), at 11.

[41] According to Law 1 (1991), the Supreme Court's composition was determined in large part by the Judicial Council (Article 11), which itself was headed by the President of the Republic (Article 104).

number of occasions by one of his government ministers.[42] Yemenis, including parties to the GCC Initiative, therefore had no means at their disposal to compel the president to act and had no legal avenue to channel their disputes.

Adjustments: Throughout 2012 and 2013, many Yemenis complained of worsening governance, which they blamed on a number of factors (including much of what is set out in the previous section).[43] As a result, when it was decided in January 2014 to extend the transition by a year (see later in this chapter), it went without saying that interim governance would have to change. The NDC decided that the then-president should "change the government in a manner that achieves competence, integrity and national partnership." It was also agreed that this same approach should be applied to other central institutions and to the governorates.[44] That wording did not amount to a solid commitment to bring about real change to governance, first because the absence of a specific mechanism on how competent administrators would be introduced into government significantly reduced the likelihood that it would happen and also because it did not amend the president's decision-making authority. Pursuant to that agreement, relatively minor changes were made to the government's composition, and many Yemenis continued to complain of the president's unilateral decision-making power.[45] Shortly after the sudden and total elimination of fuel subsidies that pushed many Yemenis even deeper into poverty, the capital was taken over by Ansar Allah, which then demanded substantial change.[46] On September 21, 2014, a new agreement was entered into, according to which a new government would be formed within one month (Article 1).[47] The agreement provided

42 Senior Yemeni Official, interview with the author (September 2019).

43 Some Yemenis even argued that oversight over government expenditure was close to nonexistent during the transition; Senior Yemeni official, interview with the author (May 22, 2020).

44 See NDC Outcomes, The Republic of Yemen (2013–2014), Section 4, Chapter 2, at 293.

45 Members of Ansar Allah reacted very negatively to that agreement, arguing that it violated the NDC's requirement that true participation be established. Observers also noted that after the agreement was announced, government business retreated behind closed doors; see Marieke Brandt, "The Huthi Enigma: Ansar Allah and the 'Second Republic'," in Marie-Christine Heinze (ed.), Yemen and the Search for Stability: Power, Politics and Society after the Arab Spring, I. B. Tauris (2018), at 172–174.

46 There is significant speculation that Ansar Allah's takeover was the outcome of an agreement with former President Saleh and the military units that he still controlled, and the presidential decision to eliminate fuel subsidies was merely a pretext; see for example Basheer al-Bakr, "Ali Abdallah Saleh: The Last Dance with the Houthis" (علي عبدالله صالح... الرقصة الأخيرة مع الثعابين), Al-Araby al-Jadeed (December 4, 2017).

47 See Peace and National Partnership Agreement (September 21, 2014) (in the author's possession).

that the new government should be "technocratic" and should ensure "broad participation of political constituencies." It also provided for a complex and multistage government formation process that would involve all major groups (Article 2). The agreement introduced power-sharing at the president's level, by providing that the president "shall appoint political advisers from Ansar Allah and the [Hirak]," but failed to firmly establish how decision-making would change (Article 2). Finally, the agreement provided a very large number of priority areas that the new government would have to satisfy, including lowering the price of petrol to a specific amount that was set out in the agreement for a period of three months at least (Article 3) and "increasing the social welfare fund by fifty percent" (Article 4(1)). Ultimately, the agreement made little difference, and the entire transition was halted less than four months later (see later in the chapter).

PREPARING FOR THE NDC

First Phase: The Implementation Mechanism provided that the transition should take place in two phases (Article 7). The first started on the day on which the GCC Initiative and its Implementation Mechanism entered into force and ended with early presidential elections, which were to take place no more than ninety days later (Article 18(a)). The Implementation Mechanism imposed a number of time-bound obligations on the parties, only some of which were respected. The parties generally respected deadlines to put in place power-sharing arrangements but generally did not respect deadlines to move Yemen toward a democratic system of government, which did not bode well for the country. In accordance with Article 10, the opposition JMP nominated a candidate for prime minister who formed a government of national unity that consisted of an equal number of ministers from the GPC on the one hand and the JMP on the other (other groups, including the Hirak and Ansar Allah, were left out). The parliament adopted the amnesty law within the deadline that was imposed by Article 3 of the GCC Initiative).[48] The presidential elections took place on February 21, 2012, which was within the agreed ninety-day deadline set out in Article 6(b) of the Implementation Mechanism.[49] On the other hand, the Mechanism also required the

[48] Law 1 (2012), which granted "absolute amnesty" to President Saleh (Article 1) and to other senior officials (Article 2) and which also required for the parliament to adopt a "national reconciliation and transitional justice" law (Article 3).

[49] Article 18(c) required the parties not to nominate any candidate other than then Vice President Hadi, a commitment that they respected, as a result of which he obtained 100 percent of the vote in an election in which he was the only candidate and in which 64.5 percent of the

government and the vice president to "immediately" establish a "liaison committee" that would be responsible for "initiating an open conversation about the future of the country [...] and for involving youth in determining the future of political life" (Article 15(g)). The decree establishing the liaison committee was issued on May 6, 2012, some five months late, an early indication of the parties' lack of commitment to the roadmap. Decree 13 (2012) established an eight-member committee for the purpose of encouraging "all sides to participate in dialogue" (Article 1) in a way that guaranteed "the formation of a preparatory committee by 30 June 2012" (Article 2). Even at that early stage, it was clear that the two-year transition period would have to be extended as a result of avoidable delays by the president and government.

Preparatory Committee: The transition's second phase commenced on the day on which President Hadi was elected to office and was intended to end after a new constitution entered into force and after a new president had taken office pursuant to that new text (Article 7(b)). The main task during that period was to convene and organize the NDC, which was tasked with addressing the country's major institutional issues and was to include "all forces and political actors, including youth, the Southern Movement, the Houthis, other political parties, civil society representatives and women" (Article 20). The preparatory committee was formed on July 14, 2012, two weeks past the deadline. Decree 30 (2012) included a list of all of the committee members, which mainly consisted of political representatives but also included some civil society representatives (Article 1(c)).[50] The committee's mandate consisted of determining how many individuals should participate in the dialogue conference; how the conference participants should be selected; the conference's internal organization (including the working groups that should be established); and the conference's internal bylaws (Article 4(1)). In keeping with the terms of the Implementation Mechanism, the committee was required to decide each individual issue by consensus, barring which the president would be required to decide the matter on his own (Article 5).

Rules of Procedure: Shortly after it commenced its work, the committee formed a working group that included some of the more technical members for the purpose of drawing up the dialogue conference's rules of procedure. The committee included a full draft of the NDC's rules of procedure as an annex in its Final Report, which was adopted with only a small number of

population voted, the lowest participation rate of any national election since 1997. See United Nations Development Programme, "Early Presidential Elections in Yemen" (2013), at 46.

50 The list of preparatory committee members was extended to include five additional members on September 17, 2013; see Presidential Decree 46 (2012).

changes as the NDC's formal rules.[51] There were very few points of divergence given that there was general agreement that the NDC should decide all issues through consensus, which lowered the stakes considerably.[52] The Rules therefore provided that the NDC should be composed of a General Assembly, a President (who was President Hadi), a Presidium, a Consensus Committee, nine working groups, a Disciplinary Committee, and a Secretariat (Article 7).[53] The working groups were required to debate and ultimately vote on issues that fell within their specific mandates. The working groups were obliged to seek consensus on all issues, which was defined as approval by 90 percent of attending members (Article 41(2)). All matters were also to be put to the General Assembly for final approval, which was also required to adopt all decisions by a 90 percent majority, provided that those who objected were not from the same constituency (Article 34(2)). If the 90 percent threshold was not met in any one of the working groups or the General Assembly, the matter was to be referred to the Consensus Committee, which itself would seek to reach consensus on the issue, in the absence of which the matter would be put to a vote subject to a majority requirement of 75 percent of members present, barring which the matter would be referred to the President of the Republic who would seek to reach consensus (Articles 34(2) and 41(2)).[54] The one issue that the Preparatory Committee could not agree on was how the Presidium should be composed. This was a crucial matter as the Presidium was to be responsible for chairing the General Assembly's sessions and for setting the agenda (Article 18). In addition, Presidium members were ex officio members of the Consensus Committee.[55] The Preparatory Committee therefore drew up two possible means through which the issue could be settled and referred the matter to the president. The president ultimately decided that the

[51] The Rules were issued in the form of Presidential Decree 10 (2013).

[52] Senior adviser to the Preparatory Committee, interview with the author (May 12, 2020).

[53] Working Groups were established in each of the following areas: the Southern issue; the Saada issue; issues of national dimension including national reconciliation and transitional justice; good governance; military and security issues; independent agencies; rights and freedoms; and sustainable development.

[54] The Consensus Committee was to be composed of the President of the Republic, the heads of all nine working groups, and an unspecified number of members drawn from the Preparatory Committee (Article 9). For more on the rules, see Christina Murray "Yemen's National Dialogue Conference" unpublished manuscript. Department of Public Law, University of Cape Town (2013).

[55] The Consensus Committee was described as meeting "periodically" and "weak and unable to resolve controversial issues," see George Anderson, "Yemen's Failed Constitutional Transition," in Territory and Power in Constitutional Transitions, George Anderson and Sujit Choudhry (eds.), Oxford University Press (2019), at 318.

Presidium should consist of himself and six deputies (Article 10).[56] President Hadi was also designated as the NDC's president (Article 2).

Representation: While the Rules of Procedure were decided relatively easily, the Preparatory Committee struggled for months to determine the NDC's size and exact membership. Given that the most recent parliamentary elections had taken place nine years prior, the relative importance of individual political groups was impossible to measure. So therefore many groups were concerned that if they were represented by a small number of participants in the NDC, that could be interpreted by others as a sign of weakness.[57] A number of options were discussed, and ultimately it was decided that the NDC should consist of 565 participants, of which 50 percent should be from the south, 30 percent women, and 20 percent youth.[58] All of the major political forces would be represented, including the GPC with 112 representatives, 85 for the Southern Hirak, 35 for Ansar Allah, and 62 that President Hadi was entitled to appoint on his own. Forty members were reserved for civil society.[59] Despite that agreement, the final result was far from satisfactory for a number of reasons. One of the main difficulties was that the Hirak did not have a unified structure and many of the various trends within the movement refused to participate in the transition. A number of attempts might have been made to resolve those challenges, including engaging locally through trusted actors to identity major trends within the Hirak and exploring options for how to make them engage.[60] Instead, the chosen method appeared to consist of selecting some southerners based on undeclared criteria in the hope that, through their participation, the NDC could reach an agreement and that the rest of the Hirak would eventually fall in line. In fact, because very little progress had been made on implementing the Preparatory Committee's twenty points and because overall security and living standards continued to decline throughout the transition, it became increasingly difficult to convince

56 See Article 10 of the NDC's Rules of Procedure.

57 Senior international official, interview with the author (May 12, 2020).

58 The proportion of southerners in Yemen is difficult to estimate but is unlikely to exceed 20 percent. National authorities decided that 50 percent of the NDC's participants should be southerners to encourage greater southern participation in the dialogue process.

59 Political groups generally nominated their own representatives. For the civil society component, organizations were encouraged to apply, following which the Preparatory Committee carried out a selection process; see Katia Papagianni, "National Dialogue Processes in Political Transitions," Civil Society Dialogue Network Discussion Paper No. 3, European Peacebuilding Liaison Office (EPLO), at 9.

60 Ali Saif Hassan, "Yemen: National Dialogue Conference: Managing Peaceful Change?," Accord, Iss. 25 (April 2014), 54.

southerners to support the transition.[61] If anything, the south may have been coalescing around a more militant strand of separatism during that time.[62] In addition, as noted previously, the NDC was not and could not be the forum in which high level negotiations on existential issues could take place, which contributed to the general failure to address some of the country's most pressing problems.

CONSTITUTIONAL PROCESS

Dialogue Conference: The conference opened on March 18, 2013, was originally intended to end in September 2013, but ultimately only finally concluded its work on January 25, 2014. In accordance with the Implementation Mechanism, the NDC commenced with a General Assembly meeting, which received very heavy coverage in national and international media. The working groups then carried out a first round of deliberations over a period of weeks, which were captured in a series of interim reports. The General Assembly then debated the contents of those reports in a second meeting. The working groups met for their second and final round of meetings (by which time media coverage had waned considerably), in which each group adopted a certain number of final "Outcomes." The General Assembly then met on one final occasion in January 2014 to formally adopt these Outcomes.[63] Many of the sessions were observed by local organizations and were assisted by international organizations that offered substantive expertise.[64] The NDC has been described as a historic moment for Yemen. Many Yemenis maintain that the mere fact that different political factions assembled and discussed a common vision for the future in a formal setting was an impressive achievement.[65] In addition, the participation of

[61] Many of the southern factions that did accept the invitation to participate in the NDC eventually withdrew their participants in response to the deteriorating context; see Maged al-Madhaji, "How Yemen's post-2011 Transitional Phase Ended in War," Sana'a Center for Strategic Studies (May 19, 2016), at 10; see also Maysaa Shuja al-Deen, "Federalism in Yemen: A Catalyst for War, the Present Reality, and the Inevitable Future," Sana'a Center for Strategic Studies (February 2019), at 14.

[62] See "Yemen's Southern Question: Avoiding a Breakdown," International Crisis Group, Middle East Report Number 145 (September 25, 2013).

[63] See NDC Outcomes, The Republic of Yemen (2013–2014) (available at www.ndc.ye).

[64] Most notably, the United Nations made a number of experts available (including individuals who were members of the United Nations' Mediation Support Unit).

[65] See Moosa Elayah, Luuk van Kempen, and Lau Schulpen, "Adding to the Controversy? Civil Society's Evaluation of the National Conference Dialogue in Yemen," Journal of Intervention and Statebuilding, External Research Report, San Antonio, TX: MESA Conference (2018).

women and youth, even if many were affiliated to traditional political groups, in discussions of national importance and on a sustained basis was also considered to be a major transformation for the country.[66] Just as importantly, the NDC managed to reach detailed agreements on many issues, including the enforcement of political and human rights, and the improvement of representation for women, new oversight mechanisms, anti-corruption mechanisms, etc. The final published versions included close to 1,800 Outcomes, all of which were theoretically binding on the state and would have to form the basis of the new constitutional arrangement. Predictably, many of the Outcomes were predetermined by the old elites, while others were difficult to navigate and were sometimes even contradictory or lacking, which created significant challenges for the Constitutional Drafting Committee (see next subsection).[67] By and large, however, it is very likely that any future Yemeni constitutional text will be inspired by many of the Outcomes.

Constitutional Committee: In accordance with Article 22 of the Implementation Mechanism a Constitutional Drafting Committee (CDC) was formed on March 8, 2014.[68] The CDC's mandate was to prepare a new draft constitution that should "be in conformity with the will of the people as reflected in the NDC's recommendations and decisions that were included in the final Outcomes document."[69] The Implementation Mechanism provided that the CDC should complete its work within three months,[70] but the decree that established the CDC provided that the final referendum on the constitution should take place "not more than one year after the CDC is established."[71] The CDC was also required to adopt all its decisions unanimously, barring which a threshold of 75 percent would have to be met.[72] Much of the CDC's work was straightforward, given that many of the Outcomes could easily be reworded and incorporated into the draft constitution. Chapter II of the final draft on rights and freedoms was heavily inspired by the Outcomes, and even included a limitation clause (Article 134). The draft also provided generous social and economic rights but no provision was made to ensure that

[66] See Mareike Transfeld, "Yemen: GCC Roadmap to Nowhere," SWP Comments 20 (May 2014), at 6.

[67] Ibid., at 6.

[68] See Presidential Decree 27 (2014).

[69] See Presidential Decree 26 (2014), Article 2(1).

[70] Article 22, Implementation Mechanism.

[71] Presidential Decree 26 (2014), Article 6. Given that Presidential Decree 26 (2014) was issued on March 8, 2014, and that the Implementation Mechanism's time limit for the entire transitional period was due to expire on March 23, 2014, Presidential Decree 26 (2014) effectively amended the Implementation Mechanism without specifically stating that it was doing so.

[72] Presidential Decree 26 (2014), Article 15.

they would not remain aspirational. The draft also established a presidential system, in which a popularly elected head of state forms a government and is responsible for establishing and implementing the state's policy; the president has the authority to appoint and dismiss ministers; and the parliament does not appear to have any power to withdraw confidence from either the president or any of the government's ministers. There were, however, two major sources of complication that caused significant delay. First, there were a number of important contradictions in the NDC's Outcomes that had to be resolved by the CDC, which provoked significant debate. By way of example, the NDC included two different Outcomes on appointment mechanisms to the Constitutional Court. The Good Governance Working Group decided that the Constitutional Court's members should be "elected by a general assembly of judges."[73] At the same time, the State Building Working Group decided that 70 percent of the Court's judges should be elected by the "general assembly of judges," 15 percent by the Bar Association, and the remaining 15 percent by the Council of Faculties of Sharia and Law in state universities.[74] Apart from the fact that these Outcomes were contradictory, the CDC was faced with an important dilemma: Many of its members were acutely aware that the judiciary was replete with regressive and corrupt judges, and so held the view that either version of the NDC's decision on this specific issue would cause the newly formed Constitutional Court to be dominated by those same elements, and so decided not to follow either Outcome. Instead, and only after significant debate, the CDC eventually decided that "[t]he President of the Republic shall nominate half of the [fourteen] members and the Supreme Judicial Council, universities and the Bar Association shall nominate the remaining half" (Article 329). All of the nominees to the Court would have to be confirmed by a three-fifths majority in the upper chamber of parliament. In a clear illustration of what was wrong with the NDC's organization and working methods, its deliberations and decisions on this issue had close to no impact on the final outcome.[75] Second, there were a number of

[73] See Final Report for the Second Semester of the Working Groups, Working Group on Good Governance, September 2013, paragraph 30.

[74] See Final Report for the Second Semester of the Working Groups, Working Group on State Building and Constitution Principles and Foundations, August 2013, at 24.

[75] In fact, the CDC came close to eliminating the Supreme Court altogether. In the final few days of the drafting process, some of the more strident southern members argued that the number of national institutions should be reduced and that there was no need for a final court of appeal at the national level. Ultimately, that proposal was not adopted and the Supreme Court was maintained. In another example, the limitation clause that was introduced into the final draft was not provided for in the NDC Outcomes either.

fundamental gaps in the Outcomes, most important of which was the lack of detail on the federal system of government (see next section). As a result of these difficulties, the CDC only completed its task in January 2015, far later than expected.[76] In the meantime, security in the capital had deteriorated to such an extent that the entire CDC travelled to Abu Dhabi in October 2014 to complete its deliberations.

FEDERALISM

Rationale: At the start of the transition, it was widely accepted, even by many in the former ruling party, that in order for a democratic Yemen to remain united, the injustices that had been carried out by the Sana'a-based authorities in the south, in Saada province in the north, and elsewhere would have to be addressed. Many of the Sana'a-based elites considered that better governance would improve the delivery of services, which itself would be sufficient. At the same time, however, they were aware that many Yemenis on the opposite side of the debate would not have been satisfied by that approach and would also not have trusted it as a starting point. They were therefore willing to consider the establishment of a federation that would allow significant local autonomy, but were not willing to consider the possibility of outright independence or anything that might ultimately lead to independence.[77] Many southerners, who were on the opposite side of the spectrum in this debate, were in favor of secession. Some even considered the Yemeni state to be a form of northern occupation of south Yemen.[78] Many of these same individuals were also aware of the challenges that they faced, including opposition from many in northern Yemen and even regional and world powers. As a form of compromise, some southerners were therefore willing to accept the establishment of a federation. Those who participated in the NDC generally supported the establishment of a two-region federation, which would at least see the former South Yemen reconstituted as a federal region with institutions through which the local population could govern their own internal affairs. Their position did not take into consideration the wide diversity of views within the south on how internal affairs should be organized. By the same token, some senior figures within the Sanaa-based authorities saw federalism as an opportunity to contain the

[76] The draft constitution is available in Arabic at www.constitutionnet.org/ar/vl/item/lymn-mswd-dstwr-lymn-ljdyd-lm-2015.

[77] See "Yemen's Southern Question: Avoiding a Breakdown," International Crisis Group, Middle East Report Number 145 (September 25, 2013), at 13.

[78] Ibid., at 3.

increasingly powerful Houthi movement, and argued in favor of creating a federal region that would include Ansar Allah's most important power base and that would not have access to the types of resources that would allow it to thrive.[79]

National Dialogue: The Implementation Mechanism indicated that the NDC should have as one of its main objectives to "address the issue of the south in a manner conducive to a just national solution that preserves the unity, stability and security of Yemen" (Article 21(c)). On that basis, the Preparatory Committee was the first formal body to speak directly to this issue, and in doing so possibly stepped outside of its mandate. In Annex 2 of its final report, it established a list of twenty points, eleven of which relate specifically to the southern issue and to the type of actions that would have to be taken to address southern concerns. The twenty points were discussed on a number of occasions with President Hadi and his team who formally supported their implementation but ultimately made very little progress in implementing them during the remainder of the transition period.[80] When the NDC commenced its work, a Southern Working Group was established.[81] However, in its first session, the Working Group was restricted to discussing the historical causes of the crisis between north and south, which meant that very little progress was made in the first six months.[82] Pursuant to that worrying lack of progress, in September 2013, a sixteen-member subcommittee was

79 Senior Yemeni official, interview with the author (May 22, 2020).

80 See "Yemen's Southern Question: Avoiding a Breakdown," Middle East Report Number 145 (September 25, 2013), at 6.

81 The Preparatory Committee also established two working groups that had direct relevance to this issue. The "Southern Working Group" would be tasked with determining the "roots and content of the southern problem" and the "method for solving the southern problem." Meanwhile, the State Building Working Group was required to determine the "form of the state" and the "system of government." See "Final Report of the Technical Committee to Prepare for the Comprehensive National Dialogue Conference," Republic of Yemen (December 12, 2012), at 12. Ultimately, however, the State Building Working Group deferred to the Southern Working Group on the issue of whether Yemen should be established as a federation; see NDC Outcomes, The Republic of Yemen (2013–2014), at 94.

82 The Southern Working Group's first session consisted of a series of presentations on the history of the south and on the marginalization and oppression that it suffered after unification. It had been decided that participants could raise points of clarification during these presentations but could not offer points of discussion, which led to a large number of disagreements over what constituted a point of clarification and what did not. Senior International Official, interview with the author (May 15, 2020). That account is supported by the Southern Working Group's interim report, which consists almost entirely of a list of the political, legal, economic, and cultural means through which the south has been marginalized, and ended without discussing any possible solutions; see NDC Outcomes, The Republic of Yemen (2013–2014), at 30–36.

formed to accelerate discussions on the southern issue.[83] The subcommittee consisted of eight southern members and eight northern (the subcommittee was therefore referred to as the "8+8"). The subcommittee was widely criticized for failing to resolve the same representativity issues that the NDC suffered from. Some observers considered that the southern participants were not adequate representatives of the south, which painted the subcommittee's discussions with a lack of seriousness.[84] The subcommittee issued its final report on September 15, 2013, which stated in unequivocal terms that a new "federal state" should be established, and that each federal region must be primarily responsible for economic development within its borders (including the exploitation of natural resources) and therefore should have political and administrative powers (Article 2).[85] Finally, the subcommittee found that the number of regions should be established by a "mechanism" that should work alongside the constitutional drafting committee and that should reach a consensual conclusion (Article 3). The Southern Working Group adopted almost the totality of the subcommittee's findings with a number of important differences. Controversially, the Working Group recommended that the NDC should delegate President Hadi to "establish and chair a committee to define the regions" and that the committee's decisions "shall be binding."[86] It also heavily restricted the options from which the committee could choose. It stated that the committee should consider establishing Yemen as an option of either six regions, two regions, or anything in between.[87] When those recommendations were announced at the General Assembly's closing session, many representatives withdrew in protest, in large part because the NDC was not given an opportunity to offer its opinion on the question.[88]

Regions Committee: On January 27, 2014, a new twenty-one-member committee was established to decide the number of regions (the "Regions Committee"). The committee's mandate was highly restricted and consisted of "studying and deciding whether Yemen should be established as a federal of six regions (four in the north and two in the south), two regions, or any other

[83] See Erica Gaston, "Process Lessons Learned in Yemen's National Dialogue," United States Institute of Peace, Special Report 342 (February 2014), at 3–4. The formation of the 8+8 committee does not appear to have been in conformity with the NDC Rules of Procedure.

[84] Senior international official, interview with the author (May 12, 2020).

[85] See "Outcomes of the 8+8 Committee on the Southern Issue" (September 15, 2013) (in the author's possession).

[86] It should be noted that the NDC's Rules of Procedure do not explicitly authorize the NDC to delegate the President of the Republic on substantive and procedural issues; see Article 15.

[87] NDC Outcomes, The Republic of Yemen (2013–2014), at 40.

[88] Shuja al-Deen (2019), at 13.

option between those two options that achieves consensus."[89] The committee was also required to take into account a small number of factors, including "current reality, geography, history and culture."[90] Economics was not listed as one of the factors. A number of parties immediately complained about the manner in which the committee was composed, including the lack of transparency on how members were selected, and the relative weight that had been allocated to specific parties.[91] The committee met for the first time on January 29, 2014 and, contrary to the NDC, its deliberations were largely carried out behind closed doors. The CDC issued its final report on February 10, 2014, which decided that Yemen should be divided into six regions.[92] The announcement was immediately rejected by Ansar Allah, on the basis that it "divides Yemen into poor and wealthy regions"[93] and on the basis that the committee's mandate was not respected.[94] The Socialist Party was also strongly opposed to the committee's decision but reluctantly signed off on the report so as not to halt the transition process.[95] Despite all of this opposition, the constitutional committee carried out its work without even acknowledging that the proposed federal arrangement had been rejected by

89 Presidential Decree 2 (2014), Article 2.

90 Ibid.

91 In particular, members of Islah complained that their party was given the same relative weight as much smaller political groups, while the Socialist Party complained that it was not allowed to select its own representatives; see Khaled al-Hamadi, "Yemen: The Socialist Party and the Islah Unhappy about the Region Committee's Formation" (اليمن: الاشتراكي وقواعد الإصلاح مستاؤون من تشكيل لجنة الأقاليم), al-Quds al-Arabi (January 30, 2014).

92 See Final Report of the Regions Committee (February 10, 2014). According to one account, the Regions Committee met on three occasions only. Senior international official, interview with the author (May 15, 2020). The Regions Committee's proposed map for the future federation matched almost exactly maps circulated months before that were attributed to the GPC and Islah; see, for example, "Proposed Regional Map by Islah and the GPC Establishes Six Regions" (خريطة الأقاليم المقترحه من الاصلاح والمؤتمر سته اقاليم), Al-Dali' News (December 17, 2013). Some observers have argued that this suggests that the number of regions and their boundaries had been pre-agreed; Senior international officials, interview with the author (May 2020).

93 "Vocal Rejection of the Decision to Divide Yemen into Regions" ("رفض متصاعد لقرار تقسيم اليمن لأقاليم"), Abda Ayesh, Al-Jazeera Net (February 15, 2014); "The Houthis: Federalism Divides Yemen into Wealthy and Poor Areas" (الحوثيون: الفدرالية تقسم اليمن إلى غني وفقير), Mansoura News (February 11, 2014).

94 Representatives of Ansar Allah noted that the need for consensus was not respected. They also noted that their member who had been nominated in Presidential Decree 2 (2014) that established the Regions Committee declined to participate in any of its meetings, but was nevertheless named as a signatory on its final report. Other leading figures complained that the six-region formula was adopted "to satisfy individual interests." See "The Socialist Party Leads the Wave of Opposition… While the Democratic People's Party Leads Supporters" (فيما الاشتراكي يتزعم موجة المعارضين.. والشعب الديمقراطي يتزعم المؤيدين), al-Hawyah, February 17, 2014.

95 See Shuja al-Deen (2019), at 14–18.

some of the country's principle political actors.[96] The Region Committee's final decision was never confirmed by the NDC's General Assembly.

Constitution Drafting: The decree that established the CDC specifically required it to apply the six-region formula, which left it with close to no flexibility, despite the fact that many of its members were aware how explosive that arrangement could be.[97] On the other hand, as the CDC commenced its work, it quickly became apparent that it would have to design much of the federal arrangement on its own with no political input from the NDC, political parties, or other state institutions. This was mainly the result of the fact that, in their discussions on federalism, Yemeni political actors invested most of their efforts in determining how many federal regions should be established. They expressed very little interest in discussing which powers should be exercised by those regions, most probably because the general assumption was that federal regions would exercise almost all governmental powers within their territory anyway.[98] Ultimately, close to a quarter of the CDC's final draft relates to details of the federal system of government that the NDC never even considered. For example, Chapter 5 of the draft constitution sets out extensive lists of powers for which each level of government should be responsible. Article 335 provides that the federal authorities should be exclusively responsible for "air navigation, civil aviation, meteorology and regulation of marine navigation," "intellectual property," and "national environment protection and climate change policy," among many others; Article 337 provides that the regional governments should be exclusively competent over "lands and real estate in the region," "agriculture," "tourism," and "telecom services," etc.; finally, Article 338 provides that "wilayas and localities" are exclusively responsible for "civil defense," "regulation of markets," and "medium and small enterprises," etc. The CDC also provided for a National Revenue Fund and a Board that would be responsible for drawing up a yearly National Revenue Division Act (Article 357). In another example, the CDC established three different police forces (federal, regional, and local;

96 Based on my own personal observations during 2014.

97 Presidential Decree 26 (2014), Article 2.

98 Senior international official, interview with the author (May 7, 2020). That assumption was likely partly informed by Iraq's federal system, which is one of the region's only federations and certainly the federation that has generated the most amount of interest in Yemen. In Iraq, the Kurdistan Region exercises almost full autonomy and exercises almost all governmental functions in its territory. It is very likely (but very difficult to definitely establish) that when discussing the possibility of establishing Yemen as a federation, Yemeni actors were generally expecting that federal regions would exercise the same level of autonomy as the Kurdistan Region.

Articles 335, 337, and 338). All of these radical changes to Yemen's state institutions were entirely the work of the CDC, mainly because the NDC had never considered how the federal government should function. That approach was highly problematic, mainly because the CDC was not tasked with this type of work, and did not have sufficient time and expertise to create a functional system. Most importantly perhaps, the CDC listed the six regions that had been decided by the Regions Committee (Article 391). One of the CDC's members who was particularly close to Ansar Allah refused to sign the final draft, causing significant controversy in response.

Breakdown: By the end of the transition, a large number of the country's main political actors had been either alienated or antagonized. Former President Saleh, his relatives, and much of his party were hostile toward the transition right from the start and were provoked by the removal of so many of their members from the security services. Many of the groups that made up the Hirak were also highly unfavorable because of the historical context and grew increasingly agitated by the failure to implement the Preparatory Committee's twenty points, declining living standards, and the establishment of the six-region federation. Ansar Allah, also antagonistic from the start, openly declared its opposition to the six-region federation and to the government of national unity's composition and performance. By the time the draft constitution had been completed, the entire transition was extremely vulnerable. The CDC completed its draft on January 15, 2015, close to one year after the entire transition was supposed to have ended. In the meantime, security had deteriorated significantly. By that time, Ansar Allah had taken control over large parts of the country, including the capital. On January 20, 2015, Ansar Allah occupied the presidential palace and demanded, among other things, that the draft constitution be amended to reflect their position on federalism.[99] In February 2015, Ansar Allah issued a "constitutional declaration," which amended the 1991 Constitution in part by providing for a presidency council.[100] By March 2015, the president and much of the government had fled the country. In response, an international coalition of countries with Saudi Arabia

[99] See "Yemen: The Revolutionary Committee Issues a Constitutional Declaration to Organize the Rules of Governance during the Interim Period" ("اليمن: اللجنة الثورية تصدر إعلاناً دستورياً لتنظيم قواعد الحكم خلال المرحلة الانتقالية"), Saba Net (February 6, 2015); an unofficial translation of the constitutional declaration is available at www.constitutionnet.org/vl/item/yemen-revolutionary-committee-issues-constitutional-declaration-organize-foundations.

[100] See "The Revolutionary Committee Issues a Constitutional Declaration to Organize the Foundations of Governance during the Transitional Period in Yemen" (February 6, 2015) (in the author's possession).

in the lead initiated a blockade and bombing campaign, citing the need to break Ansar Allah's control over the capital as one of their motivating factors.

Conflict and Uncertainty: At the time of writing, the conflict had not ended, the country's territorial integrity had fallen apart, and commitment to constitutional legitimacy was fraying. In late 2020, President Hadi's governing coalition expanded to include southern separatists, and his administration had partially returned to Aden, which had been given the status of temporary capital. His government still enjoyed near unanimous support from the international community and still purported to respect constitutional legitimacy, although there was significant dispute as to whether that was still possible under the circumstances. Much of southern Yemen was controlled by different groups, not all of which recognized President Hadi's legitimacy, and some of which were taking steps toward unilateral secession. In the meantime, Ansar Allah remained in control over much of northern Yemen including Sana'a, amended the 1991 constitution to establish a "sovereignty council," which nominally exercised the role of chief executive, but which many argued was merely a front for the real power brokers in the north. The entire transition and the future of the draft constitution that was completed in January 2015 remained uncertain. Most importantly, despite successive diplomatic initiatives, peace negotiations had yet to yield any major breakthroughs.

4

Libya

BACKGROUND

Colonial Legacy

Ottoman period: The territory that today makes up the Libyan state was captured by the Ottoman Empire in 1551. Much like the rest of the Empire's north African possessions, by the beginning of the eighteenth century, locals eventually achieved significant autonomy from Istanbul. By the 1830s, however, members of the ruling dynasty were at war with each other, causing Ottoman troops to reimpose direct control over the territory in 1835 in order to preempt any European designs over it. The Empire applied the law of provincial administration in the territory, which eventually allowed the establishment of a municipality as an administrative unit. By the 1870s, several urban centers had local advisory councils that were responsible for overseeing public works. The country remained poor in comparison to other North African territories, but by the start of the twentieth century, commercial centers, courts, and other institutions had been established and had contributed to the emergence of a local elite.[1]

Colonial period and independence: Italy invaded the country in 1911, leading to a brutal conflict and occupation of the country. By one estimate, approximately 30 percent of the population was killed by colonial forces from 1912 to 1943. Conditions were particularly poor in the east, which contributed to feelings of marginalization in the country. At the end of the Second World War, Libya had one of the lowest living standards in the world. Infant

[1] Lisa Anderson, 'Nineteenth-Century Reform in Ottoman Libya', International Journal of Middle East Studies, Vol. 16, No. 3 (August 1984), 324–348.

mortality stood at 40 percent and illiteracy at 94 percent.[2] Following Italy's defeat in the war, Libya's future became a matter of international concern. The future of Libya was debated by the newly formed United Nations, which ultimately decided that the territories comprising Cyrenaica, Tripolitana, and Fezzan should constitute an independent state no later than January 1, 1952.[3] A United Nations Commissioner was appointed to assist in that process, through which he exercised considerable influence on the entire transition.[4]

National Assembly: One of the first issues that had to be decided was how the country's future constitution would be written, and in particular who would be responsible for negotiating and drafting its contents. Following a prolonged negotiation process, the United Nations decided that a National Assembly should be tasked with adopting a constitution but that its members should be appointed and not elected. The United Nations justified the decision on the basis that elections would be "time-consuming, costly, and difficult" while at the same time underplaying the complications that an appointed assembly would bring.[5] The Commissioner recommended that a preparatory committee should be composed to address some of the practical issues surrounding the Assembly's work. The Commissioner also recommended that, for the sake of convenience, the preparatory committee should have an equal number of representatives from each of the three provinces, then argued that this constituted a precedent that should be followed for the Assembly's own composition. This caused a significant amount of consternation in many circles,[6] mainly as a result of the fact that Tripoli's population was three and fifteen times larger than Cyrenaica's and Fezzan's respective populations.[7] It was also highly problematic given that the Commissioner was aware that each of the three provinces had its own preferences with respect to the future form of the state, and that by shaping the Assembly's composition in the way that he did he was giving greater weight to specific voices, thereby

2 See Omar I. Fathaly and Fathi S. Abusedra, "The Impact of Socio-political Change on Economic Development in Libya," Middle Eastern Studies, Vol. 16, No. 3 (October 1980), 225–235; Waniss Otman and Erling Karlberg, The Libyan Economy: Economic Diversification and International Repositioning, Springer-Verlag (2007), at 99; and Dirk Vandewalle, A History of Modern Libya, Cambridge University Press (2012), at 30–31 and 42.

3 See United Nations General Assembly Resolution A/RES/289(IV)A (1949).

4 See Adrian Pelt, Libyan independence and the United Nations: A Case of Planned Decolonization, Yale University Press (1970).

5 In addition, several members of the United Nations insisted that elections should not take place while the British and French militaries remained on the ground; see Ibid., at 221.

6 See Ibid. at 477.

7 See Ibid., at 221.

increasing the likelihood that a specific outcome would be reached.[8] Despite all of these objections, it was decided that the Assembly should consist of sixty members (twenty from each of the three provinces). The selection process was delegated to one prominent and traditional source of authority in each of the three provinces, which allowed them to pack the Assembly with their own ideological allies. For Cyrenaica, the future king was given the power to appoint the province's twenty representatives, despite the fact that he had just returned from a thirty-year exile in Cairo.[9] The end result was of questionable legitimacy: a body that was entirely appointed by a handful of individuals, that was under heavy international influence, and whose makeup skewed the drafting process in favor of a particular political outcome.

Deciding on Federalism: The full Assembly met for the first time on November 25, 1950 and decided shortly thereafter to delegate the task of drafting the constitution to a committee of eighteen members, which itself composed a drafting subcommittee of six members (both had an equal number of representatives from each of the three provinces).[10] That subcommittee met very regularly with the Commissioner and with other United Nations staff. The members appeared to have been willing to reach an agreement despite the circumstances, which partially compensated for the Assembly's skewed membership. The Commissioner argued in favor of allowing Libyans to "take their own responsibilities and decisions" and establish a system of government that was "adapted to the country's particular traditions and needs."[11] At the same time, the Commissioner also favored establishing Libya as a federation "because of the country's geography and demographic structure: a small population living an islandlike existence in a huge ocean of sand."[12] The Commissioner did not give significant weight to Libya's socioeconomic status or to the impact its colonial legacies might have on its capacity to manage a complex federal system with three regional and one federal governments. Assembly members from Cyrenaica and Fezzan agreed that Libya should be established as a federation out of concern that a

[8] The Congress Party, one of the most significant political forces in the country, was heavily present in Tripoli and favored a unitary state. The Commissioner's proposed manner of proceeding undermined the party's position in favor of other political forces who favored a federal arrangement; see Ismail Khalidi, "Constitution of the United Kingdom of Libya: Background and Summary," MIDDLE EAST JOURNAL, Vol. 6, No. 2 (Spring 1952), 221–228.

[9] Vandewalle (2012), at 47.

[10] See "Collection of the National Assembly's and the Constitutional Subcommittee's Minutes," National Constituent Assembly, May 1951 (on file with the author).

[11] See Pelt (1970), at 515.

[12] See Ibid., at 513.

unitary state would be dominated by Tripoli. Members from Tripoli were too small in number to oppose that outcome.[13]

The 1951 Constitution

System of Government: The National Assembly unanimously adopted the new constitution in October 1951. The final text organized the country as a federation, with three federal regions, under a monarchy.[14] Article 36 set out a list of exclusive federal powers (including foreign affairs, national defense, and taxation powers), Article 38 set out a list of concurrent powers (in which policy was to be adopted through federal legislation, while the regions were responsible for implementation), and Article 39 provided that all residual power belonged to the regions. The king meanwhile had considerable authority, including the power to dissolve parliament (Article 65), and to appoint and dismiss the prime minister (Article 72) and all ministers (Article 78); half the members of the upper chamber (Article 95); and all members of the Supreme Court (Article 143). Meanwhile, ordinary Libyans were given close to no consideration, given that all of their basic rights could be regulated by legislation without limitation.[15]

Federalism Abandoned: After the 1951 Constitution came into force, despite already wielding very wide authority, the king pursued a number of means to eliminate whatever limitations existed on his authority. Political parties were banned in 1952, and all candidates for election to the lower house had to be nominated by the government.[16] Following the discovery of oil in 1959, the central government's financial resources grew exponentially, increasing the incentive to centralize decision-making.[17] In response, in 1963, federalism was abandoned and central rule reimposed, bringing Libya in line with

[13] See Henri Habib, POLITICS AND GOVERNMENT OF REVOLUTIONARY LIBYA, Le Cercle du Livre de France Ltée (1975), at 70–82; see also Khalidi (1952), at 224 (in which the author, a member of the United Nations Secretariat who was assigned to the United Nations mission in Libya, states that the United Nations Council for Libya also encouraged the Constituent Assembly to adopt a compromise between the two perspectives that was based on a recommendation that was prepared by the United States).

[14] For more on the drafting of the 1951 Constitution, see CONSTITUTIONAL DEVELOPMENT IN LIBYA, Ismail Raghib Khalidi, Khayat's College Book Cooperative (1956). An unofficial translation of the 1951 constitution is available at www.constitutionnet.org/vl/item/libyas-constitution-promulgated-national-constituent-assembly-7-october-1951-abolished.

[15] See, for example, Article 26, which provided that "[t]he right to peaceful association shall be guaranteed. The exercise of that right shall be regulated by law."

[16] See Cherif Bassiouni, "Historical Background," in LIBYA: FROM REPRESSION TO REVOLUTION, Cherif Bassiouni (ed.), Martinus Nijhoff Publishers (2013), at 43; Vandewalle (2012), at 49.

[17] See Fathaly and Abusedra (1980), 225–235.

the regional trend of centralized control over all affairs of state.[18] All of the 1951 Constitution's provisions establishing the basics of a federal system (including the provisions establishing exclusive federal powers and concurrent powers) were repealed and not replaced. The senate was to be an entirely appointed body, thereby further increasing the king's personal authority. Article 176 of the amended constitution provided that Libya was to be "divided into administrative units," which were to be administered by "local and municipal councils." Decree 13 (1963) provided that there should be ten units, and that each unit should be headed by a governor to be appointed by the Minister of Interior, who was responsible for determining the governor's powers (Article 4). Libya's increased oil wealth brought some benefits to the general population, but the state's growing patronage network further entrenched divisions within the population.

1969 Coup

System of Government: In 1969, Muammar Gaddafi, a relatively junior military officer, organized a coup d'état and ruled the country uncontested until 2011, making him one of the longest serving dictators in the region. A five page "constitutional declaration" replaced the 1951 Constitution and established a self-appointed Revolutionary Command Council that had both supreme executive power and legislative authority, matching developments in Egypt and elsewhere.[19] Over the following few years, Libya's system of government underwent a number of major reforms, including the establishment of the "Jamahiriyan era," which introduced what has been termed "popular power," as expressed through a very particular institutional framework.[20] A multi-tiered and indirect legislative system was established involving "People's Congresses, People's Committees, syndicates, trade unions and professional leagues, and the General People's Congress."[21] Political parties

[18] See Habib (1975), at 87.

[19] The term "Constitutional Declaration" has never been properly defined but has been used by ruling authorities in countries throughout the region, including Egypt and others, to convey a sense that the legal instruments in question enjoy higher legitimacy than ordinary legislation. The underlying assumption, therefore, is that "Constitutional Declarations" should not be challenged by state institutions, including the courts. An unofficial translation of the 1969 constitutional declaration is available at www.constitutionnet.org/vl/item/libyan-constitution-1969.

[20] See "The Great Green Charter of Human Rights of the Jamariyan Era," adopted by the General People's Congress of the Great Socialist People's Libyan Arab Jamahiriya, June 12, 1988.

[21] See "Constitution of the Great Socialist People's Libyan Arab Jamahiriya," adopted by the General People's Congress, March 2, 1977.

remained banned, but all of society was required to join the Arab Socialist Union, which served to organize political activity in favor of specific outcomes.[22] Gaddafi formally resigned from his positions in the Libyan state but granted himself the title of theoretician and "leader of the revolution," which meant that he maintained ultimate decision-making authority without any form of oversight whatsoever.

Libya in 2010: By the end of 2010, Libya had made significant socioeconomic progress but its political system was markedly undemocratic, even in comparison with regional standards. Despite all the changes that had taken place, the state still shared a number of characteristics with other states in the region, including the existence of a central government, local government, public service, and a judiciary. However, a number of fundamental practices and principles were entirely absent. The separation of powers had essentially never been practiced in Libya, not even as a fiction; political parties had been banned for more than half a century; there had not been any national elections of any kind (not even of the fraudulent kind) in living memory; and the judiciary was subject to direct control by the ministry of justice, and was undermined by revolutionary and military tribunals that were not bound by procedural laws. Many parts of the country (particularly the east and south) were marginalized, received comparatively little investment from the state's budget, and had their growth opportunities stifled by an overbearing centralized system of government.[23] The regime faced significant internal opposition, which it met with violence, including through arbitrary detention, forced disappearances, and the practice of inhumane punishments (including amputations, flogging, etc.).[24] By the end of 2010, despite several years of improving relations with western states and some effort to modernize the state, Libya's state of repression was subsiding only very slowly, and had at that point yielded only very modest gains in the protection of civil and political rights.[25]

[22] Gaddafi explained in a 1971 speech that "we need no parties whatever their slogans; the people are the party"; quoted in Henri Habib, LIBYA: PAST AND PRESENT, Aedam Publishing House Limited, Third Edition (1981), at 156.

[23] Many commentators have argued that eastern Libya in particular was marginalized, which has been taken to explain why eastern Libya played such a prominent role in the uprising against Gaddafi. Others have noted that there is little basis to argue that specific geographic areas were marginalized by the previous regime; see, for example, Wolfram Lacher, POLITICAL FRAGMENTATION IN LIBYA: STRUCTURE AND PROCESS IN VIOLENT CONFLICT, I.B. Tauris, 1 edition (2020), at 73.

[24] For more see Ronald Bruce St. John, Libya: Continuity and Change, Routledge, Second Edition (2015), Chapter 3. See also 'Summary of Amnesty International's Concerns in Libya', Amnesty International, March 14, 1991.

[25] See "Libya of Tomorrow: What Hope for Human Rights?," Amnesty International, 2010.

2011 CONSTITUTIONAL DECLARATION

The National Transitional Council: After the fall of both Ben Ali in Tunisia and Mubarak in Egypt in early 2011, an initial round of protests in eastern Libya quickly evolved into a full blown civil war.[26] A coalition of opponents and defectors from the regime formed a National Transitional Council (NTC) in March 2011 for the purpose of overthrowing Gaddafi's regime. A number of western powers intervened militarily on the NTC's behalf, which internationalized the conflict. The NTC's existence and its operation were justified by the exigencies of the conflict, but it was far from legitimate. The NTC's membership initially tilted in favor of eastern provinces, a natural consequence of the fact that liberation commenced in the east and spread to the west from there. In addition, its membership was essentially self-appointed, with no democratic legitimacy to speak of, and consisted mainly of recently defected members of Gaddafi's regime; former exiles who had more of a technocratic background; as well as local lawyers, academics, and activists. All of this was made worse by the fact that the NTC's members were not fully committed to institutional rules on individual mandates and decision-making, which proved to be highly detrimental to the entire transition process. These factors did little to remedy the historical grievances of negative relationships between communities in the country and arguably worsened them even at this early stage of the transition.[27]

Elections First: One of the NTC's first actions was to draft a new constitutional document that would replace Gaddafi's system of government until a permanent constitution could be negotiated. The NTC's legal committee was required to lead that process. One of the main issues that had to be resolved was how the transition process should be organized, and in particular whether elections should be organized before the future permanent constitution was drafted. Not entirely coincidentally, the debate on that issue was taking place at exactly the same time in both Egypt and Tunisia. In June 2011, an early version of the document provided that the NTC itself should be responsible for overseeing the drafting of the future permanent constitution, and that the first round of elections should only take place after the permanent constitution was adopted. However, according to one of the drafters of that document,

[26] "Muammar Gaddafi in His Own Words," John-Paul Ford Rojas, *The Telegraph*, October 20, 2011; "Saif al-Islam Threatens the Protesters... and the US Considers the 'Proper Response'" ("سيف الإسلام القذافي يتوعّد المتظاهرين.. وأمريكا تدرس الرد المناسب"), Al-Arabiya, February 21, 2011.

[27] See Christopher S. Chivvis and Jeffrey Martini, Libya after Qaddafi: Lessons and Implications for the Future, Rand Corporation (2014), at 37.

leading members of the NTC amended the draft before it was formally circulated to the NTC to provide that elections should take place before the drafting of the constitution started.[28] According to that same account, leading members of the NTC expected to outperform rivals in an election and therefore pushed for this arrangement to satisfy their own short-term self-interest. Indeed, Libya's branch of the Muslim Brotherhood argued that only an elected body could legitimately oversee the drafting of a permanent constitution. More generally, after half a century of autocracy, there was a popular demand for elections that was close to impossible to resist. There was also a concern that the many militias that had emerged during the conflict would not have accepted demobilization or submitted to anything other than a legitimate government, which could not have come into existence other than through elections.[29] As a result, the draft document (entitled "Constitutional Declaration") was adopted on August 3 and (at the time) provided that an election should take place, and that the elected body should be responsible for appointing a constitutional drafting assembly. Several of the NTC's most prominent members were absent and it has been alleged that the quorum requirements were not satisfied.[30]

Lack of Transparency: One of the main criticisms that can be made against the Constitutional Declaration is that it was not the result of a transparent and consultative process. The Constitutional Declaration was finalized on August 3, 2011, close to a month before the capital was liberated and close to three months before Gaddafi's capture and death.[31] What this means is that at the time when the Declaration was being drafted, a large proportion of the population was not even aware that a constitutional document was in discussion, which guaranteed that their voices would not be taken into account. Commentators have also noted that even in cities that were liberated early on

[28] See Khaled Ziwo, "Law 4 (2012) on the GNC Elections and Its Impact on Libya's Political Life," in Assessing Legislation for Libya's Reconstruction: Project Report, Suliman Ibrahim and Jan Michiel Otto (eds.), Universiteit Leiden and Center for Law and Society Studies, Benghazi University (2012), at 23.

[29] Interview with senior international official, February 17, 2020.

[30] See Peter Bartu, "The Corridor of Uncertainty: The National Transitional Council's Battle for Legitimacy and Recognition," in Peter Cole and Brian McQuinn (eds.), The Libyan Revolution and Its Aftermath, Hurst & Co (2015); and Duncan Pickard, "Claiming Legitimacy: The Founding Weeks of the National Transitional Council of Libya," June 2, 2014 (unpublished). According to one senior international official, the NTC's membership was never clearly and firmly established, which meant that its membership was fluid, mainly because all decisions were in fact being taken by a small number of leading members, as a result of which a quorum could never be established. Interview with international official (March 26, 2020).

[31] See Liberation Declaration, National Transitional Council (NTC), October 23, 2011.

in the conflict, including Benghazi, the negotiation process was so opaque that only a small number of individuals were able to participate in a meaningful way.[32] This had a number of immediate consequences: Apart from preventing some of the country's leading jurists and thinkers from commenting on the document's contents it also established a precedent of incomplete consultation and elitism that incentivized the use of alternative means (including threats and violence) to impact high level discussions on constitutional arrangements. In addition, given that many of these alternative means were successful in forcing change, the NTC's approach contributed to the general feeling among many actors that everything was subject to change.

Alternative Approaches: Clearly, circumstances were difficult. Aside from the legacies of fifty years of totalitarian rule, the conflict's front lines were constantly shifting, creating a deep sense of insecurity among those individuals who were responsible for planning Libya's future. At the same time, however, the NTC's chosen manner of proceeding was not inevitable. There were many possible alternatives. Perhaps most obviously, circumstances in 2011 did not favor the drafting and adoption of a single constitutional document that addressed all issues relating to the transition. Libya's transitional constitutional framework could have been negotiated and adopted in phases, with priority given to establishing a framework that would satisfy immediate governance needs (including the means through which the country was going to be governed during and immediately after the conflict), while leaving the final decision on the way in which the constitution was to be negotiated and drafted until after a consultative and national dialogue process could be organized on the issue. Significant time could have been dedicated to carrying out consultations with relevant political groups and with those individuals who might have been in a position to offer constructive comments, which would have set a positive tone for future policy-making efforts in the country.

Substantive Overview: Insofar as its substantive content is concerned, the 2011 Constitutional Declaration is woefully inadequate.[33] The system of government that it established was highly inadequate, in large part because of the Declaration's large number of omissions. The document starts by setting out a

[32] Some international officials have stated that a popular debate did take place in Benghazi at the time, but Libyan officials and observers disagree with this assessment; interview, leading academic from Benghazi, February 13, 2020.

[33] An unofficial translation of the 2011 Constitutional Declaration is available at www.security-legislation.ly/node/32001. The Arabic original is available at www.constitutionnet.org/ar/files/interim_constitution-3_aug_2011_arabic_signed.pdf. For a contemporaneous analysis of the 2011 Constitutional Declaration, see Zaid Al-Ali, "Libya's Draft Interim Constitution: An Analysis," Constitutionnet, September 5, 2011.

number of basic rights, including freedom of speech and association (important precedents for Libya). It quickly moves on to organize both legislative and executive power. Article 17 provides that legislative authority was to be exercised by the NTC, which was responsible for enacting legislation, for "establishing the State's general policy," and for "guaranteeing national unity, the safety of the national territory, embodying and propagating values and morals, ensuring the safety of citizens and expatriates," etc. Meanwhile, Article 24 provides that executive authority during the interim period was to be exercised by an "executive office," which was to be appointed by the NTC and would enjoy strong oversight powers over the executive.

Substantive Deficiencies: The Constitutional Declaration barely mentions the existence of a judiciary; it states briefly that the courts are independent (Article 32) and that all people may petition the courts (Article 33) but does not provide any specific measures that would allow the protection of judicial independence, nor does it provide for the existence of a judicial council or even the existence of a supreme or constitutional court. It is not even that these matters are referred to future legislation; they are simply not mentioned at all. Instead, the NTC merely allowed the preexisting Supreme Court to serve as the country's highest judicial authority, while enacting only minor reforms to its composition and structure.[34] The Constitutional Declaration says nothing about what procedure the NTC needed to follow to pass legislation and does not impose a clear obligation on the executive to apply and respect the law. It also does not dedicate any space to explaining what the legislature's mandate and powers will be, i.e. whether it will simply inherit the NTC's powers or otherwise. It establishes an Audit Bureau (Article 28), without stating how it will be composed, staffed, and financed.

Transition Roadmap: Second, the Constitutional Declaration established a road map for Libya to transition to democracy. Without stating so explicitly, the document provided that the interim period should consist of two phases, the first that would start immediately on the Constitutional Declaration's publication, and the second that would commence after "liberation," which would trigger a succession of events (including elections, the drafting of a new permanent constitution, and yet another election). The bulk of the Constitutional Declaration's transitional provisions are included in a single provision (Article 30). It provides that the NTC should form a government within thirty days of Libya's "liberation," and that the government would have

[34] The Supreme Court was established by virtue of Law 6 (1982). The law was amended by Law 33 (2012), which amended Law 6's provisions relating to retirement age and retirement pensions, and changed the court's organizational structure.

at most ninety days to promulgate an electoral law, appoint the members of an electoral commission, and commence the procedure for organizing the elections. It also provides that the elected legislature (the General National Congress (GNC)) should appoint a constitutional drafting committee that would have sixty days to prepare a final draft constitution. The draft would then have to be approved by the GNC and would be submitted to a referendum within thirty days. In the event the draft was rejected by the Libyan people, the drafting committee would then have thirty days to prepare a new version. After the constitution was approved, the GNC would then have to enact a new electoral law within thirty days, and elections would have to be organized at most 180 days after the electoral laws were approved.[35]

Unrealistic Timeframe: The transition roadmap was designed pursuant to a number of factors, including that specific political forces had preexisting networks that they were hoping would allow them to sweep the elections if they were organized quickly enough. International organizations, including but not limited to the United Nations, followed a checklist approach to post-conflict democratic transitions that prioritized elections. The difficulty, however, was that the transition's roadmap was ludicrously ambitious for any country, let alone one with so few democratic traditions to speak of, such as Libya. The idea that a new constitution could be drafted in a mere two months and that a national debate on the draft should last only a month was remarkably naïve and cavalier, particularly considering how high the stakes were. The issue was not just that the deadlines could simply not be met but also that the consequences of violating constitutional procedures in a country that is presumably seeking to establish the rule of law could potentially be devastating. Perhaps even more concerning was the electoral timetable, which barely allowed any time to consider a series of consequential issues, including what type of electoral system should be adopted, what the best timing for elections was, and whether other measures could be incorporated into the transition that could work against potential excesses or abuses by the newly elected authorities.

[35] The UN Secretary General issued a report to the Security Council on Libya on November 22, 2011, in which he commented on the transition plan for the first time, albeit very briefly. His only comment on the timetable was that it was "challenging," particularly "in a country where there has been limited or no electoral experience in over 45 years." Also, his only comment on behalf of specific measures was to urge the Libyan authorities to "enhance the representation of women and the engage in consultation with civil society, including young people and women"; see S/2011/727 (2011).

Long-Term Consequences: All of these deficiencies constitute clear evidence that the country's most senior policy-makers were out of their depth. The Declaration was so deficient that it was bound to have long-term consequences: It simply did not provide enough guidance on how the interim period should be managed, as a result of which the GNC would have no choice but to add to it and amend it on a regular basis (almost ten times between 2011 and 2019), whether because it was necessary or convenient to do so. The result was that the only standards that would guide the GNC's behavior were its own instincts, which should have been a major cause for concern given how inexperienced its members were likely to be and how motivated they were likely to be by short-term self-interest.

2012 PARLIAMENTARY ELECTIONS

Libya after Liberation: After all military operations against the previous regime's forces were declared over, the country was in an uncertain state. A number of irregular and regular militia forces emerged during the conflict. Most were nominally integrated into the state but did not respond to a unified command structure, and had different views on whether the post-conflict governments and parliaments were sufficiently legitimate. Many were in control over their own part of territory (including different parts of individual cities). Others controlled individual institutions (including, for example, the international airport). The result was a high degree of chaos and volatility in the country that was impossible to ignore and increased over time. At the same time, the period starting end of 2011 witnessed an explosion of organized debates and dialogue sessions on the country's future system of government. The environment was so free that it has been described as a "golden age" in comparison to what preceded it and to what came after.[36]

The Electoral System: Pursuant to the Constitutional Declaration, the NTC drafted an electoral law in January 2012 that provided for a mixed parallel system according to which 120 seats should be allocated under two different majoritarian systems and another 80 would be allocated through proportional representation. The drafters were primarily motivated by a desire to allow a wide spectrum of political actors to be represented in the GNC; to reduce the likelihood that significant proportions of the population might feel disenfranchised; and to mitigate the effects of Libya's very weak political party

[36] Interview with leading academic, February 13, 2020; interview with leading international officials, February 13 and 17, 2020.

culture.[37] The disadvantage of the chosen system, however, was that it was likely to lead to a deeply fragmented legislature that would have significant trouble in composing a government, let alone formulating coherent policy. This was likely to be compounded by the fact that the future legislature was due to come into existence without any strong state institutions that could mitigate the new parliament's lack of experience.

Results: The elections eventually took place on July 7, 2012.[38] The parliament was populated by dozens of political forces and parties, many of which suffered from a lack of experience, ideology, and/or vision for how their country should be managed. This was made worse by the fact that many of these parties were connected to militias who were more than willing to use force, exacerbating an already fragile security situation. It was estimated that sixty-one seats were won by Islamists, who remained generally unified, and who were determined to widen religion's influence on the state. Sixty-four seats were won by the National Forces Alliance, but the Alliance fragmented shortly after the election, leaving the Islamists as the largest organized group. The remainder of the seats were won by local interest groups or individual members, who were incapable of formulating national policies and who had only limited influence.[39] Considering the very considerable challenges that Libya faced at the time, the GNC's lack of capacity, its inexperience, poor work ethic, and internal divisions, combined with the Constitutional Declaration's lack of clarity, were extremely problematic.[40] The GNC only finally managed to grant confidence to its first government in November 2012, which itself was considered to be highly ineffectual.[41]

37 See Ziwo (2012) at 23.

38 See, for example, "General National Congress Elections in Libya: Final Report," The Carter Center, July 7, 2012. The Secretary General of the United Nations wrote in a report to the Security Council that "amid the constraints imposed by a compressed electoral timetable, a volatile security environment and lack of previous experience in electoral administration, the elections were a remarkable achievement"; see S/2012/675.

39 See Wolfram Lacher, "Fault Lines of the Revolution: Political Actors, Camps and Conflicts in the New Libya," SWP Research Paper, Stiftung Wissenschaft und Politik, May 2013, at 9.

40 See "Libya's Political Transition: The Challenges of Mediation," Peter Bartu, International Peace Institute (December 2014) ("Behind the façade of government, there was little depth in any sector and no experience with parliamentary and executive procedures, including consultative processes and transparent decision-making mechanisms").

41 Among other problems, the government took close to no action to integrate irregular militias into the armed forces. A series of initiatives were launched and abandoned, often within months, allowing security concerns and challenges to fester over a period of years, eventually spiraling totally out of control. See "Crumbling States: Security Sector Reform in Libya and Yemen," Yezid Sayigh, Carnegie Middle East Center (June 2015).

Impact on Constitutional Process: Importantly, the issue of who would negotiate and draft the future constitution was still not fully resolved on election day. In the period immediately prior to the elections, important forces used threats and various forms of intimidation to force through a number of changes.[42] A resurgent "federalist movement" that was concentrated in east Libya was concerned that, given the electoral system that was in place at the same time, Tripoli and the rest of west Libya were likely to dominate the GNC and the constitutional drafting committee that it was due to appoint.[43] Their concern was that this would prolong the deprivation that east Libya suffered under the previous regime. The GNC was a temporary body whose work could be undone by a subsequent legislature, but the federalists could not accept that the country's permanent constitution would be dominated by western interests with no guarantees that their own perspective would be taken into account.

Changes to the Constitutional Declaration: In the period immediately preceding the GNC's election, the NTC succumbed to the pressure and amended the Constitutional Declaration to provide that the future constitutional drafting assembly should be directly elected and that its internal composition should match the 1951 National Assembly's composition (twenty members for each of the three regions). This last minute amendment, combined with the fact that candidates were nominated only after voter registration took place, contributed to voters' sense of confusion about what they were voting for: They had originally understood that the elections were to determine the contents of the final constitution, but now voters were no longer certain. It also reemphasized how poorly organized the policy formation process was: lacking in transparency, uncertain, and subject to change with no prior notice and even on a poorly thought out whim. The GNC had to decide whether to adhere to the NTC's last minute amendments of the constitutional declaration and organize elections for a constituent assembly, or whether it should reverse it and simply appoint a drafting body itself. The matter was only finally resolved in February 2013 (seven months later),

[42] During that same period, armed militias surrounded the GNC and forced it to adopt Law 13 (2013), which excluded from public office individuals who had occupied senior state positions prior to the 2011 uprising. As a result, many of the individuals who had set the course for Libya's transition through the adoption of the Constitutional Declaration were excluded from the political scene altogether.

[43] Libya has traditionally subdivided into three provinces: western Tripolitana province (the most populous by far), eastern Cyrenaica province (the second most populous), and southern Fezzan province (the least populous by far).

when the GNC adopted Law 17 (2013), according to which the CDA would be elected after all.[44]

Criticism of the CDA Law: A number of major criticisms were offered against Law 17 (2013). First, Article 5 maintained the 1951 Constituent Assembly's membership ratio, and provided that each of the three regions should have twenty representatives. This automatically meant that the weight of western votes was heavily diluted in comparison to votes in the east and south. This was partially mitigated by the fact that all of the CDA's decisions had to be adopted by a "two thirds plus one" majority and that the CDA's members sought to achieve a high degree of consensus on all major issues (see later). Second, although the Constitutional Declaration was amended to extend the constitutional drafting process to 120 days (from 60),[45] the deadline for completion nevertheless remained far too ambitious. Considering the slow pace of reform and the absence of progress on constitutional dialogue at the highest levels, it was impossible to imagine that the CDA could come close to completing its work within that short timeframe. Inevitably, the deadline was missed, further undermining any chance that the country might have had to strengthen the rule of law. Finally, no provision was taken to deal with growing voter apathy. Turnout in the CDA elections was modest in comparison to the 2012 GNC elections. Prospective voters numbering 1,102,000 registered in 2014, which was far lower than the 2.8 million who had registered and the 1.76 million who had voted in the GNC elections. The low turnout immediately had a negative impact on the CDA's popular legitimacy within the country.

CONSTITUTIONAL DRAFTING ASSEMBLY

Drafting History: The CDA elections finally took place on February 20, 2014 and the CDA's sessions started in April 2014.[46] The CDA published a first partial draft of the future constitution in December 2014, which essentially consisted of reports that had been written by the committees rather than a consolidated draft of the future constitution. The CDA was severely criticized

[44] Law 17 (2013) was approved in July 2013.

[45] See Constitutional Amendment No. (1) of 2012 (March 13, 2012).

[46] Several constituencies, particularly among ethnic minorities in south Libya, organized an electoral boycott. As a result, many of the seats were not filled on the day when the CDA started its work. Some of the seats were filled later on in the process. The CDA's official website was available at www.cdalibya.org but has since been removed. It is recoverable from the Internet Memory Machine.

as the draft demonstrated how little progress had been made in the months that had passed.[47] A second draft was published in October 2015, by which time the CDA lost much of what was left of its credibility.[48] In March 2016, slightly more than two-thirds of the CDA's members travelled to Salalah, at the invitation of the Sultanate of Oman and of the United Nations Support Mission to Libya, with a view to reaching a final agreement on the constitution.[49] What was supposed to be the final draft was published in April 2016,[50] but it was never formally adopted by the parliament given that the CDA members who had boycotted the Salalah negotiations successfully petitioned a court to annul the draft.[51] During the period that followed, efforts were made to encourage boycotting members, and various committees were formed to bridge differences that made only slow progress. On July 29, 2017, the CDA managed to adopt what was widely considered to be the final draft.[52] At the time, some observers considered the CDA's achievement to be highly significant, and as a possible new lease of life to the entire transition.

CDA's Links to Political Groups: Law 17 (2013) was widely interpreted as barring candidates from being affiliated to political parties.[53] The result was that most CDA members were formally independents who were not linked to the country's political forces. They were nevertheless grounded in the main ideological questions that were in dispute in the country.[54] The members had

[47] An unofficial translation of the first draft is available at www.constitutionnet.org/vl/item/libya-initial-draft-constitution-2014-english.

[48] The October 2015 draft is available (in Arabic) at www.constitutionnet.org/ar/vl/item/Lybia-Draft-Constitution-2015.

[49] Some members refused to participate for a variety of reasons, including concerns over foreign involvement; interview with senior international official, February 13, 2020.

[50] An official copy of the April 2016 draft is available at www.constitutionnet.org/ar/vl/item/Libya-draft-constitution-19-april-2016-ar. For an unofficial English-language translation see www.constitutionnet.org/vl/item/draft-libyan-constitution-april-2016-non-official-english-translation.

[51] See Omar Hammady, "The Role of Civil Society in the Libyan Constitution-Making Process," in Tania Abbiate, Markus Böckenförde, and Veronica Federico (eds.), Public Participation in African Constitutionalism, Routledge (2017), at 169.

[52] The fact that the CDA managed to meet on July 29, 2017 and that it successfully reached an agreement came as a major surprise to many observers; interview with leading academic from Benghazi, February 13, 2020.

[53] "The 2014 Constitutional Drafting Assembly Elections in Libya," The Carter Center (June 2014), at 21. Article 9 of Law 17 (2013), which set out the eligibility requirements for all electoral candidates, only prevented members of the GNC and the interim government from participating.

[54] Jason Gluck, "Constitution-Building in a Political Vacuum: Libya and Yemen in 2014," International IDEA Annual Review of Constitution-Building Processes (2014), at 46. One international official who worked closely with the CDA stated in an interview with the author that the CDA's members were genuine independents and did not conceal any affiliations; interview, senior international official who worked closely with the CDA, February 13, 2020.

deeply held views on whether the Libyan state should be federal or unitary, religiously inspired or more secular leaning, among other issues.[55] There were, however, a number of factors that diminished the entire constitution-making process' ability to positively impact Libya's transition. First, because the political balance of forces was not properly represented in the discussions, the discussions focused almost entirely on resolving ideological differences without focusing on how Libya could transition to and begin implementing the final text that was agreed. To transition to the vision set out in the CDA's final draft, political forces and armed groups would have had to relinquish control over specific institutions in accordance with a specific plan that would have had to include specific guarantees. Because of its independent membership, the CDA was not in a position to design that plan or to offer guarantees, which greatly decreased its ability to offer a workable solution. In addition, the CDA could not even meet with political party representatives to take their demands or interests into consideration. Because of how unpopular political groups were in the country, CDA members were largely unwilling to meet with them in public. There were very limited opportunities for the CDA to consult with political forces to obtain feedback from them or try to convince them to support the draft. As a result, it is not clear to what extent the country's main political forces agree with the final draft's content (even though outside groups did impose their views on more than one occasion, often by threatening CDA members). This raises the possibility that after the fighting stops, the country's new powers may discover that they dislike the CDA's final draft, or that it does not meet many of their expectations. This in turn means that they may ultimately reject the final draft, whether by blocking a referendum or by encouraging Libyans to vote against it; or they could simply refuse to comply with the final draft's provisions if it ever comes into force.[56] To make matters worse, deteriorating security further reduced opportunities to organize public hearings, including with other state institutions, which means that the CDA could not organize dialogue sessions with representatives from specific institutions either.

Pressure on the CDA: While the CDA may not have been able to consult with political parties, it was subject to pressure by the parties and other forces. Armed groups used their influence to force through a number of changes to the draft. By way of example, early drafts of the constitution included specific provisions on transitional justice, which was a major popular demand

[55] Interview, senior international official who worked closely with the CDA, February 13, 2020.

[56] At the time of writing, many of Libya's main political forces appear to be actively blocking any attempt to organize the referendum.

throughout the region. The October 2015 draft's provision stated that transitional justice measures should include an effort to "uncover and document human rights violations [. . .] because of violations and military operations" (Article 190). The provision's reference to "military operations" would have been particularly worrying to a number of militias, in particular the self-styled Libyan National Army. The wording was maintained in the April 2016 draft (Article 197) but was ultimately excised when the April 2017 draft was published (Article 180). In the final July 2017 draft, the provision was cut down to its bare minimum, allowing significant scope for subsequent legislation to define the mechanisms in a way that will not allow any investigations of possible crimes that might have been committed by armed militias recognized by the Libyan state (Article 181(1)). Some observers attributed this important substantive change to direct pressure from specific armed groups.[57]

The LPA Negotiations: Around about the time that the CDA published its first draft of the constitution, Libyan and international officials were growing increasingly concerned that political polarization was worsening security in the country (see later). The CDA's slow progress strongly suggested that a separate process should be launched to address immediate governance concerns while the country waited for it to complete its discussions. As a result, in January 2015, the United Nations launched a political dialogue process with a view to reviving the political process and consolidating state institutions. Negotiations continued for months, ultimately culminating in the signing of the Libyan Political Agreement (LPA) in December 2015.[58] The LPA purported to establish a completely new system of government, including a new executive and a redesigned legislature that were intended to remain in place until the final constitution entered into force. The negotiations that led to the LPA had an indirect but important impact on the CDA's mandate. As a result of the fact that new interim arrangements were being negotiated elsewhere, all the CDA could do was negotiate on the final settlement, a governance structure that the country would strive to achieve at some later, unspecified date. The CDA was no longer responsible for negotiating how the country could transition toward that final settlement, nor could it even participate in those discussions.[59] That dynamic was cemented by the fact that those individuals who participated in the LPA negotiations were not formally connected

[57] Interview with leading academic, February 13, 2020.

[58] The English version of the agreement is available at https://unsmil.unmissions.org/sites/default/files/Libyan%20Political%20Agreement%20-%20ENG%20.pdf. The Arabic version is on file with the author.

[59] According to an international official, at the early stages of the dialogue, the United Nations intended to invite a CDA representative as part of the independent group. The CDA decided

to the CDA or its members. The CDA's reduced mandate is demonstrated by the final draft's provisions on transitional measures. Chapter 11 is extremely short, with virtually no detail on how any of the draft constitution's arrangements should come into existence. By way of comparison, the Kenyan, South African, and Colombian constitutions' respective transitional provisions are 4,268, 9,688, and 8,417 words long. Libya's Chapter 11 contains 688 words. It may be that this does not matter, since the details of the transition can be decided elsewhere; however, it does illustrate to what extent the CDA's work was decoupled from the LPA's transitional arrangements.

JULY 2017 DRAFT CONSTITUTION

Fundamental Principles: This new de facto substantive mandate had a number of implications. First, the CDA's final draft does not clearly set out what the state's new objectives, or its raison d'être, are. Chapter 1 of Libya's final draft is entitled "Fundamental Principles" but mainly consists of general provisions that are not particularly fundamental. For example, Article 12 provides that Libya's foreign relations should be based on the principle of national sovereignty and independence. Article 14 deals with political asylum; Article 26 provides that funds belonging to religious endowments should be kept separate from the state treasury; and Article 27 discusses the role and form of traditional family values. As it currently stands, only one article appears to be specifically geared toward Libya's particular circumstances: Article 2 relates to the state's identity and to language issues, which have been controversial from the start. Libya's many ethnic minorities speak languages other than Arabic and have sought to have their status recognized and protected. Some members of these communities have also sought extensive autonomy from Libya's central government, and on more than one occasion have sought inspiration from the Kurdistan Regional Government's place within the Iraqi constitution. Others have raised the concern that any formal recognition of linguistic or cultural diversity could threaten national unity. Article 2 seeks to establish a compromise on this issue, and is similar in spirit and content to equivalent provisions that have been adopted in many other countries, including Iraq (Article 4). It recognizes Libya's linguistic and cultural diversity, and states that languages such as Amazigh, Targhey, and Tebu should be protected as a general obligation (as opposed to a limited obligation toward the relevant

that it should not be part of the political negotiations. Interview with international official, March 27, 2020.

communities), but at the same time it maintains Arabic as the country's sole language of state. This formula represents a very significant advance from the position in the past and from the prevailing discourse among some groups back in 2011.

Individual Rights: The July 2017 draft provides for generous civil, political, social, and economic rights that sometimes go beyond regional standards. Article 65 provides that any restriction of a basic right must be "necessary, clear, limited, and proportional with the restrictions' objectives," which is a very clear and strong formulation of principle that should serve Libya well if it is ever applied. A number of provisions on women's rights are particularly impressive, including a state obligation to provide equal opportunities to men and women (Article 16) and to eliminate "social customs" that detract from women's dignity (Article 49). At the same time, in many respects, the final draft limits itself to matching regional progress on these same issues. It restricts itself to rewording how specific rights are formulated, rather than reconsidering the framework within which rights are protected. Article 43, on the right to peaceful assembly, makes no reference to any form of limitations, which means that the legislator will be left to decide whether peaceful protesters have to give advance notice to the authorities of their intention to protest. The July 2017 draft also does not resolve the status of social and economic rights. The draft provides the right to health (Article 48), education (Article 52), work (Article 56), and food and water (Article 47), among many others, but does not provide any indication as to whether they are directly enforceable or not.

Presidentialism: The 2011 Constitutional Declaration sought to prevent the excesses of one-man rule by establishing Libya as a parliamentary system (making it only one of three in the region, with Iraq and Lebanon). However, Libya's weak political party culture and weak institutions contributed to the breakdown that followed the GNC's election. In response, the CDA's December 2014 draft provided for a semi-presidential system of government, and was clearly motivated by a desire to limit the potential for abuse that a powerful presidential system would represent for Libya. It included a number of mechanisms that were designed to subordinate the president to the legislature. Among other things, the president was to be indirectly elected by the Shoura Council (Article 50); the president had to appoint a prime minister from the electoral coalition that had the largest number of seats in parliament (Article 74); and the president had very little scope to dissolve the parliament, and could only do so following a request by the prime minister or twenty-four members of parliament (Article 68). Since then, the draft constitution has come almost full circle. After six years of totally chaotic politics, the July 2017 draft establishes a fully presidential system.

Government Formation: Chapter 3 sets out the details of how the presidential system is supposed to function, and places the president firmly at the top of the state's hierarchy of power. The final draft provides for the president to be directly elected by the people (Article 100) and to be solely responsible for forming a government (Article 104(1)). The type of balancing act that was introduced in some post-2011 constitutions (including Tunisia and Morocco) between heads of state and parliament during the government formation process is nowhere to be seen in the final Libyan draft. Instead, the July 2017 draft more closely resembles the government formation process that is provided for in Syria's 2012 constitution. Most importantly, the president's candidate for prime minister does not have to be affiliated to any particular party, or to have been elected to parliament (Article 113). Parliament can withdraw confidence in the government, but the threshold requirement for this will be very hard to meet (two-thirds of members) (Article 115). Meanwhile, the president is solely responsible for determining government policy (Article 104(2)) and the government (which the president appoints) is responsible for implementing that policy (Article 117(1)).

Dissolution of Parliament: One of the issues that the CDA tried to address in the final draft was the presidential practice of dissolving parliaments at will. As a result, Article 109 stipulates that the president can only dissolve parliament if the general population consents in a popular referendum. The objective that the drafters sought to satisfy here is perfectly legitimate, but the sheer cost of organizing a referendum makes Article 109 completely impractical. In addition, Article 109, which allows the president to dismiss the parliament for "obstructing the state's policy," appears to contradict Article 67, which states that the parliament has the power to ratify state policy. Read in conjunction, those two provisions assume that it is parliament's responsibility to fall into line with the president, rather than for the two institutions to work together to create a state policy that satisfies the maximum number of people.

Public Finance: Just as importantly, the sections on public finance and natural resources make it clear that the president will not have any competitors for control over the country's purse strings. Chapter 8 is dedicated to public finance and is extremely short by modern standards. It stipulates that all revenues must be deposited in the state treasury (Article 165) and that the state's finances should prioritize a number of principles, including the unity of the state's finances (Article 165(1)). Chapter 8 does not provide any clear redistributive mechanisms that would require the government to invest in, or provide additional resources to, provinces that are economically stressed (Article 22, one of the constitution's fundamental principles, does require the state to seek to achieve social justice, but it remains unclear whether the article will be directly enforceable and what relationship it will have with Chapter 8). Chapter 8 does include some reference to local interests, but it is clear that in the final analysis, the president will have the upper hand in shaping the country's finances. Chapter 9 on natural resources, which is also extremely short on detail, centralizes ownership and management of natural resources at the central government level (Article 169). The president will therefore have very significant discretion in deciding how to invest the state's funds.

Decentralization: Earlier drafts sought to establish a federation, but by 2017 the overwhelming desire for simplicity in Libya's governance system pushed the CDA in favor of a more traditional approach. Chapter 6 of the final draft provides for three levels of government: the central government in Tripoli, the governorates, and the municipalities (Article 144). However, the final draft does not give any precise idea of what the governorates and municipalities will look like, how they will function, or what they will do. Almost everything is left for future legislation. What this suggests is that the CDA has been unable to come to any final agreement on what powers the country's future local authorities should have and has decided to defer the matter to the country's future elected officials. Article 145 states that local governments shall enjoy "financial and administrative independence," which suggests that they will not be able to shape their own local policies.

BREAKDOWN

Conflict and uncertainty: The CDA's proceedings took place over a three year period against a backdrop of a country that was falling apart. By mid-2014, the GNC's popularity had declined markedly, given lack of action on security and services, as well as the growing perception that its members were self-serving.[60] The GNC therefore adopted Law 10 (2014) that provided for the

[60] See "Seeking Security: Public Opinion Survey in Libya," National Democratic Institute and JMW Consulting, November 2013 (which notes that in May 2013, 37 percent of Libyans described the GNC's performance as either poor or very poor, and that this figure had increased to 60 percent in September 2013); see also "Libya Stability at Risk," Karim Mezran and Jason Pack, Foreign Policy, May 2, 2013; "Libyan PM Dismisses Army Officer's Plot to 'Rescue' Country," Ghaith Shennib, Reuters, February 14, 2014; "Libya: Wide Popular Opposition to the GNC's Decision to Extend Its Mandate" ("ليبيا: معارضة شعبية واسعة لقرار تمديد ولاية المؤتمر الوطني العام"), Mostapha al-Jaree', al-Maghreb, December 28, 2013; and "Libya: Struggle to Survive as Services Collapse," International Committee of the Red Cross, December 9, 2015.

election of a new House of Representatives (HoR) that would take over the GNC's responsibilities. The elections took place in June 2014, and the HoR that emerged included a significantly lower proportion of Islamists than within the GNC.[61] Many GNC members feared a legislative backlash from the newly elected body and so therefore refused to recognize it.[62] Both bodies set up their own governments (one in west Libya and the other in the east), neither of which recognized the other, thereby worsening the security vacuum in many parts of the country.[63] In December 2015, the United Nations sought to resolve this growing divide through the Libyan Political Agreement, but the HoR never fully recognized some of its key provisions. After close to three years of failed initiatives to mediate a solution (interrupted momentarily by the CDA's final vote in July 2017), the United Nations announced preparations to organize a "National Conference" in April 2019 in which a "road map to conclude the transitional period with either simultaneous parliamentary and presidential elections or through phased elections" was due to be announced.[64] However, ten days before the conference was due to take place, and when the United Nations Secretary General was in Tripoli, another major round of fighting commenced, when the Libyan National Army (which was mainly based out of eastern Libya) announced an effort to "liberate" the western regions, including the capital (which was formally under the control of the GNC and the governing authorities established by the LPA). Unsurprisingly, as a result of these as well as other developments, the CDA's draft could not be referred to referendum or adopted through other means. Intense fighting between the two sides ended in June 2020 after the Libyan National Army failed in its attempts to control Tripoli. In November 2020, the United Nations launched a new effort to resolve Libya's conflict through the

61 Turnout was estimated at 42 percent of the 1.5 million registered voters. In addition, because Law 10 (2014) provided that all candidates would run in single member constituencies as individual candidates, the HoR's membership actually represented a small minority of Libya's population.

62 See "At a Glance: Libya's Transformation 2011–2018," Democracy Reporting International, June 18, 2019, at 28.

63 Since the dispute emerged, the two bodies have been trying to wrestle control over a number of vital services and resources from each other, including control over the Central Bank and oil export terminals.

64 See "Remarks of SRSG Ghassan Salamé to the United Nations Security Council on the Situation in Libya," United Nations Support Mission in Libya, March 20, 2019; and "All Parties in Libya Must Seize Critical Chance to Forge Inclusive, Stable Future ahead of National Conference, Special Representative Tells Security Council," United Nations, March 20, 2019. Seventy dialogue sessions were organized to help prepare for the National Conference; see "The Libyan National Conference Process: Final Report," Center for Humanitarian Dialogue, November 2018.

Libyan Political Dialogue Forum (or LPDF), which was set up to establish a new roadmap toward elections and to form a new transitional executive authority that could govern the country in the meantime. A decision was quickly reached to organize elections in December 2021. In addition, a joint committee that was formed specifically in order to discuss the constitution's future agreed to organize a constitutional referendum before the elections. At the time of writing, it remained unclear if this timeframe would be respected.

5

Jordan, Morocco, Sudan, Algeria

JORDAN

Ottoman Period: Prior to the nineteenth century, much of the territory that today makes up the modern Jordanian state was only sparsely populated and was not subject to formal governance rules. Tribes, many of which were grouped together in confederacies, controlled much of the territory and applied tribal law.[1] During the nineteenth century, in response to growing military threats from European powers, the Ottoman Empire sought to broaden its tax base and the numbers of potential recruits it could draw from during times of conflict. The empire therefore expanded its geographic reach, including in the territory east of the Jordan river. New settlements were established, the area under cultivation was expanded, and modern governance frameworks were introduced. This included, among other things, the introduction of districting and the election of local representatives to a range of local councils; of taxation: and of commercial and criminal codes.[2] Security for the general population improved during this period, as did agricultural output and overall economic activity, which attracted merchants from across the region. Ottoman authorities also moved to coopt powerful tribes into the new governance framework. Tribal leaders assumed office in the new administrative system that was being established, which translated into access to funds and further enhanced their influence.[3] Jordan's experience under the Ottoman period was therefore defined by the imposition of policies that were

[1] Eveline van der Steen, Near Eastern Tribunal Societies during the Nineteenth Century: Economy, Society and Politics between Tent and Town, Routledge (2013).

[2] See, for example, Eugene L. Rogan, Frontiers of the State in the Late Ottoman Empire: Transjordan, *1850–1921*, Cambridge University Press (1999).

[3] Abujaber Raouf Sa'd, Pioneers over Jordan: The Frontier of Settlement in Transjordan, 1850–1914, I.B. Tauris (1989); Yoav Alon, "Sheikh and Pasha: Ottoman

formulated without any local input, which depended in part on the cooptation of influential families into local government.[4] The system brought unequal benefits to the local population, a situation that continues to this day.

British Mandate: After the Ottoman withdrawal following the end of the First World War, the United Kingdom moved to establish a mandate in Jordan. Members of the Hashemite family (who claimed legitimacy through lineage from the Prophet Mohammed's family) were encouraged to settle in Jordan and to establish a monarchy. The Hashemites were originally residents of the Hijaz in modern-day Saudi Arabia, and so therefore were foreign to the territory that they were being invited to rule. It took close to a decade for British officials and the new monarch to adjust to each other and settle on a system of government.[5] In 1928, an Organic law was drawn up by British officials that granted the monarch almost limitless authority without subjecting him to any form of accountability. The monarch was granted both executive and legislative power (Article 12); could appoint and dismiss the prime minister and all ministers at will (Article 20); called for elections; and could dismiss the parliament without limitation (Article 19(3)). The cabinet was formally part of parliament (Article 25) and the parliament was headed by the prime minister (Article 32). Meanwhile, ordinary Jordanians were formally granted some basic rights, but these were set out so briefly (speech, association, and assembly were all provided for in a single twenty-one-word article; Article 11), and without any indication as to how far legislation could go in limiting those rights, that they were effectively meaningless. Judges were also not granted any effective protections against interference in their work (Article 42).[6] The monarch used the authority that had been granted to him to prevent any form of democratic control, and therefore dissolved the parliament in 1931 after it refused to sanction the financing of a desert patrol unit.[7] The second document that was entered into, the Anglo-Transjordanian

Government in the Syrian Desert and the Creation of Modern Tribunal Leadership," Journal of the Economic and Social History of the Orient, Vol. 59, No. 3 (2016), 442–472.

4 The Ottoman legislature, which was convened in 1908 and 1914 and which was consultative in nature only, included one representative from Jordan only. Kamel S. Abu Jaber, "The Legislature in the Hashemite Kingdom of Jordan," The Muslim World, Volume 59, Issue 3–4 (1969), 220–250.

5 Among other things, this involved limiting the then-monarch's spending, which British officials considered to be profligate; see Nathan Brown, Constitution in a Nonconstitutional World: Arab Basic Laws and the Prospects for Accountable Government, State University of New York Press (2002), at 46.

6 Adel Al Hayari, Constitutional Law and the Constitutional Order: A Comparative Study (القانون الدستوري والنظام الدستوري الاردني), Dar al-Thaqafa (1972).

7 Abu Jaber (1969).

Agreement, allowed this highly undemocratic system to be controlled by British officials, who imposed legislation and government action through ministerial advisers.[8] The Agreement provided that the monarch would act based on the advice of the British High Commissioner (Article 5); would adopt all legislation that the British required (Article 4); and that the British would maintain armed forces in the country, which the monarch could not do without the express consent of the High Commissioner (Article 10).[9] These two legal instruments were adopted with close to no local or popular input. The British and the monarch also opted to maintain the Ottoman policy of coopting tribal leaders into their system of government. Both of these practices are still in force to this day (see later sections).[10]

1947 Constitution: In 1946, the United Kingdom decided to end the mandate, and entered into a new bilateral treaty with the monarch that repealed and replaced the 1928 Anglo-Transjordanian Agreement.[11] With that change, a growing number of local actors demanded greater democratic accountability in government but that demand went unheeded. A new constitution was adopted, which was heavily inspired by the Organic Law and maintained the same internal power dynamics. The new constitution provided that the monarch was the commander in chief of the armed forces (Article 26); had full control over cabinet appointments (Article 27) and dismissals (Article 28); was given legislative authority (Article 33); and was also responsible for appointing the speaker of parliament (Article 43). An upper chamber of parliament was created but was entirely appointed by the monarch (Article 29) and was given the upper hand in the legislative process (Article 49). The monarch, in any event, was still empowered to reject any legislation that had been adopted and could adopt temporary legislation in the event the parliament was not in session (Article 53). Judges were still not given effective

[8] Brown (2002), at 47.

[9] Agreement between His Majesty and the Amir of Transjordan (1928).

[10] E. Theodore Mogannam, "Developments in the Legal System of Jordan," MIDDLE EAST JOURNAL, Vol. 6, No. 2 (Spring 1952), 194–206; Abu Jaber (1969) (according to which all the representatives that were elected from 1931–1946 were drawn from thirty-six prominent families only); and Yoav Alon, THE MAKING OF JORDAN: TRIBES, COLONIALISM AND THE MODERN STATE, I.B. Taurus (2007).

[11] See Treaty of Alliance between his Majesty in respect of the United Kingdom and his Highness the Amir of Trans-Jordan, March 22, 1946, Treaty Series No. 32 (1946). The Annex to the agreement allowed the United Kingdom to maintain armed forces in the country (Article 1); obligated Jordan to make facilities available to the United Kingdom (Article 2); exempted the United Kingdom from taxation (Article 7); and provided that the United Kingdom would provide financial assistance to meet the cost of maintaining Jordan's own armed forces (Article 8).

protection, given that the cabinet (which was appointed by the monarch) was solely responsible for determining the conditions in which judges could be dismissed (Article 55). Speech, association, and assembly were still only dealt with in twenty-one words (Articles 17 and 18).

1952 Constitution: In mid-May 1948, following the first Arab–Israeli war, the Jordanian army won control of the West Bank of the Jordan River. A new government was formed that included Palestinian ministers and a new parliament was elected, half of whose members came from the West Bank (some of whom were members of radical movements). In 1950 the newly elected parliament adopted a resolution that purported to unify the West Bank and Jordan. The government formed a commission to draw up a new constitution that would introduce greater democratic legitimacy, and in particular in order to make government answerable to parliament. The new constitution was ultimately adopted in 1952 but offered few meaningful concessions. The system of government remained essentially the same: The monarch maintained full discretion to nominate and dismiss prime minister and ministers alike (Article 35); appointed all the members of the upper chamber (Article 36); and exercised indirect control over the courts (Article 98). Royal decrees were required to be countersigned either by the prime minister or by the relevant minister (Article 40) but this did not constitute an effective limitation on royal prerogative given the monarch's power to appoint and dismiss ministers at will. The only significant departure is that the parliament was given some authority to exercise oversight over the government. It could now theoretically withdraw confidence and also prevent the adoption of international treaties (Article 33), but the ever present threat of dissolution combined with the unreasonably high threshold to withdraw confidence (two-thirds of all members; Article 56) ensured that it could never be exercised effectively.[12]

Martial Law: The 1952 Constitution's few elements of progress encouraged the parliamentary opposition to exhibit its independence from official state policy on a number of issues (including foreign policy), while the government made moves to expand basic freedoms. In response, political parties were banned, the government dismissed, the parliament dissolved, and the monarch declared martial law.[13] In the thirty-five years that followed, political parties were not permitted to contest elections and the monarch remained

[12] The threshold was reduced to a majority of members in 1953 but was still hardly used as an effective oversight mechanism.

[13] Number 1328.

solely responsible for determining the composition of government.[14] The Muslim Brotherhood was the only organized political movement that contested elections throughout that period, albeit formally as independents and not as official members of a political party.[15] Importantly, several waves of refugees and displaced persons flowed into the country throughout that period, including in 1967 when Jordan lost control of the West Bank to Israel, in 1991 after Kuwait was liberated from the Iraqi army and after the 2003 invasion of Iraq by the United States and the United Kingdom. These developments caused consternation in some circles that Jordan's original inhabitants had possibly become a minority in the country. This encouraged the state to reinforce longstanding practices inherited from the Ottoman period that were designed to privilege some groups of citizens over others, which manifested itself in a number of ways, including in the electoral law.[16]

Outbreak of Protest: In 1989 unrest and rioting broke out after the government introduced austerity measures.[17] In response, modest efforts were made to liberalize governance. Political parties were legalized and were permitted to contest elections.[18] A new parliament was elected, and a royal commission was appointed to draw up a strategy for modernizing and democratizing the state.[19] Despite these small advances and the ascension of a new monarch to the throne in 1999, power dynamics and the behavior of institutions and office holders remained the same. In 2001 the monarch dissolved parliament and left the country without a parliament for two years, during which more than 200 provisional laws were adopted. In 2007 another parliament was elected, which was dissolved in 2009.[20] Throughout this period, many Jordanians complained of deteriorating purchasing power in a context where cost of

[14] From 1952 to 2011, seventy-two governments were formed with thirty-four Prime Ministers.

[15] See Muhannad Mubaidheen and Zaid Eiadat, "The Muslim Brotherhood in Jordan: Establishment, Development and Future" (الإخوان المسلمون في الأردن: التأسيس والتطور والمصائر), in Islamic Movements in the Arab World (الحركات الإسلامية في الوطن العربي), Center for Arab Unity Studies (January 2013).

[16] See "Jordan: Parliamentary Elections and Political Reform" (الأردن: الانتخابات النيابيّة والإصلاح السياسيّ), Arab Center for Research and Policy Studies (February 27, 2013); and Laurie A. Band, "Palestinians and Jordanians: A Crisis of Identity," Journal of Palestine Studies, Vol. 24, No. 4 (Summer 1995).

[17] Curtis R. Ryan, Jordan and the Arab Uprisings: Regime Survival and Politics beyond the State, Columbia University Press (2018), at 24.

[18] Najib Ghadbian, Democratization and the Islamist Challenge in the Arab World, Routledge (1997).

[19] Jordanian National Charter (1991).

[20] Many Jordanians allege that the 2007 elections were tainted by "blatant electoral fraud"; see, for example, Muhammad Abu Rumman, "Jordan's Parliamentary Elections and the Islamist Boycott," Carnegie Endowment for International Peace (October 20, 2010).

living was already unreasonably high, as well as growing rates of unemployment, which in 2010 stood at 29 percent for young Jordanians (by 2019, the rate had increased to 35 percent). Modest efforts to reform the state were carried out in the 2000s, all of which had only a limited impact.[21] Starting on January 14, 2011, Jordanians took to the streets to demand the resignation of the government and that deteriorating economic conditions be addressed. Contrary to expectations, younger members of some of the country's tribes, including those that were most closely associated to the monarch, participated in the protests to demand real limitations on the monarch's power. More specifically, many demanded that Articles 30 (according to which the monarch is "immune from any liability and responsibility") and 35 (which allowed the monarch to appoint and dismiss cabinets at will) be amended.[22]

2011 Constitution: In April 2011 the monarch composed a commission to propose constitutional amendments. The commission consisted of ten members, all of whom were staunch supporters of the system of government as it existed at the time. Members included the oldest living former prime minister; the speakers of the senate and of the chamber of deputies; the president of the court of cassation; a former prime minister; a former president of the court of cassation; and four former ministers. The commission did not include anyone who was not or had not at one point been a senior state official. It did not include any independents, academics, constitutional experts, or even anyone who formally supported the suggestion that the constitution should be amended.[23] The commission worked confidentially for three months and did not carry out any public consultations, making the amendment process among the most untransparent in the region. Some civil society organizations and political parties submitted proposals to the commission, but there is no indication that they were taken into consideration. After the commission's proposed amendments were published, they were adopted by the parliament with a small number of changes and without any meaningful

21 See Marwan Muasher, "A Decade of Struggling Reform Efforts in Jordan: The Resilience of the Rentier System," Carnegie Endowment for International Peace (May 11, 2011).

22 Sean L. Yom, "Tribal Politics in Contemporary Jordan: The Case of the Hirak Movement," Middle East Journal, Vol. 68, No. 2 (Spring 2014).

23 Prior to the formation of the Royal Commission, several of the individuals who would eventually become members stated publicly that they were opposed to any amendment of the constitution, and in particular that they were opposed to any amendments that might reduce royal prerogative; see Sufian Obeidat, "The Amended Constitution of Jordan: Analysis and Recommendations," Unpublished (2012).

opportunity for public debate.[24] The 2011 amendments made little difference to the country's overall governance framework. The monarch remained immune and was still solely responsible for composing cabinets. The threshold required to impeach ministers was set at a majority of members (Article 54(2)) but the threat of dissolution remained. A constitutional court with the power to carry out judicial review was established but all members were to be appointed by the monarch, which effectively meant that the court would serve as a check against the parliament and not the exercise of the royal prerogative (Article 58 (1)). Some changes were made to the rights provisions, including the introduction of a requirement that newspapers can only be suspended pursuant to a court order (Article 15(4)), but overall the system remained unchanged.

Further Concentration of Power: A small number of additional amendments, which once again touched upon the separation of powers, were introduced to the constitution in 2014 and in 2016. The government presented the proposed amendments, without forming a royal commission as in 2011, the public was not consulted, and the parliament adopted the changes by wide margins.[25] The amendments generally increased the royal prerogative.[26] Article 127 was amended in 2014 to officially give the monarch the sole power to appoint the director of the General Intelligence Department (GID), the director of the gendarmerie, and the head of the armed forces. The monarch had already been exercising these powers for decades, which meant that the amendment merely codified an existing practice.[27] The requirement that specific decrees be countersigned by the prime minister and the relevant minister was also amended (Article 40(2)). The monarch was therefore constitutionally authorized to unilaterally appoint the crown prince; the chairs of the Judicial Council and of the Constitutional Court; and the Speaker of the Senate and all its members; and could dissolve the Senate, accept the resignation of any of its members, and also relieve any of its members of their membership.[28] A system of government that was established a century ago under foreign rule remained unchanged.

24 Mohammed Torki Bani Salameh, "Political Reform in Jordan," World Affairs, Vol. 180, No. 4 (Winter 2017), 47–78.

25 Rana al Sabbagh, 'Inside Jordan's Proposed Constitutional Amendment', Al-Monitor (September 1, 2014).

26 Osama Al Sharif, "Jordan's King Pushes to Expand Military, Intelligence Authority," Al-Monitor (2014).

27 "Inside Jordan's Proposed Constitutional Amendment," Al-Monitor (2014). Available at www.al-monitor.com/pulse/politics/2014/08/jordan-constitution-amendment-king-government.html.

28 The monarch's ability to unilaterally appoint the other listed officials was already protected by other articles in the constitution (Articles 36, 58(1), 127). For more on the 2014 and 2016 amendments, see Ziad Abu Rish, "The Façade of Jordanian Reform: A Brief History of the

MOROCCO

Pre-colonial Period. Morocco's monarchical system of government traces its origins to 1631 and claims religious legitimacy through lineage from the Prophet Mohammed's family. For centuries, the monarch ruled through a network of agreements that together constituted the state. The agreements consisted first of a pledge of allegiance by specific communities to the monarch. This would allow the central authority to levy taxes within that community, in exchange for which the community would have access and form part of the central authority and enjoy guarantees, including security. Collectively, the monarch's administration of these arrangements was managed by a court (the 'Makhzen'), which survives to this day, although it has undergone several major evolution (see later). Through these arrangements, the Makhzen exercised at least some measure of control over the main cities and part of the countryside through alliances with specific tribes, military forces, religious authorities, and the merchant class. But by the very nature of the fact that communities engaged with the monarch on a contractual basis, Morocco remained decentralized during this period.[29] It also meant that that the country did not evolve into an absolutist monarchy, first as a result of the limits on monarchical authority that the transactional relationships established but also because many communities throughout the territory refused to pay taxes to the monarch (even though they recognized his symbolic authority) and therefore remained outside any formal control. Those communities that did not pledge allegiance nevertheless considered themselves connected to the monarch by virtue of his religious authority, and would call on him in specific circumstances, including to resolve disputes. The political system that these arrangements produced was generally inflexible and incapable of adapting to the growing number of challenges that the country was facing, including radical changes to trading patterns and foreign intervention.[30] The result was that the population as a whole suffered from a general lack of development, including the continuing practice of slavery.[31] European military and commercial encroachments in the second half of the nineteenth

Constitution," Jadaliyya (May 31, 2016); and Sufian Obeidat, "Jordan's 2016 Constitutional Amendments: A Return to Absolute Monarchy?," Constitutionnet (May 27, 2016).

29 Edmund Burke III, Prelude to Protectorate in Morocco: Precolonial Protest and Resistance, 1850–1912, University of Chicago Press (1976), at 12.

30 Ibid., at 151.

31 See Gérard Cholvy, 'Itinéraire d'un colonisateur', Revue des Deux Mondes (March 2008), at 44–45.

century prompted some reform and resistance to colonial expansion.[32] These efforts were largely ineffectual, in part because the political system was incapable of mobilizing resources fast enough.

Colonial Period: In 1908 many Moroccan elites were dismayed by the monarch's failure to protect the national territory. They attempted to modernize the country, in part by drawing up a draft constitution that recognized basic rights, reduced the monarch's powers, and strengthened the separation of powers.[33] Ultimately, however, the monarch rejected the text, partially because of the country's precarious economic and military situation, and instead in 1912 signed a treaty with France that formally placed Morocco under a protectorate (parts of northern Morocco were placed under a Spanish protectorate).[34] The agreement provided that its objective was to establish a "new regime including the administrative, judicial, educational, economic, financial and military reforms that the French government will consider useful" (Article 1). The agreement formalized the country's military occupation (Article 2) and also granted the French Resident General the right to promulgate all decrees (Article 5). As a result of these arrangements, Morocco remained without a constitution or an elected parliament until independence, and executive authority was exercised by decree and was totally unaccountable through democratic means. The signing of the treaty also contributed to popular unrest, including a series of armed rebellions. During the Protectorate, France's policies were heavily influenced by Hubert Lyautey, a military officer who was appointed Resident General from 1912 to 1925. Lyautey's ancestry was deeply entrenched in royalist traditions, as a result of which he was personally inclined to maintain and strengthen many of Morocco's traditional centers of authority. In that sense, Morocco is relatively unique within the region, given that in most other countries, colonialism eviscerated or substantially reduced the influence of whatever pre-colonial administration existed. Lyautey's approach was met with dismay by much of the general population, which hoped that French influence would lead to greater protections for individual rights. Instead, colonial authorities relied heavily on the monarch, who continued to arbitrate disputes, chaired government meetings, and appointed senior government officials.[35] French officials also enhanced the authority of traditional religious authorities and institutions, as well as tribal leaders.

[32] Douglas Porch, THE CONQUEST OF MOROCCO, Farrar, Straus and Giroux (2005), at 240.

[33] Burke (1976), at 45.

[34] Protectorate Agreement between France and Morocco (March 30, 1912), Le Memorial Diplomatique (April 7, 1912).

[35] Daniel Rivet, LYAUTEY ET L'INSTITUTION DU PROTECTORAT FRANCAIS AU MAROC: 1912–1925, L'Harmattan (1996), Volume 2, at 139–140.

Morocco's administrative system was also centralized, including through the establishment of a police force that covered the kingdom's entire territory.[36] The Makhzen ultimately inherited all of the means that had been developed when Morocco achieved independence in 1956. Meanwhile, the country's economic system was redirected toward providing grain for metropolitan France. The basic rights of ordinary Moroccans evolved only very slowly. Deep social inequalities (including, in some cases, slavery) and the deeply unequal treatment of women were allowed to persist and were only addressed gradually and over a period of decades.[37] Colonial authorities offered the general population improved basic services if they did not resist, while at the same time employing extreme violence against those that did.[38]

Independence: Starting in the late 1940s the independence movement intensified and grew increasingly violent. The monarch began distancing himself from the Protectorate and sought common cause with the Istiqlal party, a nationalist party that was established a few years prior, which itself recognized the importance that the general population still attributed to the monarch's traditional authority.[39] Despite French repression, Morocco's independence was negotiated against the backdrop of Algeria's war of national liberation, which was leveraged by the monarch to negotiate from a position of strength. Independence was formally granted in 1956. As the colonial authorities withdrew, a new struggle began over what system of government should be established and who should dominate the new state. During the early independence period, the nationalist movement; left-wing, and republican groups; elements within the military; and a vibrant protest movement competed with the monarchy for control. Some hoped to marginalize the monarchy completely or to establish a one-party system that would be dominated by the independence movement. The monarchy's survival was not a foregone conclusion, and so it responded first through violence and second by establishing a constitutional system of government that marginalized and fragmented the opposition.[40] The Makhzen itself had evolved somewhat. A set

36 George Joffe, 'Monarchy, Legitimacy and Succession', Third World Quarterly, Vol. 10, No. 1, Succession in the South (January 1988), 221.

37 See Gérard Cholvy, "Itinéraire d'un colonisateur," Revue des Deux Mondes (March 2008), at 49.

38 Jonathan Wyrtzen, Making Morocco: Colonial Intervention and the Politics of Identity, Cornell University Press (2015), at 56.

39 Joffe (1988), 207.

40 The period starting from independence and until the 1990s is commonly referred to as the "years of lead" ("سنوات الرصاص" in Arabic); see Fadoua Loudiy, Transitional justice and Human Rights in Morocco: Negotiating the Years of Lead, Routledge (2014).

of royal decrees (or "Dahirs") clarified how part of its composition was determined.[41] New actors, including the leaders of the Istiqlal party and of the armed forces (which were formed around a core of French-trained officers), were incorporated, while more traditional actors, including rural notables, were lesser both in number and in importance.[42]

1962 Constitution: The monarch provided for the establishment of a constitutional commission, which was to be composed of representatives of most of the country's political parties (excluding the National Union, a radical offshoot of the Istiqlal party, whose leaders were directly hostile to the monarch) to draft the country's first constitution. However, following internal disagreements on who should lead the commission's deliberations and the sudden death and replacement of the monarch, the council was abandoned.[43] Instead, the 1962 Constitution was drafted by the newly enthroned monarch and a small group of advisers. It was published in November 1962 and approved in a referendum twenty days later.[44] The final text clearly put the monarch in control of the state, while granting only marginal influence to the political opposition (which quickly grew restless). It sets out a short list of "political rights" (including movement, speech, and association but not assembly). Article 9 provides that rights cannot be curbed in the absence of a law, but given that the executive was granted very significant legislative power that limitation was far from effective. The constitution also included a very short list of social and economic rights (including the right to work, culture, and strike but not education or health) but without clearly indicating that these rights are directly enforceable. Meanwhile, the 1962 Constitution provided that the monarch enjoyed "sacred status" (Article 23); could unilaterally appoint and dismiss the prime minister and all ministers (Article 24); headed the council of ministers (Article 25); was the commander in chief of the armed forces (Article 30); could dissolve parliament practically without limitation (Article 27); had legislative power on a broad range of issues (Articles 29 and 49); was the head of the high judicial council (Article 33); and was also not subject to any constitutional accountability mechanisms. Parliament, meanwhile, could only legislate in a small number of areas

[41] See, for example, Dahir (June 21, 1947) (which states that the Makhzen consists of a prime minister, a minister of justice, a minister of religious endowments, a director of protocol, a deputy prime minister, and a number of assistants).

[42] Paul Silverstein, "Weighing Morocco's New Constitution," Middle East Report Online (May 7, 2011).

[43] See Mohammed Hashas, "Exceptionalism Examined: Constitutional Insights Pre- and Post-2011," Instituto Affari Internazionali (2013), at 5.

[44] Brown (2002), at 51.

(which did not include security issues; Article 48); the judiciary was not given any real means through which its independence could be protected; and there was close to no wording on local governance. Most importantly, the King was granted unrestricted and implicit power (Article 19), which remained unchanged until 2011. The 1962 Constitution divided Morocco's political scene. Some leading nationalist parties campaigned in favor, while others (including far-left parties) rejected the text in part because of the monarchy's continued control over the country, and because of the process through which the text was adopted.[45]

Constitutional Instability: During the period that followed, the monarchy developed the patronage system by granting economic benefits to nonpolitical institutions and groups in exchange for their support. Those new arrangements were under constant renegotiation, as a result of which Morocco's constitution has undergone seven major amendments since independence.[46] All of these constitutions had a number of common features. They all deviated only marginally from the original system of government that was established in 1962. Second, all of these constitutions were produced by small numbers of individuals who were closely connected to the monarch, while opposition parties and the general population were generally not consulted.[47] In 1965 after security forces repressed demonstrations by students, the unemployed, and manual laborers in Casablanca, a state of emergency was declared.[48] The monarch governed through decree and without a sitting parliament for five years. In 1970 a new constitution was enacted that increased the power of the monarch, and marginalized the parliament (in part by restricting parliamentary immunity) and some of the institutions that the monarch relied on most, including the armed forces, even further. In 1971, elements within the military attempted to carry out a coup d'état against the monarch, which forced him to downgrade his reliance on that institution and to reach out to the same opposition parties that he had marginalized during the previous ten years. In 1972 a new constitution was drafted that reverted back to many of the 1962 Constitution's arrangements, which allowed the monarch to continue to

[45] Driss Maghraoui, 'Constitutional Reforms in Morocco: Between Consensus and Subaltern Politics', The Journal of North African Studies, Volume 16, Number 4 (2011), 684.

[46] While each of the constitutions since 1962 has been presented as an entirely new text that replaces the previous text, they all draw heavily from their predecessors. Much of the wording, principles, concepts and arrangements have been maintained since 1962.

[47] On occasion, political parties were invited to submit memoranda to the monarch. That process was followed in 1992 and 1996.

[48] Khadija Mohsen-Finan, "'Mémoire et réconciliation au Maroc," Politique Étrangère, Vol. 72, No. 2 (Summer 2007), 327–338.

exercise both executive and legislative power, while allowing parliament a marginal role only.

Limited Liberalization: By the early 1990s the political dynamic within the country underwent an important evolution. Following the fall of the Berlin wall, domestic and international forces were increasingly vocal on Morocco's human rights record. In addition, the violence in neighboring Algeria encouraged Moroccan opposition parties to exercise a certain amount of self-restraint.[49] In 1992, this led to the adoption of yet another constitution. The new text, marginally more liberal than its predecessors, provided stronger protections for basic rights; strengthened the prime minister (who was still appointed unilaterally by the monarch; Article 24); allowed opposition parties some additional scope to be involved in governing the country; and established a constitutional council (Article 76). In 1996, a new constitution reinforced some of the countermeasures against liberalism, including by providing an appointed upper chamber that would work against the elected lower chamber. Contrary to past constitutional processes, political parties did not engage in any meaningful discussions about royal prerogatives. Increasing domestic and international pressure led to the establishment in 2004 of an Equity and Reconciliation Commission, which was mandated to investigate disappearances and arbitrary detention from 1956 to 1999, but was formally prevented from establishing any form of individual responsibility.[50] In its final report that was published in November 2005, it offered a number of recommendations, including to "strengthen the separation of powers and to prevent all interference by the executive in the judiciary's work."[51]

Morocco on the Brink: In late 2010, despite progress on a range of socio-economic indicators, Moroccan society was struggling. The literacy rate was just under 60 percent of the population, and the education sector in general suffered from glaring inequalities.[52] Inequality was persistently high and increasing (with the poorest 10 percent of the population accounting for 2.7

[49] See Mounia Bennani-Chraïbi and Mohamed Jeghllaly, "The Protest Dynamics of Casablanca's February 20th movement," Revue francaise de science politique (English edition), Vol. 62, No. 5–6, Arab Uprisings, Reflections on Revolutionary Situations in Context (2012), at 107.

[50] Dahir Number 1.04.42 (April 10, 2004). The Commission's establishment was facilitated by the fact that a new monarch was enthroned in 1999, who sought to turn the page on his father's tenure.

[51] The Commission's full report is available at https://hmcwordpress.humanities.mcmaster.ca/Truthcommissions/wp-content/uploads/2019/01/Morocco.IER_.Report-FULL.pdf.

[52] Aomar Ibourk and Jabrane Amaghouss, "Regional Dynamic of Educational Inequality in Morocco: An Empirical Investigation," International Journal of Education Economics and Development, Vol. 5, No. 3 (2014), 209–226.

percent of consumption, far worse than in countries such as Egypt and Syria).[53] Only 37 percent of the population had access to safe sanitation services. The urban/rural divide was particularly marked, with 87 percent and 32 percent, respectively, having access to safe drinking water. Politically, the country was still liberalizing but the general population was growing increasingly detached from formal politics. In the 2007 parliamentary elections, the largest parliamentary party obtained only 11 percent of the vote. The abstention rate was at 63 percent, the highest on record. Most mainstream political parties were regularly accused of serving the state or themselves, rather than the general population.[54] There was also a widespread perception in the country that corruption was worsening, particularly in the real estate sector.[55]

Constitutional Committee: Encouraged by developments in the rest of the region, Morocco's radical opposition, including left-wing organizations and an Islamist movement, formed the February 20th movement, named after the date on which its first mass demonstration would take place.[56] Unlike many of their regional peers, the movement did not call for the end of the regime, but rather focused on ending "despotism," which suggested a preference for reform over revolution.[57] More specifically, some protesters called for reform of royal prerogatives, the establishment of a parliamentary monarchy, and the establishment of effective anti-corruption mechanisms.[58] Faced with these demands, Morocco's controlling elites opted for continuity and stability, rather than confrontation or major reform.[59] On March 9, 2011, the monarch delivered an address that was partially designed to respond to these demands.[60] The monarch announced that a constitutional committee would be formed (and named the individual who would head the committee), which was

53 See Lahcen Achy, "The ADCR 2011: Poverty in the Arab World – Successes and Limits of Morocco's Experience," United Nations Development Programme (2011).

54 Paul Silverstein, "Weighing Morocco's New Constitution," Middle East Report Online (May 7, 2011).

55 See "Morocco Country Report," Economist Intelligence Unit (December 2010), at 11.

56 See Bennani-Chraïbi and Jeghllaly (2012), at 116.

57 See Slyomovics (2011).

58 See Mohamed al-Makhdhairi, "Morocco's February 20th Movement: The Youth Revolt while Islamists Rule" (حركة «20 فبراير» المغربية: الشباب يثورون والإسلاميون يحكمون), Bidayat Magazine (Summer 2012).

59 The same attitude and strategy has been in place for many decades. See Saloua Zerhouni, "Morocco: Reconciling Continuity and Change," in Volker Perthes (ed.), Arab Elites: Negotiating the Politics of Change, Lynne Rienner Publishers (2004).

60 The address was formally delivered to mark the completion of an ad hoc commission that had been established to recommend a new framework for decentralization. See Royal Speech, March 9, 2011, in the author's possession.

required to consult with "political parties, trade unions, youth organisations" among others. The monarch also set out seven fundamental principles, which taken together informed virtually all of the main contributions that were made by the constitutional committee. They included the need to formally recognize Morocco's cultural diversity (including Tamazight); to broaden the scope of application of basic rights and freedoms; to strengthen the constitutional council; and to strengthen the separation of powers (by providing that the prime minister should be drawn from the largest parliamentary party); among others. By establishing the committee's scope of work, the monarch essentially precluded it from venturing outside these specific areas. The Committee consisted of twenty members, mainly jurists, academics, and senior state officials. The monarch maintained a strong influence on the committee through a number of key members. The Committee consulted civil society organizations and state institutions (although the February 20th movement formally boycotted the process), and received 200 memoranda from political parties, civil society organizations, and others on what they hoped the constitution would provide for them.[61] Some commentators noted with disappointment that most of the proposals that were offered did not touch on royal prerogatives.[62] Also, there were no rules on how these proposals should be taken into consideration. Others noted in response that past Moroccan constitutional processes had never solicited public input and that the Constitutional Committee's public consultations for the first time created an environment in which the general public was encouraged to discuss constitutional reform.[63] There is little question, however, that in comparative practice, the amount of consultation that was carried out and the time that was made available did considerably limit the scope for meaningful contributions to be made.

[61] One such memorandum is representative of many of the others that were submitted in that it makes only minor recommendations, which essentially consists of maintaining the system in place at the time and reforming a small number of institutions and practices. The memorandum itself is sixteen pages long but sets out its recommendations on page thirteen, after a twelve-page introduction. The first recommendation consists of recognizing Tamazight identity, which was already provided for in the king's March 9, 2011 address. See Hussaîn Terjaoui, "Memorandum sur la Réforme de la Constitution du Royaume du Maroc," ISTIGOP (May 30, 2011), in the author's possession.

[62] Maghraoui (2011), 682 and 686 (according to the author "[i]nstead of heated debates, at least in the public sphere, there was a disturbing consensus"); see Mohamed Madani, "Constitutionalisme sans démocratie: la fabrication et la mise en oeuvre de la Constitution marocaine de 2011," in Omar Bendourou, Rkia el Mossadeq, and Mohammed Madani (eds.), LA NOUVELLE CONSTITUTION MAROCAINE À L'ÉPREUVE DE LA PRATIQUE, Éditions la Croisée des Chemins (2014), at 71 (in which the author describes political parties as having behaved as if they were part of the "deep state").

[63] "Faut-il reviser la Constitution? La réponse de Nadia Bernoussi," Medias24 (July 18, 2019).

The draft constitution was officially circulated on June 17, 2011, leaving only two weeks for public debate. The constitution was adopted by 98.5 percent of voters and with an official 72.65 percent participation rate.

2011 Constitution: The constitution goes far beyond previous rounds of amendments and introduces a number of important changes. It is almost double in length in comparison to the 1996 Constitution, which indicates a willingness to regulate the work of key state institutions. For the first time, the monarch must appoint the prime minister from within the largest parliamentary party (Article 47). The wording does not specifically state that the monarch must choose the candidate of the party's choice, but it nevertheless represents a major departure in comparison to past practice. The constitution also provides the parliamentary opposition with significant and guaranteed rights (including the right to head specific committees, to influence parliament's agenda, and to public finance; Article 10).[64] A constitutional court is established, which has the power to interpret the constitutions and to exercise judicial review (Articles 132–134). The constitution also introduces a number of key developments, including "advanced regionalisation" (Article 1). The term itself is not properly defined but it comes in response to persistent and growing complaints by the country's peripheral regions of marginalization. The relevant section in the constitution provides far more detail on how regionalization will be organized but still manages to leave out crucial detail. Article 135 provides that regional and local councils will be directly elected, while Article 138 states that council resolutions must be executed. On the other hand, no indication is given as to what powers local governments will exercise, and the relationship between central, regional, and local governments is also not clarified (Articles 140, 146) leaving open the possibility that these local authorities will remain powerless. The protection of individual rights remains mainly unchanged. Specific provisions falsely suggest that rights are limitless by formulating them in absolute terms (such as the provision on speech; Article 25), or defer entirely to subsequent law without giving any indication as to how far that legislation can go in limiting the right (such as for assembly; Article 29). These provisions are so vague that they essentially do not provide any meaningful protection. At the same time, the National Council for Human Rights is now formally recognized in the constitution,

64 Abderrahim El Maslouhi, "The Morrocan Parliament under the 2011 Constitution: Composition and Functions" (البرلمان المغربي في ظل دستور 29 يوليو 2011: دراسة في التأليف والوظائف), in Sa'ad al-Deen al-Othmani (ed.), Morocco's Experience with Constitutional Reform (تجربة الإصلاح الدستوري في المغرب), Arab International Relations Forum (2016), at 95.

and individuals can now appeal against legislation on the basis that they impose unconstitutional limitations on fundamental rights (Article 133).

Constitutional Monarchy: To this day, Morocco cannot be described as a constitutional monarchy, given that the monarch maintains more authority than most heads of state or chief executive officers in democracies. The monarch has a dual function as both the formal and effective head of state, and the head of the community of believers (through the title "commander of the faithful"; Article 41). The monarch's power is limited by law, but successive constitutions have given the monarch very significant authority without any meaningful accountability mechanisms. It is established convention that the monarch's person is immune from any legal actions, and his legal acts (known as "*dahirs*") can also not be challenged before the courts. This includes administrative acts, such as the establishment of institutions and the appointment or dismissal of judges from the bench.[65]

Royal Prerogative: The 2011 Constitution modifies some of these practices but leaves the monarchy firmly at the top of the state's decision-making process. The monarch continues to exercise very significant authority, far more than most directly elected presidents, and is not subject to any meaningful oversight. He is no longer sacred, but he remains the "commander of the faithful" (Article 41), his personality is "inviolable" (Article 46), and he is now the "supreme arbiter between institutions" (Article 42). The monarch also remains the head of the judiciary (Article 56) and continues to wield major influence over its internal functioning. Article 42 provides that royal decrees must be countersigned, which is an important advance in terms of democratic accountability, but it also sets out a significant number of exceptions. The monarch alone determines the composition and powers of the High Council of Ulema, the highest religious body in the country (Article 41); selects the Prime Minister (although he must select a member of the largest parliamentary party) (Article 47); dissolves parliament practically at will (Article 51); approves the appointment of all of the judicial council's members (Article 57); proclaims a state of exception (Article 59); and appoints half of the members of the constitutional court and selects its president (Article 130).[66] Finally, the 2011 Constitution codifies and reinforces the monarch's control over state policy. The 2011 Constitution also grants the monarch veto power

65 Mohammed Hashas, "Exceptionalism Examined: Constitutional Insights Pre- and Post-2011," Instituto Affari Internazionali (2013), at 12.

66 The draft constitution that was originally submitted for public discussion prior to the referendum mistakenly indicated that the king and the prime minister should jointly select the constitutional court's president (see Bulletin Officiel, Royaume du Maroc, 100th Year, Number 5952 bis); see Madani (2014), at 73–74.

over the state's strategic orientation by creating a complex institutional arrangement within the executive that places the monarch firmly in control. Article 92 provides for the establishment of the "council of government," which is responsible for drawing up the "general policy of the state," which must then be presented to a second executive body known as the "council of ministers" (Article 92). Article 48 provides that the "council of ministers" is presided over by the monarch, and also includes the prime minister and the ministers. Article 49 confirms that the "council of ministers" is responsible for deciding the "strategic orientation of the State's policy." What this means is that ministers draw up state policy and must submit it for approval by a second body that they themselves are the only members of, the only difference being that the monarch presides over the meetings of that second body. Effectively speaking, the 2011 Constitution provides the monarch with a veto on state policy. Some commentators expressed significant exasperation that the monarch continues to wield so much influence.[67] Others have noted that the fact that royal prerogative can only be exercised in a limited number of areas is not insignificant.[68] There is little question, however, that the current system of government, and in particular the absence of meaningful accountability mechanisms, is largely out of step with democratic processes elsewhere.

SUDAN

Egyptian and Mahdist Rule: For centuries, the territory that today makes up the Sudanese state was governed by successive sultanates covering different parts of territory, including the Funj Sultanate and the Fur State.[69] In 1820 the viceroy of Egypt invaded the country, unifying it for the first time under Turkish–Egyptian rule. For the next century and a half, Sudan's constitutional and political development remained intrinsically linked with Egypt's own situation. Egypt's purpose was to extract as many resources as possible (including slaves) from the country. To support that effort, it extended its own autocratic system of government, bureaucracy, and a court system into the

[67] Ibid., at 80–82.

[68] Abderrahim El Maslouhi, "Séparation des pouvoirs et régime parlementaire dans la nouvelle Constituition marocaine," in La Constitution Marocaine de 2011: Analyses et Commentaires, Centre d'études internationals (2012), at 99. Note, however, that past Moroccan constitutions also limited the areas in which the royal prerogative was absolute (see, for example, Article 29(2) of the 1992 Constitution).

[69] M. W. Daly, Darfur's Sorrow: A History of Destruction and Genocide, Cambridge University Press (2007); and Peter Malcolm Holt, A Modern History of the Sudan: From the Funj Sultanate to the Present Day, Weidenfeld and Nicolson (1961).

country, which was administered by a governor general who was appointed by Cairo. By 1881 Egyptian rule had collapsed as a result of the state's debt burden and other factors, which allowed a local leader (the "Mahdi"), who claimed the divine right to rule, to take control. Egyptian and Ottoman forces were defeated and a new state was established (the Mahdist State) that modeled itself on the early Islamic period. The Mahdi was the head of the state's executive, and exercised both legislative and judicial functions as well. Successors to the Mahdi were designated, each of which exercised specific functions (including, for example, treasurer and chief justice).[70] Taxation and bureaucracy were simplified from the earlier Egyptian systems but eventually reacquired much of their original complexity.

British Period: In 1898, after the United Kingdom took control of Egypt, the two countries dispatched joint military forces to recover control over Sudan. A two-page agreement (the "Condominium") was entered into between the two countries, formally in order to share sovereign control and authority over Sudan, but in effect consolidating all effective decision-making authority in British hands while granting a ceremonial role only to the Egyptian viceroy.[71] Article 3 provided that Sudan would be governed by a governor general who would be formally appointed by the Egyptian viceroy "on the recommendation" of the British government, and who could not be removed without the British government's consent. During the half century that followed, the governor general, who was granted both executive and legislative authority (Article 4) combined with military authority, answered only to London. A legal secretary was established who was responsible for drawing up legislation and regulations. The country was divided into provinces, each of which was headed by a governor who was responsible to the governor general.[72] Sudan was left without a constitution during this period, but through key statutes of constitutional character, the British encouraged obedience while maintaining and strengthening the foundations of nondemocratic rule. A few months after they took control over the country, the British enacted a criminal code that was used to limit the free expression of ideas and the right of association.[73] On occasion courts would rule against colonial authorities, but in politically sensitive cases, the courts leaned in favor of the

[70] See P. M. Holt and M. W. Daly, A History of the Sudan: From the Coming of Islam to the Present Day, Longman (2000), at 84–85.

[71] See The Sudan: 1899–1953, British Information Services (1953), at 51–52.

[72] P. B. Broadbent, "Self-government," International Affairs, Vol. 30, No. 3 (July 1954), 326.

[73] Mark Fathi Massoud, Law's Fragile State: Colonial, Authoritarian and Humanitarian Legacies in Sudan, Cambridge University Press (2013), at 49.

colonial authorities.[74] Throughout their period of domination over the Sudan, British colonial officials maintained that their primary interest was to serve the local population. That view was supported by the fact that there was no plan to settle Europeans in the country and because the colonial government only employed a small numbers of foreign officials, which supposedly supported the development of a national administration based on the assumption that the Sudanese were not capable of governing themselves.[75] Simultaneously, however, British colonial authorities imposed their control over the country by introducing segregation, and racism in the country, particularly toward southerners, and by deforming the identity of the local population through legislation and government policy. The effect was that the British legacy on the eve of independence was a deep sense of national disunity.[76]

Independence: The issue of Sudan's future status grew in importance as a result of a number of factors, including that the United Kingdom was withdrawing from many of the territories that it controlled. By 1943, pressure from the nationalist movement on the colonial authorities led them to establish an advisory council, which was widely considered to be unrepresentative and ineffectual.[77] In 1947, this was replaced by an executive council and a legislative assembly, the membership of which consisted of a combination of appointed, directly elected, and indirectly elected members.[78] In 1952, the Egyptian revolution accelerated the race toward independence.[79] Prior to the revolution, the Egyptian authorities had insisted that Sudan should remain a part of its own national territory, which complicated discussions on to whom the United Kingdom should surrender power.[80] The new revolutionary government prioritized securing British withdrawal of the region and so encouraged their Sudanese counterparts to press in favor of complete independence and the departure of British forces.[81] The United Kingdom's hand was forced

74 Ibid., at 62.

75 See, for example, "Letter from Sir R Howe to Sir o Sargent," FO 371/73472, no 343 (January 4, 1949), quoted in Douglas H. Johnson (ed.), Sudan: British Documents on the End of Empire, Part I: 1942–1950, Series B, Vol. 5, The Stationary Office (1998) at 351.

76 See for example Noah R. Bassil, The Post-Colonial State and Civil War in Sudan: The Origins of Conflict in Darfur, I.B. Tauris & Co. (2013), at 88.

77 Peter M. Holt, "Sudanese Nationalism and Self-determination: Part II," Middle East Journal, Vol. 10, No. 4 (Autumn, 1956), 368–378.

78 Ordinance 9 (1948), Legislative Supplement to Sudan Government Gazette (June 15, 1948).

79 Broadbent (1954).

80 The Egyptian government even went so far as to unilaterally declare Egypt and Sudan united and published a constitution for Sudan, which did not gain significant traction within Sudan; see Robert O. Collins, A History of Modern Sudan, Cambridge University Press (2008), at 59.

81 Ibid., at 62.

and an agreement in 1953 established the mechanism through which the Sudanese could decide their own future.[82] The agreement provided for a three-year transition period, during which the governor general was to exercise his powers "with the aid of" a five-member commission (only two members of which were Sudanese) (Articles 3–4). A Constituent Assembly (Article 10) would have first to decide whether Sudan should remain united with Egypt and then draw up a constitution "compatible with the decision that shall have been taken" (Article 12). The agreement also provided for the adoption of a Self-Government Statute, which purported to codify institutional arrangements that would govern Sudan during the transition.[83] The arrangements were classically colonial and post-colonial in nature: Close to no detail was given on individual liberties (Article 7), some of which were not even mentioned (including freedom of assembly); the governor general had full control over the executive, including through the appointment of the cabinet (Article 13) and could not be held accountable for his actions; the governor general appointed a large number of parliamentarians at his discretion (Article 31); and the governor general also appointed the chief justice (Article 83). At the end of 1953, a new parliament was elected that declared independence on January 1, 1956. In December 1955, on the eve of independence, the Self-Government Statute was modified and readopted as a Transitional Constitution.[84] The new text provided that a five-member "sovereignty council" was to be indirectly elected by the parliament, although the composition of the first such council had already been determined and was recognized by the Transitional Constitution (Article 10). The council exercised head of state functions, including acting as commander in chief of the armed forces (Article 11) and appointing the chief justice and all members of the high court (Article 97(1)). There were no practical means through which council members could be removed from office, apart from a finding that the member had violated the constitution, which required the support of three-quarters of the members of the entire parliament, including appointed members (Article 22), an impossible threshold and one typically reserved only for directly elected heads of state. The council was required to elect a chair (Article 14) and all its decisions were to be taken by

[82] Agreement between the Government of the United Kingdom of Great Britain and Northern Ireland and the Egyptian Government concerning Self Government and Self-Determination for the Sudan (February 12, 1953), Treaty Series No. 47 (1953), Her Majesty's Stationery Office; see D. K. Sen, "Recent Constitutional Developments in the Sudan," India Quarterly, Vol. 10, No. 3 (July–September 1954), 225–247.

[83] Ibid.

[84] Mohamed Ahmed Mahgoub, Democracy on Trial: Reflections on Arab and African Politics, Andre Deutsch (1974), at 177.

majority (Article 16). Parliament also elected the prime minister (Article 23), who in turn nominated all the ministers (Article 24(2)).

Instability and War: Despite the apparent consensus of opinion in favor of independence, the country's significant internal divisions have since contributed to over half a century of violence and volatility. The country's main political groups have been sharply divided on which system of government should be adopted, whether Islamic law should be imposed, and whether and to what extent state power should be concentrated in the capital. In particular, communities in the west, east, and south argued in favor of arrangements that would redress historical marginalization, including greater autonomy, cultural rights (given that large numbers of Sudanese do not speak Arabic as a mother tongue), religious freedom, and access to public investment in infrastructure.[85] Meanwhile, centrist forces that were concentrated in the capital had very little appetite for genuine action in favor of decentralization. These divisions have had a number of consequences. First, prior to 2019, the country had been governed by civilians for only thirteen years, spread over three periods (1956–1959, 1964–1969, and 1986–1989), each of which failed to negotiate a permanent democratic constitution.[86] Instead, on all three occasions, civilian authorities applied the 1956 Transitional Constitution, applying minor amendments only as it became necessary to do so. Efforts to negotiate a constitution were obstructed by major political, economic, and security challenges and endless debates on whether Sudan should be established as an Islamic republic.[87] Second, the failures of the political class to reach agreement encouraged elements within the armed forces to view themselves as the only anchor of stability in the country. They have therefore carried out three separate military coup d'états (in 1959, 1969, and 1989), which led to five periods of three years of military rule in the country. The military-led governments adopted the 1973 Constitution and the 1998 Constitution, both of which concentrated power in the hands of the president (albeit to varying degrees). The 1973 Constitution did not originally establish Sudan as an Islamic republic but ruling authorities moved in that direction over a number of years, ultimately imposing Islamic penal laws in 1983. The

[85] See, for example, Ahmed T. el-Gaili, "Federalism and the Tyranny of Religious Majorities: Challenges to Islamic Federalism in Sudan," Harvard International Law Journal, Vol. 45 (2004), 503.

[86] For an account of some of the issues that were raised during the constitutional negotiations that took place from 1956 to 1959, see H. Kumarasingham (ed.), Constitution-Maker: Selected Writings of Sir Ivor Jennings, Cambridge University Press (2014), at 207–216.

[87] Mahgoub (1974).

1998 Constitution formally established Sudan as an Islamic republic.[88] Remarkably, all three military regimes were brought to an end through civilian-led revolutions, the most recent of which took place in 2019 (see later).[89] Third, and perhaps most importantly, Sudan has lived through decades of internal conflict, leading to millions of dead and displaced. Various peace initiatives and negotiations that took place throughout that period failed to end the conflict.

2005 Interim Constitution: For a combination of reasons, including a changed international environment following the 2001 attacks on the World Trade Center, negotiations to end the conflict between north and south resumed. In 2005 a Comprehensive Peace Agreement between the government of Sudan and the Sudan People's Liberation Movement/Sudan People's Liberation Army ended the civil war. Pursuant to that agreement, a new interim constitution entered into force that for the first time established a plural system of government that explicitly limited the national executive's authority.[90] The new text proposed to resolve the relationship between north and south first by establishing a Government of Southern Sudan (Part 11), which would exercise wide powers (Schedule B), and second by providing that, within six years of the Interim Constitution's entry into force, a referendum would be organized in Southern Sudan to allow the people to decide whether the south should secede from the north (Article 219–222). In addition, the Interim Constitution maintained that Islamic Sharia would be a source of legislation for nationally enacted legislation that applied only to the north (Article 5). The independence referendum took place in 2011 and led to the establishment of South Sudan as an independent country. The loss of South Sudan's oil revenues precipitated a number of economic shocks, which worsened after South Sudan itself descended into civil war.[91] At the end of 2019, Sudan's economic situation ranked only slightly above Yemen's.[92]

2014 Dialogue: In January 2014 following several rounds of protests that were violently repressed by security services, the government organized a

88 See Kristine Mo, 'CONTESTED CONSTITUTIONS: CONSTITUTIONAL DEVELOPMENT IN SUDAN 1953–2005, Chr. Michelson Institute (May 2014).

89 See W. J. Berridge, UPRISINGS IN MODERN SUDAN: THE "KHARTOUM SPRINGS" OF 1964 AND 1985, Bloomsbury Academic (January 2015).

90 For more on how the 2005 interim constitution was negotiated, see Zaid Al-Ali and Philipp Dann, "The Internationalized Pouvoir Constituant – Constitution-Making under External Influence in Iraq, Sudan and East Timor," MAX PLANCK YEARBOOK OF UNITED NATIONS LAW, No. 10 (2006), 423–463.

91 Khalid Hassan Elbeely, "The Economic Impact of Southern Sudan Secession," INTERNATIONAL JOURNAL OF BUSINESS AND SOCIAL RESEARCH, Vol. 3, No. 7 (July 2013), 78.

92 See, for example, Economist Intelligence Unit, Sudan Country Report, October 29, 2019, at 18.

national dialogue conference for the purpose of debating possible changes to the system of government, individual rights, peace building, economic reform, and foreign relations. The dialogue process ended in October 2016 and resulted in hundreds of recommendations on a range of issues, including constitutional reform.[93] Many critics argued that the government manipulated the proceedings to prevent or reduce the likelihood that any meaningful recommendations would be made.[94] In fact, the constitutional amendments that were entered into following the dialogue run contrary to what was agreed by the delegates. By way of example, Recommendation 12 of the dialogue's governance working group states that Sudan's "federal system of government should be developed."[95] Instead, the amendments reconcentrated significant power in the president's office, first by granting the president the power to appoint all state governors (who were previously elected; Article 179 (a)), and second by increasing the powers of the National Security and Intelligence Services (NISS).[96] Neither of those amendments were provided for by the dialogue, and caused for the system of government to regress back in favor of the arrangements that were in force under the 1998 Constitution.

Revolution: In December 2018 a protest movement led by the Sudanese Professionals Associations (SPA),[97] opposition political parties, and others unified under the banner of the "Forces of the Declaration of Freedom and Change" (FFC).[98] Their stated objective was to remove al-Bashir from power through peaceful protest and to form a national transitional government.[99] On April 11, 2019, following months of sustained protest and civil unrest, a newly established Transitional Military Council (TMC) removed al-Bashir from power and granted itself supreme executive power. Shortly after seizing power, the Military Council announced that it intended to administer the country for

93 See National Dialogue Outcomes, on file with the author.

94 For more, see Nasredeen Abdulbari, "Post-National Dialogue Constitutional Amendments in Sudan: Undermining Fundamental Rights and Decentralization?," Constitutionnet, December 14, 2017.

95 See National Dialogue Outcomes, on file with the author.

96 See 2017 Constitutional Amendments, entered into on May 3, 2017, on file with the author.

97 The Sudanese Professionals Association is an alliance of Sudan's largest professional groups, namely the Central Committee of Sudanese Doctors, the Sudanese Journalists Network, and the Democratic Lawyers Association.

98 An English language translation of the FFC's founding statement is available at www.sudaneseprofessionals.org/en/declaration-of-freedom-and-change/.

99 Article 1 of the Declaration of Freedom and Change provides that the movement's objective was "[t]he immediate and unconditional end of General Omar Al Bashir's presidency and the conclusion of his administration."

the following two years, which was immediately rejected by the FFC.[100] During the months that followed, the FFC and the TMC negotiated the contents of a transition plan toward civilian rule. The negotiations were interrupted on several occasions, most importantly in early June 2019 when security forces allegedly killed more than one hundred and injured thousands of unarmed protesters. The domestic, regional, and international response to the massacre was overwhelmingly negative, which encouraged the parties, particularly the TMC, to reach an agreement as soon as possible.[101] A breakthrough was finally achieved on July 17, 2019 when the two sides signed a document entitled the "Political Agreement for the Establishment of Governing Structures and Institutions in the Transitional Period" (the "Political Agreement").[102] The Political Agreement sets out the transitional period's main objectives, a timeframe for the transition, and the formation of a commission of inquiry. The Agreement also provides for the formation of an eleven-member Sovereignty Council and provides some indication on how the transitional parliament will be composed and how it will function. These arrangements established for the first time a power-sharing arrangement between civilian and military forces with a view to ultimately transitioning to full civilian control on a reasonable timeline.

Constitutional Charter: The Political Agreement precipitated the adoption of a "Constitutional Charter" on August 17, 2019.[103] The Charter replaces the 2005 constitution and takes the form of an interim constitution. It includes significant detail on how the Sudanese state will be organized institutionally during the following three years. The Charter provides that the sovereignty council is the head of state, and is composed of eleven members, of whom six should be civilians and five should have a military background.[104] It also provides that the council should be chaired by one of the military members for the initial period, and that a civilian member should take over on May 17,

[100] See Magdi el-Gizouli, "The Fall of al-Bashir: Mapping Contestation Forces in Sudan," Arab Reform Initiative, April 12, 2019.

[101] The African Union immediately suspended Sudan's participation in all African Union activities "until the effective establishment of a civilian-led Transitional Authority." See "The 854th Meeting of the Peace and Security Council on the Situation in The Sudan," African Union Peace and Security Council, June 6, 1989.

[102] The Political Agreement is available in both Arabic and English at http://constitutionnet.org/vl/item/sudan-political-agreement.

[103] The Constitutional Charter's Arabic original is available at http://moj.gov.sd/files/download/144. An unofficial English language translation is available at http://constitutionnet.org/vl/item/sudan-constitutional-declaration-august-2019.

[104] Article 11(2).

2021.[105] The Charter also provides that the council of ministers and the parliament should be civilian-led, and includes significant detail on how the political formation process should take place. The Charter's Article 8 sets out a list of sixteen agenda items that all state agencies are required to work to achieve during the transitional period. Many of these items are general in nature and probably not fully achievable during the transitional period (e.g. "resolving the economic crisis," Article 8(4)). Most importantly, the Charter prioritizes "[a]chieving a just and comprehensive peace, ending the war by addressing the roots of the Sudanese problem, treating its effects, taking into account the provisional preferential measures for war-affected regions, underdeveloped regions and the most affected groups" (Article 8(1)). It also provides that a mechanism should be established for drafting a permanent constitution for the Republic of Sudan (Article 8(9)), which has yet to be formed. On how the future constitution will be drafted, the only indication that is provided by the Constitutional Charter is that "a national, constitutional conference [should be held] before the end of the transitional period" (Article 8 (10)) and that a Constitutional Drafting and Constitutional Conference Commission should be formed (article 38(3)(c)). This leaves open the questions as to what the conference's objective will be; who will participate; and how the draft constitution will be prepared, debated, and endorsed.

Juba Peace Agreement: Pursuant to the Constitutional Charter's requirements, representatives of the new governing authorities in Khartoum negotiated with representatives of rebel groups in Juba, the capital of neighboring South Sudan. The final agreement (the "Juba Agreement for Peace in Sudan" or the "Juba Peace Agreement") was delayed as a result of a number of factors, including the spread of COVID-19, but was formally signed at a ceremony on October 3, 2020.[106] The Juba Agreement amends the 2019 Constitutional Charter in a number of important ways and also predetermines much of the yet-to-be drafted permanent constitution. According to the Agreement, Sudan is to be established as an asymmetric federation. A region is to be established in Darfur that will exercise a different set of powers to other parts of the country. The Agreement contains a large amount of detail on the powers that specific regions will exercise, but is close to silent on a range of issues, including but not limited to the national government's structure, the internal structure of federal regions, and the composition of revenue sharing commissions. The Agreement includes a significant amount of detail on how the

[105] Article 11(3).

[106] The full text of the Juba Peace Agreement is available at https://constitutionnet.org/vl/item/sudan-peace-agreement.

constitutional process will be organized. The Agreement provides that a conference on the system of government should take place, a timeframe, an agenda, and some indication of the participants have also been determined. However, it is still unclear what the conference's purpose will be. Finally, the Agreement establishes a complex web of transitional justice mechanisms, including truth and reconciliation mechanisms, investigations, and the possibility of pardons. In some cases, the Agreement appears to prioritize judicial mechanisms over reconciliation, although that is not stated explicitly. At the time of writing, the drafting of the country's new constitutional process had not yet begun, and the country was struggling to cope with rapidly declining standards of living, which was causing many to doubt that the transition would survive. For the transition to have any chance of success, a permanent constitution that delivers real benefits to the general population and that enjoys some form of democratic legitimacy will have to be negotiated while progress is made on interim governance, all within a reasonable timeline.[107]

ALGERIA

Ottoman Period: In 1519 the Ottoman Empire claimed sovereignty over Algeria after local elites requested their assistance out of concern that European powers could invade and take control over the country. In the centuries that followed, they established a countrywide political system that had all the characteristics of an (undemocratic) modern state. During the first century of this period, the Empire named governors (pashas) for three-year terms. By 1671 after a period of instability following accusations that successive governors were corrupt, local elites formed a governing council (divan) that had as part of its functions to elect a ruler (dey). The ruler had both administrative and judicial functions, which eliminated the possibility of any form of oversight.[108] The new system of government provided that the state treasurer was the first minister, who would traditionally replace the ruler on his death, while the state treasurer would be replaced by the commander in chief of the army, which ensured that whoever assumed the highest office in the country would first have to occupy other key offices.[109] Despite the fact that this system

[107] For a full commentary of the Juba Peace Agreement, see Zaid Al-Ali, "Summary and Analysis of Sudan's 2020 Peace Agreements," Constitutionnet (December 2020), available at https://constitutionnet.org/vl/item/summary-and-analysis-sudans-2020-peace-agreements.

[108] Claude Collot, Les Institutions de l'Algérie Durant la Période Coloniale (1830–1962), Editions du CRNS (1987), at 166–167.

[109] Jamil M. Abun-Nasr, A History of the Maghrib in the Islamic Period, Cambridge University Press (1987), at 160.

was developed locally, the Empire formally recognized the new rulers' status when it granted the title of pasha to the dey. During the Ottoman period, the national territory was organized in three provinces (beyliks), each of which had its own internal structures and subdivisions. Local councils were composed by prominent tribes and families who were granted a range of benefits including tax exemptions. In the early nineteenth century, regular uprisings and bouts of rioting and violence were taking place due to food shortages. In 1817 a new ruler was elected whose first act was to replace the entire council of ministers with individuals who were selected based on merit. These reforms were not enough to contain unrest in the countryside, which made the country vulnerable to foreign invasion.

Colonial Period: In 1830 the French army invaded and occupied Algiers, bringing the Ottoman period to a sudden end. A nationwide rebellion erupted, which involved the establishment of a new state over the ruins of the defunct Ottoman authority. A number of key reforms were entered into during this period, including redrawing internal boundaries.[110] The leaders of the rebellion were ultimately defeated in 1847, leaving French authorities virtually unopposed during the century that followed. On July 22, 1834 the government of France issued an ordinance that delegated a military governor general, who was answerable to the ministry of war, to administer both military and civilian affairs. Article 5 provided that all future ordinances relating to the future of the country would be prepared by the governor general and issued by the ministry of war.[111] France established a classically colonial enterprise that offered the best farm land to European settlers for the purpose of extracting resources to benefit the mainland. The settler population eventually grew to one million in number. As a corollary of that system, the original population of Algeria was subjected to arbitrary rule. They were not represented in the parliament and were left without options in the case of abuse of authority by colonial officials. This inequitable system remained in place until national liberation 130 years later. In 1844 the governor of Algeria established the Arab Bureaus (Bureaux Arabes) for the purpose of "organizing the colonial enterprise," which included pacifying the local population through force of arms and transforming societal and economic norms.[112] Officers in the Bureaus exercised both administrative and judicial functions, thereby continuing the

[110] See Raphael Danziger, Abd al-Qadr and the Algerians: Resistance to the French and Internal Consolidation, Africana Publishers (1977).

[111] See Collection Complete des Lois, Décrets, Ordonnances, Réglemens et Avis du Conseil d'État, Éditions Officielles (1834), at 200–201.

[112] Collot (1987), at 40.

Ottoman practice of preventing any meaningful form of oversight over executive officials. French officers were accused of arbitrary behavior, including acts of summary and brutal justice.[113] In order to reinforce France's capacity for control, the large administrative boundaries that had been developed during the rebellion were abandoned in favor of small units that would be easier to control. In 1848 France's new constitution provided that Algeria was integrated into the national territory, although it was also clearly indicated that it would be governed through its own "separate" laws (Article 109). The text also provided that Algeria should be represented in the national legislature (Articles 21 and 46), although no indication was given as to whether the local population would participate in the elections, a major point of contention that would last until independence. In 1881 a Code of Indigenous People (Code de l'Indigénat) was adopted, which subjected Muslim Algerians to a series of penalties that were not applicable to European settlers and excluded Muslims from the civil code in matters of personal status (marriage, inheritance, etc.). The governor general maintained the power to impose administrative detention in a variety of cases that were deliberately kept vague. All of these practices were left without any meaningful oversight.

Liberation: Following the end of the Second World War France made only modest progress toward democratization in Algeria and refused to countenance any discussion of independence. After countless acts of violence against the civilian population, nationalist Algerians formed the National Liberation Front (FLN) and a national liberation army for the purpose of waging a war of national liberation against colonial rule.[114] In 1956 the FLN met clandestinely to establish the institutions that would execute the war and that would establish a vision for the postwar period. A National Council for the Algerian Revolution was established as the representative assembly of a sovereign and independent Algeria. The council deliberated on a number of fundamental issues, including the shape and form of the future independent state's constitution. The council met for the last time in June 1962 in Tripoli, Libya, where it adopted its plan for the implementation of the "popular

[113] John Ruedy, Modern Algeria: The Origins and Development of a Nation, Indiana University Press (1992), at 73.

[114] On May 8, 1945, as France celebrated its own liberation from Nazi Germany, Algerians organized marches to demand independence. The French military and settler militias responded with indiscriminate violence leading to approximately 7,000 dead over a period of days; see James McDougall, A History of Algeria, Cambridge University Press (2017), at 179–180.

democratic revolution."[115] The program called for a popular revolution that would be led by the rural population and would be assisted by urban working class and young Algerians. From 1954 to 1962, a brutal conflict raged that left hundreds of thousands dead. On March 19, 1962, a series of agreements were entered into between France and the FLN, which required for Algerians to be consulted on whether they supported independence (a foregone conclusion). The agreements also provided that, in the event Algerians did choose to become independent, "the Algerian state will freely determine its own institutions and will choose the political and social system that will be best suited to its interests."[116] Those agreements, as well as France's scorched earth policies and the FLN's response, caused the near totality of the settler population to flee the country, mostly well before sovereignty was formally transferred to the new authorities. This led to the takeover of the country by the FLN, a militarized revolutionary force that was both deeply divided and had little interest in competing for elections or in democratic accountability. In fact, early disagreements on how power should be exercised were resolved militarily.[117]

1963 Constitution: Independent Algeria inherited a number of legacies from its colonial past, including undemocratic institutional arrangements and the fact that the state was left entirely in the control of a liberation movement that itself was deeply divided. The intense competition within its various circles, which was resolved through less than democratic means, left an indelible mark on the early post-independence period and can still be felt today. An effort to draw up a constitution started immediately after independence and was deeply impacted by this competition. In September 1962 a constituent assembly was elected from a single list of FLN candidates. One of the leaders of the independence movement was nominated as its speaker. Deliberations commenced and various options for how the future system of government would be organized took place. However, the FLN's monopoly on the assembly was still too inclusive for some of its leaders, who argued that the assembly was not properly authorized to draft the constitution, and that the task should be left to the party and its leadership only. By April 1963, the president of the republic had won undisputed control over the party's politbureau, which he then directed to draw up a draft. A few months later, a

[115] See Azghīdī Muḥammad Hasan, The Soummam Conference and the Developments of Algeria's Revolution of National Liberation 1956–1962 (مؤتمر الصومام وتطور ثورة التحرير الوطني الجزائرية، 1956-1962), Dar Houma (2005).

[116] See Article 1, Section A, Chapter II, March 19, 1962 Governmental Declarations in Relation to Algeria.

[117] Ruedy (1992), at 194.

meeting of party loyalists was organized in a cinema where the party's own draft of the constitution was presented.[118] The assembly's speaker had not been consulted and objected strenuously to the draft's contents and resigned in protest.[119] The decision to task an appointed committee to draw up a constitution behind closed doors would be repeated several times over the next half century. Subsequent processes also included public consultations, which had very little if any impact on the concentration of power in the hands of the president. The end result was that the 1963 Constitution was blatantly undemocratic. It established a hyperpresidential system, in which a single individual controlled the executive completely and had sufficient leverage to control parliament and the judiciary as well. Algeria was clearly established as a socialist state, a principle that virtually all state bodies were required to uphold (including the judiciary; Article 62), and Islam was established as the "state religion" but not a source of legislation (Article 4). The Constitution provided that the National Liberation Front was the only political party that was authorized to operate in the country (Article 23); that all members of the legislature should be nominated by the Front (Article 27); and that basic rights could not be used to undermine national unity, state institutions, the people's socialist ambitions, and the Front's unity (Article 22). The president of the republic was also to be nominated by the Front (Article 39) and was the ex officio head of the high judicial council (Article 65). Subsequent constitutions tweaked some of these arrangements one way or the other but always made sure to main the overall framework.

1976 Constitution: In the years that followed, the then-president sought to marginalize rivals by further concentrating power in his hands. In 1965 the military responded by carrying out a coup d'état. The president was jailed and eventually exiled, which brought the internal rivalries within the ruling class to an end. The 1963 Constitution and the parliament were suspended and the country was left without a fundamental document for the following eleven years. A "council of the revolution" was established that was dominated by the military and maintained the FLN's monopoly on power. By 1976 the military regime sought to establish a constitutional basis for its own system of governance. A "national charter" was adopted by referendum, followed by a constitution later on in the same year. The 1976 Constitution was much longer than its predecessor and proposed to steer state and society in a more firmly socialist direction. At the same time, however, many of the 1963 Constitution's most fundamental pillars were maintained. This included the FLN remaining the

[118] See Hervé Bourges, L'Algérie à l'épreuve du pouvoir (1962–1967), B. Grasset (1967).
[119] See Ferhat Abbas, L'Indépendance Confisquée, Flammario (1984).

only party that was permitted to operate in the country (Articles 94 and 95). The system of government also remained firmly presidential. The president remained firmly in control over the government formation process (Article 113); could dissolve the parliament at any moment and without giving reasons (Article 163); and remained ex officio head of the high judicial council (Article 181). The Constitution purported to promote socialism through a number of means, including an apparently generous list of rights, including social and economic rights. However, the Constitution undermined the exercise of those rights, first by not making them justiciable and second by providing once again that the exercise of those rights could not undermine national unity; the state's internal and external security; and the "socialist revolution" (Article 73).

1989 Constitution: By the mid-1980s Algeria's political system was stable but had seriously mismanaged macroeconomic policy, such that the country was left highly vulnerable to a rapidly changing world economy. By 1988, a sharp decline in crude oil prices, high inflation, and unemployment sparked large-scale protests and rioting that were met with brutal repression by the military. Hundreds of protesters were killed as a result. Reeling from the shock of this violence, senior officials conceded that the political system should be liberalized in part through the adoption of a new constitution. The FLN's monopoly of political power was brought to an end and Algerians were given the right to establish associations "of a political nature" (Article 40). The explicit limitation on the free exercise of rights contained in the previous two constitutions was eliminated and replaced with a milder obligation to "protect the independence of the country" (Article 58) and to "loyally serve the national collectivity" (Article 59). The president of the republic remained all powerful, maintaining full control over the government formation process (Articles 74 and 75), could dissolve the parliament at will (Article 120), and remained the head of the high judicial council (Article 145). A constitutional council was established that was given the right to exercise judicial review (Article 159) but of which the president of the republic nominated the chair unilaterally (Article 154). In 1990, municipal elections were organized and in December 1991, the first round of parliamentary elections took place, in which the Islamic Salvation Front secured close to a majority of the seats. The military responded by suspending the constitution, cancelling the elections altogether, and arresting thousands of the Front's members and leaders. The president of the republic resigned and was replaced by a "high state committee," a provisional council that exercised executive and legislative power for a two-year period. A civil war ensued between armed Islamists on the one hand and state security forces on the other. The years that followed witnessed intense fighting between Islamist insurgents and the state that led to tens of thousands of dead and huge economic losses.

1996 Amendment: In 1996, as part of the overall effort to normalize state and society, the military established a power-sharing arrangement with elements within the FLN. As part of that arrangement, the 1989 Constitution was reinstated with a number of amendments. The new text maintained and even reinforced the hyperpresidentialism that defined all previous constitutions. An upper chamber was established, one-third of which was directly appointed by the president (Article 99), and that would serve as a bulwark against any radical forces that might emerge in the lower chamber. The president still controlled government formation, could dissolve the parliament at will (Article 129), and was still the head of the high judicial council (Article 154). Importantly, the right to form political parties now included a prohibition against the formation of any party that could be formed "on the basis of religion, language, race, gender, corporation or region" (Article 42). The wording was clearly designed to prevent the reemergence of another Islamist party. In 1999 Abdelaziz Bouteflika, a veteran member of the FLN and of successive administrations in the Algerian state, was elected president after all the other candidates withdrew following allegations of vote tampering. Other amendments were also entered into during the 2000s, including a formal recognition of Tamazight as one of the national languages in 2002 (Article 3) and the elimination of presidential term limits in 2008 (Article 74).

2011 Uprising: By 2010 the chasm between the ruling elites and the general population had grown inexorably, perhaps beyond repair. Aside from the periodic rounds of bloodletting that had taken place over previous decades, many Algerians complained of economic stagnation. Despite vast reservoirs of natural resources, by 2010 youth unemployment stood at 22 percent, a figure that had grown to 29 percent by 2019. Meanwhile, inflation stood at 16 percent, a deadly combination for many. Perhaps most importantly, however, ruling elites appeared to have no idea what ordinary Algerians were expecting of them, and also appeared to believe that minor amendments to preexisting constitutional arrangements would appease popular demands for change. This has been demonstrated on two separate occasions in the past decade. In 2011 president Abdel Aziz Bouteflika launched a constitutional reform effort to appease the population, which had taken to the streets during the region-wide uprising.[120] However, the process that was adopted lasted so long and was

[120] See Azzedine Layachi, "Untenable Exceptionalism during the Spring of Upheavals," in Ricardo René Larémont (ed.), Revolution, Revolt and Reform in North Africa, Routledge (2014).

executed by the state so unenthusiastically that the general population hardly noticed when the process was completed. The process itself involved a number of different stages and actors that might have served the country well in a different context and if it had been implemented by different people. In May 2011 two separate consultation processes were launched, one of which focused on national development and the second on political dialogue. The consultations lasted for months and were wide-reaching, but the outcome was never published. In April 2013 an expert committee was composed to translate the outcome of the consultation process into amendments for consideration. The draft was finalized in May 2014 but was only published months later, following which yet another round of consultations was launched.[121]

2019 Uprising: The amendments were formally adopted in 2016 and reintroduced term limits, but the public felt almost no change in the way government functioned.[122] This was partly because President Bouteflika suffered a stroke in 2012, after which he was almost totally paralyzed and was absent from public view for significant periods of time, often because he was outside the country for treatment. Many Algerians speculated that Bouteflika was no longer involved in administering the country, which reemphasized the view that elections were a sham. Despite his condition, Bouteflika stood for reelection in 2014. He was pushed to the ballot box in a wheelchair. Algerians responded with much consternation and derision (one mock campaign poster urged voters to support the president for reelection, whether he was "dead or alive") but were at least reassured that this would be the last time that Bouteflika would stand for high office. And yet, in February 2019, Bouteflika announced through a spokesman that he was running for a fifth term in office and that he would initiate yet another national dialogue on constitutional reform. A few days later, Algeria's largest and most sustained protest movement in its history was launched to protest the announcement and the state of politics in the country. Millions took to the streets in virtually all parts of the country, week after week for over a year, to demand major structural reform.[123]

[121] See Wissam Benyettou, "Will Algeria Start 2016 with a New Constitution?," Constitutionnet (November 24, 2015).

[122] Article 210 provided that if the constitutional council finds that constitutional amendments do not affect the "general principles that govern Algerian society," they can be adopted without recourse to a referendum on the condition that a three-quarters majority is obtained in the legislature. The constitutional council made such a determination through creative legal reasoning. See Nimer Sultany, LAW AND REVOLUTION: LEGITIMACY AND CONSTITUTIONALISM AFTER THE ARAB SPRING, Oxford University Press (2017), at 280–286. The amendments were adopted without a referendum.

[123] Amel Boubekeur, "Demonstration Effects: How the Hirak Protest Movement Is Reshaping Algerian Politics," European Council on Foreign Relations (February 27, 2020).

In April 2019 the military once again intervened directly in politics by unceremoniously removing Bouteflika from office and in December 2019 organized a presidential election. The new president (who in the past had served as minister on four different occasions and as prime minister once) campaigned on a promise of constitutional reform and so tasked a small committee of handpicked experts to produce a new draft constitution in just three months. As in Morocco and Jordan, the president provided detailed instructions on the type of changes that he expected the committee to make.[124]

2020 Constitution: In May 2020 the expert committee's draft amendments were released.[125] Unsurprisingly, the draft maintained a firmly presidential system of government. The president retained control over national defense, government formation, and appointments (Article 95). The president was empowered to appoint the prime minister "after consulting the parliamentary majority" (which means that the president can choose any candidate he wants) and to dismiss the prime minister at will (Article 95(7)).[126] The prime minister nominated ministers but the president appointed them, which clearly suggested that he could block the nomination of any specific minister (Article 102). The president's appointment authority extended to state officials that were supposed to exercise oversight over him, including the head of the supreme audit institution, the president of the high court, among others (Article 96). The president maintained the absolute right to dissolve parliament, for whatever reason (Article 156). He also remained the head of the judicial council (Article 187). There were also some improvements. The president could still declare a state of emergency virtually at will but could only do so for thirty days. The period can only be renewed by a joint session of parliament (Article 112). This was a clear improvement to the previous system, which allowed limitless states of emergency. Overall, the draft constitution represented more a continuity of the historical Algerian framework structured around a powerful president. Despite some institutional innovations, the proposed amendments were so modest that they were met with derision by

[124] See "Révision de la constitution: le Président Tebboune nomme le Pr Laraba à la tête d'un Comité d'experts," Radio Algerienne (January 8, 2020).

[125] One of the members of the expert committee has since stated that the draft amendments are inadequate and has withdrawn from the committee. Following the publication of the draft changes, a public consultation process was organized, during which authorities claimed to have received close to 2,000 suggestions from the general public. See Zaid Al-Ali, "Algeria's not-so-new (Draft) Constitution: Betraying Hirak's Radicalism?," Constitutionnet (June 4, 2020).

[126] By way of comparison, Morocco's 2011 Constitution forces the monarch to appoint a prime minister who must be drawn from the largest parliamentary party.

large segments of the general population, who were unconvinced that the changes would make any difference in the state's functioning.[127] The referendum took place in November 2020. Two thirds of voters approved of the new text, but turnout was particularly low at 23 percent of eligible voters. Despite the promise of a new beginning, at the start of 2021, Algeria appeared to be stuck in the same cycle of long absences by the head of state for medical treatment abroad, while the country continued to languish without the major reforms that it needed.

* * *

[127] See, for example, Mustapha al-Iraqi, "In Algeria, to Each President a Constitution" (في الجزائر ، لكل رئيس دستوره), al-Itihad (June 4, 2020) (in which Mustapha Bouchachi, a prominent human rights lawyer, describes the proposed amendments as maintaining "the same unitary and totalitarian system").

PART II

Revolution

6

Purpose
(or Who Decides What a Constitution Is for?)

INTRODUCTION

Iraq was once a wealthy country but its population has been run into the ground due to a series of catastrophically bad policy decisions that were fueled by an absence of accountability. By October 2019, Hundreds of thousands of poor and marginalized Iraqis were in the streets taking major risks to life and limb to demand change. Three different high level committees were established to propose amendments to the constitution in ways that addressed the protesters' demands. One evening in late December 2019, as one of the committees prepared to meet in a conference room in a key government institution's offices, they found that the committee chairman (a senior government official) was engaged in conversation with a small group of individuals. They were protesters who had been brought in to the government department by a third party to describe how they had been kidnapped and tortured by the security services. One of the three dominated the conversation. He spoke fluidly and without hesitation on why he supported the protests, including rampant poverty and unemployment. He described how he was targeted by masked men who detained and tortured him for weeks while they tried to make him sign a statement confirming that he would not participate in any future protests. He refused to sign and was released after contacts mobilized support within the ministry on his behalf. He seemed strong, fearless, and full of integrity. The committee members listened to his account respectfully until he and his fellow protesters excused themselves and left. The committee commenced its session and discussed a number of issues, including how the judiciary's performance could be improved. Two hours later, the chairman called a break. The members moved to another room where dinner was waiting. As soon as they started the meal, a committee member who was also a senior government adviser said "you know, despite it all, Iraqis can't complain. The constitution really does serve them well."

In early March 2011 a group of young Egyptians met in a conference room to discuss their transition to a new future. The attendees were brought together by a neutral actor who tried to have a wide spectrum of views represented in the discussion. There were nationalists, conservatives, social democrats, Islamists, and others. All had been on the frontlines during the uprising, and very few of them had met before, as a result of which much of the earlier part of the discussion amounted to a sharing of experiences of rallying family, friends, and colleagues; confronting the police; and the joy of hearing of Mubarak's departure from office. During one of the breaks, a woman with long reddish hair whose views included a mixture of progressive, nationalist, and xenophobic views told a lanky and bespectacled participant who was also an Islamist that their support toward the end of the uprising was crucial to winning the battle against the police. The conversation shifted to elections, including when they should take place; whether they should be parliamentary, presidential, or both; and what electoral system should be adopted. Finally, the participants discussed the future constitution, the main issue being how it should be drafted. A guest speaker was asked to introduce the topic. His presentation consisted entirely of a series of questions. He asked the participants who, in their view, should draft the new constitution. One of the participants responded without hesitation that "we have lots of great academic experts in this country. They should write the constitution." It wasn't clear if all the participants agreed but no dissenting views were expressed.

In early 2011 Jordanians were taking to the streets in their tens of thousands demanding reforms. For over twenty years, the state recognized that there would have to be serious reform and so organized a series of dialogue processes and published major white papers to set out major ideas. Very little came of it, and so by 2011 protesters were demanding more deep-seated reform, including a major reimagination of the national constitution. Demonstrations were generally orderly. Security services did not respond violently and protesters did not threaten the seat of power. Nevertheless, in private, senior officials expressed significant consternation that the protests were being led by Islamists who were hoping to undermine the king. A private lawyer who was intimately connected to the state volunteered to carry out a full review of the constitution, including its historical origins and design flaws, with a view to recommending amendments that would preserve the system while improving existing mechanisms. The intent was that the review would be published privately and distributed freely, in the hope that it could improve public discourse about what could be achieved through constitutional reform.

The lawyer prepared a first draft, which was circulated to a number of leading Jordanian, Arab, and international lawyers who offered their comments. Around that time, government officials were working behind the scenes to block the publication. "You have to understand", one of them said. "The constitution is a red line for us."

In late 2019 Lebanon's popular uprising was causing significant consternation in official circles. Protesters were enraged at proposed regressive taxes despite increasing poverty and inequality. The most prevalent popular slogan to emerge during the protests was "all of them means all of them." The slogan established the people as a single unified entity, no longer separated by religion or ethnicity, and also unified the political class into a single class of conspirators who were intent on defrauding ordinary people. Protesters did not have a leadership structure, and for the most part did not have a clear strategy other than to express their extreme anger through acts of civil disobedience. Almost every day, dozens of roads and major arteries would be closed off simultaneously, bringing the national economy to a halt for weeks at a time. In an effort to reassure protesters that their interests were being taken into account, the president of the republic gave a television interview to a major broadcaster. The discussion focused on the cause of protests, including the increased poverty. Halfway through the interview, the president expressed exasperation at the fact that none of the protest leaders had put any demands to him. One of the journalists offered that "it's a popular revolution. They don't have leaders." The president responded that "if they don't have people that are part of the state to represent them, then they should emigrate."

In 2013, at a private dinner in Tunisia, a group of lawyers and judges discussed the latest developments in their country's constitutional process. The consensus between the individuals present was that some substantive progress had been made but that much remained to be done. One lawyer disagreed. In his view, none of the uprising's objectives had been achieved. He spoke at length about what the people had demanded two years prior. No real effort had yet been made to achieve social justice. Throughout his comments he repeatedly used the words "revolution" and "revolutionaries." Before he had finished, he was interrupted by a sitting judge who banged her fist on the table as she said, "it's not a revolution! Those people are criminals and delinquents."

THE TEXT'S STANDARD

Constitutional Purpose: In the context of a massive popular uprising against the state, what is a constitution supposed to achieve and who is it supposed to serve? And, perhaps most importantly, in the post-2011 era who decides what a constitution is supposed to achieve and who it should serve? These are not mere rhetorical questions as they get to the heart of how the state and political groups should respond in the face of a popular uprising; whether one can consider that popular demands for reform have been satisfied; and, ultimately, whether another uprising is likely to occur. Pre-2011 constitutions were so closely associated with individual rulers that post-2011 there was no dispute that they should be replaced. Throughout the region, political groups, experts, and others immediately engaged with each other on how the new constitutions should be drafted and what they should provide. However, in many circles, there was significant confusion as to what a constitution should achieve. In many countries, Islamists sought to use the constitution as one tool among others through which to transform society in their image. Other groups sought to use the constitution as a means to preserve their own version of society. Negotiators and drafters argued day and night over these issues through one means or another for a period of years. In some cases, the constitution was viewed as a tool of political transformation, including in Sudan where civilian groups were hoping that the 2019 Constitutional Charter would allow the country to transition from military to democratic rule.

Interpretation: Given all these competing visions, what is a constitution for? The texts of the constitutions themselves should be the point of departure in answering this question. In many cases, Arab constitutions have included statements of purpose, some of which were pages long. Many set out in extensive detail what the state's ideology is and the historic wrongs that the constitutions seeks to resolve. How should these texts be interpreted and what importance should be given to them? It is a standard rule of legal interpretation that when examining a text, we must first give the words used their literal meaning. On the question of constitutional purpose, preambles (where they exist) are the natural place to start given that they often seek to encapsulate the text's general objective and describe what type of state is being established. In the Arab region, preambles are often drafted and agreed before the rest of the text is completed, and various iterations are normally published in national media, provoking significant discussion.[1] One of the reasons why they have so much importance is precisely because they purport to establish the context within which a constitution is adopted as well as its objective. Standard rules

[1] Tunisia's final constitution was adopted in January 2014, but its preamble was in very close to final form in June 2012; see "Final Draft of Preamble to 2012 Tunisian Constitution: English Translation by Tunisia Live," Farah Samti, Tunisia Live, published at Jaddaliya, June 21, 2012; "The Preamble of Tunisia's Constitution: Agreement and Discord" ("ديباجة الدستور التونسي.. توافق وخلاف"), Ayman Madhab, Al-Jazeera, June 11, 2012.

of interpretation also provide that we must move beyond the general and seek to understand the nature of a constitutional text from the remainder of its substantive content. A constitution can establish an explicit objective in its preamble or in the body of the text, and can also underline the importance of that same objective through various means in the remainder of the text.

Statements of Intent: Sudan's 2019 Constitutional Charter sets out a large number of objectives in its preamble, so many in fact that a reader cannot distil from it a clear objective. By way of example, the preamble provides that the state's objective includes "fighting corruption, recovering stolen funds, reforming the national economy, achieving a state of prosperity, welfare and social justice" and "strengthening the pillars of social peace" and "laying the foundations for a healthy civil regime to govern Sudan." In the context, standard rules of interpretation require readers to investigate the remainder of the Charter's provisions for guidance on whether some of the preamble's wording has been given priority over other parts. Article 7(2) provides that "[d]uring the first six months of the transitional period, priority is given to working seriously to establish peace in accordance with the provisions of the transitional period program in this regard." The cabinet is also given explicit instruction to "[w]ork to stop the wars and conflicts and build peace" (Article 16(2)). In addition, Article 68 sets out in eleven subparagraphs the means through which all state agencies are supposed to work toward achieving a "comprehensive peace," while Article 39(3)(a) establishes a "peace commission." On the issue of transition to civilian rule, the Charter establishes a number of mechanisms. Apart from the fact that both the cabinet and the parliament are to be established entirely by civilian groups (apart from the ministers of interior and defense, both of whom are to be officers), the Charter establishes a Sovereignty Council that is the head of state during the transition, and which consists of five military members and six civilian members. Article 11(3) provides that "[o]ver the first twenty-one months of the transitional period, the Sovereignty Council is chaired by one of the military members, and in the remaining 18 months, it is chaired by a civilian member." The Charter's other objectives, including to "reform the national economy, achieve a state of prosperity, welfare and social justice," among many others, are not given the same weight and importance as the achievement of peace and the transition to civilian rule. The inevitable conclusion therefore is that the Charter clearly prioritizes these two objectives over all others.

Holistic Approach: Some constitutions are very clear in the objectives that they seek to achieve, but nevertheless require additional inquiry to confirm the intent, in part because specific provisions can have different meanings depending on the context. Spain's 1978 Constitution is typical of liberal constitutions in that its preamble includes commitments to democracy, the rule of law, and a respect for human rights and cultural traditions. The preamble also provides that the "Spanish Nation" seeks a "fair economic and social order," and a "dignified quality of life for all," which places Spain within a sociodemocratic tradition of placing emphasis on socioeconomic rights, particularly through the delivery of essential services to the general population.[2] On its own, however, that specific wording does not clearly indicate the constitution's own order of priorities. For that, a more holistic interpretation of the constitution's substantive provisions is necessary. The constitution provides that citizens have the right to a number of social and economic rights, including housing (Article 47) and healthcare (Article 49). In addition, Article 9(2) clearly establishes that it is the Government that is ultimately responsible "to promote conditions ensuring that freedom and equality of individuals and of the groups to which they belong are real and effective, to remove the obstacles preventing or hindering their full enjoyment, and to facilitate the participation of all citizens in political, economic, cultural and social life." At the same time, however, the constitution also limits the right of ordinary citizens to directly implement any of the constitution's social and economic rights, in the absence of implementation legislation (Article 53(3)), which places the government firmly in control of the state's policy. The constitution's goal of establishing a social order is therefore tempered by its desire to ensure that the government's policy-making power remains unfettered.

Interpretation in Context: The point can be made more clearly through a comparison with the South African text. The preamble to South Africa's 1996 Constitution also includes reference to democracy, fundamental human rights, and quality of life.[3] Those general principles are given more specific meaning by Chapter 2, which provides for a right to housing, healthcare, and education (Articles 26, 27, and 29). In contrast to the Spanish text, however, the South African constitution ensures that even in the absence of a law,

[2] See Victor Ferreres Comella, THE CONSTITUTION OF SPAIN: A CONTEXTUAL ANALYSIS, Hart Publishing (2013). Many other preambles share the same qualities.

[3] Ecuador's 2008 Constitution stands apart from both previous examples. It also includes reference to democratic values, to which it adds a commitment to "social liberation struggles against all forms of domination and colonialism." The preamble is followed by a list of the state's prime duties, which include "planning national development, eliminating poverty, and promoting sustainable development and the equitable redistribution of resources and wealth to enable access to the good way of living" (Article 3). The wording here is easily distinct from the liberal values set out in the Spanish and South African texts, and clearly illustrates the constitution's objectives.

individuals may petition a court for relief in direct application of the constitution; the courts are specifically told that, when applying a provision of the Bill of Rights (which includes social and economic rights), they "must apply, or if necessary develop, the common law to the extent that legislation does not give effect to that right" (Article 8). As a result of this and other provisions, the South African constitution's formal commitment to establishing a social democracy appears significantly stronger than the Spanish case, and can reasonably be considered to constitute one of the constitution's main objectives.[4]

Contradictions: Other constitutions may require a closer reading because their provisions point in opposite directions, which means that an attempt must be made to reconcile them. On occasion, clear contradictions can be identified, in which case the reader must reach her own reasoned view on what the constitution's true objective is, based on an evaluation of the entirety of the circumstances. In that sense, the fact that a constitution establishes a series of political, social, and economic rights without saying anything about who enjoys those rights or how they are to be enforced, and that it provides for an independent judiciary but exposes the courts to heavy influence by the parliament and the government indicate a clear order of priorities and a sense of the same constitution's objectives. By way of illustration, Iraq's now-defunct 1970 Interim Constitution did not have a preamble but included a general statement of purpose establishing Iraq as a "sovereign people's democratic republic. Its basic objective is the realization of one Arab State and the establishment of a socialist system" (Article 1). To underline its supposed commitment to the principle of democracy, the interim constitution also provided that the people are the "source of authority and its legitimacy" (Article 2). The constitution's system of government, however, established a different set of priorities. A "revolutionary command council" was established (Article 37) and granted both full legislative and executive functions (Article 42). The council was responsible for selecting its own members (who had to be drawn from the Baath party's leadership (Article 38)), who were accountable only to the council itself (Article 45). The stated objective of establishing a socialist democracy was therefore clearly eclipsed by the desire to perpetuate undemocratic rule by a closed circle of individuals.

Absence of an Explicit Statement: Some constitutions consist almost entirely of a dry elaboration of rules and make no attempt to set out any

4 See Sandra Leibenberg, Socio-Economic Rights: Adjudication under a Transformative Constitution, Juta Academic (2010).

objectives or even principles from which an objective could be extracted. In those situations, a closer reading of the constitution may nevertheless indicate what the text's objective may be, even if only implicitly. Jordan's 1952 Constitution does not have a preamble or a clear statement of principles. The constitution places heavy emphasis on organizing the functioning of state institutions, and on establishing a form of separation of powers that grants very heavy influence to the monarch. The king has the power to dissolve the House of Representatives (Article 34(3)); appoints and dismisses the prime minister (Article 35); and appoints all of the members of the constitutional court (Article 58). Chapter 2 on basic rights does not provide many of the same social and economic rights that are provided under other regional constitutions. In any event, those rights that are provided for are not directly enforceable. If the text is the point of reference in our effort to determine the constitution's objective, then in this case it may not be possible to determine a precise objective. At best, an argument can be made that the 1952 Constitution's only discernable objective is to maintain a constitutional monarchy.

Drafter's Intent: In some situations, it is justified and possibly even necessary to explore the negotiators' and drafters' intent. Where a contradiction in the text cannot be resolved, a reader may be justified in examining the archives of the constitution drafting committee (if they exist) or even drafters' and negotiators' writings, statements, and records of behavior to determine what they intended to achieve. This method of interpretation is merely an extension of the type of textual analysis set out in the previous sections: It allows us to determine, through a different means of interpretation, what a constitution's actual objectives might be. After the 2003 invasion, a number of Iraq's major political movements were determined to prevent the country from relapsing into another dictatorship by deconcentrating power along a number of lines. This became one of the major points of discussion during the drafting of the 2005 constitution, and indeed is still a point of contention today.[5] The 2005 Constitution introduced a number of elements that are designed to satisfy that objective. The preamble includes a commitment to "strengthen our national unity, following the path of peaceful transfer of power, adopting the course of just distribution of resources, and providing equal opportunity for all." The preamble also provides for the establishment of a "republican, federal, democratic, pluralistic system." What is unclear from

5 See Haider Ala Hamoudi, Negotiating in Civil Conflict: Constitutional Construction and Imperfect Bargaining in Iraq, University of Chicago Press (2013).

all of this, however, is the type of federation and state that the constitution provided for, and by extension how committed the text is to Iraq remaining a unified state. The text points in different directions. The English translation of the preamble's final paragraph provides that Iraq is a "free union," which some have interpreted to mean that individual components or geographic regions can leave that union whenever they so choose.[6] In the Arabic and Kurdish originals, the wording that is used is not a recognized term and therefore has little meaning. A number of other provisions suggest that the state should remain united and that the federation should have a strong center. For example, Article 1 provides that Iraq should remain a "single federal, independent and fully sovereign state." Other provisions give priority to laws adopted in the federal regions over laws adopted at the central level and therefore appear to point in the opposite direction (Article 115). Ultimately, given that Iraq's annual state budget and by extension its capacity to enact policy is almost entirely financed by the sale of natural resources, it is the provisions on the distribution of resources that are most determinant here. Article 111 provides that the federal government can only be involved in the exploitation of "current fields," which by extension excludes it from the exploitation of "future fields," therefore providing significant support for the proposition that the constitution's objective is to establish Iraq as a weak federation. The fact that many Iraqi negotiators and drafters set themselves as an objective to deconcentrate power adds weight to that view. Contemporaneous statements by senior officials who participated in the drafting of the constitution also point in this direction.

THE ELITES DECIDE

The Problem: But what should be done if the constitutional negotiators and drafters are not adequately representative of a country's political spectrum? "Adequate" representativity is a matter of degree, so our concern here will be limited to those constitution-making processes that were undeniably exclusionary. In such situations, the act of exploring what the drafters' intent was through an analysis of the final wording will yield at best a partial picture and at worst a totally distorted one. Iraq's 1970 Interim Constitution was exclusively

6 "The Constitutional Case for Kurdistan's Independence and a Record of the Violation of Iraq's Constitution by Successive Iraqi Prime Ministers and Ministers, the Council of Representatives, the Shura Council, the Judiciary and the Army," The Kurdistan Regional Government (September 24, 2017).

the product of the Baath party, and therefore says close to nothing about what anyone outside of the Baath party's inner circle of leaders were hoping that the constitution might achieve for them. Other major political forces, including communists, nationalists, liberals, trade unions, and religious communities, were unable to influence the final text. In early 2005 a constituent assembly was elected, but there were so many boycotts, changes in membership, and ultimately exclusions from the negotiations that the final text only reflects the will of a small number of actors (not all of whom were Iraqi).[7] Major political groups such as the all-powerful Sadrist movement were not involved in the negotiations and did not influence the final outcome of the 2005 Constitution. After the 2005 Constitution came into force, the federal government refused to apply some of the constitution's most essential pillars (particularly its federal arrangement), which meant that whatever the constitution's objective might be has not been matched by what key state institutions have been moving toward.[8]

Drafters: Iraq in 1970 and in 2005 was hardly exceptional by regional standards.[9] Prior to 2011 most constitution-making process were far from inclusive. This was true even in the immediate post-colonial period, when large numbers of political parties were active in many parts of the region and debated how their future states should be structured. Other groups and communities were influential in their own way, including lawyers, academics, and judges, many of whom self-identified as intellectual leaders who should necessarily be involved in determining their countries' constitutional culture. Religious elites in many countries (including in Lebanon, Iraq, Egypt, etc.) were highly influential and often formed political parties and movements that they could then use to influence constitutional processes in a more targeted fashion (particularly with a view to ensuring that personal status rights and fundamental rights were not granted in a way that contravened a very traditional understanding of religious values). The state bureaucracy was also influential, particularly given the role that it played in forming each specific

7 See Zaid Al-Ali, "Constitutional Legitimacy in Iraq: What Role Local Context?," in Rainer Grote and Tilmann Röder (eds.), Constitutionalism in Islamic Countries: Between Upheaval and Continuity, Oxford University Press (2012).

8 See, for example, "Republic of Iraq – Decentralisation and Subnational Service Delivery in Iraq: Status and Way Forward," The World Bank (March 2016).

9 One major distinguishing factor, however, is that post-2003 Iraq's political scene was so volatile that the parties that were dominant when the constitutional drafting process took place quickly declined in popularity, and were replaced by other parties that did not agree with their own vision. That immediate political shift quickly revealed how exclusionary the constitutional negotiation process was.

country's educational policy and cultural identity.[10] Finally, broader cultural elites, including prominent journalists and authors, played important roles in channeling and promoting ideas to the national stage. These groups of individuals played a key role in defining each country's political priorities, many of which were articulated either directly or indirectly in the constitutions that were drafted over the past 100 years.

Controlling Elites: Ultimately, however, throughout that period, genuine political power in the Arab region was concentrated in the hands of small groups of kings, presidents, military officers, and other senior executive officers (hereinafter "controlling elites"), none of whom were elected.[11] Despite the fact that they had to contend with large numbers of voices, controlling elites were in a prime position to influence their respective country's constitutional culture, including what each constitution's objective would be. The controlling elites were influenced by the general post-colonial context, which assumed the desire to build a modern bureaucratic state and to accelerate socioeconomic development in their respective countries. Mainly, however, controlling elites were determined to monopolize power, as demonstrated by the constitutional texts that they midwifed into existence and by their subsequent behavior. Ultimately, this led to the establishment of systems of government that allowed controlling elites to rule unimpeded.[12] Controlling elites also borrowed from each other, looking for inspiration from other countries across the region and associating themselves with whatever form of post-colonial and revolutionary legitimacy might allow them to neutralize oversight institutions.[13]

10 For a detailed explanation of how this took place in Iraq, see Reeva Spector Simon, Iraq between the Two World Wars: the Militarist Origins of Tyranny, Columbia University Press (2012).

11 This applied to all countries in the region apart from Lebanon, which has held elections relatively regularly and has survived on power-sharing arrangements for decades. Even in Lebanon, however, corruption and nepotism quickly took root, to the extent that specific political groups managed to ensure a monopoly of support from each of the country's various communities and the change in political fortunes became more a function of demographics than the relative failure or success of a specific party's policies. See Bassel F. Salloukh, Rabie Barakat, Jinan S. Al-Habbal, Lara W. Khattab, and Shoghig Mikaelian, The Politics of Sectarianism in Postwar Lebanon, Pluto Press (2015).

12 See, for example, Kirsten Stilt, "The Egyptian Constitution of 1971," in Constitutions in Authoritarian Regimes, Tom Ginsburg and Alberto Simpser (eds.), Cambridge University Press (2014); and Mahmoud Hamad, Judges and Generals in the Making of Modern Egypt: How Institutions Sustain and Undermine Authoritarian Regimes, Cambridge University Press (October 25, 2018).

13 Egypt's "Revolutionary Command Council" was constitutionalized in 1956. Iraq, Syria, Libya, and Sudan were all to follow that example.

Process: Controlling elites used a number of mechanisms to reinforce their influence on state structure, including dominating constitutional drafting processes. Prior to 2011 most constitutional texts in the region were drafted by individuals who were handpicked by ruling authorities specifically because of their bias toward authority and control. Libya's 1951 and Iraq's 1925 Constitutions were prepared by foreign officials and advisers with only minor input from locals. The king was directly involved in and controlled the drafting of all of Morocco's constitutions and Jordan's 1952 Constitution. Algeria's 1963 Constitution was handcrafted by the office of the authoritarian president, despite the fact that a national assembly had nominally been tasked with drafting the text.[14] The president packed a movie theater with loyal party supporters who offered their enthusiastic and unquestioning approval, leaving the assembly with no choice but to do the same.[15] Syria's 1973 Constitution and Iraq's 1970 Interim Constitution were both drafted under the auspices of harsh authoritarian regimes.[16] Egypt's 1971 Constitution was drafted by a committee of eighty individuals, all of whom were members of the National Assembly, which was intensely loyal to the president.[17] In most cases, drafting committees would be mainly populated by jurists, but have also included individuals who did not have a legal background. Controlling elites were generally unfamiliar with their countries' legal traditions and therefore provided only broad direction for what should be included in the constitutional text, leaving the detail to the drafters.[18] In practice, controlling elites were unlikely to object to legal innovations that fell outside their main scope of interest. This in turn meant that constitutional drafters potentially had enormous power to influence the outcome of a constitution-building process given that they were responsible for translating broad principles into specific constitutional rules. The drafting processes themselves were generally brief,

[14] Ferhat Abbas, the National Assembly's President, resigned in protest after an authoritarian draft was presented and after an earlier draft that favored a parliamentary system was set aside; see Ferhat Abbas, L'independence Confisquée, Flammarion (1984)

[15] Mohamed Sifaoui, Histoire secrète de l'Algérie indépendante, Nouveau Monde Editions (2012), at 81.

[16] Syria's 1973 Constitution was drafted by an appointed People's Assembly. The Assembly consisted of 173 members, 87 of whom were Baath party members; see Karim Atassi, Syria, The Strength of an Idea: The Constitutional Architectures of Its Political Regimes, Cambridge University Press (2018), at 301.

[17] John Waterbury, The Egypt of Nasser and Sadat: The Political Economy of Two Regimes, Princeton University Press, Reprint edition (2014).

[18] See, for example, Stilt (2014) (in which the author sets out the "short list of specific instructions" that President Anwar Sadat provided to the National Assembly that was tasked with drafting the constitution).

however, which reduced opportunities for drafters to engage in major innovations. Even in those cases where the processes nominally lasted months or even years (Iraq in 1925, Tunisia in 1959, etc.), the drafting processes were themselves monopolized by small numbers of individuals (some of whom were not even nationals) who generally worked behind closed doors, further reducing opportunities for outsiders to impact the discussions.[19] Finally, many drafters were selected on the basis of their conservative predisposition and party loyalty and so any attempt to introduce progressive ideas to the process would have met with significant resistance.

Outcome: It is tempting to dismiss constitutions that result from undemocratic process as entirely cynical, merely a smokescreen to conceal a harsh dictatorial system of government.[20] Some authors have argued, however, that, regardless of how they were implemented in practice, the manner in which post-colonial constitutions were constructed is evidence that they were deeply rooted in popular demands for freedom and social and economic development.[21] The evidence in support of this argument is compelling, including the fact that many post-colonial constitutions included long lists of civil, political, social, and economic rights, all of which coincided with the general population's expectations of what their respective countries should offer in the post-colonial period. The constitutional texts themselves therefore constitute clear evidence that both drafters and post-colonial rulers were aware of and wanted to be seen as satisfying popular demands for change. At the same time, controlling elites and their constitutional drafters were also careful to ensure that the rights that were granted were constructed as nonbinding promises that could be curbed by thousands of laws and regulations that restricted all the rights that ordinary people assumed they could exercise relatively freely.[22] Other authors have argued that the pre-2011 constitutions were in fact principally designed to organize state authority.[23] Indeed, as noted earlier, most Arab constitutions were enacted at a time when various groups of elites were jostling

[19] For the manner in which this played out in Iraq, see Majid Khadduri, Independent Iraq, Oxford University Press (1951), at 14–15.

[20] See Anthony Billingsley, "Writing Constitutions in the Wake of the Arab Spring," Foreign Affairs (November 30, 2011).

[21] See Nimer Sultany, Law and Revolution: Legitimacy and Constitutionalism after the Arab Spring, Oxford University Press (2017), at 63.

[22] Research institutions have since compiled all of the legislation that was adopted in each of the countries that was designed to curb all of the rights that were supposedly granted in national constitutions. See, for example, "Tunisia's Repressive Laws: The Reform Agenda," Human Rights Watch (2011).

[23] Nathan Brown, Constitutions in a Nonconstitutional World: Arab Basic Laws and the Prospects for Accountable Government, SUNY Press (2012).

against each other in a competition for political power, and so were replete with provisions that regulate the activities of state institutions. As such, security institutions, members of the legal profession (mainly judges), and a small number of political groups were all given their own spheres of influence. The constitutional texts themselves were principally designed to regulate their behavior in a way that augmented and cemented each institution's sphere of authority, while also cementing them together. The fact that the constitutional provisions on institutional frameworks were generally respected gives this second theory significant credence.

Executive Control: The pre-2011 constitutions also shared a number of design features that virtually guaranteed the constitutional degradation that eventually led to the 2011 uprisings. All of these texts included detailed provisions on how parliament should operate, specifically setting out the circumstances in which sessions could not be held, how long sessions should last, how votes should be organized, etc. Meanwhile, the texts were virtually silent on the limits of executive authority.[24] There were no provisions that indicated that governments should always operate in application of the law; states of emergency could be declared and renewed *ad infinitum*, with no clarity on their impact on rights and freedoms; the role of the executive in the legislative process was left undefined.[25] The bias in favor of whoever controlled the executive branch of government, whether king, president, or prime minister, ultimately created a further incentive for specific individuals or groups of individuals within executive circles to eliminate rivals and purge the halls of power.[26] Therefore, as time progressed, executive power was eventually monopolized by ever diminishing numbers of people (sometimes eventually reducing to a single individual, as in the case of Iraq from 1979 until 2003).[27] As the pool of individuals and groups that were involved in designing

[24] Egypt's 1971 Constitution included fifty articles (1,942 words in the Arab original) that regulated parliamentary proceedings. It only included seven articles (325 words) on how the government was supposed to function.

[25] See, for example, Sadiq Reza, "Endless Emergency: The Case of Egypt," New Criminal Law Review, Vol. 10 (2007), 532; and Lina Khatib, "Political Participation and Democratic Transition in the Arab World," University of Pennsylvania Journal of International Law, Vol. 34 (2013), 315.

[26] Syria's 1973 Constitution was the most presidential of all of Syria's post-mandate constitutions. According to Atassi, it "contained the seeds of the personalization of power that was to be confirmed subsequently"; see Atassi (2018), at 303.

[27] In Algeria, behind the scenes purges are a regular feature of political life. For example, Ferhat Abbas, president of the first post-colonial national assembly, resigned in protest over the president's autocratic tendencies, eventually leading to his arrest. In September 2015, the head of the intelligence service for twenty-five years was quietly replaced by President Abdelaziz Bouteflika. No reasons were offered. See "Algerian President Fires Intelligence Chief in a

state policy narrowed, so did the quality of decision-making. During this period, demographics in many countries spiraled out of control with booming populations fueling unemployment, poverty, and illiteracy.[28] Despite the fact that there were few if any genuine challenges to the existing constitutional orders, governments throughout the region were essentially incapable of mounting a serious policy response, which fueled the 2011 uprisings. In the end, state authority was diminished by executive overreach, which manifested itself through the desire to monopolize power for as long as possible, without paying any heed to genuine social needs.

Consociationalism: The same dynamics were in play, albeit in different form, even in those few countries that had a plural system of government, including post-2003 Iraq and Lebanon. In both cases, political parties were able to capture all institutions of state through their domination of their respective parliaments. Neither Lebanon's 1926 Constitution nor Iraq's 2005 Constitution established a mechanism to resolve disputes between governing parties or an arbiter to control or limit transgressions. Individual institutions (audit institutions, anticorruption agencies, specific ministries) became private fiefdoms of specific political parties. By early 2020 both systems were teetering on the brink of collapse. Lebanon's 1926 Constitution, the only colonial era constitution that is still in force in the Arab region, is partially informed by the "National Pact," which provides for a consociational system of government that allocates senior positions of state in part on the basis of religious affiliation and in part on electoral outcomes. The 1926 Constitution makes the judiciary totally subservient to the parliament (see Article 20) and the state has made only marginal efforts to promote judicial oversight over the executive.[29] Implementation is also informed by the legacies of a fifteen-year civil war that ended in 1990, and by the 1989 Taif Agreement,

Shake-Up of Security Forces," Carlotta Gall, *The New York Times* (September 14, 2015); see also, "Bouteflika Puts an End to Head of Intelligence General Mohamed Medien's 'Legend'" ("بوتفليقة ينهي «أسطورة» الجنرال توفيق قائد الاستخبارات"), Atef Qadadara, al-Hayat (September 14, 2015). By the start of 2019, the country's senior leadership could not mount a convincing response to a popular uprising, leading to President Bouteflika's forced resignation.

28 Although Egypt's education sector has been in desperate need of reform for decades, the state has been incapable of addressing the basic challenges that it faces. The sector's difficulties have grown significantly worse over time. Louisa Loveluck, "Education in Egypt: Key Challenges," Chatham House Background Paper (March 2012). In 2013 Egypt ranked last out of 148 countries in the ranking of primary education quality; see "Unpacking Egypt's Low Education Score in the Global Competitiveness Report," Egyptian Initiative for Personal Rights, September 25, 2013. The same difficulties are shared by other sectors, including the security sector; see, for example, Roger Owen, The Rise and Fall of Arab Presidents for Life, Harvard University Press (2014).

29 "The Regular Courts in all Its Positions: Drawing in the Colour of Water" (القضاء العادي في جميع محطاته: رسم بلون الماء), Legal Agenda (August 2018).

which provided for a number of constitutional amendments. The amendments were based on the assumption that the consociational system contributed to the conflict, and were intended to gradually move toward a more traditional form of democratic rule. The preamble provides that "[e]liminating political sectarianism is a basic national objective, to be achieved according to a transitional plan." Article 95 provides for the establishment of a National Council that will have as its objective to "study and suggest the means capable of eliminating the sectarianism." Three decades later, close to no official efforts have been made to satisfy those objectives, despite the fact that over 70 percent of Lebanese citizens now believe that religion should not influence politics,[30] and over 90 percent of Lebanese consider that state institutions are corrupt.[31] By the end of 2019, the system of government was so unpopular that it contributed to the largest popular uprising in Lebanon's history (which at the time of writing is still ongoing).

A LIBERAL STANDARD

Scholars: If neither the text of the constitutions nor the elites themselves can clearly indicate what the purpose of a constitution should be, then who can? Some scholars consider that they are in a position to do so. In their view, the actual wording and content of a constitution should not be the ultimate measure of what its purpose is, or even should be. In their view, a single universal test should be applied to measure constitutional performance in most if not all situations. Such a test would have to be general enough to be applicable to a wide range of constitutions. But at the same time it would also have to be inspired and anchored by the values of the test's authors. No matter how hard the experts or scholars try to encapsulate universal values, the end result will always reflect a particular political understanding of the state's role (in the same way that international institutions, which are supposed to reflect universal values, in fact reflect the liberal tendencies of the western officials that typically dominate them). For example, one proposal that was made by two western scholars is that to be considered successful, a constitution would have to (i) enjoy popular legitimacy, (ii) channel conflict away from violence and into politics, (iii) limit agency costs, and (iv) create public goods.[32] It would be difficult to argue against most if not all of these criteria, but there is

30 "Wave V, Country Report: Lebanon," Arab Barometer (2018–2019), at 17.

31 Ibid., at 6.

32 See Tom Ginsburg and Aziz H. Huq, "Assessing Constitutional Performance," in Tom Ginsburg and Aziz H. Huq (eds.), Assessing Constitutional Performance, Cambridge University Press (2016), at 14–23.

little question that they reflect a liberal perspective in which the constitution and by extension the state should be as intrusive as possible on society.

National Preferences: This approach suffers from two distinct problems, the first ideological and the second practical. Ideologically, people in countries that are already nominally democratic, but which suffer from very particular circumstances that are the focus of national attention, are likely to have very particular ideas about what their constitution is supposed to achieve. For example, many Latin American constitutions have as one of their main objectives to reverse the legacies of colonialism in part by reducing economic inequality. Ecuador's 2008 Constitution provides that the State's "prime duties" include "[g]uaranteeing without any discrimination whatsoever the true possession of the rights set forth in the Constitution and in international instruments, especially the rights to education, health, food, social security and water for its inhabitants" (Article 3(1)), and the "elimination of poverty" (Article 3(5)). Brazil's 1998 Constitution provides that the "fundamental objectives of the Federative Republic of Brazil" include "eradicating poverty and substandard living conditions and reducing social and regional inequalities" (Article 3(3)). In the view of many Latin American citizens, "economic development" on its own is not the objective; it is more the provision of economic development to the millions of marginalized poor that matters. The 2014 Tunisian Constitution is also clear in its intent to establish "social justice" as a matter of priority, which clearly matches the demands of the 2011 uprising (see later). The Tunisian people and political elites appear to have reached a consensus on what their constitution is supposed to achieve; so it is unclear why anyone would seek to measure that text according to a different standard. At the other end of the spectrum, if such a test is applied to religiously inclined states that seek to promote piety and conformity to a different set of values (e.g. Iran, El Salvador), the result may be that the relevant constitutions are judged to be successes or failures according to the test, but national actors are likely to be totally indifferent to the analysis if the criteria do not reflect their own national values.

National Differences: Practically any set of universal criteria will necessarily ignore the fact that constitutions are enacted in countries with widely varying starting points and are also subject to influence by a multiplicity of factors. In some countries, achieving a single one of the proposed four criteria can sometimes require sustained effort over decades. Sudan's 2005 Interim Constitution had as its main objective to end the conflict between north and south and in that sense it can be said to have been broadly successful, even though it clearly failed to satisfy a number of other measures. Its 2019 Constitutional Charter, meanwhile, prioritizes peace with all its insurgency groups and sets a path for a transition toward civilian rule within three years. If the Constitutional Charter contributes to achieving those two things but does nothing to "limit agency costs" or "create public goods," it would nevertheless be considered to be wildly successful in the minds of a vast majority of Sudanese. Conversely, if the end result of the three-year transition is that the military still has significant influence over government and policy-making, many Sudanese will no doubt view that outcome as a failure, regardless of whether or not politics is still as violent as it was in 2019.

WHO ARE THE PEOPLE?

Exclusions: If it was the drafting process' exclusionary nature that caused the post-colonial constitutions to adopt undemocratic objectives that contributed to the near collapse in 2011, then the question must become who was excluded from the drafting process, what those actors might have wanted, and whether their inclusion might have made a difference. As already stated, controlling elites across the region excluded their political rivals from the drafting processes, albeit to varying degrees. A genuine attempt to accommodate other political groups might have led to the establishment of more plural regimes, although Lebanon's and post-2003 Iraq's respective experiences suggest that the end result for ordinary citizens is not very different. What is most striking, however, is that throughout the region, the people as a whole played only a passive and indirect role in the drafting of their own national constitutions. At the time, there may not have been any convincing mechanisms or real opportunities to involve the general population in a truly participative constitution-making process. In the post-colonial period, the political environment was undemocratic and elections could obviously not have been relied on given the history of manipulation. But our objective here is not so much to correct the past as it is to learn from it and to improve the future. In addition, as indicated in greater detail in the next section, the general population today has become an unavoidable force in any discussion on major governance reform in the region. Baghdad's three constitutional amendment committees would not have been formed at the end of 2019 had it not been for a massive protest movement. The same was true of all of the constitutional reform processes that were initiated following the 2011 uprisings.

Divisions: The first issue that emerges when considering popular participation is whether the people can ever be said to share the same view on issues relating to constitutional reform, and if not then how negotiators should manage those divisions. Clearly, while there may be near consensus on a limited number of fundamental issues (e.g. national sovereignty), this tends not to extend very far. Even where a clear and uncontested majority opinion has been expressed on a key constitutional principle (e.g. adopting a parliamentary system of government), significant proportions of the population will disagree with the voice of the majority. In 2011 it would have been reasonable to assume that crushing majorities of Egypt's population supported the calls for greater freedom and social justice, but by 2012[33] and even more so by 2013,[34] it became obvious that significant proportions of the population prioritized law and order over other considerations. How then should these divisions affect the effort to incorporate the popular will in a constitution-building process? Should one set of popular preferences be prioritized over others, even to the extent of excluding other preferences altogether? Using Egypt as an illustration, the protesters who took to the streets in 2011 faced opposition from most of the state's bureaucracy and security institutions and were met with significant violence. Meanwhile, the 2013 protests that led to the removal by the military of the president were at first assumed to have been the result of a grassroots effort with no political leadership.[35] Since then, it has been widely accepted that the protest leaders enjoyed the support of a large segment of Egypt's security establishment and of its business community.[36] Should these different circumstances encourage us to give different consideration to one

[33] In Egypt's May to June 2012 presidential elections, 48.27 percent of voters opted in favor of Ahmed Shafik, who lost only narrowly to Mohamed Morsi. Shafik was former dictator Hosni Mubarak's last appointed prime minister, and served as commander in chief of the Air Force from 1996 to 2002. During his election campaign, Shafik referred to Hosni Mubarak as a "role model"; "Egyptians Learn that Democracy Sometimes Produces Tough Choices," *The Post and Courier* (May 29, 2012). Shafik also promised a return to the old order if he was elected, including the reestablishment of a strong security state; "Ahmed Shafik, Mubarak's Last Prime Minister, Is the Surprise Contender in Egypt's Presidential Race," Hannah Allam, *McClatchy Newspaper* (May 17, 2012). For more on Shafik's campaign promises, see "Text of the Candidate Ahmed Shafik's Speech at the End of His Electoral Campaign" ("نص خطاب المرشح أحمد شفيق فى ختام حملته الانتخابية"), Al-Watan News (June 14, 2012).

[34] By the end of June 2013, a large segment of Egypt's population grew so frustrated by president Mohamed Morsi's performance that millions participated in protests demanding that he resign, and subsequently appeared to support the military's decision to depose him. See "Protesters across Egypt Call for Mohamed Morsi to Go," Patrick Kingsley, *The Guardian* (June 30, 2013).

[35] Ibid. (quoting Michael Hanna, a fellow at the Century Foundation, as saying that the protests were remarkable because they were "a bottom-up, grassroots effort and not directed by political opposition leaders. In a sense, they have latched on to this expanding current. While the organisers were diligent and creative, while lacking organisation and funding, this breadth of mass mobilisation could not have transpired unless the protest movement was tapping into deep and growing frustration and disenchantment with the current course of the country and its leadership").

[36] See, for example, Ben Hubbard and David D. Kirkpatrick, "Sudden Improvements in Egypt Suggest a Campaign to Undermine Morsi," *The New York Times* (July 10, 2013); Mohamed Ali Hasan, "Al-Watan Reveals Full Details of the Communications between the Army and

group's set of political preferences over the other? It seems obvious to say that, in a revolutionary environment, and where a constitution-making process is taking place in response to a mass protest movement, the views of millions of protesters who take to the streets over a period of months and who face harsh retribution from the state cannot and should not be ignored. It is only through the effort to address the demands that those protesters make that a country and its population can hope to progress and return state and society back to stability and normalcy. At the same time, however, all mainstream views should be given their proper consideration, even if some of those views are conservative in nature and are in opposition to the desires of a determined protest movement, for to ignore any mainstream popular opinion is to run the risk of reaching an undemocratic outcome and to worsen instability.[37]

Reconciliation: The result of including the people as an actor in a constitution-making process is that different preferences will have to be reconciled. That process will be challenging but will nevertheless be facilitated by the fact that popular preferences will be expressed in very broad terms, which leaves scope for identifying points of agreement. For example, since the nineteenth century, experts on Latin American constitutionalism have argued that the struggle for independence and against economic backwardness constituted the "great dramas" of the time and that the region's constitutional frameworks should have been geared in favor of resolving those dramas.[38] More recently, Latin American scholars have identified "inequality" as the region's modern drama.[39] Clearly, if large segments of Latin America's population prioritizes the struggle against inequality, then so do many seek to maintain their positions of privilege, often on the basis that the economy

Tamarod on 3 July" ("الوطن تكشف التفاصيل الكاملة لاتصال الجيش بـ"تمرد" يوم 3 يوليو"), Al-Watan (July 4, 2015).

[37] Not all views can be considered. In some situations, it will simply not be possible to consult the general population, or a segment of the populace, or to satisfactorily enquire what their priorities might be (e.g. during an all-out conflict, such as in Syria during the civil conflict that commenced in 2012). In other situations, smaller proportions of the population will have strongly held views and a decision will therefore have to be made on which views should be considered to be mainstream (and therefore be considered during the constitutional drafting process) and which should be considered to be peripheral (and therefore be excluded), which itself requires its own in-depth discussion that is beyond the scope of this volume.

[38] Juan Bautista Alberdi, Obras de Juan Bautista Alberdi, IberiaLiteratura (2015).

[39] Roberto Gargarella, Latin American Constitutionalism, 1810–2010: The Engine Room of the Constitution, Oxford University Press (2013), at 196. For more on the drama of inequality in Latin America and the impact that it has on public acceptance of existing constitutional frameworks, see 'The Latinobarómetro Poll: When the Tide Goes out', The Economist (September 26, 2015).

and general welfare are better served under the status quo.[40] Where divisions of this nature exist, the reader seeking to uncover a population's constitutional objective will have to make her own individual assessment of whether different visions for a country's fundamental text can be reconciled, or even whether one set of objectives should be prioritized over others. In the case of Latin America, one could convincingly argue that failing to prioritize the struggle against inequality is inviting a society to breakdown as a whole, which itself would undermine one segment of the population's goal to maintain privilege. Meanwhile, in the Arab region, the result of prioritizing law and order over all other considerations has already been made clear through the 2011 uprisings.

THE PEOPLE'S MANIFESTO

How Slogans Spread: So what do the people want? In western liberal settings, the popular will is determined through traditional means, including but not limited to elections and referenda. Revolutionary environments introduce major complications to the equation, including the use of political violence as a means of coercion and the power of popular mobilization. The 2011 uprisings were among the first to take place in an era of immediate and direct communication between peoples within individual countries and across an entire region, unfiltered by political party leaders, newsroom editors, and government censors. Popular demands were developed, sloganized, and then tested on the streets. Slogans that articulated fringe demands would typically not find favor with protesters and would not gain significant traction. In contrast, slogans that successfully articulated popular preferences were met with popular approval. This would lead to individual slogans propagating through protests, which would increase the likelihood of slogans being filmed and disseminated through various platforms, including traditional media and social media platforms, exposing larger and larger numbers of audiences to the same popular slogans. The snowball effect would then result in a conversation involving millions of determined protesters over a period of weeks and months, sometimes even years, which would cause for those same slogans to be developed and refined even further.

The People's Slogan: The principal slogan that joined crowds together throughout virtually every country in the region was "the people want the downfall of the regime" (الشعب يريد اسقاط النظام). Protesters in Tunisia were the

40 See Andre Gunder Frank, Capitalism and Underdevelopment in Latin America: Historical Studies of Chile and Brazil, Monthly Review Press (1967).

first to formulate this demand, and it quickly spread throughout the region, although not everywhere and not always all at once. Protesters in Morocco generally refrained from using this particular slogan, for a combination of reasons, including a general understanding that Moroccans are attached to some of their traditional institutions, including the monarchy. Protesters generally focused their attention on specific aspects of the ruling regime (including, for example, corruption) as opposed to the regime's very existence.[41] Meanwhile, the demand spread rapidly through Egypt, Libya, Yemen, and Sudan, among others. In Iraq, the 2011 protests generally eschewed calls to end the post-2003 order, and focused instead on demanding specific reforms, including action against high level corruption. By 2019, however, after close to a decade of government inaction, the popular mood had changed and the protest movement adopted the slogan.[42] The same evolution took place in Lebanon and in Algeria.[43]

The People: The people want the end of the regime. Those few words densely packed together a number of important concepts that directly address the dynamics set out in the previous subsection, and therefore the phrase is worth breaking down into its component parts. First, protesters self-identified as "the people" (الشعب), which is by itself a major innovation. Before, during, and after the colonial period, citizens and residents of the region were always at the receiving end of action by local rulers and invaders, and were never consulted on the types of policies that might satisfy their own needs. Through the use of the term "the people," the protest movement sought to reimpose the people as a new category of actor in each country's political dynamic, in opposition to other preexisting groups, including specific political parties, trade unionists, or particular communities (geographic, demographic, religious, or otherwise). Through their repeated use of the term, protesters were distinguishing themselves from the elite pact that had been in force since the colonial period, as well as the fact that they were excluded from it. In Iraq, protesters' sense of exclusion by the state was so extreme that a complementary slogan was widely adopted, which read "I want a nation."[44] Popular

[41] See, for example, anti-corruption slogans sung at a football stadium in October 2019 such as: www.youtube.com/watch?v=6hJ-fjQhCYQ.

[42] See Zahra Ali and Safaa Khalaf, "In Iraq, Demonstrators Demand Change – and the Government Fights Back," *The Washington Post* (October 9, 2019).

[43] Dozens of online videos show how often and in what numbers protesters adopted the slogan. See, for example, www.youtube.com/watch?v=j_aW9joLXJs (for Lebanon) and www.youtube.com/watch?v=ROyb1lno6qM (for Algeria).

[44] See Zahra Ali, "Iraqi Demand a Country," Middle East Research and Information Project, 292/3 (Fall/Winter 2019).

sovereignty was therefore now a core demand of the protest movement. "The people" defines the protest movement as broadly as possible, in response to the compartmentalization by the elite pact of society into winners and losers. "The people" were now determined to sweep all those categories away in favor of each country's entire citizenry. As noted previously, the "people" were obviously an amorphous group, which was not necessarily limited to those who were excluded from the elite pact (for example, the unemployed).[45] Many trade unionists, bureaucrats, and even members of the security sector were acutely aware of their declining socioeconomic status and therefore joined the protests.[46] This movement toward popular unity did not include all components of society (each group's respective leadership was often less enthusiastic than the rank and file) nor did it extend far beyond the first victories against the ruling regimes.

Want: Second, protesters did not only impose themselves as a physical and a political presence but were also taking action to shape their own destiny: Now, they were saying, not only do the people exist but they also "want" (يريد). For more than a hundred years, ruling regimes had prevented the broader community of citizens living under their control from expressing its views openly. Many countries never organized elections (including countries such as Iraq, where referenda on presidents were organized instead), others organized sham elections (including Yemen, where opposition candidates called for all citizens to support the incumbent president), and all countries practically eliminated opportunities for speech (including by prohibiting any discussion of senior officials' health). That period of oppression had been crumbling for some time but by 2011 was firmly at an end. During the uprisings, protesters adopted a radically different approach. They were not responding to any specific action on the part of their national governments; they did not take to the streets to express displeasure at the passing of a new constitutional reform or the passage of a new law. The people had taken to the streets because they "wanted" to impose an agenda that was independent from whatever their national governments were devising.

The Regime: Third, protesters clearly identified whom their action was directed against, namely the "regime" (النظام). The term's main characteristic is its comprehensiveness. The people were not making demands in relation to a

45 Amin Allal, "Becoming a Revolutionary in Tunisia, 2007–2011," in Joel Beinin and Frédéric Vairel (eds.), SOCIAL MOVEMENTS, MOBILIZATION, AND CONTESTATION IN THE MIDDLE EAST AND NORTH AFRICA, Stanford University Press (2013).

46 Marie Duboc, "Challenging the Trade Union, Reclaiming the Nation: The Politics of Labor Protest in Egypt, 2006–2011," in Mehran Kamrava (ed.), BEYOND THE ARAB SPRING: THE EVOLVING RULING BARGAIN IN THE MIDDLE EAST, Oxford University Press (2014), at 247.

political party or a specific institution (such as the police, the courts, or even the presidency). The demand was directed against the entire functioning of government, including constitutional arrangements such as the elite pact, executive immunity, presidents for life, as well as institutional mechanisms that deliberately allowed for corruption and nepotism to thrive.[47] For a period of a few hours, there was some disagreement in Egypt about this specific term, in response to Hosni Mubarak's offer to delegate his powers to his newly appointed vice-president, Omar Suleiman.[48] The mass of protesters in Tahrir Square and elsewhere in Egypt immediately rejected the initiative, but there were different views about how that rejection should be conveyed. For some, the view was that the focus on the "regime" should be replaced by the "president." Very quickly, however, protesters reverted to the slogan's original formulation, which continued to be the preferred message of protest even after Mubarak was forced from office.[49] Protesters were in agreement: Their struggle was not uniquely against a specific individual but targeted an entire system of government. In Algeria and in Sudan, protesters continued to set the regime in their sights even after their respective presidents were removed from office in April 2019.

Downfall: Finally, protesters were plain in their intent. For the regimes, they saw only one possible form of remedial action, which was its "downfall" (اسقاط). Apart from in Morocco, where protesters were more measured in their demands, protesters demanded not only reforms, a new president, or even a new government but also a complete break from the past. The regime's downfall could only mean one thing: a constitutional, legal, and institutional revolution. Given that the "regime" consisted of a specific set of rules that held the states' institutions together, a new arrangement would have to be devised, this time not for the elite pact's benefit but in favor of the "people." In Iraq, the 2019 protest movement insisted on electoral reform and early elections as a first step toward achieving that aim. In their view, a constitutional reform effort

[47] For Lebanese and Iraqi protesters, their regimes were principally defined by consociational and sectarian arrangements. The 2011 protest movement in both countries focused on those arrangements as a matter of priority. See, for example, slogans from Lebanon's largest demonstration in 2011 at www.youtube.com/watch?v=SHo3aTEMLlU.

[48] See Anthony Shadid and David D. Kirkpatrick, "Mubarak Refuses to Step Down, Stoking Revolt's Fury and Resolve," *New York Times* (February 10, 2011).

[49] Throughout 2011 and a large part of 2012, while Egypt was under the control of the Supreme Council of the Armed Forces, protesters alternated between demanding the fall of "the regime" and the "fall of the field marshal." See www.youtube.com/watch?v=T9JmBTotCWQ. In Tunisia, after the first government after the fall of Zine El Abidine Ben Ali was composed, protesters insisted on its dismissal, by demanding the "downfall of the regime." See "Police Join Protests in Tunisia," Al Jazeera (January 23, 2011).

carried out by the members of the same political class could never be successful.

Social Justice: Through their demand that the regime should be collapsed, the protest movement established part of a substantive goal, which was the desire to eliminate an entire system of government. But by what should that system be replaced? Here consensus within the protest movement already starts to break down, as there is not a single unifying aspiration that was shared by all protesters throughout the region. There were, however, individual concepts that were adopted by protesters throughout the region, and that formed the basis of slogans and other demands throughout the region, including the demand for "social justice." In Egypt, protesters very quickly came to demand that any new regime should deliver "bread, freedom and social justice." "Bread" in this context represented a demand for improved economic opportunities and an end to hunger. "Freedom" was connected to the same idea of the "people" being in opposition and demanding the downfall of the "regime." The reference to "freedom" was to be understood as a demand for less state interference in the exercise of civil and political rights. "Social justice" is a more flexible term, particularly given that it has never been properly defined.[50] The term does include some features that, within the context, can be used to at least give an idea as to its meaning. The use of the term "social" in particular suggests that protesters favored policies that were aimed at redressing ills that were suffered by the population as a whole. Given that each of the region's societies includes affluent members who do not require any specific redress, the intent here is therefore not to benefit every member of society individually but to improve society as a whole through an improvement of citizens' relationship with each other.

THE DRAFTERS' RESPONSE

Preambles: Did the post-2011 constitutional drafters listen? A reading of the post-2011 constitutions suggests that they were at least aware of the demands that were being made. The preambles to the Egyptian (2014), Tunisian (2014), Moroccan (2011), and Syrian (2012) constitutions as well as the Sudanese Constitutional Charter (2019) constitute strong evidence that the drafters

[50] Some practitioners and scholars consider the use of specific undefined terms to be advantageous in the context of contentious constitution-making processes, and as a means to absorb and possibly even defer contentious debates that might otherwise prevent a final agreement on the text. See, for example, Markus Böckenförde, "From Constructive Ambiguity to Harmonious Interpretation: Religion-Related Provisions in the Tunisian Constitution," American Behavioral Scientist, Vol. 60, No. 8 (2016), 919–940.

sought to address the concerns that were being expressed by the protesters and revolutionaries.[51] All of these preambles offer historical and political narratives, which are designed to encapsulate the state's ideology, and also to divorce the new state from previous generations of ruling authorities or at least to reinforce the importance of certain segments of the existing ruling elite. Although each of these constitutions include idiosyncrasies that reflect unique national circumstances (e.g. the role of the monarchy in Morocco or the sense of international isolation in Syria), there are themes and principles that recur in all of the preambles. All of the texts without exception make reference to the people's or the nation's place in the world community, sometimes through the mention of international institutions and at other times by providing an account of the nation's contributions to world history. More importantly, the texts also strongly emphasize popular sovereignty and social justice, sometimes to the extent that these principles are repeated several times within just a few lines. In fact, the post-2011 constitutions contained so many references to social justice that there are too many to list.

Post-2011 preambles: To name but a few examples, the preamble of Egypt's 2014 Constitution states that its purpose is to "achieve freedom and social justice together" (an exact reflection of the popular slogan cited previously), that the Egyptian people believe in "democracy as a path, a future, and a way of life; in political plurality; and in the peaceful transfer of power," and that all people have the right to "[f]reedom, human dignity, and social justice." The preamble of Tunisia's 2014 Constitution provides that the constitution has as its objective to establish the "framework of a civil state founded on the law and on the sovereignty of the people," and that the constitution seeks to "build on national unity that is based on citizenship, fraternity, solidarity, and social justice." According to the preamble of Morocco's 2011 Constitution, the state seeks to establish a "democratic State of Law" through "participation, of pluralism and of good governance," and also develops a "society of solidarity where all enjoy security, liberty, equality of opportunities, of respect for their dignity and for social justice." The Syrian preamble states that the new constitution establishes a number of principles, including the "rule of the people based on elections, political and party-based pluralism, [...] social justice, equality, equal opportunities, citizenship, and the rule of law." Finally, Sudan's 2019 Constitutional Charter cites social justice prominently on more than one occasion. In its preamble, it states that the negotiating parties "[s]trive to implement measures to achieve [...] a state of prosperity,

[51] The 2017 draft Libyan and 2015 draft Yemeni constitutions do not include preambles.

welfare and social justice." Meanwhile, Article 41, which is the first provision of the rights and freedoms chapter, provides that "the human rights and fundamental freedoms contained in the document [...] shall be considered the cornerstone of social justice, equality and democracy in Sudan."

Pre-2011: The wording used in post-2011 constitutions can be contrasted against preambles of the previous generation of constitutions. Although the latter made some reference to progressive values that are similar in nature to the desire to achieve "social justice," these were often secondary concerns in comparison with the-then ruling authorities' political aims, including the establishment of socialism and the monopolization of power by undemocratic forces. The preamble to Morocco's 1996 Constitution made quick reference to international organizations and obligations, and to the need to establish peace and security in the world and made no mention of the needs or aspirations of ordinary people. Syria's 1973 Constitution essentially consisted of a historical narrative from the point of view of the Syrian Baath party. The need for "Arab unity" was emphasized on several occasions, as well as the "establishment of a socialist order." The preamble also stated that "[f]reedom is a sacred right and popular democracy is the ideal formulation" but only after several references were made to the Baath party's special role in guiding state and society. The preamble to Egypt's 1971 Constitution was clearly drafted with progressive ideals in mind. Multiple references are made to the "dignity of man," although no clear explanation is offered as to what human dignity consists of. The preamble also committed the state to a broadly progressive agenda that was perfectly suited to the 1970s, including the "integration between science and faith, between political and social freedom, between national independence and social affiliation." Tunisia's 1959 Constitution was the only text that would not be out of place among post-2011 constitutions. It made reference to "human dignity, justice and liberty," the "sovereignty of the people," "respect of human rights," and "citizens' right to work, health care and education" (roughly equivalent to the modern conception of social justice in the Arab region). The major difference between the 1959 Constitution and its successor was the former's moral conservatism, for example, when it specifically stated that the text had as one of its main objections to "protect the family."

Fulfilling Promises: The evolution from the earlier generation of Arab constitutions to the post-2011 texts could not be clearer. Constitutional drafters from 2011 to 2014 were clearly conscious of the need to respond to the demands of the people and adopted the exact same terminology that was used in demonstrations throughout the region (even in Syria). As such, the constitution's stated aims, as expressed in their preambles, overlap to a very large extent with the popular aspirations of the people. But while the change in rhetoric is obvious to see, the mere fact of catching the drafters' attention had already been achieved in the immediate post-colonial period. Did the drafters of the post-2011 constitutions establish institutional mechanisms, principles, and rules that would give meaning to terms such as social justice?

For there to be a chance that the post-2011 constitutions would respond to the popular demands for change, a number of conditions would have to be satisfied. At a bare minimum, advocates in favor of change would have to have a clear vision of the types of substantive changes they wanted to see introduced. In addition, their vision would also have to include specific ideas about how the constitutional negotiation and drafting process should be constructed in order to allow these discussions to take place.

7

The Individual (or the Search for Meaning)

INTRODUCTION

In late 2019 hundreds of thousands of Iraqis took to the streets in response to decades of high level corruption, massive youth unemployment, dysfunctional public services, and abusive treatment by the security services. In their view, the state and the constitutional system that underpinned it were collapsing. In a clear sign of their sense of marginalization from the state, the most common popular slogan carried by protesters communicated a simple demand, "I want a nation."[1] A civil disobedience campaign was organized lasting months. Central squares were occupied in more than a dozen cities. Universities and schools were forced to close their doors. Protesters made a number of demands, including a new electoral system and early elections, which many hoped would lead to much of the country's corrupt and inept ruling class being replaced by better quality lawmakers. Many protesters considered that constitutional reform should take place if and when early elections based on a new electoral system were carried out.

Security forces were called in to bring the protests under control, resulting in hundreds of deaths and thousands of wounded. Security officials shot dozens of unarmed protesters in the face with military grade tear gas canisters, which penetrated the skull, crushing the brain and causing smoke to bellow from ears, nose, mouth, and eye cavities.[2] Many deaths were blamed by the Prime Minister and other senior officials on an unnamed "third party," which was never formally identified. Prominent journalists and civil society activists who were linked to the protests were assassinated in the street. Protesters were

[1] The slogan was motivated by a sense that the state institutions that were created in 2003–2005 did not constitute a functional basis for a viable nation state. See Zahra Ali, "Iraqis Demand a Country," Middle East Research and Information Project, 292/3 (Fall/Winter 2019).

[2] "Iraq: Teargas Cartridges Killing Protesters," Human Rights Watch, November 8, 2019.

arrested and some were kidnapped. Some protesters signed documents stating that they were members of terrorist organizations, confessions that they say were extracted during torture.[3] Senior security officials threatened others with annihilation in broad daylight and on camera.[4] Meanwhile, the justice system was essentially silent. Only a few arrest warrants were issued against security officers who were clearly using disproportionate force against protesters, and even fewer were actually prosecuted for human rights violations.

In response to this dramatic situation, state institutions promised a series of reforms. One of the first measures that was taken was to redesign the electoral law in favor of a system that would theoretically allow more independent oversight over political parties. In addition, by October 2019, three different state institutions established their own constitutional revision committees despite the fact that protesters were determined that constitutional reform should only take place after early elections. One of the committees was composed entirely on an ethno-sectarian basis, with all members being drawn from mainstream political forces.[5] The other two committees consisted of independents, activists, and academics and also a small number of representatives from the protest movement.

Close to none of the discussions that took place revolved around the relationship between the individual and the state and focused instead on rebalancing the relationship between state institutions (each of which was controlled by specific political groups). Two of the three committees adopted an "article-by-article" approach to their discussions, which necessarily reduced the scope for major changes and ensured that the near totality of suggested amendments consisted of minor improvements to wording and discrete arrangements. Both committees flew past the 2005 Constitution's section on civil and political rights, including Article 19 that guaranteed due process rights, without suggesting any significant changes. Daily violations of basic rights by the state did not register as a major concern that should be redressed. Instead, the two committees were absorbed by issues that would not have any direct impact on ordinary people's lives. At one particular session that took

3 See "Human Rights Special Report: Demonstrations in Iraq – 2nd Update," Human Rights Office, United Nations Assistance Mission to Iraq (UNAMI), November 5–December 9, 2019, at 6.

4 See statements by the chief of police in Dhi Qar province (in Arabic), on January 8, 2020, available at https://twitter.com/SajadJiyad/status/1214968950959857664 (also on file with the author).

5 The committee's composition was subject to very significant criticism. In response, seven academics were invited to serve as advisers to the committee. The academics were not chosen on a sectarian basis but they were invited to participate only once.

place in December 2019, members discussed Article 61(6)(b)(iii), according to which the parliament can relieve the President of the Republic from their official duties following a conviction for "high treason" before the Federal Supreme Court. The entire session was dedicated to whether a definition of "high treason" existed under Iraqi law, and which body should be responsible for trying the president. That discussion took place in a highly charged atmosphere: the prime minister had just resigned, triggering Article 76 of the constitution, which provided that the President of the Republic should charge the nominee of the largest parliamentary bloc with the formation of a new government. The president had received the nomination but refused to discharge his duties, on the basis that the nominee was highly unpopular and could cause further unrest in the country. In a letter to the speaker of parliament, the president offered to resign.[6] This context was not mentioned during the committee's deliberations, but it was clear that the president's allies and enemies were both positioning their arguments in response to recent developments. Similarly, at one of the other committee's regular meetings organized in the same week, members argued for hours whether Article 64, which set out the circumstances in which parliament could be dissolved, should be amended to allow the President of the Republic to dissolve the parliament without the prime minister's consent.

Dynamics within the third committee were different. It was smaller in size, which meant that individual members had a greater impact on the discussion. As it turned out, at least two of the members were determined to bring about change, which sometimes led to serious discussions about reform. In December 2019 the committee's chair had decided to focus attention on possible changes to the court system. The courts were essentially incapable of preventing regular human rights abuses,[7] and their standing in Iraqi society was declining rapidly.[8] The chair asked one of the two progressive members (not a lawyer) to prepare a series of recommendations for discussion. At the session, he offered a number of key reflections on the judiciary. First, the court system is nominally independent but is politically aligned to the parliament

6 See Letter from President of the Republic to the Speaker of Parliament, December 26, 2019 (on file with the author).

7 See "Report on the Judicial Response to Allegations of Torture in Iraq," United Nations Assistance Mission to Iraq, February 2015.

8 See "Iraq Country Report," Arab Barometer, 2019 (an opinion poll that shows support for the judiciary dropped from 54 percent in 2011 to 38 percent in 2018, a 16 percent drop); see also Munqith Dagher, "100 days of Adel Abd al-Mahdi's Government," IIASS, February 2019, at 9 (an opinion poll that shows respondents evaluated the Iraqi courts' performance at an average of 4.3, on a scale of 1 to 10).

and by extension to the government. Article 61(5)(a) of the 2005 Constitution provides that parliament is responsible for appointing the president and members of the Federal Court of Cassation, the Chief Public Prosecutor, and the President of Judicial Oversight Commission. Those individuals together make up the entirety of the High Judicial Council, which itself is responsible for administering all of the judicial internal affairs.[9] The committee member therefore argued that, through those arrangements, the parliament and government indirectly have a hand in everything that happens in the judiciary. Second, the committee member insisted that the judiciary's work was highly opaque. The Public Prosecutor and the Judicial Oversight Commission are both responsible for overseeing different aspects of the judicial process, but were under the High Judicial Council's control, which meant that there could be no effective oversight. All of the Oversight Commission's members were judges, who were highly collegial with their colleagues on the bench and worked in secrecy. None of its reports and decisions were publicly available. The committee member concluded that in the circumstances it was no surprise that the courts offered no assistance to ordinary people in situations where security officials were engaging in blatant human rights violations.

The member suggested a number of possible changes that could help resolve that situation: Reform the process through which the High Judicial Council's members are appointed to reduce the legislature and the government's influence over its internal policies; amend its composition to include nonjurists, so as to reduce the influence of collegiality; separate the Public Prosecutor and the Oversight Commission from the Judicial Council, to increase the chances that they will act independently and exercise real oversight; and amend the composition of the Oversight Commission to include a majority of nonjurists and provide for the publication online of all its decisions as well as an annual report. All of the other committee members but one responded negatively to each of these suggestions. One member who was a law professor noted that Supreme Court judges in the United States were confirmed by the Senate, and that there was therefore no basis for disentangling Iraq's judiciary from the parliament. Another member, who theoretically represented the protest movement, could not hide his hostility to the mere suggestion that things could be improved. The Judicial Council would necessarily be corrupt no matter how it was composed. Judges would never accept inspection carried out by laymen. It was all hopeless, he said. One member representing the bar association ended by arguing that there was

[9] See Law 45 (2017), Article 2.

in fact no need to engage in any reform of the court system whatsoever. The session ended with the member who had proposed all of the reforms asking, "So what do we do? Are the streets not full of protesters?" His lament was met with barely a shrug.

A private lawyer who was connected to the halls of power was invited to join one of the committees as an informal adviser. After attending a few meetings and taking note of how all the deliberations appeared to be ignoring the popular demands for change, he decided to make an intervention. The following day, during a break in the discussions, he addressed all of the members. People had taken to the streets in massive spontaneous uprisings to demand fundamental change, which was why these high level discussions on the constitution were taking place. However, the only concern that appeared to be motivating discussions in the committee room was tilting the balance of power in favor of one political group and away from that of their political rivals. He implored the committee members to focus their attention back on what should have been the main concern of the discussion, which was the demand for freedom and social justice. This he said meant that the main area of focus should be to redress the relationship between the individual and the state. As soon as he ended, one of the members responded dismissively, "Your concern is misplaced. Iraqi citizens have the most generous rights in the region. We are on the only free country in the region."

FREEDOM

Preconditions: The 2011 uprisings focused enormous attention on basic freedoms and the general framework for the protection of basic freedoms in national constitutions. Aside from the decades of oppression, the violence that was inflicted on protesters during the uprisings themselves made it inevitable that constitutional negotiators would dedicate significant attention on this issue. As indicated in more detail later, drafters introduced a number of changes to their respective constitutions' sections on fundamental rights, only some of which have a chance of benefiting the general population. To be clear, however, no effort by the drafters can successfully improve the protection of basic freedoms unless a number of preconditions are satisfied. First, as indicated in Chapter 8, the hyper-presidential system of government that is so prevalent everywhere in the region must be abandoned, not only because it excludes other political actors from government but also because it necessarily strips the general population of its basic rights. If and when hyper-presidentialism is abandoned in favor of a more democratic political environment (as was achieved in Tunisia), the competitive political environment could result in significant benefits for the general population. The transition could also result in individuals or groups of individuals leveraging institutions such as the courts (that are no longer under the total control of the chief executive) for their own benefit. First and foremost, however, drafters must understand the problem with the way in which the constitution is constructed and propose adequate solutions.

Clawback Clauses: Arab constitutions have long been criticized for limiting fundamental rights and freedoms, but all societies limit fundamental rights in some form; every piece of legislation that regulates human activity carries with it at least the potential for the limitation of some right. Freedom of expression is limited by the prohibition against defamation. Freedom of movement is limited to make public transport more efficient (through traffic lights), to protect law and order through the detention of criminals, and for economic reasons, including the desire to protect local labor markets by preventing large-scale immigration. Many constitutions specifically require parliament to determine how each right should be limited. Where these provisions can be validly criticized it is because they do not limit the extent to which fundamental rights and freedoms can be controlled. These provisions are commonly referred to as "clawback clauses" because they recognize the existence of a specific right while at the same time clawing back whatever benefit might have flowed from that right.[10] For example, Article 8 of Tunisia's 1959 Constitution provided that "[f]reedom of opinion, expression, the press, publication, assembly and association are guaranteed and exercised according to the terms defined by the law." Article 25 of Libya's 1951 Constitution provided that "[t]he right of peaceful meetings is guaranteed within the limits of law." Article 47 of Egypt's 1971 Constitution provided that "[f]reedom of opinion is guaranteed. Every individual has the right to express his opinion and to disseminate it verbally or in writing or by photography or by other means within the limits of the law." These provisions follow an identical pattern: They merely announced that the right existed, and that it was subject to restriction, without providing any indication as to how far that restriction could extend. In practice, hundreds if not thousands of laws were passed that so restricted those rights that they rendered the rights themselves completely meaningless. For example, in accordance with the 1959 Constitution, Tunisia's criminal code provided that it was a criminal offense to possess or distribute "tracts that can harm

[10] C. R. M. Dlamini, "Towards a Regional Protection of Human Rights in Africa: The African Charter on Human and Peoples' Rights," The Comparative and International Law Journal of Southern Africa, Vol. 24, No. 2 (July 1991), 189–203.

public order or good morals" (Article 121(3)).[11] In Egypt, under the 1971 Constitution, rules were passed that prohibited any public criticism of the police, the army, or the courts.[12] It became almost impossible to criticize the state, which meant that freedom of expression was essentially nonexistent, despite Article 47's very broad and apparently generous wording.

Rewording: Following the 2011 protests, despite the context, the overwhelming majority of drafters failed to improve the general framework for the protection of rights. For the most part, the drafters maintained the framework in place while simultaneously throwing sand in protesters' eyes with new wording that was extremely unlikely to have any impact. Generally speaking, drafters introduced two main changes to provisions on rights and freedoms. First, drafters simply reworded the provisions that they had inherited from the past by introducing wording that sounded more forceful but did not make any substantive difference. Article 7 of Jordan's 1952 Constitution originally only provided that "[p]ersonal freedom shall be guaranteed." Jordan's colonial period having only just ended, the statement was designed to affirm that Jordanians and others who lived in the country could live their lives free from oppression. In keeping with that logic, Article 8 set out some due process rights (including that "[e]very person detained [. . .] should be treated in a manner that preserves human dignity") and Article 9 provided that Jordanians could not be deported (a standard colonial practice). In 2011 the ad hoc committee that was tasked with proposing amendments to the Constitution turned their attention to Article 7. In the context of popular demands for greater freedom, the committee included a new second paragraph according to which "[a]ny infringement on the rights and public freedoms or sanctity of private life of Jordanians is a crime punishable by law." The wording appears forceful and may have impressed some leaders when they read it. However, on closer inspection, it is confusing and is probably completely meaningless. Article 15 provides that freedom of expression is guaranteed provided that it is exercised within "the limits of the law." Given that Article 7(2) now provides that public freedoms cannot be infringed, does this mean that legislation can now no longer limit freedom of expression as provided for under Article 15? That would lead to unlimited freedom of expression, and would also mean that much of the Constitution (including part of Article 15) would have to be

[11] Article 121(3) was introduced to the Criminal Code through Law 43 (2001). For more, see "Tunisia's Repressive Laws: The Reform Agenda," Human Rights Watch (2011).

[12] See Article 133 of Egypt's Criminal Code, as amended on April 22, 1982 (according to which any person who defames a public official, a security official, or any person who is responsible for public service shall be imprisoned for a period not exceeding six months).

disregarded, which is clearly not what the drafters intended. In that case, is Article 7(2) intended to mean that infringements of freedom of expression that are not permissible under the law should be criminalized? That would also be nonsensical given that it casts the net far too widely. If that principle were ever applied, it could lead to perverse effects given that state officials would be extremely reluctant to take any action for fear that they could then be charged with a crime if they were found to have made a mistake. The result of all this confusion is that despite its strong wording, Article 7(2) has had no impact in practice. In another example of the type of minor changes in wording that took place post-2011, Syria's 1973 Constitution provided that "[c]itizens have the right to meet and demonstrate peacefully within the principles of the Constitution. The law regulates the exercise of this right" (Article 39). That provision was replaced in 2012 with the following wording, "[c]itizens have the right to assemble and demonstrate peacefully and to strike from work within the principles of the Constitution and the laws that regulate the exercise of these rights" (Article 44). These mild terminological differences will not make any difference to the way in which ordinary citizens can exercise their rights, particularly in countries such as Syria.[13]

Subsequent Law: In other cases, drafters argued that the solution to the web of repressive laws that had been passed prior to 2011 was simply to remove the reference to subsequent law altogether, which would then guarantee that the rights themselves could not be limited by legislation. By way of example, whereas Article 47 of Egypt's 1971 Constitution provided that freedom of expression should be exercised "within the limits of the law," Article 45 of Egypt's 2012 Constitution provided that "[f]reedom of thought and opinion is guaranteed. Every individual has the right to express an opinion and to disseminate it verbally, in writing or illustration, or by any other means of publication and expression."[14] Article 31 of Tunisia's 2014 Constitution removed the reference to subsequent law that was included in Article 8 of the 1959 Constitution. Morocco's 1996 Constitution had previously stated that "[n]o limitation, except by law, shall be imposed on the exercise of" freedom of expression (Article 9), whereas the 2011 Constitution provides that "[t]he freedoms of thought, of opinion and of expression under all their forms are guaranteed" (Article 25). However, deleting the reference to subsequent law cannot make any difference, given that all rights in all countries are subject to

[13] Other examples include Article 15(1) of Jordan's Constitution and Article 52 of Algeria's 2020 Draft Constitution.

[14] The provision was readopted without any substantial change in Article 65 of Egypt's 2014 Constitution.

at least some form of limitation. Given that in most countries, the state's institutional framework remained firmly intact, with its traditions and culture, these amendments were never likely to have any impact. By way of example, the adoption of the 2014 Constitution had no impact on Article 121(3) in Tunisia's Criminal Code, which was still in force at the time of writing in early 2021. The drafters were either deliberately mischaracterizing their work or had genuinely misunderstood the problem.

Impact: For the most part, these modest changes have not made any difference in practice. In Morocco, following a wave of protests, fifty-three members of a protest movement were condemned in April 2019 for having participated in a "conspiracy aiming to undermine state security." Some were given twenty-year prison terms. When a journalist criticized the court's decision, he himself was condemned to four months in prison for having "offended a magistrate." In Algeria, throughout 2019 and 2020, individuals were also regularly arrested merely for having participated in protests, for expressing support for the protests on their social media pages, or for carrying flags other than the national flag.[15] In Iraq, security services responded to the 2019 protests with extreme violence. Hundreds were killed, but the courts only carried out a handful of prosecutions against the state.[16] In 2019, Jordanian authorities arrested and detained and charged a large number of individuals who criticized state officials. Even in Tunisia, which has made significant advances in other ways (see later), courts have applied what appears to be arbitrary standards in the protection of rights. In one case, an activist published a short text on her Facebook page that sought to caricature the state's measures to guard against COVID-19. The activist's writing adopted a Koranic style, which was deemed to be offensive to public morals by the court, which sentenced the activist to six months in prison.[17] In another case, a student was expelled from his university for six months for having criticized the university's administration in an online post. The student appealed the decision but the court maintained the penalty despite procedural irregularity on the university's part.[18]

[15] In one case, scores of protesters were given one-year prison sentences for having carried an Amazigh flag.

[16] At a point when 354 protesters had been killed and 8,104 had been injured during protests that had been ongoing for months, only two security officers had been prosecuted; see "Iraq: New Protester Deaths Despite Order Not to Fire," Human Rights Watch (December 4, 2019).

[17] "Tunisia: Blogger Emna Chargui Sentenced to Six Months in Prison for Social Media Post," Amnesty International (July 15, 2020).

[18] See Administrative Court Decision 4104074 (October 22, 2019), unpublished.

Defining Limitations: If these minor changes in wording make no difference, what might have been done to meet the popular demand for greater freedom? The answer is to acknowledge that rights must be limited, while at the same time seeking to prevent the arbitrary application of limitations in the future. Aside from their clearly undemocratic features, the pre-2011 constitutions' main failing point was that they did not give any indication to the executive, legislature, and judiciary of what types of limitation were permissible and which were not.[19] Even where the courts were under no pressure to find in favor of the government, they simply had no criteria on which to base their decision. Constitutional negotiators and drafters who are genuinely interested in delivering freedom to the region's population should focus first and foremost on the issue of limitations. More specifically, they should clearly articulate the process through which limitations can be made and the reasons on which they must be based. This can be achieved by incorporating what is referred to as a "limitation clause," which is a constitutional provision that has as its sole purpose to set out the criteria that must be satisfied in order for a limitation to be constitutionally valid.[20] In comparative practice, limitation clauses typically set out a list of grounds for which rights can be limited, including public order and public health, which democratic and undemocratic governments alike very often use to justify their actions. In order to be effective, however, constitutional frameworks must go further and introduce concepts such as "proportionality."[21] Proportionality is a German legal concept that was originally developed at the end of the nineteenth century, and has since been adopted in dozens of countries (including Tunisia, see next subsection). By introducing it into their national legal systems, states are committing to carrying out some form of analysis when deciding whether a limitation of a right is constitutional or not. Each country has developed its own test, but most involve a number of the same elements. These include the "worthy purpose" test, according to which a limitation will only be constitutionally valid if its purpose or objective is worthy in a democratic society; the

[19] Some pre-2011 Arab constitutions did include provisions that provided some indication of how rights and freedoms could be limited but the wording was so modest and the general context so unfavorable that they hardly made any difference in practice. By way of example, Article 7 of Tunisia's 1959 Constitution provided that basic rights could only be limited "by law and in order to protect the rights of others, public order, national defense, economic development and social renaissance."

[20] See Dawood Ahmed and Elliot Bulmber, "Limitation Clauses," International IDEA Constitution-Building Primer, Vol. 11 (2017), 1–33.

[21] Most limitations clauses do not actually use the word "proportionality." Courts have interpreted the clauses as requiring proportional limitation.

suitability test, according to which a limitation must have a rational connection to the objective; necessity, according to which a limitation must impair a right as little as reasonably possible to be valid; and balance, or proportionality, which requires an analysis as to whether the reasons for regulating the right can justify the degree to which the constitutionally protected right will be harmed.[22]

Tunisia: As early as 2011 a group of Tunisian legal experts were determined that their new constitution should incorporate a modern limitation clause. They met with representatives of major political groups to argue in favor of including a reference to both proportionality and necessity in the future constitution's limitation clause. After the Constituent Assembly commenced its work, many of the members were unfamiliar with the concept and were concerned that it could have consequences that they were incapable of anticipating at the time. As a result, they initially favored individual limitation clauses that would be applied to specific rights and would be very limited in scope.[23] Two and a half years after the constitutional process commenced, drafters had finally accepted to include a general limitation clause but its wording was only slightly improved in comparison to the 1959 Constitution.[24] During the constitutional process' last few months, as the deliberations moved from the Constituent Assembly to the National Dialogue and the Consensus Committee, the community of experts lobbied specific negotiators to have their preferred wording adopted. The limitation clause was not among the issues that were threatening to destabilize the country, but the negotiators adopted the recommendations that were made to them on this issue anyway. In its final session on the drafting constitution, the Constituent Assembly adopted the provision by a wide margin, even though Assembly members barely discussed its provisions during the previous three years.[25] The final constitution provides that "limitations can only be put in place for reasons necessary to a civil and democratic state" and that there must be "proportionality between these restrictions and the objective sought" (Article 49).

[22] See Vicki Jackson, "Constitutional Law in an Age of Proportionality," THE YALE LAW JOURNAL, Vol. 124, No. 8 (June 2015), 3094–3193.

[23] Article 2.26 of the first draft of Tunisia's constitution (circulated on August 14, 2012) provided that "[f]reedom of the media and of publication may not be restricted unless by virtue of a law protecting the rights, reputation, safety and health of others."

[24] Article 48 of the fourth draft of Tunisia's constitution (circulated on June 1, 2013) provided that "[t]he law will determine the limitations that can be imposed on the rights and freedoms that are included in this Constitution and their application on the condition that it does not compromise their essence. The law can only take away from these rights to protect the rights of others or based on the requirements of public order or national defense or public health."

[25] Article 49 was adopted by 164 votes in favor, 4 abstentions, 6 against.

Yemen: The introduction of both proportionality and necessity was considered to be a major victory for the general population, and attracted significant attention in the legal community throughout the region. Yemen's National Dialogue Conference established a rights and freedoms working group, which had reached a large number of decisions on how rights and freedoms should be framed but did not discuss the possibility of adopting a limitations clause. The Dialogue Conference ended only a few days before Tunisia's 2014 Constitution was formally adopted and so did not take notice of these last minute changes. Later on in 2014 the constitutional drafting committee was required to prepare a draft constitution based on the Dialogue Conference's outcomes. The committee's work on rights and freedoms advanced fairly quickly, first as a result of the work that had already been done during the Dialogue Conference but second because the entire chapter was not particularly controversial or politically charged. Early on in the drafting process, a small number of independent experts met with the drafting committee to advocate in favor of incorporating a robust limitations clause. The drafters listened to the experts and offered a number of comments and questions in response without taking the matter further. In October 2014, after they had already moved their sessions to Abu Dhabi, the drafters sought to finalize the draft's section on rights and freedoms. The seventeen-member constitutional drafting committee typically met either in small working groups to discuss specific substantive issues or in plenary to take final decisions and set the agenda for the coming period. A small group of members that had a specific interest in the protection of rights met to review the latest draft of the chapter on rights and freedoms. The members decided to include a specific limitation clause and to include a reference to proportionality, which was the first time the issue was ever seriously considered in Yemen, albeit in modified form.[26] The following month, the draft was put to plenary with a view to finalizing the wording. The committee worked in a large conference area and displayed all draft provisions on a screen, which focused everyone's attention to very specific questions but also encouraged them to argue endlessly about

[26] Article 63 of the October 2014 draft provided that "[r]ights and freedoms set forth in this constitution shall not be subject to obstruction and derogation; they may not be prejudiced in any shape or form. In situations where the law provides for regulating these rights and freedoms, these regulations may not restrict or limit the origin, essence and implications of a right. Restrictions may only be introduced when necessary with the aim of protecting rights of others, public order, public health or public morality and to the minimum level possible under a civil democratic State and such restrictions should be general." Article 67(2) provided that "[t]he principle of proportionality between crime and punishment shall be taken into consideration."

minor changes in phrasing. When the proposed limitation clause was displayed on the screen, one of the members exploded in anger, and argued that the proposed wording would drastically limit executive power in ways that would lead to chaos and said that it was without precedent in comparative practice. The committee's rapporteur displayed Article 49 of Tunisia's Constitution on the screen and calmly read it aloud for everyone's benefit. But at that point, the complaining member had already invested too much energy in his criticism to back down and demanded that the article be deleted at once. A shouting match ensued that could be heard from outside the halls, in which other voices demanded that the draft provision be maintained. The matter was eventually deferred to a later date to allow members a further opportunity to deliberate the matter bilaterally. Ultimately, the draft was amended but the final draft maintained a general limitation clause.[27]

Impacting Culture: The introduction of Article 49 has had an immediate impact. It has given state officials a clear and rational basis for debating whether specific measures are constitutionally valid. By way of example, in 2017, the Tunisian ministry of interior proposed a raft of measures in response to terrorism-related concerns. Among other things, a system was proposed that would force all Tunisians to carry with them at all times a biometric card that would be instantly readable by security forces. Draft legislation to that effect was drawn up and referred to the parliament's human rights committee. The chairman invited the relevant officials from the ministry for a hearing, where he asked whether and if so how the proposed system could be reconciled with Article 49. Following a discussion on the matter, the committee concluded that while the draft legislation's purpose was worthy in a democratic society, the proposed measure was a clear limitation on the right to privacy that was not proportionate to the objective and so asked that the ministry revisit its proposal.[28] However, despite the clear progress that Tunisia has made, the reform was not the result of a major discussion within the legal community, or even within the Constituent Assembly. The Assembly's official minutes, which recorded every word that was spoken during the formal plenary sessions

[27] Article 134 of the final draft provides, "Rights and freedoms set forth in this constitution shall not be subject to obstruction and derogation; they may not be prejudiced in any form; and in cases where the law provides for restrictions to regulate these rights and freedoms, these restrictions may not prejudice the origin, essence and content of a right. Restrictions may only be determined when necessary with the aim of protecting rights of others, public order or public morals and to the minimum level necessary for these purposes as required by the foundations of the civil democratic State, provided that such restrictions shall not be confined to a special case."

[28] Interview with senior Tunisian official (April 4, 2018).

and is close to 2,000 pages long, records only eight uses of the word "proportionality" over a three-year period, all of which were made only in passing. For example, on January 18, 2013, one representative made a general intervention in which she made fourteen separate points. At around halfway through, the representative stated that "an article should be added that defines the laws that limit freedoms. Such laws must respect the rule of proportionality and the rule of necessity so that in the future in order to prevent any regression in the protection of these rights."[29] The only reaction that the suggestion elicited during the session was from the chair of the rights and freedoms committee, whose only comment was to say, "[o]n limitations, I would simply like to ask some of my colleagues when they refer to proportionality and necessity, aren't proportionality and necessity limitations on those rights?"[30] The next reference to proportionality was made half a year later, and once again only in passing.[31] The debate in Yemen was even more restrained given that the National Dialogue Conference never even considered a limitations clause. The debate on whether to include a limitations clause took place in 2014, exclusively within the Constitutional Drafting Committee and a tiny number of foreign advisers. The impact of the absence of public debate in the Constituent Assembly and in much of the legal community is that even after Article 49 was formally adopted its practical impact was still limited. By way of example, in the example of the university student cited previously, neither the student's lawyer nor the court appear to have made any reference to Article 49 throughout the proceedings.[32] In Yemen's case, the 2015 Constitution was ultimately not adopted so we do not know what impact its limitation clause would have had, if any.

SOCIOECONOMIC RIGHTS

Colonial Self-justification: Social and economic rights are cornerstones of modern constitutional design. But even before they became binding

[29] See Intervention by Representative Salma Mabrouk (سلمى مبروك), National Constituent Assembly Minutes, Plenary Sessions, Tome 1, Assembly of the Representatives of the People (2020), at 306.

[30] See Intervention by Representative Farida al-Abidi (فريدة العبيدي), National Constituent Assembly Minutes, Plenary Sessions, Tome 1, Assembly of the Representatives of the People (2020), at 315.

[31] See Intervention by Representative Reem Mahjoub (ريم محجوب), National Constituent Assembly Minutes, Plenary Sessions, Tome 2, Assembly of the Representatives of the People (2020), at 1076.

[32] See Administrative Court Decision 4104074 (October 22, 2019), unpublished.

constitutional principles, they were widely recognized as underpinning the state's normative legitimacy. As states started becoming more accountable and responsive to popular demands, they understood that the general population was increasingly expecting adequate health care, education opportunities, social security, and other such benefits that guarded against the inequities that the majority of the population inherited at birth. When the colonial enterprise commenced, its architects understood that many of their own domestic constituencies considered the entire colonial enterprise to be abhorrent while subjugated populations were deeply suspicious of foreign control over their lands. Indeed, countrywide uprisings took place in virtually all of the countries, sometimes on more than one occasion and sometimes sustained over decades. As such, they argued that colonialism was justified because it would allow the socioeconomic development of the subjugated populations.[33] At times, British and French officials bolstered their respective occupations by comparing themselves favorably with their imperial competitors. In reference to their government's occupation of Morocco in the early twentieth century, French officials regularly conveyed the message that they were purely motivated by altruistic motives, including that "unlike other countries, France does not colonise to exploit, but in order to civilise."[34] A number of initiatives were therefore introduced, each of which was formally designed to benefit the locals but which would also further the colonial enterprise. Educational initiatives in countries such as Iraq and Morocco were in part designed to convince the local population of the colonialists' good intentions, and were also intended to create local constituencies that would serve the colonialist enterprise's interests.[35] Agricultural reforms increased prosperity among some Egyptian farmers, and also led to increased output, satisfying a British domestic market.[36] The British also promoted the rule of law in countries such as Sudan, first to perpetuate the idea of their own civilizing mission but also to maintain order, repress nationalist movements, and defend the United Kingdom's imperial presence.[37] Ultimately, while there were some advances, socioeconomic surveys that were conducted toward the end of the colonial

[33] See, for example, Noah R. Bassil, The Post-Colonial State and Civil War in Sudan: The Origins of Conflict in Darfur, I.B. Tauris & Co. (2013), 59.

[34] Robin Bidwell, Morocco Under Colonial Rule: French Administration of Tribal Areas 1912–1956, Frank Cass (1973), at 3.

[35] Ibid., at 237.

[36] Steven A. Cook, The Struggle for Egypt: From Nasser to Tahrir Square, Oxford University Press (2013), at 20.

[37] See Mark Fathi Massoud, Law's Fragile State: Colonial, Authoritarian, and Humanitarian Legacies in Sudan, Cambridge University Press (2013), at 82–83.

period describe how the crushing majority of the population were made to suffer horrific living conditions.[38]

Post-colonial Legitimacy: Following the departure (in some cases, expulsion) of Britain, France, and Italy from the region starting in the 1940s, the new governing authorities moved quickly to consolidate their control over the state. Following the colonial example, this involved justifying whatever form of government that was established by arguing that it was necessary for national development. Colonialism had benefited too few locals, encouraging massive disparities in wealth and opportunity in the region. Postcolonial rule in the region was theoretically designed for the good of ordinary people. On occasion, radicals were invited to participate in government (including the Communist Party, which held a number of ministerial portfolios in Sudan and Iraq) to design and implement redistributive policies that were formally intended to undo colonial rule. In the Cold War context, this often involved large scale expropriations, economic protectionism, and large scale subsidies in favor of local industry and land redistribution to individual farmers, which were wildly popular with the general population. Were the new controlling elites truly intent on improving socioeconomic conditions for ordinary people, or were their actions merely designed to obfuscate their power grab? Whatever the case may be, the new elites had learned from their colonial predecessors of the need to acquire internal legitimacy through socioeconomic development initiatives. The new ruling authorities were also acutely aware of the need to ingratiate themselves with the international community. They were therefore careful to pay lip service to internationally recognized norms (including popular sovereignty and the rule of law).[39] In any event, the policy of state intervention had an immediate and positive impact on the general population.[40] There were drastic reductions in poverty and infant mortality, and dramatic increases in school

[38] See, for example, The World Bank, The Economic Development of Iraq: Report of a Mission Organized by the International Bank for Reconstruction and Development at the Request of the Government of Iraq, Johns Hopkins Press (1952), 1.

[39] See, for example, the preamble to Morocco's 1996 Constitution, which provides in part that "Aware of the need of incorporating its work within the frame of the international organisations of which it has become an active and dynamic member, the Kingdom of Morocco fully adheres to the principles, rights and obligations arising from the charters of such organisations, as it reaffirms its determination to abide by the universally recognised human rights. Likewise, it reaffirms its determination to continue its steady endeavours towards the safeguard of peace and security in the world." Also, see Roger Owen, THE RISE AND FALL OF ARAB PRESIDENTS FOR LIFE, Harvard University Press (2014), at 54.

[40] Owen (2014), at 32.

enrollment and life expectancy.[41] In Egypt, the employed saw their income double between 1952 and 1967 while life expectancy increased by three to four years.[42]

Constitutional Commitments: During the immediate post-colonial period, the state was determined to bring about socioeconomic development through its interventionist policy. The constitutions that were adopted during this period recognized some accompanying rights but did not do so in a way that would make any difference, mainly because courts were not fully independent during that period but also because socioeconomic rights themselves were considered to be unenforceable. Many of the earlier texts did not recognize any socioeconomic rights at all. The rights to education and health are not recognized by Tunisia's 1959 Constitution, Egypt's 1953 Constitutional Declaration, or Iraq's 1958 Constitution Declaration. With time, almost all of the main rights would be recognized in the constitutions that were in force, with the exception of those texts that were not replaced and remained generally unamended (as in Tunisia and Lebanon). Egypt introduced the rights to both education and health in 1971, which provided that "health services" should be provided, including "in the villages" (Article 16), and that "[e]ducation is a right guaranteed by the State" (Article 18). Both Egypt and Iraq prioritized the struggle against illiteracy, but Iraq's 1970 Interim Constitution was far more ideological, providing that "[e]ducation has the objective of [...] developing the general educational level, [...] creating a national, liberal and progressive generation, [...] proud of its people, homeland and heritage, [...] and that struggles against capitalist ideology, exploitation, reactionism, zionism, and imperialism for the purpose of realizing the Arab unity, liberty, and socialism" (Article 28). Other rights such as the right to work were provided by many countries (with the notable exception of Morocco), while the right to housing was not provided anywhere.

Decline: Starting in the 1970s, the interventionist approach was gradually abandoned in favor of neoliberal economic policies, and gradually accelerating over time.[43] State-owned enterprises were privatized, subsidies were slashed, and socioeconomic entitlements were significantly reduced, in favor of free market principles in the hope that a new capitalist class of entrepreneurs could create sufficient wealth that would then trickle down to the rest of

41 Tarik M. Yousef, "Development, Growth and Policy Reform in the Middle East and North Africa since 1950," THE JOURNAL OF ECONOMIC PERSPECTIVES, Vol. 18, No. 3 (Summer, 2004), 96.

42 Ibid., at 91–116; Cook (2013), at 71–72.

43 Yousef (2004), at 97; and Sadri Khiari, TUNISIE, LE DÉLITEMENT DE LA CITÉ, Editions Karthala (2003), at 75.

the population. Regardless of the reasons for which these policies were adopted, their effect was unquestionably negative.[44] The guarantees that were set out in the constitutions had no impact; even when they were provided, human development indicators and socioeconomic data all reflected an increasingly desperate situation: booming populations, growing unemployment, stubborn levels of poverty and illiteracy, staggering levels of corruption, etc. On the eve of the 2011 uprisings, the absolute numbers of people living in poverty and without access to adequate services were unacceptably elevated in the crushing majority of countries. In 2010 more than one in five Tunisians lived in poverty or extreme poverty.[45] Poverty rates in much of the region were either similar or worse: almost 19 percent in Iraq in 2012 and nearly 27 percent in Egypt in 2010.[46] Unemployment rates were just as dire. Tunisia's in 2010 was some 13 percent, Egypt's 12 percent, and Yemen's 18 percent. Youth unemployment rates were even worse: Tunisia's 29 percent, Egypt 24 percent, and Yemen's 34 percent.[47] Regional rates followed similar patterns. Economists and demographers predicted with remarkable accuracy that the economic crisis would worsen significantly as the population grew increasingly younger, and there is every reason to believe that these trends will continue.[48] The International Labour Organization (ILO) estimates that youth unemployment will keep rising in much of the region,

[44] Ibid., at 76. See also Cook (2013), at 177.

[45] "Mesure de la pauvreté, des inégalités et de la polarization en Tunisie, 2000–2010," Rebublique Tunisienne, Ministere du Developpement, Regional et de la Planification, Institut National de la Statistique, October 2012. The World Bank's final country brief on Tunisia prior to the 2011 uprising offered significant praise to the Tunisian authorities and estimated the national poverty rate to be at 7 percent, which it described as being "amongst the lowest in the region." The country brief has received significant attention for misjudging (some say misreporting) Tunisia's situation. Indeed, with the revolution only a few months away, the report's first sentence read "Tunisia has made remarkable progress on equitable growth, fighting poverty and achieving good social indicators." See "Country Brief," The World Bank (April 2010), http://siteresources.worldbank.org/INTTUNISIA/Resources/Tunisia_CB_EN_final.pdf.

[46] Note that World Bank data on poverty in Iraq for year 2010 is not available. See "World Development Indicators," World Bank, available at https://databank.worldbank.org/data/source/world-development-indicators/preview/on.

[47] Figures are rounded to nearest whole number. See World Bank, "Development Indicators." Many of these countries' unemployment rates would increase after the uprisings.

[48] Gilbert Achcar, The People Want: a Radical Exploration of the Arab Uprising, University of California Press (2013), at 117 (quoting Ammar Ali Hassan, director of Cairo's Middle East Studies and Research Center, and Abdel-Wahab Elmessiri, coordinator of the Kefaya movement, in an interview that was carried out in 2008, both of whom foresaw the popular uprising. The author writes "Elmissiri even foresaw 'a populist uprising in the form of a catharsis that could destroy everything'. Hassan thought that Egyptians had been more politicised in 1977 but acknowledged that living conditions were 'much worse' than they had

reaching 29 percent in the Middle East and 31 percent in North Africa by 2019, whereas the peak rates in other world regions that year are not expected to exceed 18 percent.[49] Between 2007 and 2011, 250,000 Iraqis turned 18 every year, increasing to 290,000 annually from 2012, and yet there are only enough new jobs being created for approximately 10 percent of that number.[50] Similar numbers were being reported throughout the region, with predictable consequences, including social unrest and mass migration.[51] Hunger was also widespread in the Middle East and North Africa before the uprisings, and continues to be so. The number of individuals suffering from chronic undernourishment doubled from thirteen million people in 1990–1992 to twenty-five million people in 2010–2012.[52] During the same period, the proportion of undernourished people also increased from 10.4 percent to 12.8 percent.[53] Hunger was particularly bad in Yemen, where in 2010 almost 26 percent of the population was undernourished.[54] To make matters worse, the food that is available to the region's poor is often of such poor quality that it has led to an additional health crisis – the rise of noncommunicable diseases related to diet.[55]

been then. Elmessiri [. . .] pointed to the impressive wave of worker's strikes and the unprecedented strikes by civil servants then occurring in the country").

49 Section 3.3, AHDR 2009 chapter on education.

50 USAID–Tijara Provincial Economic Growth Program: Assessment of Current and Anticipated Economic Priorities in Iraq, USAID/Tijara, Report for Prime Minister's Advisory Committee (PMAC) (October 4, 2012), at 43, at http://pdf.usaid.gov/pdf_docs/pnadz673.pdf.

51 See Marc Lynch, The Arab Uprising: The Unfinished Revolutions of the Middle East, Public Affairs (2012), at 68 ("Economic woes escalated, the middle class disappeared, the poor scrambled for survival, and youth found all doors closed to them. Sectarian and tribal conflicts broke out unpredictably. Labor strikes intensified and proliferated"). See also Philippe Fargues, "Mass Migration and Uprisings in Arab Countries: An Analytical Framework," The Graduate Institute Geneva, July 2017.

52 See the State of Food Insecurity in the World by FAO, available at www.fao.org/3/a-i3027e.pdf.

53 Regional overview of food insecurity FAO, at 1.

54 There was great variability in hunger indicators between different countries, but there were few if any bright spots. A 2009 report by the United Nations Development Programme report stated that between 1990 and 2004 "Saudi Arabia, Egypt, Lebanon, Jordan, Morocco and Yemen . . . recorded increases in both the absolute numbers and prevalence of undernourishment, while Syria and Algeria achieved very small reductions in prevalence but none in numbers." Arab Human Development Report 2009, Hunger Chapter. Available at www.undp.org/content/dam/undp/library/corporate/HDR/ahdr2009e.pdf.

55 In Egypt, cardiovascular diseases accounted for 40 percent of all deaths in 2013. In 2010, mortality from cardiovascular diseases, cancer, and diabetes, or chronic respiratory diseases of adults aged thirty to seventy was 28 percent, compared to a global rate of 19.7 percent for the same year. See World Bank, "Development Indicators." In 2015, there were 7.8 million new cases of diabetes (close to 8 percent of the population). See Maddison Sawle, "Egypt's Working Poor Are Facing a Silent Killer: Bad Food," Mada Masr (January 3, 2017), https://madamasr.com/en/2017/01/03/feature/society/egypts-working-poor-are-facing-a-silent-killer-bad-food/.

Inequality: What made the situation even more intolerable for the masses of poor across the region was that small segments of the population were thriving just as their situation deteriorated. Virtually all countries in the region provided near-perfect chances for children from the most advantaged backgrounds to enter school and reach secondary level, whereas almost none came close to providing the same opportunities for children from the least advantaged backgrounds.[56] In Morocco, between 2008 and 2012, the richest fifth of the population had a 95 percent chance of having a skilled attendant available at birth while the poorest fifth had only a 30 percent chance.[57] The World Bank's data indicates that from 2004 to 2010, the top 20 percent of the population of Syria, Yemen, Morocco, and Egypt controlled between 41 percent and 48 percent of their respective country's wealth, while the bottom 20 percent controlled 7 percent and 9 percent, respectively.[58] In Tunisia, the National Institute of Statistics found that, despite growing national GDP, the Center-West and the South West of the country suffered from disproportionately high poverty and extreme poverty rates (which explained why, in December 2010, the Tunisian uprising began in the center of the country).[59] Informal settlements throughout the region (most notably in Egypt) were decades old and suffered from failing basic services, particularly when contrasted with planned areas.[60] In general, regional educational opportunity and attainment has been comparatively poor; even in the best cases it has fallen short. Egypt's situation is the most concerning of all: in 2010–2011, it ranked 131 out of 139 countries in quality of the education system, with similar rankings in quality of math and science education and quality of management of schools, respectively.[61] In 2016, one out of five schools were said to be unfit for use, due to lack of water and sanitation facilities.[62] In Morocco, quality of the overall educational system ranked 105.[63] Literacy has also remained

[56] Section 3.2, AHDR 2009 chapter on education.

[57] Morocco UNICEF data retrieved in 2018, available at https://data.unicef.org/country/mar/.

[58] World Bank, "Development Indicators."

[59] Mesures de la pauvreté, des inégalités et de la polarisation en Tunisie 2000–2010, Statistique Tunisie, October 2012, available at www.ins.tn/fr/publication/mesure-de-la-pauvret%C3%A9-des-in%C3%A9galit%C3%A9s-et-de-la-polarisation-en-tunisie-2000-2010.

[60] See "Cairo: A City in Transition," Cities and Citizens Series, UN Habitat and American University in Cairo (2011), at 14.

[61] It also ranked extremely poorly (126 out of 139) in the quality of primary education. See World Economic Forum's Global Competitiveness Report 2010–2011, available at www3.weforum.org/docs/WEF_GlobalCompetitivenessReport_2010–11.pdf.

[62] www.unicef.org/egypt/education.html

[63] Morocco's quality of primary education ranked 100 out of 139 countries. See World Economic Forum's Global Competitiveness Report 2013–2014, at 285, www3.weforum.org/docs/WEF_GlobalCompetitivenessReport_2013–14.pdf.

stubbornly low throughout the region, ranging from just 54 percent in Yemen in 2004 to a paltry high of 81 percent in 2004 (the last year for which comparable data is available). Especially disquieting are the gaps between male and female literacy – in Yemen, one of the most extreme examples, the two figures were 73 percent versus 35 percent.[64] Health systems are also severely lacking – inefficient, understaffed, and underfunded.[65] Budgetary constraints have been blamed for these deficiencies, particularly following structural adjustment programs. This has led to an incessant stream of deeply demoralizing stories throughout the region, including poorly trained staff causing accidents that often led to injury and even death on a regular basis.[66]

Post-2011: After decades of repression and missed opportunities, constitutional drafters wanted to be seen to be addressing the popular demand for change. This was reflected not only in the post-2011 constitutions' preambles (Chapter 6). It was also reflected in the constitution's substantive provisions on socioeconomic rights. The list of rights was now much longer and each individual right was also far more detailed. Through their interventions, drafters sought not only to assert the existence of a whole series of rights that had never been recognized before but also to provide significant detail as to how they should be exercised. For example, in relation to education, virtually all of the post-2011 constitutions now make reference to the quality of state education, while some give some indications of how the curriculum should be constructed. Morocco's 2011 Constitution now provides that citizens have the right to "modern, accessible and high quality education" (Article 31). Tunisia's 2014 Constitution introduces a right to education and provides that the "necessary resources" must be made available by the state to ensure that

64 World Bank, "Development Indicators." See also the Tunisia, Iraq, Egypt, and Morocco statistics pages, UNICEF, available at www.unicef.org/where-we-work.

65 In the words of the 2009 *Arab Human Development Report*, "shackled by bureaucratic inefficiency, poor professional capabilities and underfunding; and health risks from new infectious diseases are on the rise." Health Chapter. A World Health Organization 2012 publication refers to Djibouti, Iraq, Morocco, Sudan, and Yemen as having a "critical shortage of health workers," based on a WHO benchmark of 2.3 health workers per 1,000. See World Health Organization, "Human Resource for Health Observer", 2012, available at www.who.int/hrh/resources/observer10.pdf.

66 A peer-reviewed study that examined forty-five research studies on medication errors in the Middle East in 2011 from five peer-review databases, indicated that medication prescribing error rates ranged between 7.1 percent and 90.5 percent, and medication administration errors between 9.4 percent and 80 percent. The study found that "poor knowledge of medicines was identified as a contributory factor for errors by both doctors (prescribers) and nurses (when administering drugs)." See Zayed Alsulami, Sharon Conroy, and Imti Choonara, "Medication Errors in the Middle East Countries: A Systematic Review of the Literature," European Journal of Clinical Pharmacology, Vol. 69, No. 4 (2013), 995.

education will be "high quality" (Article 39). Libya's 2017 draft constitution also makes references to the quality of education, which it states must be "in accordance with international standards and the teachings and values of the Islamic religion" (Article 60). Yemen's 2015 draft constitution provides that education should "promote a scientific approach to thinking, criticism and analysis" (Article 44), and that university education should conform with "global quality standards" (Article 46). Egypt's 2012 Constitution provides that "[e]very citizen has the right to high quality education" (Article 58). Meanwhile, the 2014 Constitution includes ten separate provisions that relate to education (Articles 19–25, 80, 81, 238), in which there are three separate references to "global quality criteria" and two other references to the "quality of education." Other rights were given the same treatment, including the right to health, which in many countries must also be of satisfactory "quality" (e.g. Tunisia, Article 38). The right to work was generally maintained from the earlier generation of constitutions, but with considerably more detail, including the right to collective bargaining (Egypt 2014, Article 13), the right to safe working conditions (Libya 2017, Article 65), and a commitment that work should be allocated "on the basis of competence and fairness" (Tunisia 2014, Article 40).

Unenforceability: Despite all of this additional detail, on their own, these provisions make close to no difference for the general population. These provisions should be read in the context of the longstanding debate on the status of socioeconomic rights. Traditionally, many legal systems recognize a distinction between civil and political rights (sometimes referred to as first generation rights) and socioeconomic rights (sometimes referred to as second generation). According to this distinction, the first category of rights is of such fundamental importance that it is directly enforceable, which means that claims can be brought before the courts to challenge state actions that interfere with them. The second generation, however, should not be directly enforceable for a combination of reasons, including that they are of a lower order of importance but also because, by their very nature, they would require heavy planning and investment for the rights to be satisfied. According to this view, the implementation of socioeconomic rights should be a matter of policy best left to the government rather than the judiciary.[67] As a

[67] India, which drafted its constitution shortly after declaring independence, followed this approach and placed these rights in a chapter of the constitution titled "Directive Principles of State Policy." It expressly made these rights nonenforceable. Article 37 of the Constitution of India provides that "The provisions contained in this Part shall not be enforceable by any court, but the principles therein laid down are nevertheless fundamental in the governance of the country and it shall be the duty of the State to apply these principles in making laws."

consequence, the vast majority of courts throughout the region will not accept jurisdiction if a claim were brought that seeks to force the state to take action pursuant to any of the above provisions.[68] The rights that are listed in the constitutions and that drafters spent so much time rewording are therefore merely intended as a list of aspirations. Knowingly or not, in the post-2011 period, constitutional negotiators and drafters accepted this rationale, despite its obvious flaws. The budgetary argument is incorrect on its face, given that many civil and political rights are just as costly and sometimes even more so than specific socioeconomic rights (including, for example, due process rights, which require the establishment and proper functioning of entire court systems, etc.).[69] Second, an increasing number of countries is recognizing that the free exercise of civil and political rights without accompanying socioeconomic rights is not only inhumane but it actually makes it close to impossible for many to exercise their civil and political rights.[70] Early on during South Africa's own constitutional negotiation process, Nelson Mandela personally intervened on this question when he stated that a

> simple vote, without food, shelter and health care is to use [civil and political] rights as a smokescreen to obscure the deep underlying forces which dehumanise people. It is to create an appearance of equality and justice, which by implication socioeconomic inequality is entrenched. We do not want freedom without bread, nor do we want bread without freedom. We must provide for all the fundamental rights and freedoms associated with a democratic society."[71]

[68] One partial exception to this trend is the Egyptian administrative courts, which will enforce socioeconomic rights if a claim for enforcement is accompanied by a claim that the state has discriminated against the plaintiff (on the basis that prohibitions against discrimination are directly enforceable). For example, in one claim, a parent brought a claim against a hospital that had refused a rare and expensive treatment for his son. The court found in favor of the plaintiff, not on the basis that the refusal to provide the treatment was a violation of the son's right to health, but because the hospital had not provided a rational explanation for why that specific treatment was denied when other treatments that were just as expensive were being granted to patients. As a result, the administrative court found that the hospital's denial of treatment amounted to a violation of the constitution's anti-discrimination clause (Article 53). See Decision 14109 (2015), unpublished.

[69] See Stephen Holmes and Cass Sunstein, The Cost of Rights: Why Liberty Depends on Taxes, Norton (January 2013).

[70] See David Bilchitz, Poverty and Fundamental Rights: The Justification and Enforcement of Socio-economic Rights, Oxford University Press (2008).

[71] Nelson Mandela, "Address: On the Occasion of the ANC's Bill of Rights Conference," in A Bill of Rights for a Democratic South Africa: Papers and Report of a Conference Convened by the ANC Constitutional Committee, African National Congress Constitutional Committee (1991), 9–14; quote is on page 12.

A large number of countries has followed that lead and now no longer recognizes the difference between the different category of rights, mainly based on the principle that the individual must have equal access to all these rights to live a dignified life.[72] Finally, if constitutional drafters are serious about socioeconomic rights, they should be aware of existing institutional practices that tend to exclude their application, and the fact that making them directly enforceable forces other branches to take them seriously.[73]

Debate: However, despite the historical context and despite the huge pressure for change, no meaningful debate between stakeholders appears to have taken place in the post-2011 period. Instead, the reform effort consisted entirely of piling on more detail to provisions that remain entirely unenforceable. To be totally clear, it is not that negotiators and drafters debated whether socioeconomic rights should be directly enforceable and decided against it. It is that they did not debate the matter at all. For example, Yemen's National Dialogue Conference's Rights and Freedoms Working Group provided that the state should be obliged to build hospitals, "medical research centres," and "emergency units in all districts and provincial centres." In Tunisia, negotiators reached consensus on virtually all socioeconomic rights within a few months of the start of the process. For example, the first draft of the constitution provided that "every citizen is entitled to work. The state exerts all effort to ensure the availability of work in a sound and fair environment."[74] That same wording was maintained without any change in the following three drafts. Some change in favor of greater gender equality was introduced in the final draft, which includes the words "male and female" besides the word "citizen."[75] Egypt provides a partial exception to this trend. In 2013, one member of the constitutional committee appeared to raise the issue of enforceability during a plenary session, which is probably the only time that the issue was raised throughout the region. During the discussion on education rights, Naser Ameen made what can be described as a unique contribution. "The right to education, to health and to housing should be redrafted on the basis of the popular demand that they should be considered to be rights of the people," Ameen argued. "If housing, education and health are considered to be rights, then there will be a commitment on

[72] See Jody Heymann, Aleta Sprague, and Amy Raub, ADVANCING EQUALITY: HOW CONSTITUTIONAL RIGHTS CAN MAKE A DIFFERENCE WORLDWIDE, University of California Press (2020).

[73] See David Bilchitz, "Are Socio-Economic Rights a Form of Political Rights?," SOUTH AFRICAN JOURNAL OF HUMAN RIGHTS, Vol. 31 (2015), 86–111.

[74] Article 2.14, first draft of the Tunisian constitution (August 2012).

[75] Article 40, Constitution of the Republic of Tunisia.

the state to deliver."[76] What Mr. Ameen was clearly suggesting was that socioeconomic rights should enjoy the same status as civil and political rights. However, none of the other members appeared to have reacted to that intervention. Instead, they focused on minute details that were almost comical in their irrelevance.[77] In the end, the Egyptian drafters maintained much of the CDC's structure and formulations and satisfied themselves with introducing a number of changes that will likely not make any practical difference to the general population. The 2014 Constitution provides that specific percentages of the annual state budget should be allocated to specific social and economic issues. For example, Article 18 provides that "no less than 3% of Gross Domestic Product (GDP) [should be allocated to] to health." The only problem, however, is that the provision has been totally ignored since the Constitution entered into force. Put in global context, this is surprising given debates in South Africa and Colombia around socioeconomic rights and the development of progressive models to enhance accountability.

Future Treatment: Can the popular demand for social justice be reconciled with an outdated distinction between different categories of rights that leaves socioeconomic rights unenforceable and hardly worth the paper that they are printed on? A senior finance ministry official from any country in the region would likely say that the resources simply do not exist to guarantee all socioeconomic rights for all people, but this assumes that other current expenditures under national budgets should remain essentially the same and that if rights are included in the constitution, everything should be included immediately. It also does not take into account the fact that there is simply no alternative to satisfying this popular demand, not only because of the moral imperative but also because to ignore the demand would be to invite yet another social explosion at any moment. In fact, one of the reasons the distinction survives to this day is because much of the general population is simply not aware that it exists (it would be safe to assume that many drafters are

76 Minutes from the C50's fifth meeting (September 11, 2013), at 18.

77 One somewhat humorous example of these debates is members' discussion of whether the provision on the right to health should use the term "health" or "health care." Some members argued that "heath" would be more inclusive and comprehensive, but in the end a decision was taken in favor of "health care" on the basis that "only God could guarantee health." In another example, members disagreed as to whether the constitution should provide for a comprehensive health care system that covers "all diseases." Some members argued that the wording was too broad, on the basis that it could be understood to mean that the state should provide coverage for cosmetic surgery. Minutes from the C50's twenty-first meeting (November 6, 2013).

also unaware). The only acceptable course of pursuit is therefore to eliminate the distinction altogether and to treat all rights as fundamental and directly enforceable. This would entail first that individuals can petition central and/or local authorities (depending on the legislative framework that is in force) on issues arising out of the application of specific socioeconomic rights. Second, in the event central or local authorities fail to adequately protect specific rights, claims can be brought to the courts to compel action.

Enforceability: Some countries that formally do not recognize a distinction between different categories of rights nevertheless treat specific rights (mainly socioeconomic rights) differently in that they require the government to improve their protection "progressively." In South Africa, socioeconomic rights and other fundamental rights are all contained in the constitution's "Bill of Rights," and are covered by that chapter's justiciability guidelines.[78] South Africa's constitution does, however, consider that these rights might pose challenges that civil and political rights do not. In particular, whereas state measures to guarantee the exercise of the freedom of assembly do not typically consume significant portions of the annual budget, immediate application of the right to health care to every citizen could lead to massive overhauls of the state budget in ways that may not be possible. As a result, the constitution includes specific wording that recognizes the state's budgetary constraints. For example, it provides that "everyone has the right to have access to adequate housing" but that the state is only obligated to act "within its available resources, to achieve the progressive realisation of this right."[79] This provision recognizes that some socioeconomic rights may implicate state budgets in ways that some civil and political rights do not. For this reason, the constitution only requires the state to act within available resources. This provision also recognizes that it may take time to build institutions to administer these rights, and so the constitution allows for the progressive realization of them.[80] The enforceability of these provisions is not questioned in South Africa, but each case does raise complex questions regarding how these rights should be enforced, and when it would be reasonable for a court to force the government to ensure protection of a particular right.[81] The constitution provides courts with the necessary flexibility to enforce socioeconomic rights

78 Article 8 of the Constitution of South Africa (1996) provides that "The Bill of Rights applies to all law, and binds the legislature, the executive, the judiciary and all organs of the state."
79 Article 26.
80 Ibid.
81 *Government of the Republic of South Africa & Ors* v. *Grootboom & Ors* 2000 (11) BCLR 1169. Available at www.escr-net.org/caselaw/2006/government-republic-south-africa-ors-v-grootboom-ors-2000-11-bclr-1169-cc.

while still respecting resource and time limitations.[82] The constitution of Colombia goes one step further by creating a special mechanism to ensure that individuals always have a course of action to protect their constitutional rights, particularly in situations when the ordinary courts are unable to satisfy their function. The constitution created a special constitutional action called a 'tutela' that tries to address the difficulty many vulnerable people face in gaining access to justice. Individuals who are denied constitutional rights can approach a court at any time alleging this infringement and the court must make a decision within ten days. In practice, this remedy has allowed Colombians who do not have access to legal representation to make their submissions to the Colombian courts in the form of short letters, and sometimes even in the form of oral messages. This mechanism is today studied around the world for its innovative approach to the enforcement of civil, political, and socioeconomic rights.[83] Where there are many violations of the same type, the courts have also sought to allow them to be collated and then sought to address some of the systemic problems that have faced the realization of rights in this area.

Impact: There is today a vigorous debate on the impact that direct enforcement has had in practice. Some scholars and others have noted that judicial remedies are typically only available to individuals who have access to legal representation, and that the most marginalized segments have very little hope of seeing their constitutional rights realized in court. Others have noted that courts have limited reach and that whatever judgments they render can at best affect only small segments of society at a time.[84] Still others have noted that, despite the little means at their disposal, courts have made significant progress, which is an argument in favor of even stronger remedies.[85] A final argument has been that, regardless of the court remedies that are available, the fact that socioeconomic rights are justiciable has forced governments into a "culture of justification" (Chapter 8).[86] What this means in practice is that governments

[82] Article 172(1)(b).

[83] The relevant passages of the Colombian constitution are in Article 86, which also provides that courts must respond to the request in less than ten days. See, for example, "Social and Economic Rights," International Institute for Democracy and Electoral Assistance (August 2014).

[84] See D. M. Davis, "Socioeconomic Rights," in Michel Rosenfeld and András Sajó (eds.), The Oxford Handbook of Comparative Constitutional Law, Oxford University Press (2012), at 687.

[85] See, for example, David Landau, "The Reality of Social Rights Enforcement," Harvard International Law Review, Vol. 53, No. 1 (2012), 189.

[86] See David Dyzenhaus, "Law as Justification: Etienne Mureinik's Conception of Legal Culture," South African Journal on Human Rights, Vol. 14 (1998), 11–37.

in many countries can no longer formulate their policies without any public debate. Their actions must be justified publicly, which contributes to debate about whether goals set by constitutional provisions are being met, which is considered by some to be achievement enough.[87] For countries that have experienced massive upheaval caused in large part by the failure to exercise the enforcement of these rights, there appears to be little choice but to build on these experiences, perhaps with a view to developing local mechanisms that will see greater parts of the population having their rights protected. To proceed otherwise would be to invite disaster.

WHAT ARE COURTS FOR?

Pre-2011: As already noted, substantial judicial reform must be achieved in order for the popular demand for freedom and social justice to be achievable. Prior to 2011 judges throughout the region were extremely unlikely to find against the state in politically sensitive disputes, particularly in disputes that involved political dissidents or allegations of abuse. Under the colonial period, in most countries, judges were forced to adapt to an unnatural constitutional environment. Nominally, a local monarch was sovereign, but real executive authority was being exercised by a foreign agent that was not subject to judicial control. In Sudan, there was no sovereign, but judges were always made aware which cases were considered to be politically sensitive. In Algeria, the law itself created different categories of citizenship that judges did not and could challenge despite their obvious discriminatory nature. Judges were therefore unable to carry out their functions, particularly when it came to protecting vulnerable and poor defendants against the state. That dynamic was eventually carried over to the post-colonial era. Constitutions paid lip service to judicial independence but the protections were so bare that they were essentially meaningless. Many constitutions would simply limit themselves to stating that judges were "independent" and "subject to no authority other than the law" (Tunisia 1959, Article 65). In countries where both executive and legislative power were in the hands of unelected officials (including in Morocco, Algeria, Libya, Egypt, Iraq, and elsewhere) that essentially meant that judges were subject to the control of unelected and unaccountable officials. Iraq's 1970 Interim Constitution only had two articles on the judiciary (forty-seven words altogether) that said nothing of importance whatsoever. Sometimes national constitutions provided for the establishment of a judicial council,

[87] See Davis (2012), at 687.

but details on composition, mandate, and powers were never given (Tunisia 1959, Article 67). Even in Egypt, where judges did display significant independence over a significant period of time, the national constitution itself provided very little protection against executive control. What that meant is that judges could be dismissed, forced into retirement, transferred, etc. through pressure from either the executive, the legislature, or both. Sometimes the constitution specifically provided that the judiciary was headed by the chief executive, as was the case in Morocco, Algeria, and Syria, among others. In all of these cases, whenever individual judges would act against the interests of the state, the executive rarely hesitated to retaliate. Finally, the educational system throughout the region consisted almost entirely of rote learning, a simple application of the law, without any critical thinking as to whether executive action or the law were in conformity with the constitution. The impact that all of this had over the long run was that, in the best case scenario, judges grew accustomed to keeping their heads down and to doing the best they could without attracting too much attention to themselves. In the worst case scenario, the courts were packed with judges who considered that their main role was to protect the state and who would always charge defendants with maximum penalties unprompted.

Post-2011: When the constitutional negotiation processes started throughout the region, one of the main questions that should have been asked was how to resolve the deep institutional and cultural problems that colonial and post-colonial control had created within the judiciary. Instead, there was barely any discussion of what if anything was wrong with the judiciary. In many countries, the task of proposing reforms was deferred to the judiciary itself.[88] In others, constitutional negotiators and drafters would draw up the reforms. But in any event, there was hardly any genuine debate, given that virtually everyone agreed that the main changes had to consist of introducing more independence to the judiciary. This would be achieved through a number of means, including by specifically providing for the establishment, mandate, and composition of the judicial council in the constitution itself and not

[88] In Egypt, the ten-member 2013 committee of experts that was tasked with reviewing the constitution included six judges. The 2012 Constituent Assembly's president was a senior judge, who has served as head of the court of appeals and the judicial council. In Iraq, the three constitutional amendment committees that were composed in 2019 deferred to the High Judicial Council for recommendations on how the judiciary should be reformed. In 2016 Iraq's Prime Minister adopted a reform proposal that was unanimously adopted by the Council of Representatives and also deferred to the judiciary for recommendations on how corruption within the judiciary should be addressed; see Zaid Al-Ali, "Premature Excitement about Iraq's New Government Reforms," *The Washington Post* (August 14, 2015).

leaving the matter to legislation. For example, Tunisia's 2014 Constitution provides that the Supreme Judicial Council "ensures the sound functioning of the justice system and respect for its independence [. . .] proposes reforms and gives its opinions on draft laws related to the judicial system [. . .] for making decisions on the professional careers of judges and on disciplinary measures taken against them [. . .] for preparing an annual report." Meanwhile, Article 112 provides that the Council "is composed of judges, the majority of whom are elected, in addition to judges appointed on merit, while the remaining third shall be composed of independent, specialized persons who are not judges." Similar changes were introduced in other countries, although not always with the same degree of independence, particularly in countries that are still subject to a hyper-presidential system of government. In those countries, the chief executive was often named as the head of the judicial council, which he would then control through appointments (see Chapter 8).

Constitutional Court: A significant number of countries have also established constitutional courts (Morocco, Algeria, Tunisia, Egypt, Syria, Jordan, Iraq, Kuwait, etc.). Generally, the courts were mandated to ensure that legislation is in conformity with their respective constitutions, which suggests that ruling authorities should be subject to the law. But judging from the controversy over appointments, the issue is far from having been resolved. Egypt's struggle with this issue is illustrative of how controversial it can be. Egypt's supreme constitutional court enjoys the highest profile in the region and has been subjected to a number of appointment mechanisms since it was first established. The 1971 Constitution was silent on the court's composition, and Law No. 48/1979 granted the president of the republic the authority to select the court's chief justice and granted him a significant amount of influence over the court's general membership. Although the president always nominated the court's most senior member as the chief justice, that practice was reversed after the court's opinions on policy matters were increasingly in opposition to the president's own perspective. The president of the republic asserted his legal right to appoint the person of his choosing for the position of chief justice by selecting an individual known for his loyalty to his administration, thereby undermining the court's independence and credibility.[89] The 2012 Constitution did little to resolve this matter: It merely referred the issue to future legislation. The 2014 Constitution reversed that trend by reestablishing the court as totally independent from all other government bodies, with a clear constitutional provision to protect it from any potential encroachments in the

89 For more, see Tamir Moustafa, The Struggle for Constitutional Power: Law, Politics and Economic Development in Egypt, Cambridge University Press (2009).

future. The new constitution provided that the court's general assembly was exclusively responsible for selecting the chief justice and her deputies (Article 193). Since then, in 2019, an amendment was entered into which now provides that the president of the republic selects the chief justice from among the five most senior deputies in the court (Article 193). In Tunisia's case, negotiators adopted a balanced appointment mechanism for its constitutional court that was designed to prevent any single branch of government from dominating the court (see Article 118). The stakes remained too high, however, as a result of which six years after the constitution entered into force, the court was yet to be appointed.

Impact: The post-2011 debate on judicial reform has been limited to increasing the courts' institutional independence from the other branches of government. What this does is preserve virtually the entirety of the pre-2011 judiciary while at the same time establishing it as its own self-regulating body with virtually no outside interference. Given that most if not all of the senior judges who will form the leadership of the new bodies will necessarily have inherited many of their instincts from the pre-2011 period, the new independence that they will have been granted by post-2011 constitutions will not make any difference to the general population. There is already a mountain of evidence that pre-2011 practices are still being followed, some of which has already been cited in this chapter. One need merely carry out an online search using terms such as "court," "penalty," "abuse," "protester," and the name of any specific country in the region (including Tunisia) and the search invariably returns a virtually endless list of high profile political cases where a judge has acted to protect the state against unemployed protesters. That outcome should not be surprising: Additional independence does not lead to better performance, or to a more humane or responsive approach without special consideration of the judiciary's particular culture and a clear strategy on how it can be resolved.

Judicial Culture: What was missing throughout the post-2011 period was a genuine debate on how judges currently engage in decision-making, on what the role of a judge should be, and what could be done to resolve these problems. If such a debate had been carried out, it would inevitably have led to the conclusion that many judges in the region are heavily biased against defendants, particularly when they are accused of threatening state security. For countries that are genuinely interested in protecting freedom and in establishing social justice for their citizens, a serious effort must be made to resolve that bias as a matter of urgency, which can only be achieved through a complex strategy that addresses both cultural legacies of the past as well as the institutional deficiencies that are so obvious to everyone. To repair the culture of judges in the context of a new constitutional and democratic environment, first and foremost what is required is an agreement on what a judge's mission is. Past practices, according to which judges considered themselves to be servants of law and order as defined by unelected autocrats, should not continue. Given the historical context, and the long term challenge of rebuilding the state's legitimacy, the role of a judge must and should be to protect personal freedom from the abuse of executive authority while at the same time helping to achieve social justice for the general population. Second, a strategy to repair judicial culture should involve establishing progressive bodies specifically in order to imbue the entire judiciary with a more humane culture. After the fall of Apartheid, South Africa established a new constitutional court to be the final arbiter of the meaning of the constitution. The Court's role was to protect and enforce the values of the new constitutional order mainly by upholding the promise of rights that embody the hopes and aspirations of those who struggled against apartheid. The first Court was established in the first half of 1995, about a year after South Africa's first democratic election, with the appointment of eleven justices who were specifically selected for their commitment to the protection of fundamental rights.[90] All courts were empowered through the supremacy clause to be guardians of the values established in the new constitution, but the Constitutional Court played a guiding role through its central importance in the judiciary and its progressive character, through which it was able to influence the functioning of the entire judiciary.[91]

Oversight: Another commonsense reform would be to break the judiciary's monopoly on judging its own performance. Reporting on the judiciary's performance is highly opaque throughout the region and is typically controlled by the judiciary's leadership. Accountability measures such as judicial inspection are carried out exclusively by judges, a practice that is frowned on in many other contexts because it creates scope for judges to protect each other out of a sense of solidarity or as a means to lessen criticism of the judiciary's own performance. Similar mechanisms in other parts of the world have contributed to allowing corruption and incompetence to thrive. On occasion, dysfunction grew to such an extent that governing authorities established full vetting authorities that had has their purpose to investigate

[90] Heinz Klug, "South Africa's Constitutional Court: Enabling Democracy and Promoting Law in the Transition from Apartheid," University of Wisconsin Legal Studies Research Paper No. 1530 (2008), at 174.

[91] Kate O'Regan, "Justice & Memory: South Africa's Constitutional Court," DÆDALUS, THE JOURNAL OF THE AMERICAN ACADEMY OF ARTS & SCIENCES, Vol. 143, No. 3 (2014), 174.

every single judge in the entire country by auditing their financial holdings.[92] In Arab countries, as noted previously, all reforms should be tied to the effort to protect individual freedom and to establish social justice. The solution cannot be to allow the executive or the legislature to control the processes as that would create perverse incentives. As a result, any future reform of the judiciary's internal structures should incorporate more laymen to the judiciary's internal accountability processes, particularly reporting and internal inspection.

* * *

[92] Jan van Zyl Smit, "Restoring Confidence in the Judiciary: Kenya's Judicial Vetting Process, Constitutional Implementation and the Rule of Law," Constitutionnet (undated).

8

Government (or the Weight of History)

INTRODUCTION

Prior to 2011 my professional and personal interests were narrowly focused on a small number of issues, including Iraq. Countries such as Tunisia were relatively unknown to me. While I had many opportunities to visit, I reasoned that my family had not fled one dictatorship for me to go holidaying in another. My first visit to the country therefore took place in May 2011 while the transitional authorities were still considering how the new constitution should be drafted. I met with a large number of individuals who generously shared their views on the options that were in consideration at the time. A prominent human rights activist who was a member of the High Commission to Achieve the Goals of the Revolution, on Political Reforms and Democratic Transition said to me that he did not expect the drafting of a new constitution to be difficult. "Tunisia is one of the world's most homogeneous countries," he said. "We do not have any important ethnic or religious minorities and we hardly have any disagreements. 95% of our population is Arab, Muslim, Sunni and of the Maliki school."[1] He ended with a comment

[1] That view proved to be less than accurate. The November 2014 presidential election results revealed that Tunisia is deeply polarized, with the north favoring an octogenarian establishment candidate who campaigned on the basis of a promised return to stability, while the south mainly supported the second post-revolution interim president, who was secular but supported by the country's main Islamist party. For more information on how deep the divisions run, see « Présidentielle: Tableau interactif des votes par circonscription, la Tunisie coupée en deux, Siliana et Sidi Bouzid se démarquent, » HuffPost Tunisie (November 26, 2014). Geographic divisions are manifesting themselves in increasingly worrying ways; see, for example, Eileen Byrne, "Tunisian Brothers Text Home: We Are in Libya and Everything's Fine," *The Guardian* (July 15, 2015) (describing an incident in which thirty-three young Tunisians from a poor desert town crossed into war-torn Libya in an attempt to escape their own poverty; the article quotes a Tunisian from the same town as saying "[s]ome are just fed up

that struck me as curious: "In my view, the new constitution should be around ninety articles long." The comment seemed futile given that a single article could range from just a few words in length to several pages but I did not question him on that point considering the amount of other issues that were on the table. None of my other interlocutors during that short visit mentioned the length of the future constitution, and so I did not make anything of it at the time.

A few months later, in September 2011, I was in Tunisia again, where I attended a public event on the transition. Two major public intellectuals offered their views on the constitutional process, which at that point had not yet started. There were possibly five hundred people in attendance and the event was televised by a national broadcaster. The first speaker was a professor of public law, also a member of the High Commission, and a dominant figure in policy-making circles at the time. He also downplayed the challenges that the future negotiation process would create for the country and said in passing that he and a group of colleagues were preparing a draft of the constitution and that they had found that the ideal length was ninety articles. When his turn came, the second speaker, also a leading academic in constitutional law, responded impatiently that the length of the constitution was irrelevant. What mattered he said was uprooting the legacies of colonialism, including the reliance on security forces to impose policies that are designed to serve narrow interests. There was so much tension that after the session concluded, the two speakers barely glanced at each other. During another meeting that took place a month later the issue came up again. The head of a key state institution told me privately that in his view the new constitution should be 120 articles long. A newly elected MP from the Islamist Ennahda party responded that the exact number of articles was irrelevant. At this point, it was hard not to be intrigued but I still did not understand the focus on the number of articles, let alone the reference to colonialism given that France had withdrawn close to sixty years earlier.

A few months later, I obtained a copy of the ninety-article draft constitution that the speaker referred to in September 2011. I read it carefully and finally understood the relevance of this unusual debate: The draft was heavily inspired by Tunisia's 1959 Constitution, which itself was eighty-eight articles long. The only major departure as far as I could tell was the introduction of

with the poverty and unemployment here; the arrogance of the north [of Tunisia] towards the south").

presidential term limits.[2] It was only then that I understood that a deep political divide had already formed by the time my first visit had taken place in May 2011. It turned out that on the one hand many Tunisians were not particularly opposed to the system of government as it existed prior to 2011, and sought to maintain most of its arrangements with only modest adjustments. In their view, the 1959 constitution was generally fine; it was the dictator that had corrupted it for his own benefit. The focus on the number of articles was designed to predetermine or at least influence the outcome of the constitutional negotiation process by suggesting that the new constitution should not be substantially different to its predecessor and that all that was needed was a few additional measures (including term limits) that would prevent the emergence of a new dictator. Many other Tunisians rejected that view altogether albeit not always for the same reasons. Some leaned in favor of a parliamentary system mainly because they were concerned that a new directly elected president could be of a political persuasion other than their own. According to that view, the constitution would have to be seriously redesigned, which meant that the exact length of the new constitution could not be predicted in advance.

But not everyone was motivated by self-preservation. Some Tunisians prioritized social justice over all else, and sought to redesign the system of government with that objective in mind. In their view, Tunisia's entire post-colonial system of government was in fact heavily inspired by governance during the colonial period. History, they said, was the problem and was preventing the system of government from developing in a way that could benefit the general population. In the years that followed, I saw how constitutional drafters from country to country sought inspiration from established and emerging democracies while also referring to texts and practices in their own countries that had been in force during the long period of anti-democratic rule. In most cases, the outcome was far from revolutionary. The drafters ended up merely taking what had already been in place and making minor adjustments in favor of one institution or another. Only in a small number of cases did constitutional negotiators manage to move past colonial style hyper-presidentialism in favor of a more democratic system. However, even where progress was made, much remains to be done to move from the

[2] I am in possession of four fully fledged proposals for constitutional reform that were prepared by different groups of leading Tunisian academics between 2011 and 2012. All four proposals were circulated before the end of 2011. All four are so similar to the 1959 constitution that they were hoping to replace that they were practically indistinguishable from it. The four proposals do not appear to have been formally published and are not available online.

general democratic framework that was adopted to one that satisfies the interests of the general population.

COLONIALISM

Diversity and Commonalities: Colonial powers designed and built administrations that were responsive to their specific needs and were adapted to circumstances on the ground. To a very significant extent, they built on whatever remained from the pre-colonial systems of government, including elements of the legal order and internal administrative boundaries. In many cases, they sought to accommodate local sovereigns (including in Morocco, Tunisia, and Egypt), although this was not a hard rule (Algeria). Where local sovereigns did not exist, the British established new monarchies (as in Iraq and Jordan) and the French established republics (Lebanon and Syria), with Sudan being the only case in the region where the British deliberately established a republic. Morocco's monarchy had been on the verge of collapse for some time, and was propped up by French officials with royalist sympathies.[3] Tunisia was also allowed to maintain its own hereditary head of state (the *beys*) but only as figureheads in a country where French officials monopolized power. Some countries were never fully brought under control, including Yemen where the Ottomans struggled to pacify a succession of rebellions in the north and where the British imposed a light footprint only on the condition that its security interests were maintained. The result of this diversity of circumstances and approaches is that each Arab country was administered differently. Nevertheless, regardless of the manner in which each country's colonial administration was shaped, each was defined by a number of common features.[4] This included the practice of concentrating authority in

3 See Daniel Rivet, Lyautey et l'institution du Protectorat francais au Maroc, 1912–1925, L'Harmattan (1988).

4 Similar arrangements were adopted by colonial powers in sub-Saharan Africa, where colonial traditions also have lasting influence. Yash Ghai and Jill Cottrell, "The State and Constitutionalism in Postcolonial Societies in Africa," in Law's Ethical, Global and Theoretical Contexts: Essays in Honour of William Twining, Upendra Baxi, Christopher McCrudden, and Abdul Paliwala (eds.), Cambridge University Press (2015) ("The colonizers brought the concept and organization of the state and of the constitution. [...] The legal system showed a curious dichotomy: that part of the system that applied to Europeans and other external settlers had some resemblance to the law as administered in Europe but, as far as Africans were concerned, the system was arbitrary and depended more on the whims of the colonial administrators than the imperatives of the law. [...] A police force was established, not to protect the people but to coerce them into submission to British rule. The police as an aggressive force played a key role in the foundation of the structures of British administration – a role that has continued up to the present. [...] Indeed, the British colonial state was rooted in

the hands of a single individual; the use of violence to enforce policy; the lack of meaningful accountability mechanisms; the reliance on different groups of elites; the practice of formulating policy without carrying out any meaningful consultations; and finally the establishment of an extractive economy.

Centralization: Both Britain and France established the essential features of a central administration in all the countries that they controlled in the region. This was achieved by establishing and promoting a central bureaucracy that controlled policy formation and executive action throughout the territory that existed within internationally recognized boundaries.[5] Depending on the circumstances, the central bureaucracy would either be staffed by locals or by a combination of Europeans and locals, with Britain and France maintaining an oversight capacity and final veto power in all cases. In all cases, the centralized bureaucracies were controlled either by a plenipotentiary, a single individual, or by a tiny number of individuals who were answerable to no one. In Morocco, this role was played by France's Resident General. In the Sudan, it was the United Kingdom's Governor General. These individuals answered only to their home governments, who protected them from parliamentary scrutiny and who were so far away from the subjugated populations that they might as well have been on another planet.[6] In some countries, the plenipotentiary coexisted with a local monarch or sovereign, as was the case in Morocco, Tunisia, Iraq, Jordan, and Egypt (but which was not the case in other countries, including Algeria and the Sudan). In all cases, the plenipotentiary exercised both executive and legislative authority and in most cases authority over the judiciary through appointments and other means. Nominally, the local sovereign had some measure of decision-making authority as defined by bilateral agreements with the colonial power. Whatever the arrangement, the situation for the local population was

violence and the exploitation of African peoples. [...] Colonial authorities enjoyed considerable immunity for their acts under the common law. [...] The colony's constitution could easily be amended or abrogated by the colonial government, and thus the system of government could be adjusted periodically. [...] Lord Denning said, as late as 1956: 'The courts rely on the representatives of the Crown to know the limits of its jurisdiction and to keep within it. Once jurisdiction is exercised by the Crown the courts will not permit it to be challenged.' Courts thus abandoned, for the most part, attempts to ensure legality on the part of the government – another feature that was carried over into the post-independence period.").

5 Roger Owen, State, Power and Politics in the Making of the Modern Middle East, Routledge (2004), at 9.

6 Roger Owen, Lord Cromer: Victorian Imperialist, Edwardian Proconsul, Oxford University Press (2004) (quoting Fitzroy Bell, a visiting educational expert, who in 1902 said that "despotism is the only possible system [for British rule in Egypt] and those who administer government having no House of Commons, must justify their work at the bar of the civilized world as well as the high court of history").

scarcely any different, first because the local sovereign was hardly more democratic and second because in any event they could not refuse to implement colonial policy no matter the circumstances.[7] Just as important, colonial authorities had no rival administrations to deal with outside of the capital: The central ministries in the capital were solely responsible for establishing policy for the entire country and local government in the provinces merely consisted of administrative employees whose only responsibility was to apply policies that had been shaped elsewhere.[8]

Violence: Colonial administrations also maintained and in many cases mechanized the enforcement of policy through violence. In fact, colonial rule was rooted in violence, and violence was utilized as a matter of policy. Political parties and opposition leaders throughout the region were either banned, exiled, imprisoned, or, in the worst cases, assassinated by colonial officials or their allies. Colonial authorities sometimes mobilized massive amounts of force against a virtually defenseless local population. In Sudan, the British Governor General did not hesitate to engage in illegal practices, including preventative detention,[9] and deployed armed force to repress rebellions against British rule at various points.[10] In Iraq, the British Royal Air Force perfected the technique of eradicating entire villages in less than an hour, a practice that was implemented daily.[11] French colonial officials in Morocco formally prioritized "peaceful penetration" but stated privately that "in this country, force alone imposes respect."[12] French forces cut off food supplies to the local population, prevented the harvest, and destroyed infrastructure used

[7] This was illustrated with dramatic effect in Egypt, when in 1942 the monarch refused a request by the United Kingdom to appoint a prime minister drawn from a particular political party. The British ambassador arrived at the Egyptian King's residence accompanied by British officers who were "armed to the teeth," and explained to the King that he had no choice but to abdicate the throne or "I should have something else and more unpleasant with which to confront him." See Gabriel Warburg, "Lampson's Ultimatum to Faruq, 4 February, 1942," Middle East Studies, Vol. 11, No. 1 (January 1975), 24–42.

[8] See, for example, Alex de Waal, The Real Politics of the Horn of Africa: Money, War and the Business of Power, Polity (2015), at 69–90.

[9] See Ali Suleiman Fadlalla and Mohamed Abdelsalam Babiker, "In Search of Constitution and Constitutionalism in Sudan: The Quest for Legitimacy and the Protection of Rights," in Lutz Oette and Mohamed Abdelsalam Babiker (eds.), Constitution-Making and Human Rights in the Sudans, Routledge (2019).

[10] See Lutz Oette, "Power, Conflict and Human Rights in Sudan," in Lutz Oette and Mohamed Abdelsalam Babiker (eds.), Constitution-Making and Human Rights in the Sudans, Routledge (2019), at 30.

[11] See Zaid Al-Ali, The Struggle for Iraq's Future: How Corruption, Incompetence and Sectarianism Undermined Democracy, Yale University Press (2014), at 22–23.

[12] Douglas Porch, The Conquest of Morocco: A History, Farrar, Straus and Giroux (1982), at 187.

for agriculture. The Spanish military made extensive use of chemical weapons in its campaign against Moroccan forces.[13] In Libya, Italian forces sought to crush local resistance through a genocidal campaign that resulted in the death of 30 percent of the population. Hundreds of thousands were killed in Algeria, many of whom were killed through indiscriminate violence on the day on which France celebrated its own victory against Nazi Germany. Violence could also be highly politicized: Colonial rulers rarely hesitated to exile or even assassinate local leaders who worked to undermine imperial interests.[14] At times, the use of force was delegated to local security forces that were established, staffed, and trained by the colonial powers, and who were better equipped to interfere in the daily economic and political lives of the subjects.[15] In practice, colonial powers had a strong preference for the regular police, rather than for military units, which on the whole did not receive significant investment.[16] Violence could also be very casual, with colonial officials beating and prosecuting locals, sometimes for reasons that could properly be described as petty.[17]

Impunity: Colonial rule was also defined by the absence of any genuine accountability mechanisms for the executive. The general population had no real recourse against colonial officers and their local partners before any jurisdiction, regardless of how they behaved or the consequences of their actions. Whatever actions were taken by colonial powers or their proxies, they were never held accountable for their actions. This was the result of constitutional and legal arrangements that had been deliberately enacted by the colonial powers. In many countries, there were no parliamentary assemblies to speak of. In Sudan, the first assembly to include elected members was composed in 1947, after half a century of British rule. Algeria was constitutionally a territory of metropolitan France, but the local population's electoral

[13] See Jonathan Wyrtzen, THE MAKING OF MOROCCO: COLONIAL INTERVENTION AND THE POLITICS OF IDENTITY, Cornell University Press (2015), at 56; and Porch (1982), at 187.

[14] See, for example, Rob Prince, "Tunisia: Siliana and the Heritage of Farhat Hached Sixty Years after His Assassination," Nawaat, December 5, 2012 (describing the assassination on December 5, 1952 of Farhat Hached, one of the founding fathers of Tunisia's independent trade union movement, by a French paramilitary group).

[15] Nazih N. Ayubi, OVER-STATING THE ARAB STATE: POLITICS AND SOCIETY IN THE MIDDLE EAST, I.B. Tauris Publishers (1995), at 89.

[16] Owen (2004), at 10.

[17] In his historic account of colonial violence against ordinary Egyptians, Wilfrid Blunt provides an infamous account of a beating that British army officers inflicted on a number of Egyptians. The officers were on a fox hunt and were prevented from entering private property by a number of locals. The officers beat these individuals and imprisoned them. See Wilfrid Scawen Blunt, ATROCITIES OF JUSTICE UNDER BRITISH RULE IN EGYPT, T. Fisher Unwin (1907).

rights were heavily curtailed. Even in those countries that did have an elected chamber, they had close to no authority over the monarch and had none over the colonial authorities. On the contrary, the local monarch and by extension French and British officials could dissolve parliaments at will and did so whenever it was convenient. Local populations were also deprived of any meaningful opportunity to bring claims against governing authorities before the courts. Very early on during the occupation of Egypt, Lord Cromer forced the national government to pass a law that allowed the British military to take criminal cases involving its soldiers out of the ordinary courts whenever it saw fit and to have them tried before special military courts, which would function according to their own special procedure and to which there could be no appeal.[18] Several years later, in 1914, the British declared martial law, pursuant to which Egypt was given a British governor and military matters were totally removed from the jurisdiction of ordinary courts. The British also used the exceptional powers that they had unilaterally granted to themselves to issue new legislation without any form of process, including the imposition of new taxes on the local population. Martial law was only finally lifted in 1922.[19] Even when the local populations were given the right to challenge colonial authorities before the courts, judges were made to understand which cases were considered to be politically sensitive.[20] Colonial powers were also prepared to manipulate and distort legal traditions to satisfy their own ends, which included ensuring that their own actions would never be subject to any form of legal scrutiny. In Egypt, the United Kingdom moved to exercise hegemonic control over the courts.[21] In Algeria, French officers were formally authorized to use force against locals, who were not given any right of appeal. Many of the officers who were involved in the system defended the arrangement, arguing that the effort to civilize locals was only achievable without outside interference.[22]

Elite Pact: Britain and France reinforced and modernized the tradition of partnering with different elite groups to facilitate their rule (typically referred

18 Ibid., at 24–25.

19 Sadiq Reza, "Endless Emergency: The Case of Egypt," Boston University School of Law, Working Paper Series, Public Law and Legal Theory, Working Paper No. 08-12.

20 Mark Fathi Massoud, LAW'S FRAGILE STATE: COLONIAL, AUTHORITARIAN AND HUMANITARIAN LEGACIES IN SUDAN, Cambridge University Press (2013), at 62.

21 See Isabelle Lendrevie-Tournan, "The Independence of the Judiciary: Past and Present," in JUDGES AND POLITICAL REFORM IN EGYPT, Nathalie Bernard-Maugiron (ed.), American University in Cairo Press (2015), at 43.

22 K. J. Perkins and Ken Perkins, "The Bureaux Arabes and the Colons," PROCEEDINGS OF THE MEETING OF THE FRENCH COLONIAL HISTORICAL SOCIETY, Vol. 1 (1976), 96.

to as the "elite pact"), as an alternative to establishing (or even attempting to establish) genuine popular sovereignty. Thus, in Morocco, French officials collaborated with the royal court (the Makhzen), the merchants of the country's major cities, French settlers, and tribal leaders with a view to preventing conflict between them and controlling the local population.[23] Moroccans might have expected that the French would liberate them from the control of traditional leaders, but they were disappointed to learn that, on the contrary, their power was maintained and augmented.[24] In Iraq, British authorities also promoted tribal sheikhs, many of whom were elected to parliament. The same approach was adopted throughout the region, although the precise configuration would depend on the local circumstances. These elite bargains sometimes took the form of sectarian arrangements, whether formally or informally. The kings of both Iraq and Jordan (who were in fact brothers) were both from the Hijaz area, in modern Saudi Arabia, which meant that they were less likely to be acceptable to the general population, which in turn reinforced their dependence on elite pacts to survive. This proved particularly problematic in Iraq, where the new monarch relied heavily on former Ottoman officers to govern the country, which led to large segments of the local population being excluded from high office and from the policy-making process.[25] France adopted a more formal arrangement. Apart from dismembering Lebanon from Syria, it merged Latakia and Tartus to allow Syria's Alawite population to administer itself separately. All of this further reduced the need to consult with the general population and reinforced the attachment of nondemocratic practices. It also delayed and possibly even prevented the formation of national administrative cultures for decades, which in some countries still obstructs national development today.[26]

Absence of Consultation: Finally, the colonial enterprise was wholly based on the belief that the local population had nothing to contribute to the business of governing their country. The entire administrative system was therefore designed in a way that did not invite or depend on input from the local population. That belief was perhaps best encapsulated by Lord Cromer, who was the United Kingdom's First Consul General in Egypt from 1883 to 1907. After leaving office, he wrote that

[23] Robin Bidwell, Morocco under Colonial Rule: French Administration of Tribal Areas 1912–1956, Frank Cass (1973), at 9.

[24] David Rivet, Le Maroc de Lyautey à Mohamed V: Le double visage du Protectorat, Editions Denoël (1999), at 42.

[25] See Al-Ali (2014), at 22.

[26] Ayubi (1995), at 90–91.

> We need not always enquire too closely what these people, who are all nationally speaking, more or less in statu pupillari, themselves, think best in their own interests, although this is a point which deserves serious consideration. But it is essential that each special issue should be decided mainly with reference to what, by the light of Western knowledge and experience tempered by local considerations, we conscientiously think is best for the subject race, without reference to any real or supposed advantage which may accrue to England as a nation, or – as is more frequently the case – to the special interests represented by some one or more influential classes of Englishmen.[27]

Administratively, Lord Cromer's sentiments found expression through the practice of appointing British and French advisers in all government departments, including ministerial offices, which was imposed in virtually all countries. Even when local elites organized themselves peacefully to request greater democratic accountability, colonial officers dismissed them outright. In 1928, 150 Jordanian tribal elites and intellectuals met in the form of a "national council" to request that specific provisions of the Organic Law be amended. The British Resident General at the time responded by ignoring the council and by writing that "progress towards parliamentary rule will not be accomplished until the people prove their ability to shoulder their responsibilities."[28] Needless to say, an occupation force can never ignore its own self-interest, which is why the entire colonial enterprise was bound to fail.[29]

An Extractive Economy: This was clear from the manner in which Britain and France organized the region's economy. Unsurprisingly, the entire colonial enterprise was designed in a way that would allow both countries to extract resources from the local economies that they controlled.[30] This was generally achieved through a number of mechanisms, most importantly by favoring trade relations with home countries over internal or regional trade,[31] and by forcing local labor to carry out their work in precarious conditions. As already mentioned, colonial powers strongly favored dealing with elite groups (or creating them) rather than having to bargain with large constituencies (such as labor unions). As such, Britain restructured cotton production in Egypt such that by the end of their tenure in that country, cotton represented

[27] Earl of Cromer, POLITICAL AND LITERARY ESSAYS, 1908–1913, Macmillan and Co. (1913), at 13.

[28] Quoted in Kamel S. Abu Jaber, "The Legislature in the Hashemite Kingdom of Jordan," THE MUSLIM WORLD, Vol. 59, No. 3–4 (1969), 220–250.

[29] See Zaid Al-Ali, "Constitutional Drafting and External Influence," in Tom Ginsburg and Rosalind Dixon (eds.), COMPARATIVE CONSTITUTIONAL LAW, Edward Elgar Pub (2011).

[30] Ayubi (1995), at 89–90.

[31] Ibid., at 86–87.

90 percent of the total value of exports, and 13,000 individuals owned half the cultivated land.[32] On occasion, economic exploitation took on a crude form, such as in Iraq where Britain established its own corporation to extract oil from Iraqi territory while only paying minimal royalties to the Iraqi state.[33] In North Africa, France pursued aggressive colonial policies, which saw local farmers pushed off their land in favor of European settlers.[34] In Morocco, despite initial attempts to limit colonial encroachment, by 1953, there were nearly six thousand European farms, which covered half a million hectares.[35] In Algeria, where one million Europeans settlers had settled, and despite the fact that Algeria was nominally part of metropolitan France, the native Algerian population was not entitled to the same protections under France's labor laws as their European counterparts who were living in the same country.[36]

Impact: Over time, the harsh administrative and security measures combined with the obvious self-interest that motivated economic policy created significant antagonism for the local population throughout the region. The general population was deeply impacted by the routine humiliations that colonial authorities inflicted on local rulers, despite the local population's own disaffection toward their monarchs. Future putchists and revolutionaries who agitated against the colonial occupation cited the impunity with which colonial authorities imposed policies on local rulers as an important source of inspiration for their future acts of rebellion.[37] Meanwhile, despite the process of socioeconomic development, conditions remained appalling in much of the region. In 1952, the World Bank published a mission report on living conditions in Iraq after three and half decades of British-inspired rule. The report makes for sobering reading for supporters of European imperialism.

[32] Ibid., at 91.

[33] See Daniel Yergin, The Prize: The Epic Quest for Oil, Money and Power, Free Press (2008).

[34] Charles Kuntz, Souvenirs de Campagne au Maroc, University of Michigan Library (1913), at 257 ("Il faut développer avec une volonté tenace la colonisation européenne de la Tripolitanie à l'Atlantique. Le progrès, l'avenir sont dans l'Européen. L'Arabe n'est que le symbole du passé et de la décadence [European colonization from Tripolitania to the Atlantic must be developed with a tenacious will. Progress and the future are in the European. The Arab is only the symbol of the past and of decadence]").

[35] Bidwell (1973), at 213.

[36] Although Algeria was formally incorporated into the French state, and took the form of a French département, French labor laws were not applied to the native Algerian population in the same that they were in France. See Farid Lekeal, "Pacifier par le droit social? L'applicabilité de la législation ouvrière française en Algerie 1895–1921," in Samia el Mechat (ed.), Coloniser, Pacifier, Administrer: XIXe–XXIe siècles, CNRS Editions (2014).

[37] Fawaz A. Gerges, Making the Arab World: Nasser, Qutb, and the Clash that Shaped the Middle East, Princeton University Press (2018), at 162.

It states that 90 percent of Iraqis were illiterate, and that malaria, hookworm, and bilharzia and other debilitating diseases were common. It also describes a desperate economic situation, stating that Iraq's entire industrial sector only employed 2,000 people.[38] Where socioeconomic progress had been made, it could not keep up with the local population's expectations, particularly as they contrasted their living conditions with that of their foreign rulers or indeed of the local allies, leading to predictable results.[39]

POST-COLONIALISM

Diversity: Throughout the region, colonial authorities surrendered sovereignty to specific individuals or groups. The identity of these local elites and the manner in which they obtained power varied from country to country. In Morocco, Libya, and Jordan, colonial authorities withdrew in favor of monarchs that they themselves had selected and with whom they continued to be on good terms in the post-colonial period. In Tunisia, France eliminated radical actors just as it was withdrawing, clearing the scene for the future president with whom they built a solid relationship. In Egypt and Iraq, military officers forced British forces to relinquish control after they exiled or murdered the former ruling families. Algeria won its independence through conflict, forcing France to withdraw on the FLN's terms. In all cases, the monopoly on power that had previously been exercised by colonial powers was transferred to local forces, who guarded power just as jealously. The new ruling elites proceeded by drafting formal constitutions that had the same look and feel as many western European constitutions (including the 1962 Moroccan, 1959 Tunisian, 1952 Jordanian, and 1951 Libyan constitutions). Others viewed that approach as belonging to a failed liberal model and enacted extremely short constitutional documents that were undemocratic in both form and substance and were theoretically intended to spearhead development (including the 1969 Libyan Constitutional Declaration, Iraq's 1959 and 1970 Interim Constitutions, Algeria's 1963 Constitution, Egypt's 1953 Constitutional Declaration and Sudan's 1973 Constitution). Most of the texts were drafted by individuals who were handpicked by ruling authorities specifically because of their bias in favor of state authority and control. Libya's 1951 and Iraq's 1925 Constitutions were prepared by foreign officials and

[38] World Bank, The Economic Development of Iraq: Report of a Mission Organised by the International Bank for Reconstruction and Development at the Request of the Government of Iraq, Johns Hopkins Press (1952).

[39] Bidwell (1973), at 6.

advisers with only minor input from locals. The king was directly involved in and controlled the drafting of all of Morocco's constitutions and Jordan's 1952 Constitution. Syria's 1973 Constitution and Iraq's 1970 Interim Constitution were both drafted under the auspices of harsh authoritarian regimes. Egypt's 1971 Constitution was drafted by a committee of eighty individuals, all of whom were members of the National Assembly, which was intensely loyal to the president.[40]

Commonalities: Aside from the length, format, and manner of draft of each of these constitutional texts, a number of fundamental norms, all of which were inherited from the defunct colonial period, transcended borders, system of government, and the particular political preferences of controlling elites. These norms were both adopted by the new local authorities and amplified to a significant degree.[41] The end result was almost always the same: The fate of millions of unrepresented citizens in the region depended on the personal preferences of a few individuals, who could never be held accountable for their decisions or actions. Although the constitutional and institutional arrangement evolved, sometimes to a significant extent, the state did not waver from these fundamental tenets.[42] The only possible exceptions were Sudan and Syria, neither of which were dominated by specific actors at independence. However, both countries had to deal with decades of divisive colonial policies that enormously complicated the effort to negotiate a stable constitutional environment.

Hyper-presidentialism: The new ruling authorities moved to centralize authority to the fullest extent possible, sometimes matching the powers that governors general exercised, sometimes exceeding them.[43] This was the case whether the regime was led by civilians (as in Morocco, Tunisia, Jordan) or by the military (as in Egypt, Iraq).[44] It was also the case if the ruling regime was blatantly undemocratic (Iraq, Syria, Algeria from 1963 to 1975),[45] or maintained a semblance of democratic rule (Egypt under the 1971 constitution, Tunisia, Jordan, Morocco).[46] Chief executives were entirely responsible for composing government, and for determining state policy. Often, important

[40] John Waterbury, The Egypt of Nasser and Sadat: The Political Economy of Two Regimes, Princeton University Press (2014).

[41] See Massoud (2013), at 82.

[42] Roger Owen, the Rise and Fall of Arab Presidents for Life, Harvard University Press (2014), at 21–22.

[43] See, for example, Oette (2019), at 27.

[44] Ghai and Cottrell (2015), at 178.

[45] Owen (2014), at 17.

[46] Ibid., at 23.

decisions that would impact the entire population would be taken by the monarch or president entirely on his own, who would then impose the policy through his personal control of key institutions. National parliaments were nominally responsible for adopting legislation, including the annual budget law, but national constitutions diluted their authority so much as to make them almost totally ineffectual. In some cases, this took on extreme forms. Between 1952 and 1970, Egypt had six different constitutions, none of which allowed for any type of parliamentary oversight. Iraq's 1970 Interim Constitution provided that both legislative and executive power belonged to a body that was known as the Revolutionary Command Council. That body's membership was self-selected and self-generating, with absolutely no input from any outside body. There was no oversight, and there could be no possibility of removing any of the Council's members from office. In Morocco, the 1962 Constitution granted the king legislative power on a range of issues (Articles 29 and 49). In addition, some national constitutions provided for a bicameral system, in which the second chamber would be wholly appointed by the monarch and in which it was given the upper hand in case of disagreement with the lower chamber (Jordan). Parliament could still seek to influence policy by threatening to withdraw confidence from the cabinet. However, the required majority was two-thirds of its members, which was close to impossible to meet. In any event, parliaments were kept in line by the constant threat of dissolution, which could be exercised at any point and with absolute impunity.[47] Parliaments were dissolved so often in some countries that they almost never completed a full term (as in Jordan). Chief executives also had unlimited emergency power, which they invoked regularly and often without compelling justification. Most famously perhaps, Egypt and Tunisia maintained states of emergency for decades.[48] The practice was hardly limited to those two countries, however: The Kings of both Morocco and Jordan declared emergencies of their own, dissolving parliament and banning

47 Ninette S. Fahmy, THE POLITICS OF EGYPT: STATE–SOCIETY RELATIONSHIP, Routledge (2002), at 244.

48 Egypt passed an Emergency Law in 1958. Article 3(1) provided that, during an emergency, the executive had the following powers, "Restrict people's freedom of assembly, movement, residence, or passage in specific times and places; arrest suspects or [persons who are] dangerous to public security and order [and] detain them; allow searches of persons and places without being restricted by the provisions of the Criminal Procedure Code; and assign anyone to perform any of these tasks." See Sadiq Reza, "Endless Emergency: The Case of Egypt," Boston University School of Law, Working Paper Series, Public Law and Legal Theory, Working Paper No. 08-12.

political parties at various junctures, sometimes for a period of years.[49] Finally, chief executives were in all cases the commander in chief of the armed forces, which granted them unequal access to the armed forces and to the very substantial budgets that were allocated to military spending. In some countries, presidential or monarchical control over the military was so great that the cabinet would not even have a ministry of defense. The absence of safeguards against abuse by the security sector created an additional incentive for the executive to make use of that tool whenever it considered a threat to its authority had emerged. There was no oversight over instructions that were issued by the executive to the security sector, nor were their actions subject to adequate review, nor were military or security expenditures reviewed in any meaningful form.

Centralism: Similarly, power was also exclusively concentrated in each country's capital with a view to preventing the emergence of local centers of opposition to the ruling regime. Thus, although most countries provided for the existence of elected local councils, a complex network of laws and regulations ensured that those councils could never exercise any real authority, and real power at the local level belonged to the provincial governors who were almost always appointed by the central authorities.[50] The result was that provincial authorities played no role in policy formation and could be dismissed at any moment by various ministries in the capital.[51] Local councils, whether elected or not, could be ignored or dissolved at will. In many countries, provincial governors were often drawn from security institutions, something that was also done by colonial authorities. In other cases, their principle qualification was their allegiance to the ruling party. In both cases, the governor's main task was not to oversee the social and economic development of the areas that were under their control but rather to oversee the implementation of security policy.[52] A version of that arrangement was even

[49] Lise Storm, Democratization in Morocco: The Political Elite and the Struggles for Power in the Post-independence State, Routledge (2007), at 25–26. On Jordan, see Sufian Obeidat, The Amended Constitution of Jordan: Analysis and Recommendations Study, International IDEA, Unpublished.

[50] Mona Harb and Sami Atallah (eds.), Local Governments and Public Goods: Assessing Decentralisation in the Arab World, Lebanese Center for Policy Studies (2015).

[51] Sujit Choudhry and Richard Stacey, Decentralisation in Unitary States: Constitutional Frameworks for the Arab Region, The Center for Constitutional Transitions, International IDEA and the United Nations Development Programme (2014).

[52] Fahmy (2002), at 244. The same dynamic existed in sub-Saharan Africa; see Ghai and Cottrell (2015), at 177 ("Regimes that remained civilian in form (though some, including Swaziland, had the military in the background) showed two tendencies, with some commonalities: basically, they were aimed at the concentration of power. They changed parliamentary into presidential systems – not itself a necessarily autocratic tendency, of course, but it demonstrated

adopted in Iraq after the 2003 invasion and subsequent regime change. Despite a new federal system of government and the existence of elected provincial councils, central authorities in Baghdad reserved for themselves the authority to dismiss provincial governors at any time, and passed a number of laws to remove any decision-making authority from the provincial councils.[53]

Courts: Judiciaries remained firmly under executive control in the post-colonial period. In most countries, the chief executive was formally the head of the judiciary, head of the judicial council, and responsible for composing the highest courts. The impact was that many judges, who had grown accustomed to operating under the overbearing control of colonial authorities, simply shifted their allegiances to the new controlling authorities but changed nothing in their manner of proceeding. This even applies to post-2003 Iraq, where the courts could not even prosecute members of the elite when they admitted corruption and embezzlement on national television.[54] Judiciaries in the region evolved and integrated some reformists within their ranks, which created hope that they could serve as a check on executive overreach. In Egypt, the courts were undermined in 1969 through a number of measures, including but not limited to the establishment of a new Supreme Court that was firmly under the president of the republic's control.[55] However, the Supreme Constitutional Court gradually evolved into an avenue for opponents of the ruling regime to challenge its decisions and behavior. By 1998, dozens of petitions for constitutional review were being raised every year, and the Court issued many rulings that undermined regime control.[56] Although a number of activists and commentators saw this as a unique opportunity to advance the rule of law in the heart of the Arab region,[57] the Egyptian regime

some impatience with the idea of power being in any way divided. And they emasculated systems of autonomy, such as they were, in Ethiopia, Kenya and Uganda").

[53] See Sabah Al-Bawi, "Influences of Ambiguity of Constitutional Provisions on the Administrative System of Iraq," University of Pennsylvania Journal of International Law, Vol. 33 (2012), 1165.

[54] Martin Chulov, "Post-war Iraq: 'Everybody is Corrupt, from Top to Bottom. Including Me'," *The Guardian* (February 19, 2016) (in which a leading politician, who was never prosecuted, is quoted as saying "I was offered $5m by someone to stop investigating him. I took it, and continued prosecuting him anyway").

[55] See Mahmoud Hamad, Judges and Generals in the Making of Modern Egypt: How Institutions Sustain and Undermine Authoritarian Regimes, Cambridge University Press (2018), at 107.

[56] See Tamir Moustafa, the Struggle for Constitutional Power: Law Politics and Economic Development in Egypt, Cambridge University Press (2007), at 178.

[57] Nathan J. Brown, Constitutions in a Nonconstitutional World: Arab Basic Laws and the Prospects for Accountable Government, State University of New York Press (2002), at Chapter 5.

used the constitutional authority at its disposal to pack the Court with loyalists, who did not hesitate to serve executive interests once they had captured the Court. In 2001, the president went so far as to appoint a senior official at the ministry of justice, who had drafted legislation so illiberal that the Court had only just struck down key provisions months before his appointment.[58] Executive authorities have also been known to issue outright threats against the courts or to persecute judicial officials. In Egypt, reformist judges found that their immunity had been lifted and that they were being investigated after organizing a conference on political reform.[59] In Iraq, judges were routinely imprisoned whenever they found that the government had acted in violation of the constitution.[60] In Tunisia, judges who dared challenge abuses by the executive were fired, prevented from travelling, and ostracized by the state.[61] The end result of all these actions was that the courts lost all of their potential as a mechanism to hold the government to account and, on the contrary, they had evolved into yet another mechanism of oppression against citizens who were outside the elite bargain.[62] Finally, in the rare cases when a court avoided cooptation or where a decision was issued against executive interests, the government would simply refuse to implement the decision (without making an official declaration to that effect, of course), safe in the knowledge that plaintiffs and the courts had no means at their disposal to enforce a decision against it. The end result was that 85 percent of verdicts in civil courts were never executed, another practice that was used to marginalize and punish political opponents.[63]

58 Moustafa (2007), at 198.

59 Ibid., at 215.

60 For example, one Iraqi judge who found a government confiscation order without compensation to be in violation of the constitution was sentenced to three years in jail. See Beth K. Dougherty and Edmund A. Ghareeb, Historical Dictionary of Iraq, The Scarecrow Press (2013), at 180.

61 Samer Ghamroun, "In Memory of Mokhtar Yahyaoui (1952–2015): Lessons from Tunisia's Rebel Judge," *The Legal Agenda*, November 30, 2015.

62 Moustafa (2007), at 208 ("With Supreme Constitutional autonomy lost, there are clear signs that the government is using the SCC as a weapon against both reform activists and against other branches of the Egyptian judiciary itself"). The same applied in Tunisia; see Beatrice Hibou, The Force of Obedience: The Political Economy of Repression in Tunisia, Polity Press (2011), at 117 and 119 ("judges, public prosecutors, and magistrates as a whole have acted as driving belts of the central power, notably in cases of crisis, to fight successively against student movements, leftist movements, the Baathist movement, popular revolts, trade union movements, the Islamist tendency (of course) and democratic demands. [...] The judicial system['s] function is essentially to 'protect society' – or rather to protect a certain order of society – and to ensure the proper functioning of measures of security and the realization of the pact of security").

63 Fahmy (2002), at 244. The same was also true in Tunisia; see Hibou (2011), at 117–118.

Audit Institutions: All modern states are required to maintain audit institutions, particularly if they hope to tap into international finance institutions. All countries in the region established supreme audit institutions, including Iraq's Board of Supreme Audit, Egypt's Central Auditing Organisation, and Tunisia's Cour des Comptes.[64] Over the past century, these institutions have evolved as a vital component of government. They employ hundreds (sometimes thousands) of auditors and investigators and are empowered to review government expenditures in all ministries, state institutions, and state-owned enterprises. Without this exercise, most parliaments around the world would not have sufficient information to carry out effective oversight over the government, both in terms of waste and corruption.[65] For democratic systems of government, they are a vital component of the oversight mechanism, whereas in the Arab region, heads of state have traditionally viewed them less charitably. Until recently, national constitutions never mentioned the audit institutions, which meant that their composition, mandate, and operation were completely subject to legislation, which in turn meant that they were subject to executive control. For those that did (such as Iraq's 2005 Constitution at Article 103(1)) there was such a lack of detail that the act of manipulating the exercise of their functions was straightforward. Presidents and monarchs reserved for themselves the right to appoint and dismiss the heads of auditing institutions, and ensured that whoever was in charge would report directly to the chief executive (and not to the parliament). Finally, and perhaps most importantly, none of the audit reports (many of which detailed gross mismanagement of public funds) could ever be published without the head of state's approval. As such, yet another avenue for possible oversight of the executive branch was closed off entirely.[66]

Elite Pact: In the first years of their independence, countries in the Arab region witnessed intense competition between groups of elites who were jostling against each other in a competition for political power.[67] Many of the countries' new rulers found that they either did not enjoy sufficient support to rule on their own or that specific institutions or groups had

64 The counterpart institution in the United States is the Government Accountability Office, and in the United Kingdom it is the National Audit Office.

65 See Kenneth M. Dye and Rick Stapenhurst, "Pillars of Integrity: The Importance of Supreme Audit Institutions in Curbing Corruption," The Economic Development Institute of the World Bank (1998).

66 Abdel Khalek Farouk, The Roots of Administrative Corruption in Egypt ("جذور الفساد الإدارى في مصر"), Dar al-Shourouk (2008).

67 Owen (2014), at 27.

sufficient authority to challenge their claim to power.[68] As such, presidents, kings, and prime ministers reinvigorated the elite bargains that had been established under the colonial period in order to augment their own authority, while making sure to adapt it to the new realities on the ground.[69] In practice, this meant that some constituencies were maintained as part of the new arrangements; some were abandoned and excluded altogether; while others still were introduced into the bargain for the first time, albeit with significant limits on their capacity to influence state policy. Constitutional texts were enacted and were in large part designed to regulate the activities of state institutions and other groups, while also cementing them together. In practice, this meant that the security sector (which, in countries such as Iraq, Egypt, Algeria, and Syria constituted a constituency of its own and grew to considerable size after independence), the legal profession (particularly judges), the bureaucracy, and a small number of political groups were all given their own spheres of influence.[70] Certain segments of the bourgeoisie were also permitted to survive under the new arrangement, with some formally acquiring roles in government and parliament.[71] Trade unions were also incorporated into the ruling bargain but under very specific and controlled conditions. Most famously perhaps, the Egyptian Trade Union Federation was formed in 1957 as the only body authorized to represent national workers and was entirely loyal to the state regardless of how workers were actually treated. As the new elite pact formalized, there were bound to be losers. Thus, as new ruling authorities in countries such as Algeria, Egypt, and Iraq moved to nationalize key assets throughout the territories that they controlled, a class of individuals (including merchants in cities such as Cairo, Alexandria, Casablanca, and elsewhere; local industrialists; and major landowners) quickly understood that they were to be excluded. Algeria in particular saw the departure of 1 million European settlers from its territory as the country gained independence in 1962.[72] The executive granted a certain amount of

68 Ibid., at 32–33.

69 Brown (2002), at 92.

70 Mehran Kamrava, "The Rise and Fall of Running Bargains in the Middle East," in Mehran Kamrava (ed.), Beyond the Arab Spring: The Evolving Ruling Bargain in the Middle East, Oxford University Press (2014); Owen (2014), at 15.

71 Fahmy (2002), at 242.

72 Many of these same dynamics were also present in sub-Saharan Africa. See Ghai and Cottrell (2015), at 174–175 ("In settler-based colonies, because of their vested interests, the only way to challenge colonial power was by counter-force. The response of the colonial power to that counter-force exposed its moral bankruptcy, highlighting its lack of legitimacy, and ultimately led to independence, but not before a deal had been struck between the outgoing power and the incoming elite: an elite fashioned in no inconsiderable part by the outgoing power, rather

privileges and immunity to the judiciary in exchange for its agreement not to engage in any form of review of the state's actions. Trade unionists across the region were granted guaranteed public sector employment, food subsidies, a higher minimum wage, greater pension rights, free higher education, and other benefits in exchange for political quiescence, to the extent that basic political rights such as the right to strike and assemble in protest were surrendered.[73] Parts of the bourgeoisie survived the early purges and were granted lucrative contracts by the government and were sometimes even allowed to influence economic and trade policy in exchange for a commitment not to bankroll opposition movements. The bureaucracy accepted remaining quiescent in exchange for long-term job stability and nepotistic hiring practices that allowed state employees to pass on their privileges to relatives and others.

Absence of Consultation: Colonialism created within the region's new rulers the desire to correct some of the social and economic legacies of the past but it also generated within them a savior syndrome, according to which only they were properly qualified to rule the country. A few years before he became president of Tunisia, Bourghiba equated his fate with that of his entire nation: without him, the people simply had no hope.[74] Kings, presidents, and prime ministers not only adopted colonial methods of control through the use of elite pacts and executive immunity but their impressions of themselves reinforced the idea that public consultations were a waste of time, or were perhaps even beneath them. Gamal Abdel Nasser of Egypt famously derided a leader of the official trade union federation when he dared suggest that the union had some influence over government policy. "The workers don't demand; we give," he said.[75] Nasser also challenged basic democratic principles, including the separation of powers, which he described as a "fraud."[76]

than as an agreement among the people of the colony. [...] What it bequeathed to the people on Britain's departure was a country with these communities tied together by political structures and the economy devised for their subordination, but with the additional problems of finding and creating a common identity and destiny: a state without a nation").

73 See Daniel Brumberg, "Authoritarian Legacies and Reform Strategies in the Arab World," in Rex Brynen, Bahgat Korany, and Paul Noble (eds.), POLITICAL LIBERALISATION AND DEMOCRATISATION IN THE ARAB WORLD, Boulder (1995); and see Marie Duboc, "Challenging the Trade Union, Reclaiming the Nation: The Politics of Labor Protest in Egypt, 2006–2011," in Mehran Kamrava (ed.), BEYOND THE ARAB SPRING: THE EVOLVING RULING BARGAIN IN THE MIDDLE EAST, Oxford University Press (2014), at 225–230.

74 Owen (2014), at 33 (from a French prison in 1952, Bourghiba wrote that "if my life were taken, the people would suffer an irreparable loss in losing not so much their leader and moral counsellor as the fruit of all their past sacrifices").

75 Joel Beinin, WORKERS AND THIEVES: LABOR MOVEMENTS AND POPULAR UPRISINGS IN TUNISIA AND EGYPT, Stanford University Press (2016), at 18.

76 See Hamad (2018), at 85.

In Algeria, the National Liberation Front built a state that was designed to serve local interests but had no intention of consulting the people when deciding what the state's policy should be.[77] Similarly, when asked to explain the lawmaking process in a public discussion, Saddam Hussein explained that the law was "nothing but the stroke of my pen."[78] Finally, as under the colonial period, there was no mechanism in place to control against self-interest, hence the grotesque forms of nepotism that allowed dictators across the region to appoint their children as successors or as prime beneficiaries of the elite pact. The post-colonial administrative framework, combined with the personal attributes of the individuals who now monopolized executive power and refused to acknowledge the views and opinions of their fellow citizens, ensured that countries throughout the region would remain on a despotic path.[79]

Constitutional Expression: Constitutional rules and institutional arrangements were then constructed to bring the elite pact to life: Texts throughout the region granted generous socioeconomic rights but ensured that basic political rights were very limited; security institutions and the judiciary were granted significant amounts of autonomy, immunity, and other privileges; and, the initial wave of nationalizations notwithstanding, protections for private property were instituted in favor of what remained of the bourgeoisie.[80] Where colonial-era elite pacts involved sectarian arrangements, these were almost always maintained in some form or another.[81] Vitally, however, as under colonial rule, those individuals who were not directly connected to any of these elite circles (which in some cases represented the vast majority of the population) were completely cut out from the equation. They were not given any means to influence policy and were subject to a harsh form of authoritarian rule. But the elite pact did not merely lead to an absence of consultation. It resulted in the deliberate exclusion of large segments of the population from decision-making circles. Syria's 1973 Constitution actually provided that the Baath Party was the "leading party in the state and in society," thereby totally negating the possibility that the country could ever

77 See James McDougall, A History of Algeria, Cambridge University Press (2017), at 238.

78 'Adawiya al-Hilali, "The Stroke of a Pen" (جرَّة قلم), Al-Mada Paper (February 22, 2016).

79 The same trend was visible in other parts of Africa; see Crawford Young, The Postcolonial State in Africa: Fifty Years of Independence 1960–2010, University of Wisconsin Press (2012), at 119.

80 Ibid., at 119–120.

81 See, for example, Bassel F. Salloukh, Rabie Barakat, Jinan al-Habbal, Lara W. Khattab, and Shoghib Mikaelian, The Politics of Sectarianism in Postwar Lebanon, Pluto Press (2015), at 16.

become a multi-party democracy. In any event, even if a parliament were to evolve into an avenue through which opposition voices could be expressed, heads of state had almost limitless power to dissolve them for any reason and at any time. Algeria's 1963 Constitution provided that the National Liberation Front was the only political party that was authorized to operate in the country (Article 23); that all members of the legislature were elected by the people after having been nominated by the Front (Article 27); and that basic rights such as freedom of speech could not be used to undermine the Front's unity (Article 22). The president of the republic was also to be nominated by the Front (Article 39) and was the ex officio head of the high judicial council (Article 65). In other countries, the rules were more complex but led to the same result. Under its 1959 Constitution, Tunisia's president was not subject to term limits; had control over the constitutional council's composition; was exclusively responsible for selecting and dismissing ministers; had complete administrative control over the security services; and was not subject to any form of oversight by the parliament.[82] In that context, heads of state were under no obligation to consider unsympathetic or critical views, leaving the matter entirely to their discretion. Unsurprisingly, they leaned heavily in favor of preventing opposition voices from even being expressed.

Violence: As under the colonial period, internal dissent was typically met with violence. Where individuals or groups of protesters openly criticized ruling regimes, governments rarely hesitated to deploy security services. Armies were deployed to quash popular uprisings (as in Iraq in 1991 and 2019, and Sudan in 2019) and protests against inadequate services such as electricity (Lebanon in 2008),[83] as well as corruption and socioeconomic conditions (as in Algeria in 1988, Gafsa, Tunisia in 2008, and the Egyptian bread riots in 1977).[84] Political parties were banned and heavily persecuted. The Iraqi Communist Party, which was once a dominant political force, and was a regular presence in government from 1958, was forced underground in the 1970s, and many of its members were arrested and subjected to brutal treatment. Opposition parties and voices were subjected to similar treatment throughout the region, including in Egypt, Jordan, Tunisia, Yemen, and Morocco, where even teenagers were imprisoned and subjected to inhumane

82 Clement Henry Moore, Tunisia since Independence: The Dynamics of One-Party Government, University of California Press (1965), at 182.

83 See 'Seven Protesters Die in Clash with Lebanese Troops', CNN, January 28, 2008.

84 Steven A. Cook, The Struggle for Egypt: From Nasser to Tahrir Square, Oxford University Press (2013), at 81–82.

treatment for demanding greater political freedoms.[85] This was even done within ruling regimes, which has led to an unending series of internal purges in countries as far apart from each other as Iraq in 1979[86] and Algeria in September 2015.[87] Finally, the ruling regimes pressed civil society organizations into silence, either prohibiting their activities or fundraising, or through cooptation. This extended to human rights organizations,[88] as well as to independent trade unions in countries such as Tunisia.[89] Freedom of association was highly curtailed even in smaller countries such as Lebanon.[90]

IMPACT OF HYPER-PRESIDENTIALISM

Poverty of Ideas: Colonial administrations were broadly effective at controlling small to mid-size rebellions but were not robust or flexible enough to respond to nationwide wars of national liberation (as in Algeria) or growing nationalist movements. Post-colonial constitutional systems inherited that same rigidity, which eventually caused states throughout the region to atrophy. The seeds for constitutional degradation were firmly planted when the

85 In 1976 a nineteen-year-old, Jamal Benomar (who many decades later was appointed Special Adviser to the Secretary General of the United Nations on Yemen's transition), was imprisoned in Morocco for eight years for political activism. Benomar was tortured and made to endure other forms of inhuman treatment during his period of detention. See "Memories of Morocco," Jamal Benomar, New Internationalist, Issue 163, September 1986; see also Joyce Edling, MY DEAR JAMAL (MOROCCO BOUND), New Millennium (1996), at 1–3. On Egypt, see Owen (2014), at 32.

86 See Al-Ali (2014), at 31.

87 For example, behind the scenes purges took place in Algeria in September 2015, where Mohamed Mediene, who had been the head of the intelligence service for twenty-five years, was quietly replaced by President Abdelaziz Bouteflika. No reasons were offered. See "Algerian president fires intelligence chief in a shake-up of security forces," Carlotta Gall, *The New York Times* (September 14, 2015); see also, "Bouteflika Puts an End to Head of Intelligence General Mohamed Medien's 'Legend'" ("بوتفليقة ينهي أسطورة الجنرال توفيق قائد الاستخبارات"), Atef Qadadara, al-Hayat (September 14, 2015).

88 See Moustafa (2007), at 202–205.

89 Hibou (2011), at 124–125; and Hèla Yousfi, L'UGTT UNE PASSION TUNISIENNE: ENQUETE SUR LES SYNDICALISTES EN REVOLUTION 2011–2014, Edition Med aLi (2014).

90 See Lea Bou Khater, "Understanding State Incorporation of the Workers' Movement in Early Post-War Lebanon and Its Backlash on Civil Society," Civil Society Knowledge (2019) (which describes the highly unrepresentative decision-making structures within the General Confederation of Workers in Lebanon). Despite the fact that the 1926 Constitution formally guarantees the freedom of association (Article 13), efforts in 2012 and 2013 to form an independent trade union in a leading supermarket chain were obstructed through various means. A court finally found in favor of the union six years after they launched their initiative. See Nizhar Saghieh, "Six Years Later, Spinneys Workers Win: Oppressing Unionists Is a Criminal Offense" (بعد 6 سنوات، عمال سبينس ينتصرون: قمع النقابيين جرم جزائي), Legal Agenda (January 10, 2019).

region's first generation of post-colonial constitutions reconcentrated power in the hands of the chief executive without any counterbalancing accountability measures. The constitutions favored executive privilege so much that executive power was eventually monopolized by ever-diminishing numbers of people (sometimes eventually reducing to a single individual, as in the case of Iraq from 1979 until 2003), who were solely responsible for designing macro-economic policy and for questions of war and peace. The effect was worsened by the fact that the people who happened to be in control were not particularly qualified for the positions that they occupied.[91] This was yet another consequence of colonial policies, in particular the repression and discrediting of political parties, which left very few people in place who were both capable and willing to govern. As a result, the region was infected by a poverty of ideas, leading to governance failures throughout the post-colonial period. In Libya, repression was so severe that power was seized by a low-ranking army officer with no prior experience in governance or administration. In Iraq, the catastrophic decision to invade Kuwait in 1991 was famously based on the president's misinterpretation of comments made by a foreign ambassador.

Attrition: As economic opportunity deteriorated (see Chapter 8), increasing numbers of people participated in strikes and protest actions, particularly from the year 2000 to 2011. In response, rather than engage in meaningful reform, states stepped up repression through use of the security sector, which was granted vastly increased resources to maintain the regimes in power.[92] In Egypt, during the 1990s, the proportion of police personnel grew from 9 to 21 percent of total government employment. The total number grew from 150,000 in 1974 to one million by 2002.[93] In Tunisia, starting in the 1980s, the minister of interior's budget underwent a massive expansion, and by 2010 was roughly double that of the ministry of defense. During that same period, the presidency's own budget increased by 300 times, which reflected ever increasing centralization of control, including over the security sector.[94] In parallel, basic freedoms were even more restricted than in the past. One could not even discuss the head of state's possible whereabouts or speculate about potential health difficulties when he disappeared for months at a time,

[91] See Massoud (2013), at 90.

[92] Saïd Amir Arjomand, "Revolution and Constitution in the Arab World, 2011–2012," in Mehran Kamrava (ed.), Beyond the Arab Spring: The Evolving Ruling Bargain in the Middle East, Oxford University Press (2014); Owen (2014), at 38 and 47.

[93] Sadri Khiari, Tunisie: Le Délitement de la Cité, Editions Karthala (2003), at 114.

[94] Derek Lutterbeck, "Tool of Rule: The Tunisian Police under Ben Ali," The Journal of North African Studies (2015), 813–831.

something that was increasingly common given their advanced age.[95] Even countries such as Morocco were at best mixed successes. Despite the Equity and Reconciliation Commission's recommendations (see Chapter 5, Part 1), the core demand for greater accountability for abuse of executive power has not been met.[96]

Illegitimacy: Perhaps the most outrageous and damaging display of regime entrenchment in the region was the unending number of sham presidential and parliamentary elections that were organized, some of which were so outrageous that they contributed to the protest movement's anger.[97] Constitutional amendments were carried out throughout the region to remove term limits. Although the proper procedures were generally respected, the general population understood that the regimes were now also openly undermining the rule of law for the basest form of self-interest. After the 2002 constitutional amendments that led to the elimination of term limits, Tunisians complained that the constitution was merely "scrap paper."[98] Meanwhile, the economic reforms benefited a tiny proportion of the population, which never developed its own political culture or representation and whose survival depended entirely on the executive's discretion.[99] Simply put, there was no claim left to any form of legitimacy. The potential for collapse was overwhelming and for some entirely predictable. On the eve of the 2011 uprisings, a Syrian analyst wrote that his country did "not have multiple paths or choices before it. Only two paths remain, with no other options: a total, across the board reform – in politics, the economy, the administration and human development – in conformity with democratic good governance of the political system and society, or catastrophe."[100]

POST-2011

Stability and Continuity (Morocco, Algeria, Egypt, Syria, Jordan): Despite the historical context and the overwhelming popular demand for social justice, the regional constitutional reform process was principally motivated by other concerns. All countries were starting from the same template but proceeded differently depending on the circumstances. In Morocco,

95 Cook (2013), at 197.
96 Storm (2007), at 111.
97 Kamrava (2014), at 32–33; and Storm (2007), at 50.
98 Khiari (2003), at 111.
99 Fahmy (2002), at 243; see also Owen (2014), at 52.
100 Quoted in Gilbert Achcar, The People Want: A Radical Exploration of the Arab Uprising, University of California Press (2013), at 119.

Algeria, Syria, and Jordan, the ruling elites survived the initial protests and therefore prioritized continuity and stability over all other considerations, considerably slowing the reform effort in the process. In Egypt, the monopoly on power was momentarily lost during the transition, only for it to be regained in 2013. In all these countries, the scope for reform was limited through a number of means including by hand-picking a committee that was responsible for suggesting changes and by explicitly limiting their mandate. Unsurprisingly, the reforms in those countries left the fundamental tenets of the state intact, while making only minor adjustments. Despite some minor improvements, all five countries have maintained a hyper-presidential system of government, with only slight variations between them, in which there are no effective checks on executive authority. In Algeria, Egypt, Syria, and Jordan, the chief executive is always named as the commander in chief and appoints and dismisses the government at will. In Morocco, the king must appoint the largest parliamentary bloc's nominee but can still impose his will on the cabinet by chairing the sessions whenever he pleases. All five countries' parliaments can withdraw confidence in the government but face major challenges in doing so, including unreasonably high majority requirements (usually two-thirds of members) as well as the threat of dissolution. In all five countries, the chief executive can dissolve the parliament virtually at will, with only minor exceptions (including, for example, that a dissolution cannot be ordered during a state of emergency). Notably, in Egypt, dissolution must be put to referendum, also an important exception (Article 137). In Morocco, Syria, and Jordan, the chief executive can declare a state of emergency virtually at will and for any period of time. Algeria and Egypt are partial exceptions, where the President can only declare a state of emergency for a thirty-day period, at the end of which he must obtain the approval of parliament. The chief executive exercises undue influence over oversight institutions such as the judiciary and audit institutions, mainly through unilateral appointment and dismissal powers. In some countries, the chief executive appoints all the members of the constitutional court entirely on his own, while in others he is formally named as head of the judiciary and chairs the judicial council. The only possible accountability mechanism in the circumstances is elections but real competition is close to impossible when a single individual has so much authority. In Morocco, parliamentary elections have a limited impact given that the King must appoint the largest parliamentary party's candidate as prime minister (Article 47), but, as noted previously, the King can always impose his will at any moment by chairing the cabinet's sessions. In the short term, the ruling elites in these countries have succeeded in maintaining some form of continuity and stability (with the obvious exception of Syria). A decade later, the overall picture was far from positive. All the circumstances that caused the demonstrations to take place in 2011 were still in place. Meanwhile, the pace of reform has been so slow in each of the countries that it has caused consternation among the ruling elites themselves.[101]

Conflict (Libya, Yemen, Iraq): In the remaining countries, continuity and stability could not be pursued because ruling elites lost and could not recover their monopoly on power. Surviving and emerging groups, many of which deeply distrusted each other, simultaneously scrambled for power while seeking to survive the transition. One means through which they sought to achieve that aim was to empower through the negotiations the institutions that they themselves thought they could dominate, and to limit the authority that they expected their rivals would control. The precise institutions that negotiators focused their attention on varied from country to country. Libya, Yemen, and Iraq commenced their own processes on the basis that calls for greater autonomy in various parts of both countries were so great that federalism and the vertical distribution of powers was the main point of contention. In Libya's case, it became apparent over time that support for greater autonomy was not as uniform as originally appeared, causing the constitutional drafters to settle in favor of a centralized system of government. In Yemen, there was a general acceptance that a federation should be established, but discussions were largely informed by each group's desire to limit their rivals' authority rather than to establish a functioning state (as was the case in Iraq in 2005). That logic was most clearly apparent during discussions of the number and boundaries of the future regions, as well as revenue sharing between producing regions, nonproducing regions, and the federal government. In Iraq, negotiators were consumed by federalism as a result of the Kurdistan Region's ambition to have its de facto and preexisting status confirmed in the constitution. The main issues of contention during the negotiations included natural resources; the allocation of responsibilities between the federal and regional governments; and how to manage asymmetric levels of federalism. However, none of these countries achieved a genuine agreement or stability for a combination of reasons, including process failures. Ultimately,

[101] On October 9, 2015, in a speech to the Moroccan parliament, the king repeatedly questioned the pace of legislation reform, stating "The question is: Why are the laws relating to a number of institutions still waiting to be updated, four years after the adoption of the Constitution? Why are we waiting for the new institutions stipulated in the Constitution to be set up?"; "King Mohammed's Speech before Moroccan Parliament," *Morocco World News* (October 9, 2015).

major forces in all three countries were not committed to a negotiated solution and undermined the process through a number of means, including from within by manipulating the rules and seeking to impose outcomes in the absence of an agreement, or from without by committing acts of violence. The ensuing chaos was enough to cause the Libyan drafters (who continued to work even after violence worsened) to fall back in favor of a presidential system of government that was eerily similar to what existed elsewhere in the region, in the hope that it would bring back some form of stability to the country.

Inclusivity (Tunisia and Sudan):[102] Only a small number of countries have been able to transition from hyper-presidentialism to a more inclusive form of government, although none has yet succeeded in coming close to meeting popular expectations. In Sudan, the 2019 negotiations were dominated by the attempt by the Forces for Freedom for Change to remove or at least transition away from military rule. The two sides agreed to share power for the length of a multi-year transition. The negotiations focused mainly on the amount of authority the military would retain both in the presidency (the Sovereignty Council) and in the cabinet. An agreement was reached, but by 2020 Sudan was only at the start of its transition. An election had not yet been organized and the permanent constitution had not been adopted, making the transition not yet ripe for analysis. Tunisia offers the greatest opportunity for reflection and analysis, mainly because an agreement was reached on the final constitution that moved away from the hyper-presidential model. In Tunisia, Ennahda tried to position itself as the country's dominant political force and was opposed by a combination of secular, liberal, nationalist, revolutionary, and left-wing groups. It sought to empower parliament, which it was confident it would dominate in the foreseeable future, whereas its opponents sought to empower the presidency based on the assumption that one of their own would occupy the position.[103] The bulk of the negotiations therefore focused on the relationship between the presidency and the parliament, with both sides

[102] Lebanon has had an inclusive constitutional arrangement since 1926 but cannot be described as democratic, as a result of formal and informal sectarian arrangements. A popular uprising broke out in 2019, which has by February 2021 not had any meaningful impact on the country's constitution.

[103] Successive rounds of elections have confirmed that analysis: Islamists returned a crushing parliamentary majority in Egypt and a clear plurality in Tunisia; meanwhile, Egypt's 2012 presidential elections were won by an Islamist but with a bare majority when the Islamist movement was at the peak of its popularity and with grudging support from other communities who simply wanted to defeat his rival. That trend was confirmed in later electoral cycles. In 2014, in the second round of Tunisia's presidential elections, the secular and Islamist candidates returned 55.68 percent and 44.32 percent, respectively. In the 2019 presidential elections, the Islamist-supported candidate was knocked out in the first round.

simultaneously seeking to strengthen their preferred institution and weaken the other.[104] In the end, as a result of circumstances described in Chapter 6, the final agreement did succeed in moving away from hyper-presidentialism and establishing a reasonable set of checks and balances, which has prevented either branch of government from dominating the other.[105] Tunisia's first post-transition president, the first ever to be democratically elected, was personally opposed to the 2014 Constitution's semi-presidential system and considered that Tunisia was better suited to a strong presidential system.[106] The president sought through a number of means to reconcentrate power in his own hands but was ultimately unsuccessful, mainly as a result of the country's plural politics combined with constitutional provisions that granted specific powers to parliament and to the Prime Minister.

Paralysis: At the same time, however, Tunisia's new system of government has been criticized for being too broken apart. The overwhelming focus on preventing one side of the political divide from remonopolizing power established Tunisia as a frozen republic. Since the 2014 Constitution entered into force, key state institutions, mainly including the presidency, the cabinet, and the parliament, have been unable to make meaningful progress on a number of issues that must be resolved to improve the state's delivery of services.[107] From 2015 to 2019 the country was led by an alliance between Ennahda and the then-largest secular force in the country, Nidaa Tounes. The two groups' leadership forged an alliance in order to form a government but could not form a functioning working relationship with each other or a common vision on policy as a result of the deep distrust that ran between them. Each of the two parties was concerned that whatever policy would be adopted could lead to a rise in the other's fortunes, which slowed progress considerably, sometimes to a halt, on a range of issues. Over time, the polarization was not resolved and the parliament became increasingly fractured, which made it

[104] Egypt's 2012 constitutional drafting process was informed by many of the same dynamics and reached a broadly similar outcome with some major differences (mainly as a result of the personal characteristics of specific actors).

[105] For more on semi-presidentialism, see "Semi-Presidentialism as Power Sharing: Constitutional Reform after the Arab Spring," Sujit Choudhry and Richard Stacey, Center for Constitutional Transitions at NYU Law and International IDEA (2014).

[106] See Hechmi Nouira, "Le président Béji Caïd Essebsi à Assahafa et à La Presse: 'Le système politique actuel ne peut assurer le développement et la stabilité du pays," Leaders (September 6, 2017).

[107] See, for example, Éric Gobe, "La Tunisie en 2017: Impotence de l'État et tentations autoritaires," L'Année du Maghreb, CNRS Éditions, Patrimonialiser au Maghreb, II (19) (2018).

even more difficult to reach consensus on any particular issue.[108] The parliament could not adopt a decentralization law (as required by Article 131 of the Constitution) for years, and only managed to do so a few weeks before local elections took place in 2018. Despite the considerable detail in the 100-page law, it provided only a limited part of the overall picture, given that it did not resolve many of the main aspects of the framework for decentralization, including the manner in which shared powers would be exercised (Article 13).[109] In another example, six years after the constitution's entry into force, the Constitutional Court had not yet been established as a result of the same political divisions. On the other hand, the state's actions have caused significant regressions that will necessarily have negative repercussions for the general population. Many aspects of Tunisia's macroeconomic policy, including huge expansions of current expenditure, which have been mainly financed by borrowing at the expense of capital expenditure, have continued unabated, and practically without oversight. Meanwhile, the state has still not developed a convincing strategy to modernize its administration and improve the delivery of services. The state has not developed the means to critique, let alone control, against these negative practices.

THE FUTURE

Satisfying Interests: Tunisia is the first country in the region to successfully negotiate a permanent constitution in a stable and conflict-free environment, but it will certainly not be the last. Its experience and the experiences of other countries outside the region can and should serve as an inspiration for other countries that will negotiate constitutional settlements in the near future, be it Sudan or others. The most important feature of Tunisia's process is that rival political camps came to an agreement that they felt satisfied their interests. Political negotiations, including power dynamics, are both inevitable and desirable in the context of a constitutional negotiation. Parties to a negotiation must feel that their interests have been satisfied to a sufficient extent in order to support the agreement and not work to undermine it (see Chapter 9). The only alternative to that outcome is a return to undemocratic rule or conflict. This reality does not prevent negotiations from being guided by overarching

[108] In the 2019 parliamentary elections, the largest three parties returned 19.63 percent, 14.55 percent, and 6.42 percent of the vote, respectively. Defections and floor crossing are also very common in Tunisia. Shortly after the 2019 elections, one-third of the second largest party announced their resignation from the party.

[109] Law 29 (2018).

principles that seek to achieve more than just establishing a pact between rival parties that allows them to survive or control specific institutions. The incorporation of proportionality in Article 49 of Tunisia's 2014 Constitution is an illustration of how progressive arrangements can be introduced into a constitution independently of the power dynamics between rival camps (see Chapter 8). What was missing in many countries throughout the region was the introduction of a vision for the country's political system or an underlying philosophy to inform, guide, or limit the negotiations, or even an attempt to anticipate the manner in which parts of the agreement would interact with the political context. Negotiations can and should be informed by the need to establish a functioning state that makes a serious attempt at satisfying the general population's demands. In the context of the 2011 uprisings, which took place against the backdrop of more than a century of arbitrary rule by both colonial and post-colonial authorities and in which the general population made a specific and clear demand for social justice, a greater effort could and should have been made to determine what basic principles might have been adopted in the system of government to help satisfy that demand. Examples of the types of principle that might have guided the negotiations include ending the concentration of powers in a single state body, the need to frame political culture, improving the policy-making process, and, finally, improving transparency in the implementation of government policy.

Ending Hyper-presidentialism: First and foremost, all constitutional negotiations must take into consideration the weight of history and the impact of colonial legacies. Any country that experiences mass uprisings of the type that swept across the region in 2011 and that took place in Algeria, Sudan, Lebanon, and Iraq in 2019 can and should carry out a post-mortem of its own constitutional framework. Aside from Lebanon and Iraq, all the countries where mass uprisings have taken place were defined by hyper-presidentialism, which is a vestige of a bygone age that has been widely discredited and contributes to rigidity and, ultimately, instability.[110] It should be beyond dispute at this stage that this framework should be brought to an end, but there is strong evidence that many actors throughout the region still do not agree. Algeria's 2020 Constitution adopts almost all of the characteristics of a hyper-presidential regime. In fairness, the Algerian drafters' manner of proceeding should not come as a surprise given that the constitutional process was ordered and structured by the presidency itself. More surprising, however, is how Libya's constitution-drafting assembly, which was under no obligation

[110] See Juan J. Linz, "The Perils of Presidentalism," Journal of Democracy, Vol. 1, No. 1 (Winter 1990), 51–69.

to do so, swung the pendulum back in favor of presidentialism, probably in the hope that a strong president can bring order and stability back to their country. As noted previously, however, whatever short-term stability a presidential system can bring is offset by the long-term instability that it inevitably brings. Any plural and inclusive constitutional process must frame its deliberations around the need to establish a plural and inclusive system of government, which itself must mean freeing both the legislature and the judiciary from overbearing control of the chief executive, even if the executive is controlled by a directly elected president. This is achieved through a small number of measures that are by now widely accepted in much of the rest of the world, and that are in conformity with the separation of powers. This includes, but should not be limited to, that the president should not be the head of the judiciary and should not be able to dominate senior judicial bodies through unilateral appointments; the president should not be able to dissolve parliament; and the president should not be able to unilaterally dominate the government formation process and the formation of government policy.

Political Culture: The separation of powers on its own is no longer enough to make politics work. It must be accompanied with an effort to bring order to political culture. Ideally, consolidation of a national political culture would be done organically, but throughout the region, politics is already dominated by a number of negative trends. The influence of money and undemocratic political parties has skewed political culture far more in favor of minority interests than would ordinarily be the case. The decades-long attack on political structures and ideology has also contributed to a shattered political culture in which the largest parties barely represent a fifth of voters (in Iraq it is closer to a tenth). The effect in many cases is that policy and lawmaking in both government and parliament are often chaotic, unstructured, and even improvised. When faced with deep social challenges (as in Tunisia from 2018 onward) and economic collapse (as in Lebanon and Iraq from 2019 onward), political parties have generally responded by not developing any specific strategies or policies. Specific intervention is therefore required, including by constitutional negotiators, to reduce the influence of money and to consolidate and rationalize political life in each specific country. This can only be done on a country by country basis, as it largely depends on the particular traditions that exist within each country. But one of the goals has to be to encourage an improvement in the quality of politics through a variety of means, be it through electoral laws that encourage a consolidation of parties, political party finance laws that encourage a more responsible political party culture, and mechanisms that improve the policymaking process in government.

Political Party Finance: In many countries, the influence of capital in politics is a major concern that can and should be addressed at all critical junctures, including during the constitutional drafting process. Many countries have addressed political party finance constitutionally, although the detail is often left to the legislation. These rules can help make parties more responsive to the general population's needs, but as always, are not a guarantee. The decision not to deal with this issue at all can be very costly: Tunisia's constitutional process was dominated by the desire to reach agreement between two major political camps on how the separation of powers should function, to the extent that almost no attention was given to the measures that could help organize political life in the country. The 2014 Constitution is essentially silent on this issue, and the regulations that have been adopted since are toothless (possibly because political parties in power have little incentive to adopt robust rules). The result is that all major political groups fail to disclose their accounts and are routinely accused of receiving foreign funding and serving foreign interests.[111] Iraq's 2005 constitution is also silent on this issue, and the bulk of political parties are considered to be criminal enterprises that use their proximity to power to access illicit funds, which they then use to finance their activities and election campaigns. For countries that are cognizant of the dangers of leaving this area unregulated and have sufficient scope to introduce constitutional rules to bring clarity and order to this area, there are five types of action that can be taken at the constitutional level. These include providing funding funds to parties and campaigns; introducing limits on party income and party spending; imposing disclosure requirements of party finances to the public; and the enforcement of political party finance laws by independent agencies, such as electoral management bodies (EMBs).[112]

Coordination Mechanisms: As countries transition from hyper-presidentialism to a more plural form of politics, it is more than likely that governments will consist of large coalitions of parties that will not coordinate to anything like a satisfying degree. In many cases, this will be deliberate, mainly because political parties will partially be motivated by a desire to undermine their political rivals, even if they are in partnership together. But in many other cases, the absence of coordination will be the result of a lack of initiative and the lack of a framework. Constitutional negotiators have been

[111] See, for example, Vanessa Szakal, "Party Financing in Tunisia: Violations Abound, but What about Sanctions?," Nawaat (March 1, 2019).

[112] See Sujit Choudhry and Katherine Glenn Bass, "Political Party Finance Regulation: Constitutional Reform after the Arab Spring," International IDEA and the Center for Constitutional Transitions (2014).

establishing systems of government based on the assumption that parliament will be populated by major political forces and that governments will be composed of two to three parties at most. Current trends indicate that this type of scenario will only materialize in exceptional situations if at all. Systems of government should therefore be designed in a way that anticipates and addresses that reality, including by providing for the establishment of coordination mechanisms that require government policy to be formed by the political groups that populate parliament but to do so methodically.

Policy-making: The process through which government policy is formed has traditionally been one of the weakest features of governance in the region. In many cases, this has been related to corruption, where special interests influence the decision-making process. But even outside that scenario, policy formation has often been arbitrary and suffered from a lack of transparency in terms of both process and substance. Senior state officials have adopted radical new policies only to eliminate them very shortly thereafter, sometimes within a few hours, never providing reasons either way.[113] Constitutional negotiators should seek to control that tendency through a number of means. Procedurally, constitutional negotiators should strive to make the process through which policy is formed more transparent, first because it will reduce the opportunity for complete arbitrariness and second because it will allow greater input from citizens, and in particular from direct beneficiaries of specific policies, thereby improving the final outcome. Constitutional provisions requiring policy-making to be carried out publicly would have to be constructed carefully, both in terms of what they require and so as not to over-restrict government action in areas where flexibility is required. At the same time, it will naturally be impossible to guard against all forms of arbitrary action. What is being proposed here is that constitutional negotiators can and should try to address this issue, at the very least by limiting the scope for arbitrary policy-making. One possibility could simply be to require public consultation that is both transparent and open to the public (as opposed to consultation behind closed doors, which is an invitation for abuse). Yet another possibility could be to specifically require that policies be subject to public input before they are adopted into law, while setting out some scope for exceptions. Even if such measures are required under a national constitution, there is still a risk that government will satisfy all the applicable procedural requirements only to subsequently ignore all of the advice that it has been given. Substantively, constitutional drafters should seriously consider

[113] See, for example, Gamal M. Selim, The International Dimension of Democratization in Egypt: The Limits of Externally-Induced Change, Springer (2015), at 70–71.

providing that state institutions are subject to an obligation to justify all their actions and decisions, which will open the door to judicial scrutiny. The effect will be to reduce the likelihood that arbitrary decisions are taken following public consultations, without eliminating them altogether, as indicated previously.

Policy Implementation: Just as importantly, constitutional design should consider what measures can be taken to improve the process through which policy is implemented. This can be achieved through a number of means, some of which have already been introduced in some of the region's constitutions, albeit only timidly, over the past few decades. Supreme audit institutions are one of the principle means through which oversight can be exercised on policy implementation, but in order for this to be achieved, their mandate and independence must be fiercely protected, otherwise they will fall completely under the control of the chief executive. Earlier generations of constitutions in the region did not even mention auditing as a concept. The effect was that audit institutions were all completely subject to control by the chief executive, making the work that they did worse than useless. More recently, some national constitutions recognized the existence of their respective audit institutions without providing any detail on mandate or composition. This only protected them from total dissolution but did nothing to protect their independence. After 2011 a number of constitutions took the discussion on these bodies further. Egypt's 2012 Constitution, which defined the Central Auditing Organization's mandate broadly (Article 205), provided that the chairperson was to be nominated by the president and confirmed by the upper chamber, and that a majority of the upper chamber had to approve any attempt to dismiss the chairperson (Article 202). These rules were not entirely satisfactory given that the president appointed a large proportion of the upper chamber's membership (Article 128) but it was certainly an improvement on past practice.[114]

Decentralization: In 2011, many commentators and analysts supported the view that highly centralized forms of government were a major contributing factor to inequality throughout the region.[115] Many countries

[114] Egypt's 2013 Constitution partially backtracked on this. It removed any reference to the means through which the Central Auditing Organization's leadership could be removed, which allowed the executive to remove from office the organization's then-head.

[115] See Annabelle Houdret, "Decentralisation in Morocco: A Solution to the 'Arab Spring'?," The Journal of North African Studies, Vol. 24, No. 6 (2019), 935–960; Farrukh Moriani, Mohamed al-Hammadi, and Adel al-Zawm, "Options for Future Form of Government and Decentralization in Yemen: Policy Options in Times of Change," United Nations Development Programme (2013).

were therefore encouraged to consider granting more authority to local authorities, and in particular to grant them the power to generate revenue. Many countries have since moved in that direction, or at least have tried to do so. Sudan was among the first countries in the region to include significant detail on this issue in its national constitution.[116] Iraq followed suit in 2005, but the federal arrangement has yet to be fully implemented.[117] Since 2011 a number of other countries championed decentralization as a mechanism to address poverty in the peripheries in their respective countries. In Tunisia, despite the deep distrust that touched virtually every issue, there was a consensus within the constituent assembly in favor of granting more authority to local government.[118] Since then, some legislation has been adopted to start implementing the constitution's new provisions, but much remains to be resolved, including how central government will interact with the new local authorites (particularly on shared powers).[119] Not all countries followed suit: Egypt's 2012 and 2013 processes deferred to the preexisting legal framework on decentralization, which essentially provides all decision-making should be maintained in the capital,[120] despite huge disparities in service delivery and standards of

[116] The 1998 Constitution established Sudan as a federal state, and dedicated an entire chapter to setting out how the federal arrangement would function (Chapter 6). Federal states were given the power to legislate over a range of areas (Article 111), but central authorities maintained absolute control over a number of key areas, including natural resources (Article 110). The 2005 Interim Constitution established an asymmetric system, with a separate "government of Southern Sudan," which had its own executive, legislature, and judicial branch (Part 11). Outside of the south, the territory was divided into states, each of which had their own internal bodies (Part 12). The Interim Constitution's schedules set out the powers that the national government, the government of South Sudan, and the states would exercise.

[117] See Ali al-Mawlawi and Sajad Jiyad, "Confusion and contention: Understanding the failings of decentralization in Iraq," LSE Middle East Center Paper Series, Number 44 (January 2021).

[118] See Rym Mahjoub, "From Division to Consensus: The Role and Contribution of the Consensus Committee," in CONSTITUTION OF TUNISIA, United Nations Development Programme (2017) (in which a member of the Constituent Assembly wrote that "We opposed the majority on virtually every chapter of the 1 June draft, with the exception of the chapter on local power. That chapter had not been changed by the Joint Drafting Committee and was the only point of convergence, whereas the preamble, rights and freedoms, the form of the political regime, judicial power, the transitional provisions, and the article on education posed problems").

[119] See Intissar Kherigi, "Decentralisation: The Search for New Development Solutions in the Arab World's Peripheries," Arab Reform Initiative (January 21, 2020).

[120] Article 188 provided that local councils should be elected, but Article 190 allowed for any of their decisions to be overturned by the central government in order to prevent "damage to the public interest." Worse still, Article 187 did not clearly indicate how governors were to be chosen (whether elected or selected) and made no attempt to define their powers, leaving all of these crucial matters to be decided by subsequent legislation, as has been the case for the past

living between the country's major urban centers and much of the rest of the country.[121] These reform efforts are motivated by a desire to address inequality, but it is unclear whether decentralization does lead to the types of improvements that the constitutional drafters promised, and if so what circumstances need to be in place in order for that to happen. Perhaps most importantly, it is unclear if constitutional negotiators weighed the available evidence before taking this leap.[122] There is some question as to whether some of the most impoverished provinces can raise significant amounts of revenue locally given how little economic activity exists within their territories, and whether they would have sufficient oversight capacity to prevent corruption.[123] An honest and detailed evaluation of the merits and flaws of decentralization is that it may not bring the economic benefits that so many experts and advisers have promised, or at least that it may not do so equally across all parts of a particular country. Regardless, decentralization does have real value as another means to shift away from hyper-presidential systems of government. Traditionally, centralized rule has meant that all government policy, including local policies in areas that are far removed from the capital, are determined by the personal preferences of specific individuals who have never left the capital. In that context, decentralization increases the number of voices that can participate in formulating local policy and how funds can be spent locally. The challenges in this context will be to ensure that whatever mechanism is established will give real volume to opposition voices that will have to be

few decades. Finally, earlier drafts called for a financial redistribution mechanism between provinces to remedy the gross disparities that exist in the country. That provision was deleted from the final version.

[121] "Egypt Human Development Report 2004: Choosing Decentralisation for Good Governance," United Nations Development Programme, 2004, at 22 ("By examining the tables that address urban-rural gaps in human development, one can easily identify human development disparities among the major four groups of governorates and among individual governorates; this is in spite of multiple rural develop-ment programs and efforts. Available data are not yet sufficient for estimating urban/rural indices of human development neither at national nor at governorate level, but a number of available sub-HDI indicators are revealing as regards the urban/rural human development imbalance in Egypt, even though urban/rural gaps have been narrowing during the period 1990–2002. In 2001, the average urban/rural gap at the national level was 32.3% in adult literacy rate (15+), compared to 45% in 1992").

[122] Fifteen years after Iraq's 2005 Constitution entered into force, it has not brought the type of benefits to peripheral regions that it promised. Since 2011 the country has experienced yearly rounds of popular uprisings in which government buildings are attacked and arsoned, particularly in southern provinces.

[123] Decentralization in Iraq has compounded corruption. See Ali al-Mawlawi and Sajad Jiyad, "Confusion and Contention: Understanding the Failings of Decentralization in Iraq," LSE Middle East Center Paper Series, Number 44 (January 2021).

taken into consideration when formulating local policy, and to ensure that whatever shift takes place toward greater decentralization is not accompanied by an increase in corruption (mainly by making sufficient provisions within oversight and auditing bodies). In countries such as Iraq, that has not yet been achieved, despite the establishment of directly elected local governments fifteen years ago.

9

Process Design (or on Avoiding Majoritarianism)

INTRODUCTION

From 2011 to 2012 every day brought a new development to Egypt's transition, new statements, positions, laws, arrangements, and protests. The Muslim Brotherhood and other Islamists understood that it would be in their interest for there to be an election as soon as possible. Their popularity was strong, as was their capacity to organize an electoral campaign, while their competitors had very little appeal. On the other hand, the Brotherhood expressed concern that if they were to dominate politics too soon, the international community and other forces would move to undermine them. It was for this reason that, at first, the Brotherhood sought to allay any concerns by announcing that its newly founded Freedom and Justice Party would only contest half the seats in parliament and would not contest the presidential elections. However, closer to the time, the Party reversed itself and with its other Islamist allies won close to 80 percent of the seats in parliament and won the presidency as well. The Islamists nevertheless continued to seek to reassure the international community that it would not seek to dominate politics through a number of means, including the constitutional process. After the Assembly's second iteration was finally established, a senior member of the judiciary was elected president and a well-known liberal politician was appointed rapporteur. Interventions at the Assembly's opening session called for consensus between all members. Just as importantly, leading members of the Brotherhood were messaging to the international community in private meetings that they were striving to achieve the support of at least 80 percent of the population. "If we cannot achieve eighty per cent at first, we will keep working and will not complete the process until that is achieved," a leading member said. "This isn't an election, it's a constitution. It has to be acceptable to everyone."

In the months that followed, major differences of opinion emerged on a range of issues and the Assembly's administration was less than perfect. Drafts were being circulated, without the knowledge of many members, that reflected the leadership's views only. Non-Islamist members complained that their views were not being taken into consideration and that the majority of Islamist members were breaking their promise not to amend the relationship between religion and state. At the same time, the non-Islamist camp was deeply suspicious of the Islamists' actions and interpreted every action negatively. When early drafts were circulated, much of the wording was simply copied and pasted from the 1971 Constitution. One such provision that was lifted word for word was Article 9 of the 1971 Constitution, according to which "family is the basis of society founded on religion, morality and patriotism. The State strives to preserve the genuine character of the Egyptian family – with the values and traditions it embodies – while affirming and developing its character in relations within Egyptian society." As part of the 1971 Constitution, everyone simply ignored the provision on the assumption that it was empty rhetoric that made no difference in practice. However, as part of a draft constitution that was circulated by an Islamist-dominated Constituent Assembly, the reference to the State's role in "preserving the genuine character of Egyptian family" was interpreted as meaning that morality police would be deployed to bludgeon Egyptians who did not dress appropriately in public. Throughout that period, the Assembly's leadership continued to meet privately with international observers, mainly to reassure them that the difficulties were a natural consequence of the tense negotiation process and would be resolved.

Tensions in the Assembly gradually increased. There were frequent shouting matches in the Assembly, including references to repression. Non-Islamist members could see that the Constituent Assembly's leadership was pressing ahead with the finalization process without making a serious effort to resolve the outstanding differences of opinion. They were aware that the rules of procedure allowed the constitution to be adopted with the support of fifty-seven out of a hundred members, which meant that ultimately the Islamists were under no legal obligation to compromise. All non-Islamist members withdrew and were replaced by pliant reserve members. The drafting process was finalized in November 2012, and the final draft was adopted in the December 2012 referendum. However, the results confirmed that the constitution obtained far less than the 80 percent for which the Assembly's leadership was hoping. Official figures indicated that 63 percent of voters had approved the constitution but that turnout was particularly low at around 33 percent, which meant that the constitution obtained the support of around

20 percent of the population only. The opposition was livid. Dozens of protests were organized and new coalitions were formed, all for the purpose of countering the Brotherhood and its new constitution. The Islamist president offered on several occasions to meet with the opposition to talk through their differences, but at that point tensions were too high to be resolved through mere dialogue. Nevertheless, throughout that period, the messaging to the international community continued. "Actually the approval rate in the referendum was very high," said a leading figure from the Constituent Assembly when challenged. "We are very happy with the result. It's in line with approval rates in most western democracies." In the end, the 2012 Constitution was in force for six months only.

CONTEXT

Objective: There is a tendency to detach process design from substantive discussions, to treat them as two separate issues. To design a constitutional negotiation process is to develop the milestones that need to be met, the sequence of events, and the specific rules that will govern the way in which each of the milestones must be satisfied. Ideally, a constitutional process will always be designed for two main purposes: first to increase the likelihood that a constitution will be successfully adopted without increasing the chances of conflict or violence; and second to increase the likelihood that the overall substantive objectives will also be met. In the case of the post-2011 processes, the objective was clear: to establish freedom and social justice. The terms themselves were deceptively simple, because in this case, what was required was to establish both of those things in a particular context, which meant to overcome decades of negative practices that had become entrenched within state institutions. The challenge was enormous and required very careful consideration when constructing the constitutional process. However, a number of huge challenges made that exercise far more difficult to realize.

Distrust: The constitutional processes that took place in the post-2011 period were marked by a number of characteristics that had a deep impact on how the negotiators were designed and how they played out in practice. In all of the countries without exception, the entire transition was marked by significant distrust between rival political camps, often between Islamists and non-Islamists. Decades of state-sponsored propaganda throughout the region portrayed Islamist groups as virtually indistinguishable from terrorists.[1]

[1] See Shadi Hamid, Temptations of Power: Islamists and Illiberal Democracy in a New Middle East, Oxford University Press (2014), at Chapters 2–5.

Religiously inspired rule in countries such as Sudan and civil war in Algeria in the 1990s and Iraq following the 2003 invasion were interpreted by many as a sign that no matter their rhetoric, Islamists were determined to impose their own austere style of life on society as a whole and were willing to use violence to achieve that objective. On the other hand, religiously inspired parties were persecuted for decades by states throughout the region in the name of maintaining some form of secular rule, which was widely viewed as corrupt. In the post-2011 era, this caused Islamist parties such as Egypt's Freedom and Justice Party and Tunisia's Ennahda Party to treat many of their secular rivals as if they had themselves been responsible for their persecution. Some attempts were made to bridge this political divide but these were all short lived and of limited impact. In Tunisia, following the 2011 parliamentary elections, a prominent human rights defender formed a post-election alliance with Ennahda to form a coalition government. That individual was then repudiated by his own camp, and was nearly eradicated in the parliamentary elections that followed. Ultimately, while it lasted, the alliance's only impact on the constitutional negotiations was that it allowed them to commence the formation of a government. In Egypt, some secular and liberal politicians joined with the Freedom and Justice Party's 2011 electoral alliance only to side against the party when the constitutional negotiation process started breaking down in 2012. Even in countries where the regimes survived the uprisings, the limitations that were imposed on the constitutional drafting processes were in part motivated by a desire to guard against the possibility that political rivals (mainly Islamist parties) could benefit from the uprisings. Only two countries stood somewhat apart from the rest in terms of the nature of the distrust, but not in terms of its extent. In Sudan, the 2019 uprising took place against an Islamist regime that by then was widely discredited and was ultimately dissolved. The negotiations that followed took place between two sides (the FFC and the Transitional Military Council) that were not particularly motivated or influenced by religion. The main issue of contention during the negotiations was if and how the state should transition from military to civilian rule, as opposed to the relationship between religion and state. However, due to a combination of historic reasons (including the significant levels of violence that took place during the uprising), the relationship between the two sides was just as acrimonious. Meanwhile, in Yemen, the post-2011 dynamics were informed by a large number of factors, including north–south and intra-ruling elite rivalries, among many others. Distrust between religious and nonreligious camps was certainly a factor but did not feature prominently in the negotiations.

Nevertheless, senior officials were so uneasy during the negotiations that many kept personal weapons at arms' reach at all times.[2]

Culture: The general cultural environment, which was highly restrictive mainly as a result of the limitations on speech described in Chapter 7, also played a major role. By way of illustration, state law schools, which should be dynamic environments for the free exchange of ideas, were instead transformed into static environments that specialize in rewarding an uncritical commitment to applying the law, regardless of its content or provenance. The absence of a critical element to legal education and judicial training imbued the entire legal profession with a heavily conservative and authoritarian outlook that played a key role in constitutional drafting processes throughout the region. The result was that even after the 2011 uprising, elected officials were bound by established traditions that are presented as being beyond question, including but not limited to a country's legal traditions. That impression is reinforced by, among others, each country's legal professionals and especially judges, who typically present their methods and traditions as being above reproach.[3] In practice, this cultural limitation manifested itself in a variety of ways, including the near constant references to France and the United States as sources of inspiration, despite the very significant constitutional developments that were taking place in other parts of the world, including in Africa and Latin America.

Preparation: The stifling cultural environment was compounded by how unexpected the 2011 uprisings were. Prior to the 2011 uprisings, very few actors expected that there could be an uprising throughout the region that could cause the downfall of regimes that had survived for decades, and that more than half the countries would either replace or amend their constitutions.[4] On the contrary, the understanding throughout the region was that the regimes were stable, and that in many cases presidents would be replaced by their children.[5] The impact of this state of mind was that prior to 2011 precious few

[2] Senior Yemeni official, interview with the author, May 2020.

[3] See Amr Shalakany, THE RISE AND FALL OF EGYPT'S LEGAL ELITE: 1805–2005 ("ازدهار وانهيار النخبة القانونية المصرية"), Dar Al-Shorouk (2012).

[4] See Asef Bayat, REVOLUTION WITHOUT REVOLUTIONARIES: MAKING SENSE OF THE ARAB SPRING, Stanford University Press (2017), at 135. The World Bank's final country brief on Tunisia prior to the 2011 uprising offered significant praise to the Tunisian authorities, and made no mention of human rights abuses or the widespread corruption that was common knowledge among ordinary Tunisians; see 'Country Brief', The World Bank, April 2010 (with the revolution only a few months away, the report's first sentence read "Tunisia has made remarkable progress on equitable growth, fighting poverty and achieving good social indicators").

[5] This was the case in at least Libya, Egypt, and Yemen.

actors throughout the region were seriously preparing for a transition to democracy. In other countries in other parts of the world, opposition forces eagerly anticipated their respective transitions and prepared through a variety of means, including by developing their own objectives, their positions on a range of substantive issues, their negotiation skills, etc. None of those things were done in the Arab region prior to 2011. However, even if actors within the region had anticipated the 2011 uprisings, limitations on speech and genuinely free debates would have made any organized discussions on how to manage democratic transitions extremely difficult to prepare for the transitions. At an individual level, researchers would have been able to search for information online on other transitions, be it in Kenya, South Africa, or elsewhere. However, any effort to examine these issues in an organized fashion, be it through a conference or the publication of a paper on the question, would have attracted the attention of the authorities. Even the act of studying one's own constitution for the purpose of identifying where the democratic deficit lay could only be done at an individual level. The absence of free debates on policy reform also made it extremely difficult for actors to develop their negotiation skills, including the act of compromise, and of identifying the exact extent of overlap between different parties' negotiation skills. The impact of all of these circumstances was that, in 2011, actors throughout the region suddenly found themselves overwhelmed by the post-uprising environment, which meant that actors improvised throughout, often discovering after the fact that their own actions and decisions ran contrary to their own interests.

Improvisation: Senior officials who suddenly found themselves in positions of authority in Tunisia, Libya, Egypt, and Yemen were equally affected by these dynamics, forcing them to improvise while at the same time trying to keep their composure and convey confidence. This applied to substantive as well as procedural questions. In the post-2011 transitions, leading actors had very little understanding of what they wanted beyond their own survival and what the best means were to achieve it. This was made more complicated by the fact that, at the start of 2011, many of the region's leading jurists maintained an idealized vision of their own constitutional history and reforms that were etched in the past, which they then sought to recreate. This extended to procedural matters, where in Libya, for example, the post-2011 effort to draft a new constitution was heavily inspired by the process through which the 1951 Constitution was adopted.[6] Very little thought had been given to how long the transitions should last, who should be responsible for drafting the

[6] In Libya, this trend took on an exceptional form, with many jurists, scholars, and observers arguing in favor of restoring the 1951 constitution (with some modifications). See "Assessment

constitution, how difficult the drafting process would be, what type of state should be established, and what would follow thereafter.[7] The lack of understanding on these issues was so pervasive that in early 2011 many of the main actors were adopting positions that were against their own interests. The process through which Egypt's 2011 Interim Constitution was drafted serves as an excellent illustration of this phenomenon. The committee that drafted the roadmap was entirely of the SCAF's making, and the SCAF was not under any obligation to accept its draft. And yet, Article 60 of the Interim Constitution set the country on a majoritarian path. It established a system through which one group, which in Egypt's case at the time could only be the Muslim Brotherhood, could essentially draft the constitution on its own, despite the fact that whatever electoral advantage it had at the time would inevitably be temporary. Article 60 did not even guarantee that the SCAF itself would have a role during drafting of the constitution. The SCAF could very easily have requested changes, or at least have insisted that the committee incorporate additional detail to the plan with a view to broadening the number of parties that could make their voices heard. Months after the plan was adopted, the SCAF supported the initiative to draft fundamental principles, which sought to build anti-majoritarian elements and a role for the SCAF into the drafting process, after it had already been approved and published. The entire episode was a clear illustration of how the SCAF had changed its mind about the interim constitution, and that it agreed that Article 60 should be changed. It revealed significant clumsiness on its part and a lack of appreciation of how other political groups would perceive its actions. Just as

of the 1951 Libyan Constitution According to International Standards," Democracy Reporting International, Briefing Paper 28, July 2012; Abdel Rahman Habil, "Old Constitutional Controversy Ignited in Libya," Almonitor, July 7, 2013; and Adel Abdel Hafeeth Kandir, "The 1951 Constitution in the Light of International Standards of Democracy" ("دستور 1951 في ضوء المعايير الدولية للديمقراطية"), Libya al-Mustaqbal, May 18, 2013; Bashir al-Sunni, "Libyan Constitutional Development" ("التطور الدستوري الليبي"), al-Arabiya, April 12, 2013 (reprinted from "The Libyan Nation"). A similar tendency was very apparent in Iraq, where a number of individuals argued that, following the 2003 invasion and occupation, Iraq should adopt a modified version of the long defunct 1925 Constitution. During working sessions between leading members of the Iraqi opposition in London prior to the 2003 invasion, the possibility of reintroducing the 1925 Constitution was tabled as one of two possible options to govern the interim period following the invasion; see "Final Report on the Transition to Democracy in Iraq," Final Version of the Working Document on the Conference to the Iraqi Opposition as Amended by the Members of the Democratic Principles Work Group, November 2002.

7 In March 2011 a leading Tunisian civil society activist explained to me that Tunisia's new constitution could be drafted in just a few months because Tunisia was among the most homogeneous countries in the world. As explained later in this chapter, it turned out that the constitutional negotiations were very acrimonious and lasted for two years.

importantly, while some revolutionary forces complained bitterly about the interim constitution's content and campaigned against its adoption in the referendum, they failed to follow through and impact the process in any meaningful way.[8] The Muslim Brotherhood was the clear beneficiary at the time, and appeared to have secured a major victory without having to invest any effort whatsoever.

CONSTRUCTIVE INCLUSIVITY

Definition: It is now common currency that constitutional negotiation processes are far more likely to be successful when they are inclusive.[9] Inclusivity in this context means that all actors should be represented and should participate in the negotiations. The purpose of inclusivity is generally to ensure that all major political actors reach agreement with each other in the negotiations. If they can do so and feel that the final settlement protects their interests, they are more likely to respect and apply the final text. In practice, even where there is general agreement between the parties on the importance of inclusivity, there are always disagreements on how it should be translated into practice. Questions that immediately emerge in practice are, first, how one selects the groups that are to participate in the negotiations, and, second, how many seats at the table should be granted to each group (another question that is rarely considered is how homogeneous these groups are, and how one addresses heterogeneity).[10] This was perhaps the most important issue that consumed the early part of the post-2011 transitions, with some groups arguing that everything should be decided through elections, while others still maintained that elections would result in skewed and temporary outcomes that should not guide how a permanent constitution should be drafted (see later). What was missing in the entire conversation, however, was whether there were particular arrangements that could be put in place that would assist individual countries to satisfy the general objective of achieving freedom and social

[8] Gamal Essam el-Din, "Egypt's Constitution: A Controversial Declaration," Ahramonline, March 30, 2011.

[9] See, for example, Michele Brandt, Jill Cottrell, Yash Ghai, and Anthony Regan, Constitution-making and Reform: Options for the Process, Interpeace (2011), at 10.

[10] In Iraq's 2005 constitutional process, the accepted international narrative was that the constitution was drafted by representatives of two of the country's largest communities. That narrative ignored the fact that two of the largest political groups within the country's largest community did not participate in the drafting of the constitution and in fact had been agitating against it. See Zaid Al-Ali, "Constitutional Legitimacy in Iraq: What Role Local Context?," in Raider Grote and Tilmann Röder (eds.), Constitutionalism in Islamic Countries: Between Upheaval and Continuity, Oxford University Press (2012).

justice for their people. In this case, constructive inclusivity goes beyond simply ensuring that a sufficient number of political groups are represented in the negotiations. What it seeks to achieve, in addition to political representation, is to satisfy the overall substantive objectives by going beyond political inclusivity. This will mean different things in each individual process, but it can include arrangements such as establishing independent committees that will work alongside the political negotiators, or it can mean establishing frames of reference for the political negotiators that are tied to the transition's overall objectives.

Democratic and Normative Legitimacy: Throughout the region, officials, political groups, and others struggled with how to balance the expectation that the popular will should impact the content of the constitution, with the understanding that electoral outcomes are temporary, particularly in a volatile post-totalitarian environment. In many countries, the popular urge to vote was too great and elections were organized as soon as possible. Following decades of totalitarian rule, the electoral fortunes of opposition political parties depend on a range of factors, including the level of repression that they suffered at the hands of the previous regime, or how closely they were associated to it in the population's view. In many cases, the electorate quickly switches allegiance after initial promises of immediate improvements are not met. The negotiations that led to the adoption of Iraq's 2005 Constitution illustrate this point. The parties that led the negotiations had performed very well in the January 2005 elections, which allowed them to dominate the constitutional negotiations that followed and impose a radical vision of federalism. The general understanding at the time was that these groups together represented a crushing majority of the population, perhaps as much as 80 percent. Very little importance was given to the fact that the January 2005 elections were boycotted by the country's largest political group and by a series of others. Ultimately, within a few short years, it became apparent that the groups that dominated the constitutional process represented close to 20 percent and that the federal system of government they imposed on the country was far outside the popular mainstream.[11] Other countries in the region adopted the opposite approach, which was to detach the constitutional process from elections altogether. Yemen's entire transition anticipated a presidential election in which there was only a single candidate. The rest of the process was to be led by conferences and committees, the composition of which was to be determined through negotiations. In Sudan, the 2019 Constitutional Charter

[11] Ibid.

anticipates that all the bodies that will be involved in the constitutional process will be appointed, including the national parliament. In between these two extremes, countries such as Tunisia, Libya, and Egypt tried to resolve this tension through a number of means, including allowing unelected officials to frame the constitutional process and to a certain extent to participate in the negotiations as well. The rationale for allowing unelected actors to play a role in the negotiations was never clearly articulated, which contributed to the very negative reaction that the idea received among many actors.

Appointed Bodies: Despite the number of countries that were impacted by the post-2011 uprisings, there was very little variation in the way in which the constitutional processes were organized. In all cases but one, a single body was responsible for determining the constitution's content, which in turn meant that for the most part the substantive content of each country's constitution was determined by a single constituency. The only significant variation was in whether the body was appointed or elected. In Morocco, Algeria (2016 and 2020), and Syria, the committees were appointed and were nominally expert in that they consisted of academics, lawyers, and judges. In both Egypt (2013) and Jordan, the committees were also appointed and consisted of senior state figures and representatives of state institutions, among others. In all cases, the committee's mandate was limited by the chief executive, who specifically stated which areas the committee should examine (and, by exclusion, set aside those areas that the committees should not examine). Finally, in all cases, the completion of the work was followed by a popular referendum that was approved in all cases by crushing majorities. The only exception in that regard was Jordan, where the constitutional amendment procedures only require two-thirds approval in the parliament (Article 126). Ultimately, these processes proceeded as originally planned, given that they remained under the control of the state and, by extension, of the chief executive. For the most part, the appointed body simply drew up changes in accordance with the instructions that it had received, which were then brought into force without any significant internal dissent or challenge from without.[12] Although some of these drafting committees did organize public outreach efforts, popular opinion did not play an effective role in influencing discussions beyond

[12] Algeria is a partial exception. After the 2020 draft constitution was circulated, one of the members disavowed the draft on the basis that it did not meet the aspirations of the people; see "The Reasons for Fatsah Ouguergouz' Resignation from the Constitutional Amendment Committee" (فاتح أوقرقوز" يستقيل من لجنة مراجعة الدستور لهذه الأسباب"), Tariqnews (April 15, 2020). Egypt's 2013 constitutional committee was also a partial exception, particularly on the issue of military trials of civilians; see "Egypt: Major Controversy on Military Trials of Civilians" (مصر: جدل واسع حول المحاكمات العسكرية للمدنيين), DW (November 28, 2013).

generalities that were set out in the preambles and in a few other issues. The drafting processes were all completed in either a matter of weeks or a small number of months, effectively preventing civil society from mobilizing and analyzing whatever was being done in the drafting chamber. There were very few variations to the general manner of proceeding. In Algeria, the state organized a number of dialogue processes before and after the drafting committees produced their respective drafts, but no clear rules were established on how the outcome of that dialogue process would be incorporated into the draft (in fact the results of the dialogue processes were never published). In any event, the constitutional committee's proposed amendments were so modest that there was very little chance that the dialogue process could make any difference. Egypt's 2013 process does represent an important exception to the rule that all of the constitutions were drafted by a single constituency. The constitutional committee was preceded by the appointment of a ten-member expert committee, which made suggestions of its own. Ultimately, however, very few if any of the expert committee's suggested amendments were taken into consideration. The committee itself was relatively diverse, but it suffered from the opposite problem, which was that its membership was too determined to defend narrow corporate interests to redesign the entire system of government. As a result, despite the relative political diversity of its membership, the constitutional committee only offered modest changes to Egypt's constitutional framework. There was very little scope for change, despite the feeling among some members that they had a free hand.

Elected Bodies: In the second category of cases, the constitution drafting body was composed pursuant to an election. In Tunisia, a Constituent Assembly was directly chosen by the people in an election that was contested by political parties, many of which had only recently been established. The rules provided that there should be some consultation with experts as well as with the public, but there is very little evidence that either of those formal processes had a significant impact on the draft.[13] Some civil society organizations and experts were able to influence the draft but only on discrete areas that were not particularly significant politically and through informal means (see Chapter 7). In Egypt, a parliament was directly elected and was then responsible for indirectly electing the 2012 Constituent Assembly. The rules

[13] However, see Tofigh Maboudi, "Reconstituting Tunisia: Participation, Deliberation, and the Content of Constitution," Political Research Quarterly, Vol. 73, No. 4 (2020), 774–789 (in which the author argues that 43 percent of public proposals were included in the final draft of the constitution).

through which the indirect election process was organized were never properly defined, which contributed to a significant amount of chaos, including the dissolution of the Constituent Assembly's first iteration by a court. When the second Assembly was composed, it was just as unclear whether the rules had been respected, as a result of which appeals were launched before the courts, and the proceedings loomed over the constitutional process until the end. A similar arrangement was adopted in Iraq in 2005, albeit in very different circumstances. In Tunisia, Egypt (2012), and Iraq, a huge amount of controversy erupted between the negotiating parties, and in both cases the parties leaned on poorly constructed rules of procedure that did not adequately guard against majoritarian outcomes. In Egypt's case, the rules actually specifically allowed 57 percent of the assembly to adopt the constitution. In Tunisia, the rules of procedure did not clearly specify how the Joint Committee for Cooperation and Drafting should operate and whether it could overrule the Assembly's substantive committees. Ultimately, in June 2013, when the Joint Committee was faced with the substantive committee's relatively poor progress, it imposed its own vision without consulting the committees, causing very significant controversy. Another feature of the 2012 Egyptian process is that, like the 2013 process, the Assembly was relatively diverse in its membership: it was dominated by representatives of political parties but did also include representatives from other institutions, most notably the judiciary. Ultimately, however, the content of both Tunisia's 2014 Constitution and Egypt's 2012 Constitution was determined almost exclusively by the political groups that populated the respective assemblies (mainly a combination of Islamists, nationalists, left-wing groups, and others). In Libya, the Constitutional Drafting Assembly was also directly elected, although the electoral law included a number of idiosyncrasies that skewed the results in favor of specific outcomes even before the elections took place. The electoral law provided that each of the three regions should be represented by twenty members each, despite huge demographic disparities. In addition, the electoral law was widely interpreted as barring candidates from being affiliated to political parties, as a result of which most CDA members were formally independents who were not linked to the country's political forces. The electoral law was ultimately successful in depoliticizing the process, particularly in comparison with Tunisia and Egypt. The corollary of that success, however, was that many of the country's main armed groups considered that the only possible outcome of the constitutional process could be a reduction in their own power and so deliberately acted to undermine it. As a result, when the constitutional process eventually ended in 2017 with the successful adoption of a draft by the CDA, it merely fizzled and had no impact on the country.

Dialogue Conference: Yemen's 2011–2015 transition was the only process whose design allowed multiple constituencies to impact the future constitution's substantive content. The process involved a preparatory stage in which the rules of the dialogue process and the Dialogue Conference's composition were determined, followed by the dialogue process, the outcome of which was then transferred to a constitutional committee that was charged with preparing a final draft. The Dialogue Conference was to be composed of representatives of political parties as well as from civil society. The difference between that arrangement and the outreach processes that took place in Algeria, Tunisia, and other countries is that in Yemen, civil society representatives were not just consulted; they were full members of the process with the same voting rights as political groups. In addition, the constitutional drafting committee was conceived of as a technical expert body that would draw up the final constitution based on the Dialogue Conference's outcomes. Finally, a miniature version of the Dialogue Conference (the National Body) would be responsible for signing off on the final draft before it was put to a referendum, particularly with a view to ensuring that the draft was in conformity with the dialogue conference's outcomes. These various steps were designed to allow civil society to influence the final draft, in ways that civil society in other countries could not. Regrettably, many of the Yemeni process' other features were not as well considered, and neither was the manner in which the transition plan was implemented. Ultimately, many of the bodies and groups that were originally intended to represent nonpolitical interests were heavily influenced by traditional political forces, which greatly limited civil society's capacity to influence the draft. The result was to greatly reduce whatever potential benefit might have flowed from these two groups. In addition, the rules of procedure allowed specific individuals to dominate the decision-making process on key issues, which proved to be unacceptable to a range of actors.

Direct Participation. Many practitioners and scholars have long argued that direct participation in constitution-making processes should be prioritized, first to control against whatever elite negotiations will take place, and second to improve the democratic legitimacy of the final text. However, despite the new context and the protesters' early success in imposing themselves on the regional debate, in many of the drafting processes that took place after 2011, the general population was generally unable to apply any significant pressure on drafters. Instead, drafters remained dependent on preexisting elite circles who have been largely unable to break away from the Arab region's conservative and uncritical legal traditions. Formally, an effort was organized throughout the region to counter that outcome. In Egypt, the 2012 Constituent Assembly set up an online platform through which the public's views were solicited.[14] Some political parties also tried to crowdsource the drafting of some of the future constitution's fundamental principles. Also, a number of grassroots civil society initiatives were launched to reach out to the general population, particularly outside the capital, and to solicit their views. Tunisia's Constituent Assembly organized over 160 public hearings throughout the drafting process and even amended its rules of procedure to make it an obligation for the drafters to take public comments into account.[15] In Iraq (2005), a public outreach committee was established specifically for the purpose of consulting with the general public. Other countries operated similar initiatives, some for the first time ever, including Morocco, where the general population had never been consulted on constitutional reform before 2011. However, despite all of these efforts, there is very little evidence that the general population's views made a significant difference to the final texts that were adopted for a variety of reasons. Less than 0.1 percent of Egypt's population participated through the online platform, and more than 80 percent of those individuals were urban, young, and male. Iraq's outreach process was so limited in time that it was ultimately completed after the constitutional committee was dissolved. Detailed accounts of Tunisia's public outreach campaign only list a few instances where changes were made to the draft constitution based on suggestions that were made in the public outreach campaign, none of which appeared to influence the main issues of contention. For example, the statement according to which youth is "an active force in building the nation" (Article 8) and the requirement that the internal charter of political parties must reject violence (Article 35).[16] At best, input from the general population was merely used to reinforce existing trends within the negotiations. At worst, public outreach was manipulated by specific political groups to return results that suited their particular platform (as was the case in Iraq).[17]

[14] An infographic published by the Constituent Assembly at the time claimed that 653,718 individual inputs had been made through the online platform. Twelve percent of these inputs were comments and the rest were votes on individual articles. The infographic also claimed that 981 amendments had been made to the constitution, but did not offer any indication how many changes were made pursuant to the comments that were made through the online platform. On file with the author.

[15] See Badreddine Abdelkafi, "The National Constituent Assembly and Civil Society: What Is the Relationship?," in Constitution of Tunisia, United Nations Development Programme (2017).

[16] See for example Nedra Cherif, "Participation in the Tunisian Constitution-Making Process," in Tania Abbiate, Markus Böckenförde, and Veronica Federico (eds.), Public Participation in African Constitutionalism, Routledge (2017).

[17] See Tofigh Maboudi and Ghazal P. Nadi, "Crowdsourcing the Egyptian Constitution: Social Media, Elites, and the Populace," Political Research Quarterly, Vol. 69, No. 4 (December 2016). The authors argue that "as the online public approval over draft Articles

Outcome: Despite the revolutionary environment, the post-2011 constitutional processes were also characterized by the fact that the bulk of the negotiating parties were not revolutionary in nature. For the most part, the protest movements that caused the constitutions to be rewritten did not have a clear leadership structure, which meant that they could not contest elections and could not impose themselves on the negotiations. The negotiations were therefore dominated by appointed experts or state officials, or by political parties that were principally concerned with their own survival. Combined with the other limitations set out in this chapter, the outcome of the negotiations was partially a function of these dynamics. Where there was genuine political competition between different actors, the outcome depended almost entirely on how balanced the competition was between them (Egypt, Tunisia, Yemen). The 2005 Iraqi negotiations produced perhaps the most grotesque result, in which the political groups carved up a mechanism through which they would exploit the state without making any meaningful provision for how the general population's basic rights would be protected. If there was no genuine political competition, then the outcome mainly consisted of tinkering with existing frameworks (Morocco, Algeria, Jordan, Syria). Of all of the post-2011 transitions, it was only in Sudan that the formal negotiations included a revolutionary movement. The 2019 uprising was planned and implemented by an organized political force (namely the Forces of the Declaration of Freedom and Change and, in particular, the Sudanese Professionals Association), which then went on to play a key role in the negotiations that led to the adoption of the 2019 Constitutional Charter. The Charter's radical departure from the 2005 Interim Constitution, its prioritization of peace over all other concerns, and its strategy to transition to civilian rule are clear indications of the impact that these circumstances have brought. The same is only partially true in Tunisia: The uprising was leaderless, which meant that the bulk of the negotiations were dominated by political parties that were not primal drivers of change, but civil society leaders and organizations did participate in various capacities during the negotiations and so were able to influence the final outcome, albeit not to the same extent as in Sudan in 2019.

Alternative Approach: Could history have proceeded differently? What, if anything, can be learned from all these experiences? There is obviously very little that could have been done to resolve the factors that were inherited from

increased, draft Articles were more likely to change. The results also suggest that comments and feedbacks on Articles related to individual and civil rights were more likely to be successfully incorporated in the constitution compared with those regarding political institutions."

the post-2011 constitutions at the time. However, individual decisions that were taken early on and throughout played a determining role in shaping the processes. There was nothing inevitable about the arrangements that were set in place and the outcomes that resulted from them. They are the products of political choices that were made by conservative officials without attracting the attention of the rest of the population. These early-stage decisions could easily have tilted in another direction with only minor effort in most cases. Other countries provide convincing models that could have been built on in the post-2011 processes. Kenya's constitutional process was organized pursuant to an act of parliament.[18] It provided for the establishment of both a parliamentary select committee and a nonpolitical committee of experts that were required to work alongside each other.[19] The expert committee participated heavily in the drafting process, interacting on an almost equal basis with the parliamentary committee, to the extent that the two committees took turns working on the draft and considered each other's contributions.[20] In this context, the expert committee's main contribution was to ensure the new constitution's technical viability.[21] In so doing, the Kenyan process allowed for both political and technical input, in the hope that the constitution's political legitimacy would be maintained, while at the same time improving the chances that the new constitution would deliver real benefits to ordinary Kenyans.

CONSENSUS AS A CONDITION

Balancing stability with flexibility: Because constitutions can have such a fundamental impact, the general understanding in democratic settings is that they should not be adopted through regular procedures, including, for example, the process that is usually followed when adopting a law. The rationale is that constitutions establish the political system's framework and define the general drama that all constitutional institutions should be geared to resolving. If a text were to enjoy the support of a bare majority of the population, it is very likely that its opponents would move to amend the constitution as soon as they acceded to power, which would entail a significant overhaul of key institutions of state with every electoral cycle and increase the risk of serious

[18] Constitution of Kenya Review Act (2008).

[19] Six of its nine members were citizens of other African countries.

[20] See, for example, National Assembly, "Report of the Parliamentary Select Committee on the Review of the Constitution on the Reviewed Harmonized Draft Constitution," available at https://kenyastockholm.com/2010/02/02/download-final-report-of-pscs-naivasha-retreat/.

[21] See Grace Maingi, 'The Kenyan Constitutional Reform Process: A Case Study on the Work of FIDA Kenya in Securing Women's Rights', Feminist Africa (2011).

social upheaval. As a result, in order to protect against the threat of constant instability, there is general agreement that constitutions should be adopted through an exceptional procedure. The difficulty, however, is reaching agreement on the process that should be followed and the exact majority requirement that should be met in order to adopt the constitution. Ideally, all constitutions would be supported by a consensus of both political and popular opinion. The risk in requiring consensus or a high level of acceptance in all cases is that an agreement may never be reached. Worse still, spoilers could be encouraged to block agreement. That is a risk that all constitutional negotiations face, given the level of distrust that often exists between negotiating parties. The temptation is therefore to build some flexibility in the rules of procedure that govern the constitutional negotiation and drafting process to allow for a lower threshold requirement in case consensus cannot be achieved.

Rules of Procedure: Rules of procedure typically set out the internal functioning of all the bodies that will be involved in the drafting process, including voting requirements, and not just at the process' end. The rules can vary significantly in terms of their length and level of detail, and their manner of adoption and status. Some are adopted by the constitutional committee or assembly as an internal document that can be amended through a simple majority of its members, while others require the support of a supra-majority of members. In some cases, rules of procedure are adopted in the form of a law, which means that amendments must respect the legislative process. In the post-2011 processes, each country's rules were drafted at a time when political tension was relatively low (for example, immediately following an election). In some cases, individual actors dominated the process through which the rules were adopted, which meant that they could easily influence the rules. In almost all cases, there was an underappreciation of how much damage could be caused by the rules of procedure. Principle authors were anxious to start the negotiation process and so downplayed any potential problems that could emerge. Opposition groups who acted to block various initiatives throughout the transitions were essentially silent when their respective rules of procedure were adopted. In late 2011 Egypt's revolutionary movements were offended by the contents of the "supra-constitutional principles" document that was being drafted at the time and participated in major confrontations with security forces to block them from being adopted. On the other hand, those same groups did not register the mildest of complaints when the rules of procedure were adopted, despite the many problems that they were likely to create. In Tunisia, the rules of procedure were adopted by a near unanimity of the Constituent Assembly's members despite the fact that they set the Assembly on a majoritarian path. That lack of consideration ultimately contributed to two major challenges.

Prohibiting Majoritarianism: The first was the danger that specific political actors would insist on including some mechanism through which a majoritarian constitution could be adopted. In some cases, negotiators argued that while consensus was the preferred outcome, there should always be a mechanism through which a draft could be adopted by majority in case consensus is not achievable, on the basis that nothing could be worse than deadlock. In Egypt's 2012 process, Article 5 of the rules of procedure required the Assembly to adopt the draft through consensus but ultimately allowed it to pass by a majority of fifty-seven members out of a hundred. Tunisia's rules were equally problematic. They provided that the final draft could only be approved by a two-thirds majority of the Constituent Assembly or, failing that, by a majority of voters in a referendum. In both cases, one party sought to impose its views through the decision-making process, although Tunisia stepped back from the brink before it was too late. As Egypt shows, the ultimate cost of a majoritarian approach is that it deepens distrust between major political actors, which itself can increase the likelihood of politically motivated violence. In Iraq's 2005 constitutional process, the rules were simply ignored and many negotiators were excluded based on the assumption that whatever draft was produced would be supported by close to 80 percent of the country. The outcome was that while the constitution did win close to that level of popular approval, a large segment of the political class has refused to implement some of its most important features (including the federal arrangement).[22] Libya's Constitution Drafting Assembly adopted the opposite approach and required that all decisions be adopted by a majority of two-thirds of members (Article 60). The rules did not allow for the threshold to be lowered, no matter the circumstances. The rules also provided that on issues that are of special concern to specific groups, "[c]onsensus with Assembly members representing Libyan social components that have cultural and linguistic peculiarities must be observed." Ultimately, because of the very particular manner through which its members were elected, the way in which the negotiations transpired tells us very little about what might have happened in Egypt had a similar arrangement been adopted. At the very least, however, a genuine requirement that the new constitution be adopted through consensus would have prevented the unilateral and highly divisive push to complete the 2012 Constitution. In the final analysis, the temptation to allow a lower threshold must be avoided at all costs, given that it falsely suggests that a majoritarian approach can be adopted without paying a cost.

[22] See Zaid Al-Ali, THE STRUGGLE FOR IRAQ'S FUTURE, Yale University Press (2014), at Chapter 3.

Preventing Cheating: The second risk that emerges from rules or procedures that are either poorly considered or adopted unilaterally is that they can contribute to vaguely worded provisions that can be exploited later on in the process. The reality of constitutional negotiations is that they almost always take place between actors that distrust each other deeply, and that distrust tends to grow as the negotiators try and fail to resolve many of the more controversial issues and as the deadline for completion approaches. Where the rules allow different interpretations of how to proceed, individual negotiating parties will always seek to interpret them in a manner that suits them, which can cause tensions to worsen considerably. In Tunisia, a Joint Committee for Cooperation and Drafting was established for the purpose of consolidating the different substantive committees' work, but the committees' exact manner of proceeding was not properly established by the Rules. It was not clear what should happen in the case of contradictions between two different drafts. Should the Joint Committee consult with the different committees and seek a resolution? Or should it propose a solution of its own? These issues were not resolved during the drafting of the rules of procedure, and the result was that the members of the Joint Committee tried to impose their own draft without referring back to the substantive committees, which worsened an already very tense situation considerably and contributed to a shutting down of the entire process for a period of months. In Yemen, the Implementation Mechanism and the Dialogue Conference's rules of procedure granted the president enormous decision-making power. In fact, the full extent of that authority was never properly established to the extent that it was never clear whether the decision to establish a regions committee in January 2014, or the manner in which its final decision was taken, was carried out in accordance with the rules. A more robust set of rules of procedure might have indicated, for example, that all decisions emanating from the national dialogue must be approved by the general assembly and that the decision-making process could not be delegated to another body. The rules of procedure of any constitutional process must be constructed around several objectives, but the main objective of any process should be to guard against majoritarianism by making it impossible or at least very difficult for individual actors to impose their will.

INTERIM ARRANGEMENTS

Rationale: Interim arrangements mainly consist of two things. First, where a popular uprising is successful in forcing a longstanding ruler from office, a temporary system of government must be established to administer the state until a new constitution is established. Given the context, at the very least this would entail ensuring that policy-making should not be controlled by a single individual. Even better would be to establish interim authorities that balance political realities on the ground with the basic human requirements of the general population. Second, given the state of popular anger in the country, interim arrangements should also prioritize specific areas for reform in order to deliver immediate improvements to the general population while it waits for a new constitution to be adopted. What this entails is identifying those areas that are the most in need of improvement in specific countries and seeking to deliver improvements in those areas within a reasonable timeframe. Neither of these elements was taken seriously enough in most if not all countries that were affected by the 2011 uprisings. Very many of the post-2011 transition processes failed to seriously address either of these areas, which ultimately contributed to serious failures that impacted all countries, including Tunisia. The impact was to seriously reduce prospects for overall success.

Underestimating Risks: Wherever a longstanding chief executive has been forced from office and a new constitution is to be negotiated, a temporary system of government will have to be established for the interim period. This raises a number of questions, including who will be responsible for governing the country, what powers those individuals will have, and how decisions will be taken. Whatever arrangements are adopted will also impact the constitutional negotiations that will follow. If the interim arrangements are somewhat successful, and contribute to improvements in standards of living in the country, constitutional negotiators may be inspired to maintain some of those arrangements. Conversely, where the interim arrangements prove to be a failure, negotiators are more likely to look elsewhere for inspiration. It is understandable that interim governance arrangements should be underestimated and that potential risks should be downplayed. Interim constitutions are usually drafted in unique circumstances that do not lend themselves to considering worse case outcomes. Where a dictator has just been removed from office (Tunisia, Egypt), or a civil war is about to be won (Libya) or efforts need to be made to prevent one (Yemen in 2011), very little attention is usually invested in ensuring that the interim constitution has been properly drafted. This is clearly a major mistake, which should be avoided in all cases, no matter the circumstances. There is not a single solution that can apply to all situations, but there are clearly two extreme outcomes that one should avoid at all costs.

Chaotic Governance: Some countries established a system of government that introduced total chaos, where power was transferred to a plethora of different groups and individuals who did not have a common ideology or approach to governance. That arrangement was compounded by a total absence of countervailing measures that could have controlled against the worst effects of the political system. Libya's interim constitution is an excellent illustration. The interim constitution was drafted extremely quickly, without proper consultation, and adopted despite major flaws in its design. It provided that during the interim period, a parliamentary system of government would be established. The interim constitution also provided very little indication how the parliament should function, and what types of checks would be established to prevent abuses in the parliamentary process. The interim constitution barely mentioned the courts or the security services. Very little if any consideration was given to the fact that a nascent parliamentary system in a country where political parties had been totally banned for more than half a century would need very significant assistance in order to function properly. In a few short years, well before the constitutional process was even halfway completed, basic security and public services were falling apart, ultimately leading to a complete splintering of the country. This is obviously the result of a number of factors, and cannot be blamed entirely on the interim constitution, but the text certainly did not help. In addition, the constitutional negotiators took no notice of the failure, and moved from a strong preference for a parliamentary system to a fully presidential system of government, despite the risks of a relapse into authoritarian rule.

Continued Monopolization: Other countries made the mistake of maintaining power in the hands of a single group, which would then try to use that power to skew the transition in its favor. In addition, as soon as decision-making is concentrated in this way, the incentive to carry out real consultations with other groups and to reach agreement on a path forward is greatly reduced. The impact was a series of calamitous mistakes that increased tensions during the transition, thereby making it more difficult to reach agreement. The first two years of Egypt's transition illustrate the negative effects that such an approach can generate. In the first instance, the Supreme Council of the Armed Forces assumed the position of chief executive and adopted an interim constitution without any meaningful consultation. In fact, even after the draft interim constitution was approved in a popular referendum, the SCAF decided unilaterally and without explanation to adopt a text different to what was approved. As noted previously, the SCAF sought to reverse its decision a few months later when it supported the effort to draw up the "supra-constitutional principles" document, which was done without sufficient consultation. One year later in 2012, the SCAF sought to remain in power, an effort that it abandoned only reluctantly. In late 2012 the elected president sought to increase his own power by issuing a "constitutional declaration" that sought to make his own decisions immune from judicial review. The declaration caused an uproar in Egypt and contributed to the increasing lack of trust between the two sides of the political divide.

Prioritizing Reform: Just as importantly, where millions of protesters take to the street to express deep frustration about inequality and declining standards of living, state officials must seek to take immediate measures to bring relief to the general population as soon as practically possible, or at least make a reasonable effort to achieve that aim. To proceed otherwise is to risk causing serious damage to the entire transition's legitimacy, and to decrease the likelihood that political progress will be achieved.[23] In Yemen, the Implementation Mechanism established a shortlist of priority areas for reform that the transitional government was supposed to implement, but the areas that were included in the list were so generic and so short on detail that they were essentially ignored. The government that was established pursuant to the signing of the GCC Initiative was heavily criticized for having allowed standards of living to deteriorate to a very significant degree. This was not only by omission. Specific actions, including the very sudden elimination of all subsidies, caused costs of living to spike very suddenly at a time when living standards were already in decline. In Tunisia, the transitional government that was formed following the 2011 elections also prioritized political reform and the drafting of a new constitution over all other considerations. The impact was to delay much needed economic reform and to maintain Tunisia on an unsustainable macroeconomic trajectory.[24] In 2019 Sudan adopted the opposite approach, which was to include such a long list of priority areas of reform that it was unrealistic to assume that they could be successfully implemented (although at least one area was established as a priority above all others; see next subsection).

A Plural Approach: The initial period of a transition is crucial for the entire process' success. It is during this initial period that interim constitutions are drafted, the system of government for the interim period is developed, and the interim government's reform program is established. In most, if not all, the post-2011 transitions, the interim authorities did not dedicate enough time and effort to resolve these issues, which put their respective countries on a negative trajectory from which many did not recover. The lessons from all of these experiences is obvious. The drafting of the interim constitution should be organized in a way that increases its chances of being accepted by sufficient

[23] Caroline Freund and Mélise Jaud, "On the Determinants of Democratic Transitions," Middle East Development Journal, Vol. 5, No. 1 (2013), 1–30.

[24] Ishac Diwan, "Tunisia's Upcoming Economic Challenge," Arab Reform Initiative (September 23, 2019).

numbers of political groups. It should also be done in a way that increases the chances that it will establish a functioning system of government during the interim period. What this means is that the interim constitution should be the product not only of a political negotiation but should also involve governance experts with a vision of how interim governance should be organized. In so doing, the dangers of monopolization of power during the interim period are more likely to be resolved. Finally, there is simply no excuse for delaying reforms until the end of the constitutional process. Sudan's 2019 Constitutional Charter prioritized peace between the state and the country's various warring factions, rather than delaying peace until after the constitutional process was complete. The Sudanese negotiators who drafted the Charter included that provision specifically because they understood that peace would bring dividends that a new constitution on its own would not be able to deliver. That lesson, as applied to other priority areas, including economic reform, should be learned.

FACT-BASED APPROACH

Politics and Faith: Constitutional processes are unlike ordinary legislative processes. They offer incredible opportunities to introduce major reforms to a country's political system, to basic freedoms, and to societal rules and traditions. At the same time, they are perilous exercises that can contribute to distrust, instability, and ultimately violence. However, for reasons that are not entirely obvious, the process through which constitutions are negotiated, drafted, and adopted is remarkably unscientific and at times compares poorly with the process through which ordinary legislation can be adopted. In many countries in the region and beyond, legislation is often only adopted after serious consideration is given to its possible impact on state and society. Increasingly, the legislative process includes studying the budgetary impact of bills before they are adopted; open consultations with broad segments of the population who are given sufficient time and opportunity to prepare and deliver their interventions; the publication of drafts; the solicitation of input from subject matter experts; and modeling the impact of specific provisions before they are finally adopted. Automated procedures are increasingly common and allow for greater numbers of individuals to provide input, track their input systematically, and compare versions while reducing human error or bias.[25] None of these methods were adopted in the post-2011 constitutional

[25] See, for example, Wim Voermans, Hans-Martien ten Napel, and Reifer Passchier, "Combining Efficiency and Transparency in Legislative Processes," The Theory and Practice of Legislation, Vol. 3 (2015), 279–294.

processes. Obviously, constitutional processes are far more political than most ordinary laws and the stakes much higher, which inevitably means that they are more difficult to manage. But in most post-2011 processes, the negotiations and drafting appeared to be driven by what can be described as a faith-based approach that is practically untouched by modernity. Throughout many of the processes, inconvenient facts were simply ignored in the hope that the parties would reach agreement through force of will, failing which a majoritarian constitution would be imposed in the hope that the opposition could be brought under control.

Impact: In Yemen, the National Dialogue Conference decided that the country should be reconstituted as a federation but did not come close to discussing how that federation would function. The outcomes did not include any decisions about which authorities the different levels of government would exercise; how security would be organized in the new federation; whether there would be a unified court structure; or how financial resources would be shared between the different federal regions. All of those issues were left to the constitutional committee, which was never intended to be politically legitimate. It made very little progress on the federal system during the first few months of its mandate and eventually started constructing an extremely elaborate federal arrangement after it had already left the country and was working out of Abu Dhabi. By the time they were finished, these few individuals had written the constitution's most salient sections entirely on their own, without any public knowledge of the substance of the discussions. The manner in which the work proceeded was not at all what was originally conceived, which was that all major political arrangements would flow from the National Dialogue, the political legitimacy body. It was already obvious halfway through the Dialogue that it was not on course to resolve these vital issues, but very little was done to correct the course. Instead, senior Yemeni and international officials pressed ahead, hoping that the course would correct itself, without paying sufficient attention to whether what was being done could ever be acceptable or function in practice. Similar approaches were adopted elsewhere. In Libya, the Constitution Drafting Assembly pressed ahead and eventually adopted a draft despite the fact that its deliberations were almost entirely detached from facts on the ground. At the time of writing, it is still uncertain if it will ever be put to a referendum. In both Tunisia and Egypt, parties in control circulated drafts of their respective constitutions that had not been signed off by the different sides of the political divide, markedly worsening political distrust in the process. The fact is that none of these steps would have been taken had a fact-based approach been established, which would have required a far more robust set of procedures and bodies than in the past.

Modernity: What this entails for the future is far more attention to the manner in which rules of procedure are drafted and to the establishment of bodies that are responsible for administering the drafting process. The rules should be constructed around a number of principles, including that the negotiation and drafting process should not be dominated by a single group of individuals, no matter how they are selected. If the rules accept that the constitutional process should be opened up to greater input, they should also acknowledge that it is notoriously difficult to keep record of all comments and ensure that they are being taken into account. In the post-2011 processes, including in Tunisia, which was broadly considered to be transparent and open, the process through which comments to the constitution were recorded was generally primitive, depending on rapporteurs preparing reports of meetings, the manual compilation of comments, and paper filings of written submissions, all of which are highly subject to error and manipulation. A more modern approach will allow individual commentators to access drafts and input commentary directly in relation to specific provisions or themes, which will then be automatically compiled through natural language processing, and would then be transparently made available for all interested parties to review. In order for this and other mechanisms to function properly, a secretariat would have to be composed along totally different lines to what was done in the post-2011 processes. In virtually all cases, these were composed along partisan or traditional lines, meaning that they were either composed by political representatives or by individuals who were not particularly expert at organization, particularly along modern lines. What a modern and transparent process requires is for a secretariat to include individuals with a modern skill set, including programmers who are recruited through open processes so as best to organize the process through which consultations are carried out, to ensure that all considerations are properly addressed before moving on to subsequent phases of the process.

10

External Assistance (or on Creating Order Out of Chaos)

INTRODUCTION

By the summer of 2017 most Libyans and non-Libyans alike had lost confidence that the constitutional process in that country would lead anywhere. The Constitution Drafting Assembly (CDA) had only a bare minimum of legitimacy to begin with given the low turnout rate in the elections. When it started working in 2014, the CDA was legally bound to complete the draft within a few months but suffered a large number of delays. The drafting process was paralyzed for long stretches of time, including because of basic security concerns. Drafters could not meet, some were under threat, and prospects for organizing further CDA meetings (let alone reaching an agreement) were growing dimmer by the day.

Then, very suddenly, the CDA met on July 29, 2017, and thrashed out all the remaining issues of contention on the table, managing to reach the crucial two-thirds majority that was required by its rules of procedure. Forty-four members were in attendance, and out of those, forty-three voted in favor of the final changes. Most observers were shocked to learn of these developments. Militias that were based in and around Bayda city were reported to have threatened and possibly even beaten CDA members in an attempt to force them to reverse the decision.

Many members of the international community were equally surprised by these developments. On August 9, 2017, a United Nations agency called for a coordination meeting of all relevant international actors and interested members of the diplomatic community. The agenda for the meeting included only two items, the first of which provided that "[a]n update on the constitution-making process and related political developments and a discussion on the path ahead" was to be delivered. The meeting, which was held on August 17, 2017, was well attended. All the seats on the large conference room table were occupied. Attendees lined chairs against the walls and some were standing by the entrance. I recognized many colleagues from other institutions. There were a number of senior foreign diplomats in the room as well.

As I took my seat, I noticed that the individual immediately to my right seemed hesitant, offering furtive glances and not speaking to anyone around him. I introduced myself. He responded that he was the military attaché in the embassy of a country that had major interests in Libya (which shall remain nameless here). Just as the meeting was due to begin, he explained that his embassy colleague who normally attended international coordination meetings was on leave and he was sitting in on his behalf. He then asked me relatively innocently what the purpose of the meeting that we were attending was. The attaché was asked by his embassy colleagues to attend the meeting but had not been sent the original invitation and so had no idea who else was in attendance and what we were planning on discussing. "We're going to discuss the constitution, and possible next steps," I said. He responded by asking what those next steps might possibly be. "Normally, the idea is that a referendum on the constitution should be organized," I offered. The military attaché suddenly looked horrified, and said somewhat indignantly "You're joking right?"

Before I could respond, our conversation was cut short and the meeting commenced. The meeting was chaired by a senior official who was well accustomed to delivering briefings on Libya's depressing political developments. On past occasions, his tone had been serious and somber. On this occasion, the official spoke with great confidence and optimism about recent developments. He stood upright and boomed his voice across the room. The official stated that the July 29 meeting meant that the CDA's working document was no longer merely a draft but a "constitutional proposal," with triumphant emphasis on the word "proposal." The process was now complete, the page had been turned, and there could be no further substantive discussions on Libya's future constitution. All the attendees were all urged to refer to it as a "proposal" to further underline its finality internationally. Wheels were now in motion to organize the referendum, which was supposed to take place within thirty days. The referendum would allow Libya to end its transitional period, organize fresh elections, and, hopefully, wipe away all of the moribund institutions that had been holding the country back since 2012. The official asked for all those institutions in attendance to offer their support to reach that goal. Many of the people in attendance contributed their questions and ideas on how the referendum should be organized, in accordance with what timeframe, what rules, and what procedures. One attendee asked how the referendum would be funded. Another asked if the same electoral commission that had organized previous rounds of elections would be maintained or if a new commission would be formed. Yet another attendee asked whether the referendum would be approved by simple majority or if a special threshold would be imposed. Many of the attendees wondered if there would be sufficient time to organize the referendum. Not being an electoral expert, my only contribution was to ask if anyone had formulated a view on the "constitutional proposal" itself. The chair responded that his office did not have an opinion on the text. No one else in the room offered any other thoughts.

The meeting came to a close and people started making motions to leave. I looked to my right and noticed that the military attaché now had a look of complete disgust on his face. He was still sitting, and was looking downward at the table with a deep frown and his teeth clenched. I asked him what the matter was. "All of you people are living in a Bollywood production," he said as he looked away from me. I asked what he meant and his only response was to say "If there is one thing I'm certain of, it is that there will not be a referendum in Libya. You people are completely crazy." He turned to leave. Subsequent events have since proven him right. The military attaché had access to the same information that we all had: that militias were rushing to acquire increasing amounts of military hardware; that they were vying to control resources and territory; that regional powers were supporting rival militias; insecurity was rising daily; etc. The difference between the military attaché and the rest of the attendees is that he placed more emphasis on these vital developments on the ground and no emphasis on what was happening in a conference room in Bayda between members of the Constitutional Drafting Assembly. Being an outsider to our regular meetings between internationals, he clearly considered that the attendees were engaging in a fantasy. In the absence of any form of institutional oversight, the only corrective to failing international assistance to countries such as Libya based solely on groupthink is reality and facts on the ground.

INTERNATIONAL ASSISTANCE

Pre-2011: Despite the region's desperate situation in 2011, the general population received close to no support in its struggle for freedom. To take Tunisia as one example, many western governments had provided the regime with significant political support despite horrific human rights abuses, an unending series of sham elections, and spectacular levels of corruption.[1] International

[1] See, for example, José Garcon, "'Droits de l'homme en Tunisie: Chirac blanchit Ben Ali," Libération, December 5, 2003; Vincent Duhem, "Tunisie: Quand Ben Ali était fréquentable," Afrik (January 18, 2011); John D. Banusiewicz, "Rumsfeld Meets with Leaders in Tunisia,"

organizations such as the World Bank and the United Nations were at best complacent on those same issues, and at worst could be said to be providing Ben Ali with significant international legitimacy by enthusiastically cooperating on initiatives that were designed to provide the regime with cover,[2] and by allowing the Tunisian authorities to misreport its own economic data.[3] The World Bank's final country brief on Tunisia prior to the 2011 uprising offered significant praise to the Tunisian authorities and made no mention of human rights abuses or the widespread corruption that was common knowledge among ordinary Tunisians.[4] Even foreign authors and journalists defended the state of affairs, often by arguing that Arab countries could only be ruled through the use of force or that Ben Ali's actions were supported by a consensus of public opinion.[5] People in other countries were hardly better off: In early 2011 Prime Minister Tony Blair referred to Hosni Mubarak as

American Forces Press Service (February 11, 2006) (in 2006 the US Defense Secretary described Tunisia as a "successful country" and said that the state demonstrated "the ability to create an environment that's hospitable to investment, to enterprise, and to opportunity for their people").

2 In 2005 Tunisia hosted the World Summit on the Information Society, an initiative that was endorsed by the United Nations General Assembly by virtue of its Resolution 56/183. The event was attended by 19,000 participants from 174 countries, of which only one raised Tunisia's undemocratic practices during the proceedings; see Florence Beaugé, "Tunisie: la victoire de Ben Ali, par Florence Beaugé," *Le Monde* (December 2, 2005). Equally, in 2010 the Secretary General of the United Nations named 2010 the International Year of Youth, an initiative that was originally proposed by Ben Ali in 2008, at a time when youth unemployment in Tunisia was 20 percent; see "Address by Mr. Samir Labidi, Minister of Youth, Sports and Physical Education at the Opening Ceremony of the International Year of Youth," United Nations (August 12, 2010), available at http://social.un.org/youthyear/docs/Labidi-Tunisian-Minister.pdf; in a press conference organized at the time the initiative was adopted, United Nations Secretary General Ban Ki Moon praised the "great initiative of President Ben Ali," a comment that was widely reported in the Tunisian press at the time (see, for example www.youtube.com/watch?v=T1zQgAvuNoU); see also Roula Khalaf and Scheherazade Daneshkhu, "France Regrets Misjudgement over Ben Ali," *Financial Times* (January 18, 2011).

3 Joel Beinin, Workers and Thieves: Labor Movements and Popular Uprisings in Tunisia and Egypt, Stanford University Press (2016), at 57 ("After the 2011 uprisings it emerged that the Ben Ali government had manipulated the poverty indicators, as anyone familiar with the impoverished center-west and southern regions of the country would have suspected. Revised data revealed that the poverty level was 32.4 percent in 2000 (eight times what the independent evaluation stated), 23.3 percent in 2005 and 15.5 percent in 2010. These figures do not include the 'near poor' living just above the poverty line. By another calculation, in 2014, 24.7 percent of Tunisians were living on less than $2 a day (purchasing power parity, about the same as in Egypt)").

4 See "Country Brief," The World Bank, April 2010 (with the revolution only a few months away, the report's first sentence read "Tunisia has made remarkable progress on equitable growth, fighting poverty and achieving good social indicators").

5 See Francois Bécet, Ben Ali et ses faux démocrates, Publisud (2004), at 19 ("Beaucoup voudraient ignorer ces réalités pour n'en retenir qu'une : la poigne de Ben Ali. Oui, le président gouverne sans faiblir un pays centralisé. Oui, il y a eu et il y a encore des abus, des

"immensely courageous and a force for good";[6] Ghadaffi had been reintegrated into the international fold a few years earlier and his son was admitted to the London School of Economics, where he was pursuing a doctoral degree in democratic theory and where he was invited to give the Ralph Miliband Lecture;[7] meanwhile, the United States and other western powers enthusiastically provided military support to Yemen's Ali Abdullah Saleh.[8] Given the circumstances, ordinary people throughout the Arab region realized that their only solution was to take matters into their own hands.

Questions for evaluation: After the uprisings began in late 2010, the international community engaged in a flurry of activity in a range of areas and lasting for years. The way in which the international community responded to the 2011 uprisings teaches us a number of important lessons. The first relates to how far the international community's scope of action extends, and the circumstances that lead it to vary from country to country. More specifically, it raises the question of what type of support can be offered to national constitutional drafting processes (possibilities include "technical support" or "political support"), and whether there are any practical differences between them. They also raise the question as to how international organizations decide what policy they will adopt in each specific circumstance. Finally, given how countries such as Libya and Yemen have evolved, the role that international organizations played should be examined, particularly with a view to determining whether accountability mechanisms in relation to specific actions or for acts of omission could serve to improve performance in the future.

excès et des bavures. Mais si l'on veut se donner la peine d'aller au fond des choses, de scruter avec attention ce qui s'est passé au cours des deux dernières décennies en Tunisie et chez ses voisins, on aboutit vite à la conclusion que seul un régime fort pouvait sauver l'ancient protectorat français [Many would like to ignore these realities and focus on just one: Ben Ali's grip. Yes, the president governs a centralized country without wavering. Yes, there have been and still are abuses, excesses and blunders. But if we want to take the trouble to get to the bottom of things, to examine carefully what has happened over the past two decades in Tunisia and among its neighbors, we quickly come to the conclusion that only a strong regime could save the former French protectorate]"). See also Andrew Borowiec, Modern Tunisia: A Democratic Apprenticeship, Praeger Publishers (1998), at 17 (despite the absence of any reliable data to support his claim, the author wrote that "on the event of Ben Ali's dramatic move in November 1987, a strong national consensus felt that there was no such thing as moderate fundamentalism; the Islamists had a totalitarian view of politics, including a 'seizure of power with authority over life, death and morality").

6 See Chris McGreal, "Tony Blair: Mubarak Is 'Immensely Courageous and a Force for Good," *The Guardian* (February 1, 2011).

7 See Saif al-Islam Alqadhafi, The Role of Civil Society in the Democratisation of Global Governance Institutions: From 'Soft Power' to Collective Decision Making?, The London School of Economic and Political Science (September 2007).

8 Adam Entous, "Gates Backs Big Boost in US Military Aid to Yemen," *Reuters* (February 22, 2010).

LEVEL OF INVOLVEMENT

Yemen: The international community can often play a determinant role as individual countries establish the contours of their constitutional processes. Yemen provides the most dramatic illustration of how far that involvement can extend. In 2011, the Secretary General of the United Nations dispatched Jamal Benomar, one of his Special Advisers, to Sanaa to engage with the various actors and explore whether a political solution to the crisis might be possible. Benomar, a Moroccan citizen, had previously been imprisoned for eight years in Morocco for his political activities and for demanding greater freedom of expression and association.[9] After escaping from Morocco, he eventually joined the United Nations, working in various capacities. In 2003 he was appointed senior political adviser to the United Nations Assistance Mission in Iraq and later the Secretary General's envoy to facilitate a national dialogue conference. Benomar argued with the occupation authorities and Iraq's new political elites that the transition plan that they had established should be slowed down;[10] the constitution should be the result of an inclusive process; and a national dialogue process should be launched as well.[11] After most of his ideas fell on deaf ears, he withdrew from the country just as it was about to commence its constitutional drafting process.[12] Benomar visited Yemen for the first time in April 2011, at a time when the country was on the brink of civil war. He met with a wide range of actors to better understand the dynamics of the crisis, and to decide what contribution he and the United Nations could offer.

[9] Benomar was tortured and made to endure other forms of inhuman treatment during his period of detention. See "Memories of Morocco," Jamal Benomar, New Internationalist, Issue 163, September 1986.

[10] For more on Iraq's transition plan, and the manner in which it was designed and implemented, see Zaid Al-Ali, The Struggle for Iraq's Future: How Corruption, Incompetence and Sectarianism have Undermined Democracy, Yale University Press (2014).

[11] Benomar's contemporaneous views on these issues are set out in a number of publications, including Jamal Benomar, "Constitution-Making and Peace Building: Lessons Learned from the Constitution-Making Process of Post-Conflict Countries," United Nations Development Programme, August 2003; and Jamal Benomar, "Constitution-Making after Conflict: Lessons for Iraq," Journal of Democracy, Vol. 15, No. 2, (April 2004), 81–95.

[12] See, for example, Michael R. Gordon and Bernard E. Trainor, The Endgame: The Inside Story of the Struggle for Iraq, From George W. Bush to Barack Obama, Vintage (2013) (in which the author relates a conversation between Benomar and Meghan O'Sullivan, a staff member at the US National Security Council, where the latter expresses intransigence in relation to the timing of Iraq's elections). Some of Iraq's most important political actors were determined for the constitution-making process to be decided on a majoritarian basis; see, for example, Larry Diamond, Squandered Victory: The American Occupation and the Bungled Effort to Bring Democracy to Iraq, Times Books (2007), Chapter 3.

Under his guidance, a small team of United Nations officials in Sanaa prepared a document that would supplement the GCC Initiative and provided significantly more detail on how the transition process would be managed. That document ultimately served as the basis of the Implementation Mechanism, which included all of the detail of how the transition would take place. Remarkably, Benomar's involvement in Yemen was not specifically mandated by the United Nations Security Council. Its members were formally made aware of his presence after the fact, and only provided him with a mandate after he had already been there for six months. In October 2011 the Security Council passed Resolution 2014, in which it condemned the violence and human rights violations that had been taking place, and requested that "the Secretary-General to continue his Good Offices, including through visits by the Special Adviser, and to continue to urge all Yemeni stakeholders to implement the provisions of this resolution, and encourage all States and regional organizations to contribute to this objective."[13] Benomar (and therefore the UN's) involvement in this process was made all the more sensitive by the fact that the GCC viewed Yemen as part of its sphere of influence, over which it should retain the most amount of control.

Libya: Very shortly after the start of Libya's conflict, the international community provided significant support to the NTC and its efforts to establish a transition roadmap. The United Nations General Assembly awarded it Libya's seat on September 16, 2011 and the African Union granted recognition on September 20, 2011. The United Nations also established a mission for Libya on September 16 (the United Nations Assistance Mission to Libya or UNSMIL),[14] and appointed Ian Martin as the Special Representative of the Secretary General (SRSG) on September 19.[15] The UN Secretary General also issued a report to the Security Council on Libya on November 22, in which it commented on the transition plan for the first time, albeit very briefly.[16] His only comment on the timetable was that it was "challenging," particularly "in a country where there has been limited or no electoral experience in over 45 years." Also, his only comment on behalf of specific measures was to urge the Libyan authorities to "enhance the representation of women and to engage in consultation with civil society, including young people and

[13] S/RES/2014 (2011).

[14] See S/RES/2009 (2011).

[15] The Security Council provided that UNSMIL's mandate was to "assist and support Libyan national efforts to [...] undertake inclusive political dialogue, promote national reconciliation, and embark upon the constitution-making and electoral process"; see paragraph 12 of S/RES/2009 (2011).

[16] See S/2011/727 (2011).

women." Finally, in line with a long tradition of nonintervention in domestic issues, he described the elections as a "Libyan-led process," indicating that the UN "could only provide assistance and support in line with its mandate, [given that] it is the Libyans who must agree on the electoral system and other essential elements of the electoral legislation." Special Representative Ian Martin's own view was that the United Nations should adopt a "light footprint" approach and proceed with "humility."[17] What this meant in practice was that the international community would support whatever decision the NTC would take through "technical support". It also meant, to the extent that anyone disagreed with the substance of the NTC's transition roadmap or considered its interim constitution to be inadequate, that evaluation would not be made public.[18]

Tunisia: Of all the Arab Spring countries, Tunisia was perhaps the most forgiving and the most welcoming of the international community. Dozens of organizations opened offices and began operations in the country for the first time in early 2011, transforming the country into a major hub for international development assistance.[19] After the transition gathered pace in early 2011, the United Nations did not establish a special assistance mission in Tunisia, and acted through its existing offices and agencies, including the United Nations Development Programme. Several new dynamics emerged, many of which complicated the UN's efforts to provide

[17] For an account of Ian Martin's experiences as SRSG see Ian Martin, "The United Nations' Role in the First Year of the Transition," in Peter Cole and Brian McQuinn (eds.), The Libyan Revolution and Its Aftermath, Oxford University Press (2015) (in which he states that, under his guidance, UNSMIL "endeavoured, in a difficult security context, to maintain a light footprint and deliver targeted assistance corresponding to Libyan wishes, respectful of national ownership while advocating UN principles"). Tarek Mitri, who succeeded Mr. Martin as Special Representative in September 2012 and who remained in Libya until August 2014, appeared to agree with this approach; see "Insight into the UN in Libya: Interview with Dr. Tarek Mitri, Head of the United Nations Support Mission in Libya (UNSMIL)," Issam Fares Institute for Public Policy and International Affairs, American University of Beirut (October 2012) (in which Mr. Mitri says that the UN's "primary task is offering technical assistance and advice if needed and requested. I said we will propose to the Libyans if invited to do so, and we'll offer the best of technical assistance"); see also "Libya's Political Transition: The Challenges of Mediation," Peter Bartu, International Peace Institute (December 2014) (in which the author writes that UNSMIL "was thus named in deference to Libyan sovereignty and structured to provide on-demand technical assistance with a minimum footprint").

[18] It is not clear if such an evaluation was ever made. I have been told on more than one occasion that an evaluation was made and shared with the Libyan authorities, but despite repeated attempts to retrieve it or at least to learn of its contents, I have not been able to confirm that the evaluation actually exists.

[19] Following the 2011 uprising, Tunisia became so welcoming to foreign organizations and forums that it has hosted the World Social Forum twice, once in 2013 and again in 2015.

effective assistance to the constitution-building process. The first was that much of its staff had been in their positions for several years and found themselves in a country that was shifting rapidly under their feet from a repressive environment that was hostile to democratic development to one of significant opportunity coupled with uncertainty. For internationals that happened to be in Tunisia at the time when the uprising took place, the challenge was to adapt preexisting priorities to the revolutionary environment. Second, many of Tunisia's old ideological chasms resurfaced within the offices of international organizations, with some national staff members favoring close cooperation with the country's new ruling authorities and others preferring collaboration with the secular opposition. That same division was reflected within Tunisia's new post-2011 political class, which formally welcomed international support but was actually divided on whether all forms of support should be welcomed at all times. Certain segments of the political class would seek to close the door to international involvement when it was politically convenient to do so, including when the particular type of support that was on offer was considered to be favorable to political rivals. These divisions were accentuated by the fact that the UN's political leadership in Tunisia was lacking in a clear vision for how the international organization should approach its role in the country.

SCOPE OF ACTION

Categories of Support: Theoretically, in countries that are not experiencing a severe political or security crisis but which nevertheless consider the possibility of international assistance to be beneficial (e.g. Tunisia), international organizations usually limit themselves to providing "technical support" (which is generally understood to mean the provision of expert and material support on matters of a nonpolitical nature) and avoid entering into the realm of "substantive support" (usually understood to mean providing opinions on sensitive and political matters). As a matter of general principle, national authorities are under no obligation to invite or allow international actors to provide technical assistance to their own internal processes. National authorities are entirely within their rights to consider that a constitutional negotiation process is a matter of national sovereignty, which no foreign body should be allowed to influence. That general principle would be particularly justifiable in practice if the national authorities in question were committed to reaching a positive outcome. It is also justifiable given the number of times in recent memory that external actors have manipulated and negatively influenced constitutional negotiations, without any form of accountability.[20]

National Veto: Some national officials, particularly those who monopolize access to power and policy-making, often exclude international actors merely in order to prevent progress on specific matters. On occasion, they have employed a number of mechanisms to prevent international organizations from engaging in any meaningful activity. Apart from simply preventing certain organizations and their staff members from even entering the country,[21] governments insist that whatever work an international organization carries out must be based on a program that itself must be negotiated and approved by the national authorities. The government then uses that leverage to remove any activity that could potentially threaten its monopoly on power.[22] If any of the agencies or individual staff members step out of bounds, they run the risk of being ejected from the country by the national authorities. In one relatively prominent case that took place in Algeria in 2003, a senior official from UNDP was declared persona non grata formally on the basis that he had acted beyond his mandate and encroached on national sovereignty issues.[23]

[20] See Zaid Al-Ali, "Constitutional Drafting and External Influence," in Tom Ginsburg and Rosalind Dixon (eds.), COMPARATIVE CONSTITUTIONAL LAW, Edward Elgar Publishing (2011).

[21] For example, Morocco routinely prevents western human rights organizations from working in its national territory. In September 2015, it demanded that Human Rights Watch suspend its activities in the country. See "Statement Regarding Human Rights Watch in Morocco," Human Rights Watch (October 2, 2015).

[22] Former UN official, interview with the author (January 2016) (the official in question was responsible for the implementation of a parliamentary development project in an Arab country, and described her work as thus, "I did everything except parliamentary development. Mainly, I used my budget to procure office supplies for the parliament").

[23] Paolo Lembo, interview with the author (January 2016). The incident is described, somewhat incompletely, in Dina Giurovich and Jeremy Keenan, "The UNDP, the World Bank and Biodiversity in the Algerian Sahara," in Jeremy Keenan (ed.), THE SAHARA: PAST, PRESENT AND FUTURE, Routledge (2007), at 339. More broadly, national authorities often have influence over who will staff the UN's offices that are located within their territory, sometimes because they are requested to evaluate candidates for specific positions and because they can be requested to evaluate specific staff members' performance. On occasion (usually in resource-rich countries), national authorities even fund specific positions, which are often filled by loyalists as a result. Prior to 2011, the Libyan government funded most if not all of UNDP's operations in the country, and a significant number of UNDP's staff were loyalists who worked against any form of democratic reform; Senior UN official who has served in many countries in the region, interview with the author (January 2016). The result is that a large number of international organizations choose not to invest any efforts in countries of this type. By way of illustration, International IDEA (whose mandate relates to electoral assistance and constitution building) did not have a presence in the Arab region prior to 2011. Following the 2011 uprisings, it opened offices in Egypt, Libya, and Tunisia.

Political Missions: In post-conflict situations (e.g. Libya in 2011 and Iraq in 2003) or states that are particularly fragile (e.g. Yemen in 2011), the Security Council can also broaden the UN's traditional mandate to include political support, usually through the establishment of what is referred to as a "mission." Other intergovernmental organizations, including International IDEA, also traditionally dramatically increase their involvement in crisis countries. They are also typically followed by a massive increase in civil society activity, including international NGOs. It is specifically in this type of country that controversy over the role of external actors can emerge, mainly because close to no effort has been made to define what is and what is not permissible. Theoretically, external actors are supposed to limit their involvement to what is referred to as "technical support," and to avoid "political support" except in extreme situations. As we shall see, the distinction between these two categories is essentially illusory, and the exact extent of a specific external actor's involvement will have much more to do with prosaic concerns, such as the individual personal biases of international officials, the size of an organization's budget, as well as other similar concerns.

Technical Support: As already stated, there is no agreed definition of what constitutes "technical support," leaving the term to be determined on a case by case basis by the national and international officials who happen to be involved in particular constitutional drafting processes. It is generally understood that international organizations should not be involved in making political decisions on behalf of national authorities. National authorities usually welcome, and international organizations are happy to provide, a restrictive form of technical support, which can take the form of training sessions for staff (including electoral workers; parliamentary staff; court staff), the procurement of materials on behalf of institutions (e.g. computers and other equipment), and the provision of expertise on scientific matters that have no connection to political considerations (e.g. improving agricultural yields and transport; demining, etc.). But that is where consensus ends. There are other possible forms of support, some of which could be qualified as technical in some contexts, but are sometimes considered to be controversial and therefore inappropriate by some bodies. In some cases, ruling authorities can consider that purely technical support to specific institutions represents a threat to their authority and are not shy about blocking specific initiatives. For example, in countries where the judiciary has been utilized by ruling authorities for political purposes, initiatives that are designed to improve judicial independence or transparency in the judicial sector can be blocked, despite the fact that judicial independence is a constitutionally recognized norm in all Arab countries.[24]

Substantive Advice: Technical support can even on occasion be stretched to include the provision of substantive advice on key policy issues (while making sure not to lobby in favor of any particular outcome). For example, where a state is considering what type of decentralized model of government it should adopt, international organizations can present options based on comparative practice.[25] Although this approach is often considered to be technical, it is actually far from innocent, as comparative studies and examples are never comprehensive and the examples that are used to make particular points are typically drawn from the author's biases.[26] This should not come as a surprise, as the opposite approach can lead to perverse results.[27] On occasion, national authorities are happy to allow the provision of options on sensitive policy issues, but in other circumstances, they will not allow international organizations even to observe the drafting process and will block any formal communication with them, specifically to prevent this type of involvement.[28] Finally, international organizations have been known to provide substantive advice on key issues to national offices, including by providing commentary on draft constitutions or legislation. This is typically considered to be substantive support, and is not usually regarded as being technical in nature, but many countries actually welcome this type of support and sometimes even seek it out.[29]

24 A number of initiatives that were designed to strengthen judicial independence, in particular by reducing the scope for political interference in the judicial process, were blocked by the Iraqi government from 2005 to 2014.

25 This approach was followed in Yemen, where the constitutional drafting committee worked closely with experts from the United Nations and (to a lesser extent) International IDEA, which provided information on comparative examples to the drafters.

26 These can include an author's educational background (e.g. if the author of a particular study has graduated from German educational institutions, the likelihood that her study will draw from German examples is necessarily heightened) and ideological preferences (e.g. if an expert is politically conservative, she is unlikely to draw on examples from most Latin American constitutions, many of which offer generous socioeconomic rights to citizens).

27 In one Arab country, an international organization that was providing background materials to a constitution drafting committee insisted on including in the folders of materials that were being prepared all basic laws from the region, including the basic laws of Saudi Arabia and Qatar, both totalitarian regimes.

28 In Egypt's 2012 and 2013 constitution drafting processes, the drafting assemblies did not engage with any international organizations, specifically to prevent any foreign influence over their process.

29 A number of examples of this approach exist in the region. Iraq's 2005 constitution drafting committee welcomed commentary from UNAMI's Office of Constitutional Support. Tunisia's Constituent Assembly sought substantive advice from the Venice Commission on more than

Political Support: Second, there is no agreement on what constitutes political support either. Indeed, in Libya, when UNSMIL was first established by virtue of Resolution 2009 (2011), it was provided with an incredibly vague mandate by the Security Council, which requested it to "assist and support Libyan national efforts to [. . .] undertake political dialogue, promote national reconciliation and embark upon the constitution-making and electoral process."[30] The Security Council pointedly did not request of UNSMIL that it limit itself to supporting national authorities, and did not specifically state that the support should be technical in nature. In its second resolution on the matter, the Security Council clarified the mandate somewhat by virtue of its Resolution 2040 (2012), when it stated that UNSMIL should "assist the Libyan authorities to define national needs and priorities throughout Libya, and to match these with offers of strategic and technical advice [. . .] including through technical advice and assistance to the Libyan electoral process and the process of preparing and establishing a new Libyan constitution."[31] Superficially, Resolution 2040 appeared to limit UNSMIL's mandate when it provided that all assistance should be limited to providing "strategic and technical advice," but the use of the term "strategic" in this context added significant confusion given the term's absence of a clear definition. However, the main difference, in fact, between these two versions of UNSMIL's mandate was that Resolution 2040 provided that UNSMIL should assist Libya's national authorities to "define national needs," which was tantamount to stating that the Libyans were unsure of what direction they hoped to move in and that UNSMIL should have as part of its job helping identify Libya's priorities. Vitally, however, UNSMIL's amended mandate did not appear to have any impact on the work that it was doing on the ground, which remained highly technical in nature, and which eschewed any and all political issues even as Libya's crisis intensified.[32]

Light Footprint: Interestingly, the United Nations Assistance Mission for Iraq, which was established in 2003, was mandated by the Security Council by virtue of its Resolution 1546 (2004) to "promote national dialogue and

one occasion, including to provide commentary on its draft constitution. International IDEA also provided commentary on the Libyan Constitutional Drafting Assembly's preliminary draft. See, International IDEA, Libya's Final Draft Constitution: A Contextual Analysis, Constitutionnet (2017), available here: https://constitutionnet.org/vl/item/libyas-final-draft-constitution-contextual-analysis.

30 S/RES/2009 (2001).

31 S/RES/2040 (2012).

32 See Martin (2015) (in his assessment of UNSMIL's work in Libya, Mr. Martin does not come close to suggesting that SCR2040 had any impact on UNSMIL's work).

consensus building on the drafting of a national constitution by the people of Iraq."[33] Despite the almost identical wording with UNSMIL's mandate, the two missions adopted completely different approaches. While UNSMIL favored a "light footprint" approach, UNAMI involved itself very heavily in political negotiations from 2003 onward, to the extent that it argued in favor of particular options during the drafting of Iraq's constitution.[34] Even more strikingly, the UN's heavy involvement in Yemen was carried out without a Security Council mandate at all; even when a mandate was finally granted in October 2011, it was incredibly vague in comparison to the UN's missions in countries where the UN played almost no role. Once again, the absence of a clear mandate had no impact on the ground; Jamal Benomar, the UNSG's special adviser, was enormously popular in Yemen at the time and the UN's own scope of action depended far more on the extent of his popularity than the exact formulation of a mandate by the Security Council.[35]

Contradictory Approaches: The result is a series of blatant contradictions, an incredible amount of confusion, and a number of lost opportunities, in ways that have not served the Arab region well. For example, of the issues that are traditionally considered to be purely technical, many have important political implications and vice versa. Electoral assistance is universally considered to be a technical issue, despite the fact that the implications of each chosen aspect of an electoral system are highly political, given that the exact electoral framework that a country will adopt will play a large role in determining its political makeup.[36] On the other hand, advice on judicial independence is not systematically considered to be technical, despite the fact that

[33] S/RES/1546 (2004).

[34] See Nicholas Haysom, Zaid Al-Ali, and Michele Law, "History of the Iraqi Constitution-Making Process," (December 2005), available at http://zaidalali.com/resources/academic-articles/.

[35] Interview with former senior adviser to the UN's mission in Yemen (February 2016).

[36] UNDP's Electoral Assistance Implementation Guide provides that there are two "major types of electoral assistance," including "technical assistance" and "support to international observers." The Guide provides "support to electoral assistance and planning" as well as "drafting of electoral legislation/regulations." For all intents and purposes, the Guide recognizes that these forms of assistance have important political implications. It provides in the relevant part that "[f]or the sake of this Guide, an electoral system refers to the method used to translate votes cast into seats or offices won by the competing parties and/or independent candidates. The type of electoral system (e.g., majority-plurality, proportional representation, mixed, etc.) has long-term implications for accountability, inclusiveness and representation." The Guide also states that as part of its support to elections, UNDP typically provides support to constitutional drafting processes. See UNDP Electoral Assistance Implementation Guide, 2007, at 14 and 39.

the principle is perhaps more universally accepted (at least on a formal basis) than the principle of elections.[37] Meanwhile, some international organizations have for some time approached constitution-building as a technical issue on which they regularly provide advice, while others deliberately avoid formally involving themselves in this area at all costs.[38]

Excuse for Inaction: The result of all of this is that mandates are more often than not used as an excuse for inaction rather than being a genuine impediment to providing substantive support. Those situations in which international organizations, in particular the United Nations, were actually prevented from implementing genuine reforms are the result of particular circumstances from which it is impossible to draw any broad conclusions.[39] To take but one example, what transpired in 2003 in Algeria was the result of a lopsided political dispute between some segments in the government on the one hand and the president and the country's entire security establishment on the other, in which there was essentially no contest. The UN official who was declared persona non grata was a major casualty to that dispute, and his expulsion from the country was a circumstance that is highly unlikely to be replicated elsewhere, particularly in transition countries.[40] Indeed, one of the defining characteristics of a political transition is intense political competition between rival groups in parliament, most of whom are eager for knowledge on com-

37 UNDP does not have a practice note or an implementation guide on judicial independence and has published only a small number of reports on the issue; see, for example, "Judicial Independence in Transitional Countries," United Nations Development Programme, Oslo Governance Center, January 2003. Meanwhile, the World Bank has produced so much material on this issue that it has inspired academic research on the merits of the Bank's approach. See, for example, Roberto Laver, "The World Bank and Judicial Reform: Overcoming 'Blind Spots' in the Approach to Judicial Independence," DUKE JOURNAL OF COMPARATIVE INTERNATIONAL LAW, Vol. 22 (2012), 183.

38 See Article IV, Section 10 of the IBRD Articles of Agreement (as amended in February 1989) ("The Bank and its officers shall not interfere in the political affairs of any member; nor shall they be influenced in their decisions by the political character of the member or members concerned. Only economic considerations shall be relevant to their decisions, and these considerations shall be weighed impartially in order to achieve the purposes stated in Article I").

39 Not only has the UN been extremely reluctant to involve itself in substantive matters in a number of cases, but UN agencies have even sought to prevent other organizations from providing substantive opinions on specific issues, first by arguing that the entire international community should speak with one voice, and then by insisting that the UN's voice should be the only one that should be heard. In Libya, UN electoral experts argued that all other agencies and organizations should refrain from contradicting its own position, which led to significant controversy given that many experts disagreed with the advice (or the lack thereof) that the UN was offering at the time. Ayman Ayoub, interview with the author, Cairo (November 2014).

40 Paolo Lembo, interview with the author (January 2016).

parative experiences. In many cases (as was the case in Tunisia, Yemen, Libya, Iraq, and others), national parliaments and state institutions shift from being under the control of a single party to being in a state of genuine plurality. Some parties can be relatively new with very little experience to draw from, and many seek out knowledge and information on comparative experience to bolster their own positions.[41] Thus, whatever the circumstances that led to the crisis in Algeria, they were never considered to apply to Yemen, and almost certainly would not have prevented substantive support in Libya and Tunisia from as early as 2011.[42]

Personal Biases: Second, whereas international involvement in transition countries *should* be determined by each individual country's needs, it is *actually* determined by the preferences and biases of whichever international officials happen to be based in the country in question and whichever national officials happen to be in control. This explains the UN's different levels of involvement in Tunisia, Libya, and Yemen. It also explains why, in countries such as Tunisia, where the UN sought to limit itself to a restrictive form of technical support, other intergovernmental organizations such as IDEA and the Venice Commission, and nongovernmental organizations such as Democracy Reporting International, the Carter Center, and Human Rights Watch were able to provide significant substantive support, which was generally positively received by Tunisian institutions. Based on the circumstances, it would be fair to say that the UN's limited involvement in substantive matters was more the product of its own preferences rather than a genuine restriction imposed by Tunisia's national authorities.

Needs-Based Approach: If anything, the involvement of international organizations in transitions should be based on need rather than anything else.[43] The stakes in transition countries are incredibly important. The potential for disaster is high, and knowledge about the possible consequences tends to be low, specifically considering that transition countries emerging from dictatorial rule will not have had the opportunity to engage in study and

41 This was particularly true in Tunisia, Yemen, and Libya. Based on my own personal observations from 2011 to 2015.

42 A number of international organizations provided substantive support to the Tunisian drafters and did so publicly. See, for example, the following working paper series, CONSOLIDATING THE ARAB SPRING: CONSTITUTIONAL TRANSITION IN EGYPT AND TUNISIA, Zaid Al-Ali and Richard Stacey (eds.), International IDEA and the Center for Constitutional Transitions (2013).

43 This conclusion is in conformity with positions that I have taken on this issue elsewhere; see, for example, Zaid Al-Ali and Philipp Dann, "The Internationalized Pouvoir Constituant: Constitution-Making under External Influence in Iraq, Sudan and East Timor," MAX PLANCK UNYB, Vol. 10 (2006), 423–463.

debate on democratic transition.[44] Libya's interim constitution provides an excellent illustration of this point: It does not appear to ever have been questioned by the international community, despite the fact that it clearly set the country on a negative trajectory.[45] By remaining silent on the interim constitution's very many flaws, the international community was essentially contributing to the difficulties that would inevitably emerge.[46] In the meantime, while the international community remained silent on determinant issues, significant efforts were made to encourage the Libyan authorities to include gender and youth (technical issues par excellence) in all aspects of their work, to the extent that this was mentioned in just about every Security Council Resolution relating to Libya as being a key area of concern from 2011 onward.[47]

Impact: The outcome of a more deliberate and strategic approach to substantive advice should not be construed as political interference, for a number of reasons. The first is that, although the UN Charter and other international instruments prevent international organizations from "intervening" in "the domestic jurisdiction of any state," the provision of advice does not necessarily constitute an "intervention" unless it is imposed as a condition in the context of a negotiation, which is not what is suggested here.[48] The scope for the provision of (nonprescriptive) advice in transition countries is

[44] See Al-Ali (2011), at 91.

[45] To my knowledge, I am the author of the only contemporaneous analysis that was published. See Zaid Al-Ali, "Libya's Draft Interim Constitution: An Analysis," Constitutionnet (September 5, 2011).

[46] The United Nations' failure to comment on the interim constitution was a conscious decision. Years later, in 2015, the Secretary General wrote in a report on Libya's situation that "[t]he political transition of Libya was predicated on the assumption that popularly elected institutions, namely the legislative and executive branches, would take the lead in putting the place the necessary foundations for a modern democratic state. [...] However, effective decision-making structures have not been put in place and *the responsibilities of each branch of government were not properly clarified in the constitutional declaration*. As a result, relations between the transitional legislature and the executive branch have been marked by strong competition and rivalry, preventing them from designing and implementing the required policies to ensure a successful transition process. [...] There have been significant delays in the development of the new constitution, which has not only impeded the effective functioning of the nascent institutional framework but has also prolonged and possibly exacerbated the power struggle among the political actors. [...] [T]he situation may become untenable once the body begins its work on controversial issues." See S/2015/113.

[47] See, for example, S/2011/727, paragraph 55; S/2012/129 paragraph 42; and SCR/2013/516, paragraph 36.

[48] See Article 2(7), Chapter I of the United Nation's Charter. For a more in-depth discussion of this issue, see Philipp Dann, The Law of Development Cooperation: A Comparative Analysis of the World Bank, the EU and Germany, Cambridge University Press (2013), at 256.

much larger than it is generally considered to be, and I am not suggesting that advice can be imposed in the same way that economic reforms are imposed as conditionalities by institutions such as the International Monetary Fund. In addition, based on experience from the region since 2011 (or even since the 2005 Iraqi debacle), it must be noted that the cost of silence can be so high that it should override any concerns relating to sovereignty. As already noted elsewhere,[49] a defective constitutional framework can contribute to a deteriorating security environment not only for the country in question but also for its neighboring countries.[50]

HOW ARE COUNTRY-SPECIFIC STRATEGIES DEVELOPED?

Incoherent Approaches: In addition to the above, in countries where the international community does decide in favor of providing substantive advice, there does not appear to be a coherent approach to determining what advice should be given. That much is perfectly apparent if we compare the different approaches that were taken in our three case study countries. In Yemen, the UN played a significant role in shaping the Implementation Mechanism. One of the key aspects of that document was the heavy emphasis on national dialogue, and the lack of emphasis on parliamentary elections, which (had the transition plan been allowed to play out in full) would have taken place five years after Yemen's uprising had begun. Meanwhile, there is no record of the UN ever advising the Libyan authorities not to rush to elections in 2012 and 2014, even after the UN became progressively more active on substantive issues in 2013 and 2014. On the contrary, the UN does not appear ever to have questioned whether any of Libya's three elections were well timed, whether they applied the best electoral models, or whether they contributed to increased tension and insecurity.

Risk Assessments: The fact that the UN adopted such radically different approaches would be entirely justifiable if they were actually based on a sound understanding of each country's circumstances. But were they? An analysis of the various factors surrounding each country would suggest not. If we compare the situations of Yemen, Tunisia, and Libya, particularly with a view to determining their capacity to organize elections in 2011, we are brought to the opposite conclusion. The following table is illustrative of that point.

49 See Al-Ali, (2011), at 90–91.

50 That much is obvious when one considers the situation of countries surrounding Iraq, Yemen, and Libya.

	Were key state institutions maintained?	Did the country have any experience with elections?	Did political parties/groups survive?	Did the political process survive?
Yemen	Yes	Yes	Yes	No
Tunisia	Yes	Yes	No	No
Libya	No	No	No	No

What we know from these three countries and from broader knowledge of the region is that of all the countries that were impacted by the 2011 uprising, Libya was probably the least well-placed to organize early elections. It did not have any useful experience with organizing such a large-scale effort (not even of the fraudulent kind). It did not maintain its main policy-making institutions, it did not have any experience with political parties, and did not maintain a single aspect of its pre-2011 political process. This should have suggested to any national or international officials who were involved in designing the transition process back in 2011, or who were in a position to influence its contents, that Libya should have been the last country in the region to organize elections, given the amount of effort that needed to be made to ensure that the country's transition was established on a firm footing. Instead, it organized three separate polls within two years, the most recent of which was based on "First Past the Post," which was perhaps the worst of all possible options for a country with such poor democratic traditions. Because of all these factors, elections were highly likely to return a large number of parliamentarians with no relevant experience of which to speak. The NTC largely consisted of former regime loyalists, some of whom at least had the benefit of governance experience, but it nevertheless found the business of governing revolutionary Libya to be extremely challenging. Having said that, it should have been obvious that, if the NTC suffered because of inexperience, any elected assembly that would replace the NTC would have even more trouble. Democratic legitimacy only buys elected parliaments a small amount of leeway, particularly if they are lacking capacity to formulate sound policy, while the general population suffers.

Countries in Particular Need: A convincing argument could be made that, given Libya's particular circumstances and the population's thirst for an immediate opportunity to exercise their basic democratic rights, it was simply impossible to resist the call for early elections. Even so, the NTC and the international community could have taken a number of specific approaches that might have mitigated some of the obvious risks that the country was facing. At the very least, Libya's situation in 2011 should have indicated that a solid institutional framework should have been established prior to any elections. One of the first issues that could and should have been addressed was the interim constitution, which (as already stated) was painfully inadequate. A serious effort at designing international policy on Libya should have involved a detailed study of that document and an analysis of what should have been done to remedy its inadequacies. Not only is there no evidence that such a study was carried out but there is also no indication that it would have had any impact on the international community's strategies in relation to Libya. In 2011 and early 2012 the only interest appeared to be to ensure that the 2012 elections were organized in accordance with international standards and that a sufficient number of women and younger Libyans participated.[51]

Absence of Mechanisms: All this reinforces a number of important conclusions, the first of which is that international organizations do not have effective mechanisms in place to formulate what advice should be given to specific countries. Indeed, country-specific approaches were decided on in each country by the individuals who happened to be present, and based on each of these individual's preferences and biases, many of which had nothing to do with the circumstances of the country in question. In 2011 the stakes for the region were so high that one could have expected a major brainstorming effort on the part of national and international experts with experience in democratic transitions. This was particularly true in places such as Libya after the interim constitution was published. A meeting of minds between key national officials and some of the world's leading authorities on democratic transitions in coordination with the leadership of major international organizations such as the United Nations, with a focus on the Secretary General's office, might have led to the formulation of country-specific approaches that would have averted many of the mistakes and omissions that were made. At this stage, it is impossible to say whether this more deliberate and consultative approach could have made a difference, but it would at least have involved far more reflection and planning than what actually took place.

Recruitment: The UN's highly decentralized approach to international assistance might be justifiable if the individuals who were chosen to lead each specific mission or office were chosen on the basis of their particular aptitude to support democratic transitions in a revolutionary context. Research on this question reveals that, on the contrary, individuals are retained more on the

[51] Ibid.

basis of who happens to be available when a position is vacant. One senior UN official described the selection process as "musical chairs," while another said slightly more charitably that "there is some logic to the recruitment process, but it is not the type of logic that you would have liked for it to adopt." In March 2020, the then Special Representative of the Secretary General of the United Nations to Libya announced that he was stepping down for health reasons. A replacement was announced in December 2020, but that individual declined the position for personal reasons. A second replacement was announced in January. Both the first and second replacements were high ranking UN officials from other countries and neither had any previous experience in Libya. Neither was subjected to a review process before their respective appointments.[52] One could argue that a similar dynamic was in place even in Yemen. It is beyond dispute that Mr. Benomar's impact at the early stages was overwhelmingly positive: He worked tirelessly to defuse tensions and managed to bring all of the country's major actors to the table. Having said that, there is no evidence to suggest that Mr. Benomar was selected to be the UNSG's Special Adviser because his abilities and knowledge were considered to be particularly well suited to that country. Nor is there any evidence to suggest that his strong preference in favor of national dialogue sessions, or the particular way in which Yemen's NDC was structured, were conceived based on an analysis of Yemen's situation. On the contrary, and as noted previously, Mr. Benomar's writings suggest that he had been advocating in favor of that strategy for close to a decade before arriving in Yemen in 2011. His role at the early stages of the process might have been fortuitous but it also appears to have been largely coincidental.

RESPONSIBILITY AND ACCOUNTABILITY

Assessment: A final concern of international involvement is the lack of accountability for failures at both the institutional and individual levels. This should be a major concern, given how some transitions have evolved. There is obviously a natural tendency to attribute responsibility for the outbreak of civil conflict on national authorities, but given how involved international actors have been in some contexts (including in Libya, Yemen, Iraq, etc.) the question of responsibility and accountability for external actors is a serious one that should be answered. If we were to break down this issue, we would first need to examine whether specific actions, policies, or omissions by

[52] Interviews with the author (January 2016).

international actors in a given country were a contributing factor in the outbreak of a conflict. Iraq is a case that is essentially beyond dispute: External actors pushed the Iraqis to draft and adopt a final constitution well before they were ready to do so, causing violence to quadruple in the country immediately after the new text was adopted. Specific external actors (mainly US and UK officials) were clearly culpable for having contributed to this outcome. It can also reasonably be argued that other actors such as the United Nations were culpable through omission, in particular for not having publicly raised any concerns about the constitutional negotiation process.[53] Responsibility is not as easily established in Libya, but a strong argument can be made that the international community's failure to issue warnings about the interim constitution's inadequacies, as well as its enthusiastic approach to early elections, contributed to the new ruling authorities' inability to govern the country and to the eventual emergence of rival centers of authority in the country. In Yemen, it is unclear whether much could have been done to improve the transition process' initial design, but at the very least formal objections should have been registered to the manner in which the presidential commission decided the country's federal arrangement, which ended up being one of the main drivers of the conflict.

Accountability: Assuming one can trace some form of causality between the actions or omissions taken by external actors and deteriorating political and security conditions within a particular country, one should examine whether there should be some form of institutional or individual accountability. At this stage, there do not appear to be any accountability mechanisms in place at all and at any level. For international officials, there is rarely any path but upward, regardless of their actual performance on the ground.[54] There

[53] In early 2005 the United Nations Assistance Mission in Iraq's Office of Constitutional Support carried out a review of comparable transition processes to determine which countries that had been in situations similar to Iraq had successfully negotiated their constitutions within a few months, as was required under Iraq's transition roadmap. The Office concluded that there were no successful precedents and the likelihood that Iraq would be an exception to that trend was essentially nonexistent. In addition, close to the end of the process, the Office of Constitutional Support commissioned a detailed analysis of the draft constitution, which concluded that if the draft were to be applied, Iraq would be in "grave danger," suggesting that the country could witness a new conflict. The United Nations chose not to publicize those conclusions. For the sake of transparency and completeness, I should note that I was a legal officer at the Office of Constitutional Support at the time.

[54] By way of example, in 2013, Martin Kobler (the then Special Representative of the Secretary General of the United Nations to Iraq) was accused of having been partially responsible for serious human rights abuses that were committed the Iraqi authorities. Rather than being forced into resignation, Mr Kobler was appointed as the Special Representative to Libya in 2015. See Tahar Boumedra, The United Nations and Human Rights in Iraq: The Untold

also does not appear to have been any serious attempt to hold international organizations accountable for their own failures, whether from within or without.

Specific Measures: What types of accountability measures can be used to increase the likelihood that major international players will invest greater effort to offer more constructive advice on constitution building? At the very least, one should expect an attempt to rationalize the experiences of the past few years with a view to improving performance over the coming period. One possible result of such an effort could be a clear and specific declaration of policy at the international level in relation to specific countries that move beyond obvious generalities such as human rights, transparency, and gender. Another could be a common acceptance that democratic transitions are extremely sensitive; that policy failures during transitions can lead to major conflicts that can easily spill across borders; and therefore that there is an international responsibility to contribute in as positive manner as possible to issues of process design, with a view to preventing conflict.[55] Even more useful would be periodic, mandatory, independent and public audits of individual assistance efforts. The disasters that have played out in Yemen, Libya, Iraq, Syria and other countries, and their spill-over effect across the region mean that real lessons should be learned, and that existing methods must be adapted accordingly.

Story of Camp Ashraf, Legend Press (2013). Mr. Kobler's biography states that he speaks Arabic. International officials who worked closely with him state that his Arabic was nonexistent and that he was entirely reliant on interpreters. See "Secretary-General Appoints Martin Kobler of Germany as Special Representative for Iraq," United Nations (August 11, 2011).

[55] See Guidance Note of the Secretary-General on United Nations Constitutional Assistance (September 2020). The Guidance Note includes much of these same principles, but does not firmly establish any specific mechanisms that brings them to life.

Index

CPSIA information can be obtained
at www.ICGtesting.com
Printed in the USA
BVHW041531030921
615990BV00014B/38

9 781108 429702